RESTITUTION
at the
CROSSROADS:
a comparative study

Cavendish
Publishing
Limited

London • Sydney

RESTITUTION
at the
CROSSROADS:
a comparative study

Thomas Krebs LLB, BCL, DPhil
Lecturer in Laws
University College London

Cavendish
Publishing
Limited

London • Sydney

First published in Great Britain 2001 by Cavendish Publishing Limited, The Glass House, Wharton Street, London WC1X 9PX, United Kingdom

Telephone: +44 (0)20 7278 8000   Facsimile: +44 (0)20 7278 8080

Email: info@cavendishpublishing.com

Website: www.cavendishpublishing.com

Krebs, Thomas

Restitution at the crossroads: a comparative study

1 Restitution – England 2 Restitution – Germany

I Title

346.4'2'029

ISBN 185941 646 2

Printed and bound in Great Britain

Meinen Eltern

PREFACE

The English law of unjust enrichment is a young subject. It was only in 1991, in the famous case of *Lipkin Gorman v Karpnale*, that it was recognised as a subject in its own right. In contrast, the German law of unjust enrichment is ancient, with roots reaching back to Roman law. The subject has its own heading in the German Civil Code, and is taught as part of the standard syllabus in universities.

One of the most striking differences between the common law and the civil law is that the former bases restitution on concrete 'unjust factors' such as mistake, duress or failure of consideration, while the latter works with a concept known as the 'legal ground' or 'juristic reason'. This civilian approach now appears to be encroaching on English law, mainly as a result of two cases: *Westdeutsche Landesbank v Islington* and *Kleinwort Benson v Lincoln*. It is, therefore, timely to compare and contrast these two approaches in order to see if, and how, the civilian model can be made to work against a common law setting.

Thanks are due in no small measure to Professor Peter Birks. He supervised the doctoral thesis which forms the basis of this book and continued to counsel and help long after I had left Oxford. Anyone who has ever been supervised by him will know how deep my gratitude towards him really is.

Thomas Krebs
London, July 2001

CONTENTS

Contents

Contents

Contents

TABLE OF CASES

Common law

Germany

Bundesverfassungsgericht

Reichsgericht

Bundesgerichtshof

Bundesfinanzhof

Other courts

PART I
INTRODUCTION

CHAPTER 1

SETTING THE SCENE

1.1 UNJUST FACTORS

An insurance company pays out under a policy of insurance. It overlooks the fact that the policy has lapsed. It can recover its payment.[1] A bank pays out under a cheque, overlooking its customer's stop instruction. It, too, can recover the payment from the recipient.[2] A contract to supply machinery is frustrated. The buyer has already paid the price. The buyer can recover the money he has paid.[3]

A claimant asking for restitution on the basis that the defendant has been enriched at his expense will to show not only that the defendant was enriched and that the enrichment was at his expense, but also that the defendant's enrichment was 'unjust'. In the first two examples, the enrichment was 'unjust' in the eyes of the law because the claimants were acting under a mistaken assumption. Both succeeded because they could show that they had been mistaken and that their mistake had caused the defendants to be enriched at their expense. The ground for restitution, the 'unjust factor', was 'mistake'. In the third example, the ground for restitution is traditionally known as 'total failure of consideration'. Like mistake, failure of consideration is a reason for restitution because the claimant can show that he did not really mean the defendant to have the enrichment. However, it is distinguished from mistake in that, at the time of the transfer, the claimant was not operating under erroneous assumptions, but that he *qualified* his giving, specifying a condition which had to be satisfied if the defendant was to be entitled to keep the enrichment. As in the case of mistake, the claimant has to point to a positive reason why the defendant's enrichment should be considered 'unjust' by the law. In cases of failure of consideration, the reason for restitution is that the basis of the claimant's giving has failed, that basis having been communicated to the defendant at the time of the transfer.

'Mistake' and 'failure of consideration' are central examples of the family of claims which are based on the claimant's defective or qualified intent to transfer. That family of claims itself forms part of a system of unjust factors first identified by Peter Birks. The other two families consist of cases in which restitution follows because the defendant behaved badly in accepting the enrichment, and cases in which there is an overriding policy reason demanding restitution.[4]

There is a competing model of restitutionary liability in the civilian tradition. There are indications that the common law is about to embrace that model, if that has not already happened. The civilian model is not based on concrete reasons for restitution, at least not openly. In German law, which will be our main point of comparison in this book, restitution follows if an enrichment at the expense of another lacks what is referred to as a

---

1   *Kelly v Solari* (1841) 9 M & W 54, 152 ER 24.
2   *Barclays Bank Ltd v WJ Simms Son & Cooke (Southern) Ltd* [1980] QB 677.
3   *Fibrosa Spolka Akcyjna v Fairbairn Lawson Combe Barbour Ltd* [1943] AC 32.
4   Cf Birks, 2000b, p 6.

'legal ground'. For the time being, and at the risk of oversimplification, this can be taken to refer to the absence or nullity of an underlying obligation. A payment under a contract can be recovered if later it turns out that the contract was void. In a system based on legal ground analysis, the true reasons for restitution are hidden behind several layers of abstraction. This will be demonstrated in later chapters of this book. For now, it suffices to point out that there are these two main models of unjust enrichment liability, and that the civilian model is threatening to encroach on the common law in England.

Two recent English cases stand out as throwing down the gauntlet to the Birksian typology. They are *Westdeutsche Landesbank Girozentrale v Islington London Borough Council*[5] and *Kleinwort Benson v Lincoln City Council*.[6] In *Westdeutsche*, which is discussed in detail below,[7] Hobhouse J (as he then was) based restitution on what he called 'absence of consideration', on the very absence of a valid contract underlying the transfer, in order to achieve a just result. As Birks immediately pointed out,[8] 'absence of consideration' no longer looks for concrete, pragmatic reasons for restitution, but relies on the abstract negative requirement apparently similar to the civilian '*sine causa*' (absence of cause). *Westdeutsche* could thus represent a fundamental turning point in the English law of unjust enrichment, aligning the English approach much more closely with the approach adopted by civilian systems.

The second case, *Kleinwort Benson v Lincoln* purports to remain within the established typology. In reality it undermines it in a similar fashion. In *Lincoln*, the traditional rule that there could be no restitution based on a mistake of law alone was finally abrogated by the House of Lords. Their Lordships' view of what constitutes a mistake, however, was so wide that it effectively based restitution on the nullity of the obligation which the transfer in question was supposed to discharge. The challenge in *Lincoln* is therefore surprisingly similar to the challenge in *Westdeutsche*: restitution is based not on a concrete reason for restitution such as mistake or failure of consideration, but on the absence or nullity of a supposed underlying obligation. Civilian jurists have been quick to argue that the civilian model is superior, and that English law has now all but accepted it.

Thus, in her recent book *Irrtum und Zweckverfehlung* (*Mistake and Failure of Purpose*),[9] Sonja Meier puts forward a forceful argument that the only way forward for the English law of unjust enrichment is the adoption of the civilian approach. To her, the main problem with the current typology is the unjust factor 'mistake'. She argues that it is wrong to make restitution available for every causal mistake. This, she argues, will clearly lead to too much restitution. The only way in which relevant mistakes can be distinguished from irrelevant mistakes is by adopting a legal ground approach based on the civilian model. According to her, this should be possible even in a common law system.

---

5   [1994] 4 All ER 890, QBD and [1994] 4 All ER 924, CA (references will be to the All England Law Reports, as both first instance and Court of Appeal decisions are conveniently reported there); varied [1996] AC 669, HL.

6   [1999] 2 AC 349.

7   See below, pp 6 ff.

8   Birks, 1993.

9   Meier, 1999a. Unfortunately, this book is not yet available in English, but see Meier, 2000 (summarising her argument in English); Krebs, 1999.

Meier gives examples which are meant to demonstrate the fallacy of a causal mistake approach. These all involve gifts which are made on a mistaken view of underlying facts. One person makes a donation to the Red Cross in the mistaken belief that the mayor and the vicar have made donations too. Another gives money to Friends of the Earth, not knowing that they are opposed to the additional runway at Heathrow, which he supports.[10] In such cases, a legal ground analysis would not lead to restitution because this kind of mistake would leave the legal ground of the payments, the intention to make a gift, unscathed. Meier thinks that this is the only justifiable result.

The adoption of a legal ground model would have collateral benefits, argues Meier. It would bring order into the chaos which is restitution following void transactions in English law at the moment.[11] The 'casuistry' of English law, she argues, would be replaced by an elegant, well structured and well reasoned model of restitutionary liability.

1.2 THE SCHEME OF THIS BOOK

This book is divided into five parts. Following an outline of the cases which have put the English typology of unjust enrichment into question, the second chapter gives an introduction to German private law generally. This is necessary if the remainder of the book is to make any sense at all.

Part II examines the unjust factor 'mistake'. The mainstay of Meier's argument is that 'mistake' as an unjust factor is over-inclusive and will lead to too much restitution in English law. This claim is tested against the theoretical background of mistake as a reason for restitution, and by looking at the relevant rules of English and German law.

Part III examines the unjust factor 'failure of consideration'. It will be argued that this unjust factor, properly understood, would have led to correct results in the swaps litigation. If it is interpreted restrictively, however, it leaves a gap in the law of unjust enrichment which is then filled by putative reasons for restitution such as 'absence of consideration' which are in reality alien to our system. A look at the German law will be particularly instructive, as German law has a special regime for cases of failure of contractual counter-performance within the law of contract, while, in contrast to Hobhouse J's view of English law, the category 'failure of consideration' within the German law of unjust enrichment is expressly confined to non-non-contractual cases.

Part IV is devoted to an examination of the *conditio indebiti*, the claim for restitution on the basis that an enrichment was not due. We will briefly look at policy-motivated restitution in both jurisdictions before turning to the putative general claim to restitution entitled 'absence of consideration'. The German law of unjust enrichment, as we shall see, is apparently based exclusively on the absence of an underlying 'legal ground'. It will be interesting to see how this is operated in practice. Whether it can work in a common law system is a different question. This has already been experimented with in Canada, with little success, as is argued in Chapter 13.

---

10 Meier, 1999a, p 87.
11 *Ibid*, p 363.

Part V argues that if the civilian approach is indeed adopted by English law, whether by adopting 'absence of consideration' or by a very wide interpretation of what constitutes a mistake of law, English common law will have to adapt to accommodate this. It will therefore be necessary to ask how the law of unjust enrichment can be limited, and the German experience can provide useful lessons in this context.

This book does not present an argument favouring either model of unjust enrichment liability. In other words, its author refuses to come off the fence. The advantage of the English model of unjust enrichment law is said to be that it addresses the vital question when an enrichment is considered unjust in a way which is comprehensible to the layman. This is Birks's famous phrase that restitution should follow if the claimant 'did not mean' the defendant to have the benefit. The price which English law has to pay for this is that there is a certain duplication of inquiries. The advantage of the civilian model is its elegance. Most substantive questions are not addressed by the law of unjust enrichment itself but are dealt with in the general law. This makes it possible to automate the law of unjust enrichment to a considerable extent. The price to pay for this elegance is that the German law of unjust enrichment is very abstract, although this criticism should not be taken too far, given that the substantive questions *are* dealt with, albeit not in the law of unjust enrichment itself, but in other areas of the law.

While there is thus nothing inherently wrong with the continental model, the danger which faces English law at this stage of its development is a combination of the two approaches. If the German model is about to be adopted, we should be aware of what we are doing. Otherwise, only confusion can follow.

1.3 ABSENCE OF CONSIDERATION

While Meier's challenge to the Birksian typology is mainly based on the argument that the unjust factor 'mistake' is too wide, Hobhouse J's attack on it is based on an understanding of the unjust factor 'failure of consideration' which is demonstrably too narrow. Given the importance of the decision for this book, it will now be discussed in some detail. First, however, it is necessary to introduce the reader to the somewhat confusing terminology which will be encountered again and again throughout the book.

1.3.1   A word about 'consideration'

Common lawyers first encounter the term 'consideration' when studying the law of contract, usually in the first year of their legal studies. It is thus difficult subsequently to divorce the term from its contractual undertones. In the contractual context, 'consideration' means in effect a '*quid pro quo*' – 'something of value in the eye of the law'[12] must be given in exchange for a promise in order to make it binding. Historically, however, the term 'consideration' first came into the common law as 'a thing considered', as a reason for the transfer. The 'considerations' for a promise 'meant the factors which the promisor considered when he promised, and which moved and motivated his

---

12   *Thomas v Thomas* (1842) 2 QB 851, 859.

promising'.[13] In due course, the only 'thing considered' that counted so as to give rise to an enforceable agreement was a contractual counter-performance, or at least the promise of such a counter-performance.

When we encounter the word 'consideration' again in the phrase 'failure of consideration', it is used in its original sense. A transfer is made for a reason, with a certain motive in mind: for a 'consideration', in short. When we speak of that 'consideration' failing, we do not mean that it is not sufficient to form a binding contract, or that no binding contract comes into existence. What we mean is that the transferor's motive for making the transfer has been disappointed, that the basis of the transferor's giving has failed.[14]

It is important not to succumb to the magnetic attraction of the contractual meaning of 'consideration', lest we make one of two mistakes. The first is to think that there can be no failure of consideration where a valid contract has been formed. That was the mistake in *Chandler v Webster*,[15] finally corrected by the House of Lords in the *Fibrosa* case.[16] The second mistake is a mirror image of the first. It is to think that failure of consideration can only ever be relevant in cases involving an initially valid contract. As we shall see, that mistake was made by Hobhouse J in *Westdeutsche* itself. So far, it has not been authoritatively corrected.

1.3.2 The factual background: the swaps saga

Westdeutsche was the first of the interest swap cases which reached the courts in the aftermath of the decision of the House of Lords in *Hazell v Hammersmith and Fulham*,[17] in which interest swap transactions were held to be *ultra vires* local authorities. Interest swaps are traded on the financial markets. The parties agree to pay each other interest on a notional sum. One party pays at a fixed rate (and is therefore referred to as 'the fixed rate payer'), the other at a floating rate ('floating rate payer'). If interest rates rise, the fixed rate payer will make a profit; if they fall, the floating rate payer will. To the lay person, it is not immediately clear why such apparent wagers should be entered into by rational business people, or why they should be statutorily exempted from the rules normally applicable to wagering contracts.[18] It appears, however, that the original and primary function of interest rate swaps was to insure the parties against loss arising from actual loan transactions. Thus, a party might have taken out a substantial loan at a flexible interest rate. The risk of subsequent interest rate rises is averted by entering into an interest rate swap agreement with a third party, with the notional loan sum equal to the sum of the actual loan. In this agreement, the party would be the fixed rate payer, with the result that in the event of a rate rise it would be compensated for increased servicing costs on the actual loan by receiving the corresponding amount under the swap

---

13 Simpson, 1975, p 321.
14 It must, of course, be borne in mind that no claim for failure of consideration will lie where the relevant 'consideration' has not been communicated by the transferor to the transferee at the time of making the transfer.
15 [1904] 1 KB 493, discussed below, pp 124 ff.
16 *Fibrosa Spolka Akcyjna v Fairbairn Lawson Combe Barbour Ltd* [1943] AC 32, 48.
17 [1992] 2 AC 1.
18 Financial Services Act 1986, s 63 and Sched 1.

agreement. The financial affairs of both parties become more stable, more predictable. In the markets, however, the 'hedgers' were soon joined by the speculators, hoping to make a profit from the volatility of interest rates.

Local authorities engaged in interest rate swaps as soon they became widely used in the early eighties. They frequently used them as a means of raising up-front cash to compensate for central government 'rate-capping'. Under a so called 'front-loaded' swap, the bank would pay the local authority an up-front payment, in consideration of which the interest rate payable by the local authority would be higher by one or two percent than would otherwise be the case. The bank would also charge a commission. It was their use to improve present liquidity that was considered most objectionable by the Court of Appeal in *Hazell*. However, the House of Lords, restoring the judgment of the Divisional Court, held that all swap agreements, even financially prudent hedging transactions, were *ultra vires* local authorities, rendering them absolutely void. The law of unjust enrichment was left with the task of sorting out the resulting mess (the House had refrained from expressing an opinion on the recoverability of payments under the void transactions). A wave of litigation hit the High Court. This was managed in such a way that a number of lead actions were selected to be tried, with all other actions being stayed pending the outcome of the lead actions. *Westdeutsche Landesbank Girozentrale v Islington* and *Kleinwort Benson v Sandwell* were two of these lead actions, heard concurrently by Hobhouse J in the Commercial Court. These cases were thus of a significance far exceeding the sums involved in the actual disputes before the court.[19]

1.3.3 *Westdeutsche Landesbank v Islington*

The cases involved a number of interest rate swaps which had been interrupted in mid-course. The second case, however, involved one fully executed transaction ('the first Sandwell swap'). All of them were void as *ultra vires* the local authorities. Payments made to date left the banks as the overall losers. Their claims to restitution were of two kinds. First, they put forward a personal claim at common law, in an action for money had and received. In particular, they claimed that the money had been paid for a consideration which had totally failed or, in the alternative, under a mistake. This common law claim developed in argument in a way that had 'altered its character to a claim based upon the payment of money under a void contract or alternatively money paid without consideration and without any intention to make a gift'.[20] Secondly, they maintained equitable claims based on tracing the money into the assets of the local authorities. These were founded on the House of Lords' decision in *Sinclair v Brougham*.[21] Hobhouse J allowed both the common law claim and the equitable claims to succeed.

Hobhouse J makes it clear that there 'has not been, and still is not, any general cause of action in English law for restitution for unjust enrichment'.[22] In particular he refers to an important *dictum* by Lord Diplock in *Orakpo v Manson Investments Ltd*:[23]

---

19 For essays on the swaps litigation, see Birks and Rose, 2000.

20 *Westdeutsche* [1994] 4 All ER 890, 906.

21 *Sinclair v Brougham* [1914] AC 398.

22 *Ibid*, at 912.

23 [1978] AC 95, 104.

My Lords, there is no general doctrine of unjust enrichment recognised in English law. What it does is to provide specific remedies in particular cases of what might be classified as unjust enrichment in a legal system that is based on the civil law.

Hobhouse J further cites a *dictum* by Lord Goff in *Woolwich Building Society v Inland Revenue Commissioners (No 2)*[4] also to show that there is no general cause of action in unjust enrichment:

Where a sum has been paid which is not due, but it has not been paid under a mistake of fact or under compulsion ... it is generally not recoverable.[25]

However, he is at pains to point out that the absence of a general cause of action does not necessarily denote the absence of a principle of unjust enrichment. He refers to *Woolwich* as an example of how new unjust factors can be derived from such a principle on a case by case basis.

To Hobhouse J, 'failure of consideration' is a contractual doctrine. He says:

The phrase 'failure of consideration' is one which in its terminology presupposes that there has been at some stage a valid contract which has been partially performed by one party.[26]

To an extent, this view contradicts a *dictum* by Viscount Simon LC in *Fibrosa*, which Hobhouse J cites just over the page:

... when one is considering the law of failure of consideration and of the quasi-contractual right to recover money on that ground, it is, generally speaking, not the promise which is referred to as the consideration, but the performance of the promise. The money was paid to secure performance and, if performance fails, the inducement which brought about the payment is not fulfilled.[27]

Viscount Simon is clearly drawing a distinction between 'consideration' in the law of contract (a promise for a promise), and 'consideration' in the law of restitution (a 'matter considered', an 'inducement'), which is the meaning with which 'consideration first came into the common law'.[28] This debate will be gone into in detail in Part III.

Failure of consideration can, according to Hobhouse J, never be the reason for restitution in non-contractual cases, because to Hobhouse J failure of consideration can only ever apply to contractual cases. This is the first reason why, in a case of a contract void under the *ultra vires* doctrine, he feels compelled to base restitution on 'absence' of consideration.

The second reason is the requirement that a failure of consideration must be total if restitution is to follow. Relying on the passage in *Fibrosa*, referred to above, he holds that if the other party has 'at least partially performed his obligations under the contract so as to confer some benefit upon the claimant, then the claimant cannot rely upon the principle.'[29] While it is not altogether clear that this principle is expressed in Viscount

---

24 [1993] AC 70 (cited as *Woolwich*).

25 *Ibid*, at 165.

26 *Westdeutsche* [1994] 4 All ER 890, 924.

27 *Fibrosa Spolka Akcyjna v Fairbairn Lawson Combe Barbour Ltd* [1943] AC 32, 48, *per* Viscount Simon LC; cited by Hobhouse J in *Westdeutsche*, at 925.

28 Birks, 1989, p 223; relying on Simpson, 1975, p 321.

29 *Westdeutsche* [1994] 4 All ER 890, 925.

Simon LC's *dictum*, it is undisputed that the 'total failure' requirement has been a part of English law for a long time. As Hobhouse J acknowledges, '[t]o get round the difficulty that they could not satisfy the test stated in the *Fibrosa* case, the claimants advanced various arguments which all in the end amounted to the proposition that, where there has never been any contract in law ... any sums paid under that contract can in principle be recovered'.[30] This proposition, which is accepted by Hobhouse J, is only consistent with Lord Goff's *dictum* in *Woolwich* cited earlier in the judgment[31] in so far as it is narrower: restitution does not follow because the benefit conferred was not due, but because it was transferred under a contract which turned out to be ineffective. The distinction is a narrow one, and, as Birks warns,[32] it is unlikely that it will be maintained. In Chapter 12, the 'absence of consideration' approach in English law will be discussed in detail. For the moment, it is important to note that adoption of this approach in English law would constitute a new departure. We will no longer search for positive reasons why an enrichment should be reversed, but there will be a negative requirement – the absence of consideration – which will need to be satisfied instead. The German law of restitution contains a very similar formula in § 812 I *BGB*. (§ 812 I 1 means: para 812, sub-para 1, first sentence. This notation is used throughout this book.) The German experience with that formula, referring to the absence of a 'juristic reason' for the enrichment, will be the subject matter of Chapter 11.

Islington appealed against Hobhouse J's judgment. Sandwell did not appeal, so that the important issue whether there should have been restitution in the first and fully executed Sandwell swap did not then reach the appellate courts.[33] The Court of Appeal endorsed the absence of consideration approach, although Dillon LJ, with whom Kennedy LJ agreed, thought that restitution could equally well have been based on failure of consideration.

Dillon LJ shares Hobhouse J's view, however, that 'failure of consideration' is primarily a contractual principle, relevant only to contractual counter-performances. It appears, however, that to him the term 'contractual counter-performance' is wider, encompassing cases of supposed contracts as well as actual (but ineffective) ones. To Dillon LJ, the fact that the swap transactions were void *ab initio* is thus not fatal to a claim based on failure of consideration. Dillon LJ sees absence of consideration as a principle which is primarily useful for situations in which there has been no contract at all, whether actual or supposed. To him, the paradigm case is *Woolwich*, which concerned payments made in response to an *ultra vires* demand. He argues that if recovery in that case had been based on absence of consideration, restitution would have been granted because the benefit had not been due.

Leggatt LJ states the applicable principle as follows:

> Where A has in his possession the money of B under a void transaction, B should be entitled to reimbursement unless some principle of law precludes it. If the transaction was a contract, initially valid, the question will arise whether it has been partially performed. If so,

---

30 *Westdeutsche* [1994] 4 All ER 890.
31 *Ibid*, at 913; see above, p 7.
32 Birks, 1993, p 232.
33 The issue came before the Court of Appeal some years later, in *Guinness Mahon & Co Ltd v Kensington and Chelsea Royal London Borough Council* [1999] QB 215, see below, pp 10 f.

the failure of consideration will not be total. But if the transaction was entered into by both parties in the belief, which proves unfounded, that it was an enforceable contract, in principle the parties ought to be restored to the respective positions from which they started. To achieve that, where there have been mutual payments the recipient of the larger payment has only to repay the net excess over the payment he has himself made.[34]

Leggatt LJ thus argues that, where there has been an initially valid contract, the principle of failure of consideration continues to apply, including the total failure requirement. That requirement is only lifted when there was no contract at all between the parties at any stage. As he says later in the judgment:

> There can have been no consideration under a contract void *ab initio*. So it is fallacious to speak of the failure of consideration having been partial.[35]

From a policy point of view, this is a position that is surely difficult to defend. Why should the law insist on the total failure requirement where a contract was initially valid, but was later terminated for breach, but not where no actual contract was formed, but performances were made by both sides as though under a contract?[36]

In embracing the formula which can be found in § 812 I *BGB*, Leggatt LJ goes further than either Hobhouse J or Dillon LJ, when he says that the parties 'were making payments that had no legal justification, instead of affording each other mutual consideration for an enforceable contract'.[37] Leggatt LJ is here moving uncomfortably close to a law of 'unjustified' enrichment – a state of affairs in which any enrichment is unjust, unless the transferee can show that there is some contract or other legal transaction which can justify his enrichment. Such a system would render most if not all 'unjust factors' redundant and completely change the way we do things in England.

Islington appealed to the House of Lords,[38] but only on the ground that Hobhouse J and the Court of Appeal had awarded Westdeutsche compound interest rather than simple interest. On authority, the court could only award compound interest when exercising its equitable jurisdiction. The appeal thus turned on whether Hobhouse J had been right in finding a resulting trust in favour of the bank. It was thus the second, proprietary, dimension of *Westdeutsche* that the House of Lords was concerned with, and not the common law claim for money had and received. By a three to two majority, their Lordships overruled *Sinclair v Brougham*[39] and allowed the appeal. Lords Goff and Woolf, dissenting, agreed that there should be no resulting trust, but argued that the equitable jurisdiction should be exercised nevertheless. Lords Browne-Wilkinson, Lloyd and Slynn, however, felt that it was for Parliament to extend the law in this way.

Lords Goff and Browne-Wilkinson do comment on the ground of restitution at common law, but their statements are necessarily *obiter* as the personal liability of the

---

34   *Westdeutsche* [1994] 2 All ER 890.
35   *Ibid.*
36   For possible, but in the end fallacious, arguments supporting Leggatt's view, see below.
37   *Westdeutsche* [1994] 4 All ER 890, 969.
38   *Westdeutsche* [1996] AC 669.
39   [1914] AC 398.

local authority was common ground between the parties and not at issue in the appeal. Lord Goff comments that the absence of consideration approach may have found its origin in the idea 'that a failure of consideration only occurs where there has been a failure of performance by the other party of his obligation under a contract which was initially binding'. He thinks, however, 'that the concept of failure of consideration need not be so narrowly confined'.[40] He finds 'considerable force' in academic criticisms of the no consideration approach, but is careful to point out that it 'would be inappropriate to express any concluded view' on the point.[41]

Lord Browne-Wilkinson, giving the leading judgment of the majority, does not refer directly to the absence of consideration debate. He proceeds on the basis that the ground for restitution in *Westdeutsche* was *failure* of consideration. However, it is not quite clear what he means by this phrase. It appears that there may in fact be little or no difference between Hobhouse J's *absence* of consideration and Lord Browne-Wilkinson's *failure* of consideration. Thus his Lordship says:

> The failure of consideration was *not* partial: the depositors had paid over their money in consideration of a promise to repay. That promise was *ultra vires* and void; therefore, the consideration for the payment of the money wholly failed.[42]

To Lord Browne-Wilkinson, the consideration is thus the contractual promise rather than the performance of the promise. Restitution follows because the underlying contract is void, not because the promised performance has failed. There is no distinction between this and Hobhouse J's absence of consideration. That concept, it would therefore appear, is still alive and well.

1.3.4 The *Guinness Mahon* case in the Court of Appeal

In *Guinness Mahon & Co Ltd v Kensington and Chelsea Royal London Borough Council*,[43] the issue whether there can be restitution where the interest swap transaction between the parties has been fully executed finally reached the Court of Appeal. In effect, this was the *Sandwell* appeal which had never been, as Morritt LJ pointed out.[44] The Court of Appeal decided that restitution was indeed available in such a case. Although Waller LJ expressed serious reservations about the 'absence of consideration' approach, and only agreed with the result because he considered himself bound by the authority of *Westdeutsche*, both Morritt and Robert Walker LJJ gave the new doctrine their endorsement.

Morritt LJ's judgment shows particularly clearly how very close the absence of consideration doctrine is moving English law towards the civilian model. His Lordship observed:

---

40 *Westdeutsche* [1996] AC 669, 683.
41 *Ibid*.
42 *Ibid*, at 710.
43 [1999] QB 215.
44 *Ibid*, at 275.

Though the basis of the implied promise may now have gone, in my view, the general principle must remain that an *ultra vires* transaction is of no legal effect. It must follow that the recipient of money thereunder has no right to it. If he keeps it he will be enriched. If he does not then or subsequently obtain a right to keep it, such enrichment will be unjust.[45]

And later:

Nor, with respect to Professor Birks, do I agree that there is no compelling reason to allow the bank to recover the value of its performance. The bank did not get in exchange for that performance all it expected, for it did not get the benefit of the contractual obligation of the local authority.[46]

Robert Walker LJ agreed with Morritt LJ, concluding that '[t]he injustice of the council's enrichment did not vanish because the term of a void contract ran its course'.[47] He fails, however, to point out what constitutes that injustice. This is precisely the criticism which can be levelled at restitution based on 'absence of consideration', or indeed, on 'absence of legal ground'. There are suggestions in the speech of Morritt LJ that the *ultra vires* doctrine is behind the injustice,[48] and Waller LJ's speech tends to confirm this. Nowhere in the case, however, is the actual reason for restitution clearly spelled out. If the council's enrichment is unjust because of the policy behind the *ultra vires* doctrine, that policy is not properly formulated.

1.4 MISTAKE OF LAW AND RESTITUTION FOR NULLITY

If the 'absence of consideration' approach constitutes a direct attack on the English typology of the law of unjust enrichment, the abolition of the mistake of law bar in the *Lincoln* case[49] is more indirect. *Lincoln* also involved fully executed interest rate swaps. Again the banks were the losers, and sought to obtain restitution from the councils. They were unable, however, to base their claims on absence or failure of consideration. This was because many of their claims involved payments made more than six years before issue of the writ following the House of Lords' decision in *Hazell*. The claims were therefore *prima facie* statute barred. The only hope was s 32(1)(c) of the Limitation Act 1980. That provision applies to claims based on mistake. It 'stops the clock' until such time as the mistake could reasonably have been discovered. If the claims could be based on mistake, there was thus still hope. If there had been any mistake at all, however, it had been a mistake of law. It was therefore necessary to challenge the long established rule that mistake of law was not in and of itself a ground for restitution. The claim succeeded in the House of Lords. Not only did their Lordships abrogate the mistake of law bar, they also held, by a bare majority, that the banks in these cases had indeed been labouring under a mistake of law.

The problem with this analysis is that, at the time the payment was made, everybody thought that the swap transactions were perfectly valid. The advice of most lawyers

---

45 *Ibid*, at 229.
46 *Ibid*, at 230.
47 *Ibid*, at 240.
48 *Ibid*, particularly at 229.
49 *Kleinwort Benson Ltd v Lincoln City Council* [1999] 2 AC 349.

would have confirmed this. At the time the payments were made, therefore, there was no mistake, assuming that the law was indeed what everybody thought it was. The House of Lords accept, for the sake of argument, that *Hazell* indeed changed the law. Indeed, they go so far as to suggest that the position would be no different if the payments had been made in accordance with a decision made by the Court of Appeal which is subsequently overruled. It is very difficult to see, as the minority point out, how the banks can be described to have been mistaken in such circumstances. On a more realistic view, there was no mistake here at all: the effect of the subsequent House of Lords decision is to change the law retrospectively, but, in the words of Lord Browne-Wilkinson, 'retrospection cannot falsify history'.[50] The argument that there was indeed no mistake in the *Lincoln* case will be elaborated below. If we assume that it is correct, the focus shifts away from the transferor's defective intent to the existence or otherwise of the underlying obligation. This becomes particularly clear in the speech of Lord Hope, who was part of the majority. He said:

> In my opinion, the proper starting point for an examination of this issue is the principle on which the claim for restitution of these payments is founded, which is that of unjust enrichment. The essence of this principle is that it is unjust for a person to retain a benefit which he has received at the expense of another, without any legal ground to justify its retention, which that other person did not intend him to receive. This has been the basis for the law of unjust enrichment as it has developed both in the civilian systems and in Scotland, which has a mixed system – partly civilian and partly common law. On the whole, now that the common law systems see their law of restitution as being based upon this principle, one would expect them to apply it, broadly speaking, in the same way, and reach results which, broadly speaking, were similar.[51]

A little later on, he continues:

> The common law accepts that the payee is enriched where the sum was not due to be paid to him, but it requires the payer to show that this was unjust. Whereas in civilian systems proof of knowledge that there was no legal obligation to pay is a defence which may be invoked by the payee, under the common law it is for the payer to show that he paid under a mistake. My impression is that the common law tends to place more emphasis on the need for proof of a mistake. But the underlying principle in both systems is that of unjust enrichment. The purpose of this principle is to provide a remedy for recovery of the enrichment where no legal ground exists to justify its retention.[52]

The importance of showing a mistake is thus played down and the negative requirement 'lack of legal ground' takes centre stage. What is left bears an uncanny resemblance to § 12 I: restitution based on 'absence of legal ground'.

---

50   *Ibid*, at 358.
51   *Ibid*, at 408.
52   *Ibid*, at 409.

CHAPTER 2

ESSENTIAL ELEMENTS OF GERMAN LAW

This chapter is to put the comparative discussion that is to follow into context. Even at the cost of anticipating some of the discussion to come, it is necessary to give the reader an introduction to the relevant parts of German law. Only in this way can the comparative analysis work efficiently. The first part of this chapter will give a short historical introduction. To understand the modern German law, one has to be aware of the historical background. Without this, it would be quite difficult to understand German legal style and technique – so much of it can only be explained historically. The second part of the chapter will consider the nature of codifications in general and of the German civil code in particular. For the purposes of this book, it is important to appreciate that there are fundamental differences in legal style between the civil law and the common law, which can cause significant problems if concepts from one system are transplanted into the other. The concluding two parts of the chapter will give short and necessarily superficial introductions to the two areas of law this book is mainly concerned with: the laws of contract and unjust enrichment.[1]

2.1 THE INFLUENCE OF ROMAN LAW

Germany is a civil law country. The term 'civil' indicates a tradition based on Roman law, which is one of the main distinctions between civil and common law countries. While Roman law was (and to an extent still is) taught at English universities, its study was always at best comparative, at worst historical. Never did it assume validity, and attempts by jurists such as Lord Mansfield to draw on the hidden treasure of the Roman sources were vigorously resisted and strongly criticised. On the Continent, Roman law was received into the mediaeval legal system. In studying Justinian's codification, jurists were 'discovering' their own law. The law of Rome became of vital importance for the day to day administration of contemporary law.

In Germany, the soil was particularly fertile for the reception of Roman law. There was little or no centralised political power. The 'Holy Roman Emperor' administered his 'Empire' on the road, travelling from city to city and from principality to principality. True political power was in the hands of petty kings and dukes, bishops and City States. The result was legal fragmentation on a grand scale, with such law as there was being administered mostly by laymen or the Church, not by a guild of professional lawyers as existed in England in the form of the Inns of Court. Justice was dispensed on the basis of 'common sense' or superstition (ordeals were commonplace), and differently according to the region of Germany in which a case arose. Roman law, being taught first at the Italian universities, but soon imported into Germany, provided an alternative: a legal system which deserved the name, based on logic and reason, the main contribution of Roman culture to the world. It came to assume subsidiary validity throughout most of Germany:

---

1   For much more comprehensive treatment, see Markesinis, 1997.

as the *ius commune* it was relied upon whenever local law or custom failed to provide a satisfactory answer. While Hermann Conring (1606–81) had demonstrated that Roman law had not – as had been assumed – become law in Germany by the decree of the Holy Roman Emperor Lothar I (1125–37),[2] and while it never achieved more than subsidiary validity throughout Germany, it did dominate legal practice and served to unify the otherwise fragmented 'Holy Roman Empire of the German Nation'.

In the 19th century, Roman law enjoyed a renaissance. The so-called historical school, founded by Friedrich Carl von Savigny, largely disregarded the development of Roman law that had taken place throughout the Middle Ages and went back to the ancient texts. As Basil Markesinis, Werner Lorenz and Gerhard Dannemann point out, this 'intellectual re-orientation left a strong mark on the content of the Code as a whole and the law of contract in particular, since solutions were often adopted on the basis that they had been espoused (or, which was worse, were thought to have been espoused) nearly two thousand years earlier by Roman law'[3] Finding the law in this way became a science: 'legal science'. The German term, '*Rechtswissenschaft*', survives to the present day.

2.2 A BRIEF HISTORY OF THE CODIFICATION[4]

2.2.1 The codification debate

There had been calls for a unified German code well before 1871. Arguments for and against codification were debated at length as far back as 1814 (the date is significant), by two of the foremost jurists of the time: Anton Friedrich Justus Thibaut (1772–1840) and Friedrich Carl von Savigny (1779–1861). This debate had only become possible because Roman law had run into a crisis: the German Empire and its laws had been put into question by the enlightenment and the French revolution. The French Emperor's protection enabled 16 German princes to found the '*Rheinbund*', which eventually led to the end of the 'Holy Roman Empire' when Franz II surrendered his crown in 1806. This revolution was meant to wipe out the constitution of the Empire, whose constitutional as well as private law was based on Roman law. When Art 2 of the document founding the *Rheinbund* abolished '*toute loi de l'empire Germanique*', this was not meant to include private law. However, Roman law was no longer valid as the law of the Empire, but because of the will of the relevant prince, and soon the various princes took it upon themselves to introduce changes. The Kingdom of Westphalia was the first to introduce a new set of laws, adopting the *Code Napoléon*. Here, as in Frankfurt, the *Hanse* towns, Lippe, the Duchy of Aremberg and the Grand Duchy of Berg, its introduction was the consequence of military defeat. However, full of the enthusiasm of the revolution, readable and intended for the layman, yet highly abstract to cater for all the peoples of Europe, extremely short and yet based on the sound foundation of Roman law, it was and remains a great success which survived the ultimate defeat of the revolution and the

---

2   Conring, 1643.

3   Markesinis, 1997, p 5.

4   The account which follows is oversimplified and extremely short. For much more expert and detailed treatment, see Wieacker, 1996, pp 468–88.

French Empire in France, but also on the German left bank of the Rhine, right up to the introduction of the *BGB*.

However, German national pride found it naturally difficult to tolerate a foreign civil code being in force in Germany, and after Napoleon's defeat the *Code Civil* came under increasing attack. In late 1813, August Rehberg published a short pamphlet against the code,[5] which contained some criticism of the code as a piece of legislation, but was aimed most of all at its progressive agenda based on *'liberté, égalité, fraternité'*, and the destruction of German legal heritage. Thus he writes that by founding the new code on 'the ideas of liberty and equality',[6] the revolutionaries intended 'to rob the German national of all which men of heart and feeling hold dear'. A nation 'which has to give up its established conditions, laws, customs and language', had lost its dignity, according to Rehberg.[7] Clearly, such attempts to topple the code would eventually be successful. Thibaut criticised Rehberg's approach,[8] but pointed out at the same time that the time was ripe for a comprehensive German codification. In the same year, he put forward the argument more comprehensively and forcefully in the seminal essay *'Über die Nothwendigkeit eines allgemeinen bürgerlichen Rechts für Deutschland'*.[9] For a professor of Roman Law, it was somewhat surprising to demand the quasi-abolition of his own profession. However, the picture Thibaut paints of conditions in legal Germany is a dark one. Legal fragmentation on the one hand, only held together by reference to the ancient Latin texts and the interpretation of the 'secret guild' of jurists capable of understanding them on the other, could not be a secure foundation for a modern legal system. Thibaut was further progressive enough to abhor the differences between the common man and the aristocracy, given expression in a legal system largely based on status relationships.

Savigny saw Thibaut's essay as a dangerous attempt to subvert the established order. He was firmly on Rehberg's side in advocating the abolition of the *Code Civil*. Such a step, according to him, was 'as urgent as without danger'.[10] Savigny's criticism of Thibaut's project, also published in 1814,[11] is much influenced by the spirit of the restoration. Even a German code would not be much more than a variation on a French theme. Any attempt at codification was, thought Savigny, doomed to failure. Further, it was not necessary. Roman law, as interpreted by German 'legal science', offered a much better alternative. Savigny presents Roman law not as a system based on and derived from human reason, but as objective and absolute truth – to him, the jurist's task was to identify and apply this truth. The term 'jurisprudence' was replaced by 'legal science', the search for eternal and scientific 'truths'.

This 'historical school', founded by Savigny, was very influential throughout the 19th century. Even though in the end the argument was lost, German law codified, the jurists of the historical school have left their mark on the law. Many of their insights into Roman law were relied upon when the *BGB* came to be drafted. The positivistic approach to law

---

5   Rehberg, 1814.
6   *Ibid*, p 6.
7   *Ibid*, pp 11 ff.
8   Thibaut, 1814.
9   The essay is conveniently published, together with Savigny's reply, in Stern, 1959.
10 Letter of 3 December 1913, printed in Stoll, 1927, Vol 2, No 105.
11 Savigny, reprinted in Stern, 1959, p 95.

has survived, albeit now based on the text of the code rather than the scientific interpretation of the Roman sources. Contrary to Thibaut's intention, German law has remained a law of the professors, not a law of normal people or even the judges.[12] To the present day, the great German lawyers are teachers, not practising advocates or judges. Where in England we think of Lords Mansfield, Diplock and Goff, we find Professors Windscheid, von Caemmerer, and Flume in Germany.

2.2.2 The drafting of the *BGB*

With the unification of the German State in 1871, the need for change became more pressing. Though now a single State, Germany did not yet have one single legal system. Indeed, the constitution had to be altered in order to give the *Reichstag* the right to legislate in the area of private law.[13] Prussia already had a codification, the *'Preußisches Allgemeines Landrecht'*, on the left banks of the Rhine the *Code Civil* was still valid, while the rest of the new Empire was still based on local laws and customs with the underlying subsidiary validity of Roman law. German legal science thus had to play the role the comprehensive, pan-German codification which had failed in 1814 was to have played. Bernard Windscheid, one of Savigny's pupils, published his 'Pandects' in 1862. This came to be regarded as the most authoritative text-book on the ius commune in Germany, and fulfilled many of the functions of today's code, commentaries and jurisprudence. The face of Roman law changed: the sources were re-interpreted and adapted for the needs of an increasingly industrial society.

The momentum for legal unification became ever stronger, however, and codifications were being drafted in many German States. The fruits of such efforts were many drafts, and one fully-fledged civil code, which passed into law in Saxony as late as 1863. State legislation had, for the first time since the reception of Roman law, declared its independence of legal science. It was replaced by the 'will of the people', expressed by the legislature of the constitutional State.

Had the *ius commune*, Roman law as interpreted and applied by 'legal scientists', acquired more than subsidiary validity throughout Germany, had it won the same victory as that won by the King's Courts and the common law in England, it may well be that Germany would never have had a codification.

When a first commission was entrusted with the task of drafting a civil code for the whole of Germany in 1881, the result was a code very much in the tradition of the pandectists, as they had come to be called. This was due in part to the overwhelming influence of one of the three law professors on the panel: Bernard Windscheid. Though the majority of the commission consisted of practising lawyers and civil servants, these had all been trained as pandectists: their starting point was thus the Roman law. The first draft, presented by the commission in 1887, accompanied by the detailed minutes of the first commission's proceedings, the so-called 'motives', was immediately subjected to

---

12 Cf Zweigert and Kötz, 1998, pp 144 f; Markesinis, 1997, p 9.

13 Bismarck's *'Reichsverfassung'* was based on the constitution of the *'Deutsche Bund'*, under which the *'Bundestag'* was not competent to legislate in the area of private law. It took five attempts to change the constitution accordingly, by amending Art 4 XIII by law of 20 December 1873, the so-called *'Lex Lasker'*.

fierce criticism, directed mainly at the strength of the Roman influence. It was also criticised that the draft, again in the tradition of the pandects, used wooden, artificial language and was full of cross-references to other parts of the code, which made it most difficult to understand to expert and layman alike.[14] Retaining this draft as a basis for its work, a second commission was entrusted with the task of preparing a second draft, taking account of the criticisms that had been made. This second draft, presented to the public in 1895, again accompanied by the minutes of the discussions, the 'protocols', was more enthusiastically received, although the changes made in reality failed to answer many of the criticisms levelled against the first draft: a higher level of abstraction than necessary was used, the influence of the pandects was still predominant, and cross-references to different sections of the code continued to abound.

The *Bundesrat*, which had to consider the second draft before presenting it to the *Reichstag*, did not make any important changes, and a third draft, presented in 1896 to the *Reichstag*, was passed on 18 August 1896 and received the force of law on the first day of the new century.

2.3 CHARACTERISTICS OF THE *BGB*

The main characteristic of a codification in the sense the word is used in this context is its claim to universality and comprehensiveness. What has gone before is important only in so far as it helped shape the concepts and approach of the draftsmen. The old law is now replaced *in toto* – it is not consolidated, built upon, improved or reformed. It ceases to be valid law. The codification claims to provide a coherent system, capable of producing answers for all cases that can possibly arise. To live up to this claim, it has to be drafted abstractly, keeping casuistry to a minimum. With the *BGB*, the positivism of legal science, claiming to be capable of finding an absolute legal truth in the Roman sources, was replaced with a positivism based on the codification, claiming to find answers to all conceivable legal questions within the provisions of the *BGB*. The *BGB* achieves the required high level of abstraction by three main means: the use of a 'general part', cross-referencing and general clauses. It is worth examining these techniques in a little detail.

2.3.1 The use of the 'general part'

The *BGB* contains two general parts: the first book, and §§ 241–432 of the second book both bear that title. The first book, however, does not define or explain, as might have been expected, general concepts such as 'contract', 'right' and 'duty', but takes terminology for granted and proceeds to make provisions which are applicable to all areas of law covered by the *BGB*. These are the laws of obligations, property, the family and probate. The law of obligations, as mentioned above, itself consists of a general part and a special part: the general part outlines in broad terms what rights and duties flow from an obligation between the parties (specific performance, damages, late performance,

---

14   Zweigert and Kötz, 1998, pp 144 f.

breach of contract, termination of contract etc), while the special part lists a number of specific contracts (sale, barter, donation, hire, services) and other obligations not arising under a contract, such as delict and, indeed, unjust enrichment.

German writers usually explain the technique of using a general part as 'placing common rules outside the brackets'.[15] Markesinis *et al* prefer a geometrical metaphor, describing the technique as one of 'concentric circles', with the most general rules to be found in the outermost circles, the most specialised rules in the innermost circles.[16] Probably the most 'pragmatic' metaphor was used by Heck back in 1939:[17] he likens the general part to the key to a railway timetable. That which has been explained once does not need to be explained over and over again. The main aim of the technique is thus one of *rationalisation*. This has not been achieved without paying a price: a high degree of abstraction removes a legal norm from the real-life cases which it is supposed to govern. As Markesinis *et al* put it, '[i]f there was an award for the highest level of abstraction in any code, the Bürgerliches Gesetzbuch would be a clear favourite to win it'.[18] It is questionable whether the aim of rationalisation justifies paying this price. In particular, in stark contrast to the French codification, the use of the general part makes the *BGB* virtually incomprehensible to the layperson, and indeed to the foreign lawyer.[19]

A commonplace example may illustrate the point, using 'that most common of contracts',[20] the contract of sale, as an example. In German law, a simple sale may necessitate a reference to no less than five separate parts of the *BGB*. First, the general part provides how declarations can be made so as to have legal consequences, and under what circumstances they are vitiated (§§ 116 ff). Further, it informs us that for the formation of a contract (any contract) offer and acceptance have to be declared, and provides rules concerning their communication etc. Secondly, we need to refer to the general part of the law of obligations, in order to learn what the consequences will be if one party is unable or unwilling to perform (§§ 241 ff). Thirdly, there are special rules for obligations arising from contracts (rather than in some other way) which can be found in §§ 305 ff. For instance, if performance is no longer possible, § 323 makes the promisor free of his obligation if he is not to blame for the impossibility. Fourthly, the rights and duties of seller and buyer, that is, the very content of the obligation in question, are outlined in § 433 (which is specifically directed at sale contracts): the buyer has to pay the price, the seller to transfer the property in the goods. Fifthly, we learn how the property is transferred in the third book of the *BGB*, the law of property: § 929 tells us that what is needed is delivery and an agreement that property is to pass. To complicate things still further, to approach a case in the order in which the subject-matter is arranged in the *BGB*, as was done in the above example, would probably lead to the wrong result: special rules taking precedence over general rules, the correct order is 'from back to front',

---

15   Medicus, 1997, p 15.

16   Markesinis, 1997, p 15 ff.

17   Heck, 1939, p 1.

18   Markesinis, 1997, p 15.

19   Markesinis, in giving an account of the German law of obligations, thus adopts the technique 'deconstruct and then reconstruct' (Markesinis, 1997, p xlix), ie, disregard the German structures as far as possible, concentrating on 'real' cases and 'real' decisions, which can then be compared with common law solutions.

20   Goode, 1988, p 135.

referring to the special rules towards the back of the *BGB* first and retracing one's steps from the special to the general.

The use of the general part avoids repetition, allows the *BGB* to be a good deal shorter than it would otherwise have to be, but at the price of making the code incomprehensible to a layperson. It also allows the code to be a great deal more abstract than would otherwise be possible. Everything is subsumed under ever wider concepts, and these concepts are further and further removed from everyday experience.

The 'general part approach' necessitates the use of highly abstract terminology. Thus, it is not necessary to explain under what conditions a contractual offer is vitiated, because an offer is nothing but a special kind of 'declaration' or *'Willenserklärung'*, whose conditions for validity are laid down at a much more general level in §§ 116 ff. One of the great advantages of the *BGB* is its great consistency of terminology. This is, however, absolutely necessary because its provisions are often so far removed from real life experience that inconsistencies would lead to chaos. Again, the use of such abstract terminology becomes a little less objectionable if one considers the 'target audience' of the *BGB*: trained lawyers, judges, academics. Nevertheless, in today's age, which demands increased accountability of authority, greater transparency and a more sensitive consideration for real social and individual justice, the *BGB*'s abstract nature presents a serious problem.

2.3.2 Cross-references

Markesinis *et al* explain that the general part approach 'can only function if the smallest common denominator can still serve to exclude cases to which the rationale of the rule does not apply'.[21] If that is no longer possible or practicable, the *BGB* resorts to cross-references, incorporating a rule spelled out for one situation by reference into a different context. One infamous example, which we will have to return to in some detail, is to be found in § 327, in the context of breach of contract. One option which is in certain circumstances available to the innocent party is to terminate the contract. For the details of termination, however, § 327 refers to § 346, which is a rule designed primarily for contractually agreed rights to withdraw from a contractual arrangement. This approach is used throughout the *BGB*, 'but nowhere as much as in restitution-type situations'.[22] Its frequent use in a restitutionary context is easily explained: there is no 'law of restitution' as such in the *BGB*. The remedy 'restitution' is instead made available in a number of different contexts. One of the most important restitutionary claims is contained in § 985, in the third book of the *BGB*, governing the law of property. § 985 provides that an owner of property is generally entitled to demand restitution in specie from the possessor. This vindication claim is then elaborated on by the following paragraphs, governing the relationship between owner and unauthorised possessor, the so-called *'Eigentümer-Besitzer-Verhältnis'*, a kind of unauthorised bailment relationship. Under § 292, the possessor of somebody else's chattel will be liable for any use made of the object, as well as any use he negligently fails to make. As in the English law of bailment, the possessor will, of course, be liable in damages if he negligently damages or destroys the chattel. The

---

21 Markesinis, 1997, p 23.
22 *Ibid*, p 24.

framework of §§ 985 ff is then taken as a model for other restitutionary claims throughout the *BGB*. Thus, if the claimant is entitled to restitution of a chattel under § 812 I, and the defendant was aware of his claim or otherwise *mala fide*, § 818 IV refers to the 'general provisions'. § 292 provides that where a party is required to make restitution of a chattel, his liability will, as soon as he is aware of the claim, be governed by the provisions applicable to the '*Verhältnis zwischen dem Eigentümer und dem Besitzer*', that is, § 985 ff, and in particular § 989. Thus, if a recipient under a restitutionary obligation, knowing that he is under such an obligation, damages the chattel subject to that obligation negligently, he will be liable in damages, which is a fairly obvious result. Due to the unfortunate technique of cross-referencing, such a claim is based on a 'chain of paragraphs', starting with § 812 I and culminating in § 989. This will look something like this: the claimant is entitled to damages under §§ 812 I, 818 IV, 292, 989. The problem is compounded by the draftsmen's omission to refer to the actual paragraphs: as we have seen, the *BGB* merely refers the reader to the general area of the law that is to be applied to the situation. Thus, the novice will not readily appreciate that the reference to the 'general rules' in § 818 IV in fact refers to § 292, nor is it common knowledge amongst lay-people what exactly is meant by 'the relationship between the owner and the possessor'.

2.3.3 The general clause

The choice between ever greater abstraction and painstaking casuistry can be side-stepped by using general clauses. The draftsmen of the *BGB* have used this device fairly liberally, though not to the same extent as the French *Code Civil*. General clauses are principles, maxims addressed to the judge, which 'bind and liberate him at the same time'.[23] By referring to good faith, custom and commercial practice etc, the *BGB* has been able to absorb changes in society and to stay in force, with some minor amendments, to the present day.[24] The general clause opens up possibilities for judicial development of the law, so as to reflect such changes in society. Thus, § 242, probably the most important of all the general clauses in the *BGB*, provides broadly that a contractual performance is to be rendered in accordance with good faith. However, over the years the judges have been able to derive from it concepts such as frustration ('*Wegfall der Geschäftsgrundlage*', '*clausula rebus sic stantibus*') and estoppel ('*venire contra factum proprium*'), neither of them foreseen by the drafters of the *BGB*. However, as Zweigert and Kötz point out, general clauses give rise to the danger 'of producing judicial decisions which are undirected, exuberant, and variable'.[25] Even a well-meaning judge will be encouraged to rely on his own conceptions of 'good faith', his own ideas of justice and morality, in reaching his decision, unless the general clause is given a well-defined content by established case law and/or by academic writers. The *BGB* does not place undue reliance on general clauses. As Markesinis *et al* acknowledge, it 'has made fairly prudent use of general clauses, and has generally opted for a mixture of general and special clauses which works well in practice, by covering the typical situations through the specific rules and leaving enough room for development in most other cases'.[26]

23 Wieacker, 1996, p 476.
24 On the negative side of the ledger, it has also facilitated its misuse during the Nazi era.
25 Zweigert and Kötz, 1998, p 150.
26 Markesinis, 1997, p 23.

It is important to note at this point that German courts are very much used to general clauses. Their use was absolutely necessary for a successful civil code such as the *BGB* has become, and in general the courts are well aware of their dangers. Anyone advocating the importation of general principles from German into English law should remember this.

2.4 THE GERMAN LAW OF CONTRACT

The rest of this chapter is devoted to a brief description of the substantive German law which this book will be concerned with. In this section we turn first to the law of contract.

2.4.1 Relevant provisions in the general part

To the German lawyer, a contract is merely one species of the genus 'legal transaction' (*Rechtsgeschäft*), which is defined as an act aimed at the bringing about of a legal consequence.[27] This normally consists of one or more 'declarations of will' ('*Willenserklärungen*'), which, depending on the nature of the legal transaction, will suffice to bring about the desired result. Thus, a contract consists of offer and acceptance. Both are declarations, and together they form the legal transaction 'contract'. If a contract is vitiated by mistake, duress etc, it is, strictly speaking, not the contract itself that is rescinded, but the relevant declaration which was made while labouring under the relevant mistake or under duress. Once the declaration is avoided, the contract itself falls away as an inevitable consequence.[28] As befits the structure of the *BGB*, this is still all governed by the general part. Thus, § 119 provides that a declaration can be avoided for mistake (not any mistake, but some kinds of mistake),[29] and § 123 makes it clear that the same applies if the declaration was induced by fraudulent misrepresentation or elicited under duress. § 125 provides that a legal transaction will be void if the relevant formalities (such as writing, attestation by a notary etc) are not complied with. Likewise, according to § 134 *BGB*, it will be void if it is illegal,[30] and under § 138 I *BGB* it will be void if it offends against good morals.[31] If a declaration is avoided, or if a transaction is void under §§ 125, 134, 138 or for some other reason, the law of unjust enrichment, in § 812 I *BGB*, takes over and imposes an obligation on the parties to make restitution. This, again, is in accordance with the abstract structure of the *BGB*. The general rules relating to unjust enrichment are put down once and for all in § 812 ff. They are formulated in such an abstract way as to be applicable to a variety of situations.

It is most important to point out even at this early stage that the *BGB* is consistent in its use of the word 'void' (*nichtig*). Thus, whenever the word is used, the consequence that § 812 will apply and restitution will follow is in the contemplation of the draftsman. It is

---

27 Larenz, 1989, p 314.
28 The phrase 'to avoid a contract' is nevertheless used as a shorthand.
29 For a more detailed description of §§ 119 ff, see Chapter 4 below.
30 Paragraph 134 is discussed further below, see pp 186 ff.
31 This allows German judges to strike down transactions which are contrary to public policy or in which the parties' respective bargaining positions were unequal. See further Markesinis, 1997, p 175.

thus possible to assume that whenever the legislator uses the word 'nichtig', the avoiding factors are such as to justify a restitutionary remedy (subject to defences, built into the law of unjust enrichment itself, but not affecting the reasons for restitution). This is an important point which we will come back to in Chapter 11.

The general part thus tells us essentially that a contract is formed by two corresponding declarations: offer and acceptance. It also lists a number of factors capable of vitiating such declarations, with the consequence that the contract is void *ab initio*. The rights and duties of the parties once a contract has validly come into existence are outlined in the general part of the second book of the *BGB*, the law of obligations.

2.4.2 Specific performance as primary remedy

A contract obliges the promisor to render the promised performance. This is made clear by § 241 which reads as follows:

> *Kraft des Schuldverhältnisses ist der Gläubiger berechtigt, von dem Schuldner eine Leistung zu fordern. Die Leistung kann auch in einem Unterlassen bestehen.* [By virtue of the obligation the creditor is entitled to demand that the debtor render a performance. The performance can also consist of an omission.]

Again, it is striking that this is a *general* provision, applying to *all* obligations, whether they arise from contract, delict or, indeed, unjust enrichment. In the law of contract, the provision makes it clear that the promisee's primary remedy is specific performance, not damages. However, specific performance can naturally only be ordered if the contractual performance is still possible. If a picture has been stolen or a car crashed, it can no longer be delivered. Any such order would be nonsensical. Thus § 251 provides that the right to specific performance is replaced by a right to damages in such cases. Equally, in a contract for which time is of the essence, a contractual performance will become impossible if it is late: timely performance is no longer possible, and the right to specific performance will be replaced by a right to damages.[32]

In practice, however, the more important remedy is damages. The risk of expensive and drawn-out proceedings with the aim of enforcing an order for specific performance is rarely taken, as long as compensation in the form of damages is readily available as an alternative.[33]

2.4.3 'Breach' of contract

To common law eyes, it is one of the more surprising features of the German law of contract that there is no general liability for 'breach'. Instead, the code distinguishes between two cases:

(1) The promisor is not able to perform, because performance is 'impossible' (*Unmöglichkeit*).

---

32 Note that not all orders for specific performance will be enforceable. In particular, contracts of employment are not specifically enforceable. Cf Zweigert and Kötz, 1998, pp 473 f.

33 Cf Zweigert and Kötz, 1998, p 484.

(2) The promisor performs late (*Verzug*).

This peculiarity of the German law of contract is to some extent connected with specific performance being the primary remedy: if a promisor simply refuses to perform, the court will make the appropriate order and that will normally be the end of it. It is only in cases where this is impossible that it is necessary to provide more elaborate rules. Nevertheless, this fragmentation of possible breaches of contract has been called a 'birth defect' of the German Civil Code.[34] In particular, it was overlooked that it is possible to perform so badly that the promisee would have been better off without the performance. Thus, if the purchased cattle feed leads to the death of the purchaser's herd of cows, the German law of contract did not provide a remedy beyond restitution or reduction of the price. This gap was subsequently filled by scholars and judges,[35] with the result that the promisee is now able to base himself on the contract when asking for compensation for loss suffered. This judicial creation is referred to as positive breach of contract, or 'positive *Vertragsverletzung*'.

Impossibility (Unmöglichkeit)

German law distinguishes between different kinds of impossibility. According to § 306, if a promised performance is impossible right from the start, the contract is void. This rule has been criticised and is generally regarded as wrong as a matter of policy. It is thus interpreted restrictively. In particular, if performance is subjectively impossible, that is, is not a scientific impossibility but only impossible for the promisor himself, he will be taken to have warranted to be able to perform. If § 306 does apply, the term 'void' brings the general law of unjust enrichment into play as far as either party has partly performed.

If the impossibility is not initial, but subsequent to the making of the contract ('*nachträgliche*' *Unmöglichkeit*), the distinction between 'objective' and 'subjective' is no longer relevant. It is replaced with the question whether the promisor is responsible for the impossibility. *Prima facie*, his responsibility is determined by reference to his culpability, that is, whether he brought the impossibility of performance about intentionally or negligently. Again, this is surprising to the common lawyer, for whom it is one defining quality of the law of contract that it normally imposes strict liability. In the German law of contract, liability is generally not strict. In other words, the promisor does not promise that the performance he has undertaken to render will still be possible at the relevant time, he does not guarantee performance.[36] Thus, if a house which is subject to a tenancy agreement burns down during the term of the tenancy, neither party being

---

34 Zweigert and Kötz, 1996, p 511.
35 Staub, 1904, 2nd edn, 1913. This book was immediately seized upon by judges faced with the task of filling the gaps in the new code: RGZ 54, 98 (6.3.1903).
36 This is subject to significant exceptions, however. Thus, in some circumstances a defendant will be held vicariously liable for the negligence of another, be he employed by him or not: § 278 *BGB*. If one party is late performing, he will be responsible for the delay if he fails to perform following a reminder by the other party, or indeed, if a date for performance is fixed, once that date has passed. Such delay has significant consequences: first, the other party will, once he has allowed the debtor an additional period of grace (§ 326), be entitled to terminate the contract. Second, the debtor will be responsible for any impossibility of performance supervening once performance has become due: (§ 287 2) but only if the damage would not have occurred had he performed on [cont]

responsible for the fire, the lessor will not be liable.[37] According to §§ 275 and 323 I, both parties become free of future obligations, even though the contract survives. If either party has performed in advance, for example, by paying advance rent, § 323 III refers the relevant party to the law of unjust enrichment.[38]

If, on the other hand, the promisor is to blame for his inability to perform, as in the case where the burning down of the house or the theft of his car are due to his own negligence, he will be liable. The promisee is given a choice of remedies: he can either ask for damages, or he can terminate the contract and ask for restitution under the contractual rules contained in §§ 346 ff. These are the rules of *Rücktritt*: special rules for the restitutionary consequences of contractual failure. We have seen that the general law of unjust enrichment is dealt with in §§ 812 ff. The special rules on Rücktritt are dealt with in §§ 346 ff, in the part of the *BGB* devoted to contract. These will be outlined immediately below and discussed in some detail in Chapter 6.

Delay (Verzug)

Once the time for performance has passed, the question arises under what conditions the promisee can ask to be compensated for the resulting damage or terminate the contract completely, rejecting an offered delayed performance altogether. If the contract specifies a time, or where it is clear that time is of the essence, the promisor will have to make compensation in respect of damage suffered as a consequence by the promisee, but only if he is responsible for the delay.[39] If the contract is silent as to time, this right to damages will arise once the promisee has sent a reminder and a reasonable time has passed, again subject to proof by the promisor that he was not to blame for the delay.

The promisee will only be able to reject performance if he has informed the promisor that he would reject performance if it was not rendered within a specified time. Again, this is subject to exceptions. In some cases, for instance, the promisee will have no interest in a late performance at all, for example, if the contract was for the delivery of Christmas trees before 23 December.[40] Again, the promisee will be able to terminate the contract, bringing the rules of the law of *Rücktritt* into play.

---

36 [cont] time. If the performance in question consists of the delivery of generic goods (*Gattungsschuld*) or indeed in the payment of money, § 279 provides that the debtor will be responsible for any inability on his part to deliver or pay. In the result, the difference between German law and English law will not be as pronounced as might at first sight appear. See further, Larenz, 1987, pp 255 ff, Zweigert and Kötz, 1998, pp 490 ff, 512 ff.

37 Cf RG JW 1905, 718 (24.10.1905).

38 It is said that this reference is as to the legal consequences only; in other words, if § 323 III applies, it is not necessary to go through all the requirements of an enrichment claim, they can be taken as fulfilled. § 323 III is thus interpreted as a '*Rechtsfolgeverweis*', referring to the legal consequences of an unjust enrichment.

39 As to the meaning of 'responsible', see fn 36 above.

40 § 326 II.

2.4.4 Termination of contract (*Rücktritt*)

Contractually agreed termination

The parties to a contract may agree that one or both of them will be able to withdraw from the contract in certain circumstances. Such withdrawal is called '*Rücktritt*', and its effects and consequences are provided for in §§ 346 ff BGB. § 346, 1 reads:

> Hat sich in einem Vertrag ein Teil den Rücktritt vorbehalten, so sind die Parteien, wenn der Rücktritt erfolgt, verpflichtet, einander die empfangenen Leistungen zurückzugewähren. [If one party to a contract has negotiated a right to terminate the contract, the parties are, once he exercises this right, obliged to make restitution of the performances received.]

To include this right to withdraw in a contract can be a sensible device to minimise the risk which is inherent in a transaction.[41] A buyer may, for instance, enter into a contract of sale with a car salesman who agrees to sell him the next model of a given make of car. The car salesman will not be willing to expose himself to liability if, for some reason, he might not able to procure the car on time or at all. The inclusion of a termination clause will therefore make good sense for him.

However, the use of such clauses has been limited by consumer protection legislation. Thus, the '*Gesetz zur Regelung des Rechts der Allgemeinen Geschäftsbedingungen*' (AGBG), does not permit them in consumer contract standard terms, and, even in non-consumer contracts, § 9 of the AGBG provides for the control of termination clauses which appear wholly capricious.[42] The practical importance of contractually agreed termination clauses is thus limited.

Termination by operation of law ('gesetzlicher Rücktritt')

§ 346 assumes central importance because it is incorporated by reference into other provisions of the BGB. This device of cross-referencing has been mentioned above, where some of the problems caused by its use have been referred to already.[43] These problems are particularly pronounced in this area. There is a world of difference between the right to withdraw from a contract on the basis of prior agreement and the right to terminate a contract for breach.

Impossibility and delay

§ 327 1 applies the law of *Rücktritt* to situations in which the performance contracted for has become impossible for a reason for which the other party is to blame (§ 325), or where one party has become entitled to bring the contract to an end because his partner failed to perform in time (§ 326). It is important to remember at this point that German law has not opted for strict contractual liability of the kind familiar to common lawyers, but will only make the party 'in breach' liable when he is in some way responsible for being unable to perform. If S has sold B a specific car but refuses to deliver it, the court will simply order him to make delivery. If, however, the car has been destroyed in an accident (delivery

---

41   Cf Schlechtriem, 1994, p 209.
42   Cf MünchKomm/Kötz, § 10 of the AGBG, No 3, No 19.
43   Cf above, p 19 ff.

now being impossible), S's liability will depend on whether or not he can be held responsible for the loss: in effect, whether he was negligent. If he was, B can either claim damages or terminate the contract and recover the purchase price. This strict alternative between Rücktritt and a claim in damages is generally perceived to be inappropriate, and will be discussed further below.[44]

*Rejection of unsatisfactory goods (*Wandelung*).*

§ 467 is concerned with the buyer's right to reject unsatisfactory goods in a contract of sale (*Wandelung*). It is aimed at the reversal of the contract of sale between the parties. If the contract has been fully executed, the goods are to be returned at the same time as the price (§§ 467, 348). For the details of the restitutionary regime, § 467 refers to the law of *Rücktritt*.

Consequences of Rücktritt

The restitutionary consequences of the exercise of the right to terminate a contract will be analysed at length in Chapter 6. For now, a broad outline of the most important rules will suffice. The general rule is that the parties are to make simultaneous restitution to each other (§§ 346, 348). Difficulties arise if this is no longer possible, either because the benefit conferred under the contract consisted of work or services, or of the use of a chattel under, for instance, a hire agreement, or because the goods that were transferred to the buyer have deteriorated or have been destroyed. In the former case, § 346 2 provides that the restitution debtor has to make restitution in money. The value of the benefit will then be calculated on the basis of the contract price.

If goods transferred under the contract have been destroyed or damaged, the *BGB* again focuses on the question whether the restitution debtor was negligent or intended to damage or destroy the goods. If he was, he will, in cases of minor damage, be liable to pay damages while retaining his right of *Rücktritt* (§§ 347, 351), in cases of significant damage or destruction his right of *Rücktritt* will be lost altogether (§ 351). These rules are somewhat puzzling and will require detailed analysis in Chapter 6.

2.5 THE GERMAN LAW OF UNJUST ENRICHMENT

It should first be noted that in Germany the law of unjust enrichment was never perceived to be based on any kind of implied agreement. Markesinis, Lorenz and Dannemann can thus be forgiven for covering the German law of restitution in the same volume as the law of contract. The common law reader will nevertheless regard that decision with unease, as it does have unfortunate resonances in English law, being reminiscent of implied promises in the law of 'quasi-contract'. There are no such problems in the German law.

The second point which should be noted is that the law of unjust enrichment is squarely within the law of obligations. The successful claimant in an unjust enrichment action will be entitled to have the object of his claim transferred to him – in itself, the

---

44   See below, pp 109 f.

judgment in his favour will have no proprietary effect. In Roy Goode's terminology, his right might thus be described as a *ius ad rem*, but never as a *ius in re*.[45] The strict division between obligations and property is part of the *BGB*'s heritage in Roman law.

2.5.1 Roman origins of German enrichment law

In approaching the German law of unjust enrichment, one should always be aware of its Roman origins. The very idea of making restitution dependent on the absence of a legal cause, or *'causa'*, is derived from Roman law. Thus we still find the *'condictio'*,[46] or its Germanised version, the *'Kondiktion'*, which in Roman law was a form of action ignoring differences between contract, tort and unjust enrichment. It was simply the proposition that the defendant ought to pay or, in other words, that he was in debt. As Roman law developed, different kinds of *condictio* were conceived, with different requirements that the claimant had to prove if he was to succeed. That is to say, the abstract proposition of indebtedness was differentiated according to the factual reason for the debt. Whether the *condictio* actually served to reverse unjust enrichments as such is highly controversial.[47] However, as Markesinis *et al* point out, 'these *condictiones* could be used for restitution and, indeed, were so used by the German *ius commune*'.[48] When the drafters of the *BGB* started work on their code in the latter quarter of the last century, they thus used the Roman law of *condictiones* as a blueprint for the German law of unjust enrichment.

2.5.2 The general clause of unjust enrichment

So far, we have seen that the law of unjust enrichment will apply to cases of void transactions,[49] and that the word 'void' is a keyword in the *BGB*. It triggers § 812 I, the first provision under the heading 'Unjust Enrichment', in the 'specific' part of the law of obligations. § 812 I 1 reads as follows:

> *Wer durch die Leistung eines anderen oder in sonstiger Weise auf dessen Kosten etwas ohne rechtlichen Grund erlangt, ist ihm zur Herausgabe verpflichtet.* [He who obtains something through somebody else's performance or in another way at his expense without a legal cause, is obliged to make restitution to the other.]

This provision will be discussed at length in Part IV of this book. For now, suffice it to say that by § 812 I 1 an enrichment is considered unjust if it lacks a 'legal cause'. In many cases, this will mean exactly what Hobhouse J means by 'absence of consideration': a benefit has been transferred under a supposed legal transaction. That transaction turns out to have been void, either because it was void from the beginning, or because it has since been avoided *ab initio* under the provisions discussed above. In such cases, § 812 I 1 provides that the recipient has to return the benefit to the transferor.

---

45 Goode, 1995, p 29.
46 Latin: *condicere* (to give notice), originally the *condictio* contained the words: 'And I give you notice to take a judge ...': Gaius, *Institutes*, 4. 18.
47 Cf Wolf, 1952, pp 382 f.
48 Markesinis, 1997, p 712.
49 See above, pp 21 f.

The problem with § 812 I 1 is, however, that it is considerably wider than this. As Markesinis *et al* point out, the main dilemma with general clauses 'is that with them one tends to get more than one has bargained for: their wording will often cover more than it should. The main attention within legal systems based on general clauses will, therefore, be geared towards excluding certain categories from the application of the general rule'.[50] The section has thus been narrowed considerably, first by jurists, then by judges who adopted the proposed academic solutions. For the moment, it can briefly be pointed out that German law today differentiates between 'enrichments by performance' and 'enrichments in another way'. Both have precisely defined requirements, which it has taken German jurists almost half a century to work out, and even today there is considerable controversy whether the distinction is appropriate, and where precisely it lies. There has also been a strong drive to interpret § 812 I 1 in such a way as to require positive factors for restitution (similar to the approach hitherto relied on in England). For enrichments by performance, the argument is put forward that restitution should follow where the purpose of the performance has failed. In Chapter 11, the process of narrowing down § 812 I will be discussed in detail.

2.5.3 The *condictio ob rem* or *causa data causa non secuta*

§ 812 I represents an attempt to enable the law of unjust enrichment to operate without unjust factors. However, many unjust enrichment scholars have nevertheless been trying to devise a system which contains some reference to a positive reason for restitution, even within the category 'enrichments by performance'. The second half of § 812 I provides a strong argument in favour of such positive factors, as it reads:

> *Diese Verpflichtung [zur Herausgabe] besteht auch dann, wenn ... der mit einer Leistung nach dem Inhalt des Rechtsgeschäfts bezweckte Erfolg nicht eintritt.* [This obligation [to make restitution] arises also where ... the result contemplated by the legal transaction is not attained.]

This is very similar to what English law would call 'failure of consideration': the failure of a counter-performance, or indeed the failure of the basis of the transfer. The scope of the provision in German law is, however, considerably reduced by two factors. First, many cases of failure of consideration will already be covered by § 812 I 1. In particular, this applies to all cases where a contract has turned out to be void, as we have seen above. Thus, on the facts of *Westdeutsche*, the voidness of the swap transactions would have triggered § 812 I 1 by itself, without any need to refer to the failure of the agreed counter-performance. Secondly, the provision does not apply to cases of contractual termination (as opposed to avoidance *ab initio*), because the law of contract, as we have seen, has its very own restitutionary regime, the law of *Rücktritt*. The scope of the '*condictio ob rem*' is thus much reduced. In effect, it only applies to cases of non-contractual performance, that is, where a transfer is expressed to be conditional on a certain event, or on a certain counter-performance, but where this condition is not made the subject matter of a contract. For example, the other party may agree not to report a crime to the police in return for money or a gift, and, having received the transferor's bounty, he may go back

---

50   Markesinis, 1997, p 713.

on his word.[51] The category is so narrow that it is indeed difficult to find appropriate examples. Nevertheless, the interesting thing is that the category is confined to non-contractual performances. This is very much at odds with Hobhouse J's insistence that recovery for failure of consideration should be restricted to contractual cases. It is then not surprising that those who deny the need for positive reasons for restitution (amplifying § 812 I 1), would like to throw this *condictio* on to the scrap-heap of legal history. Chapter 8 will examine the arguments in greater detail.

Those who accept that the *condictio causa data causa non secuta* is part of German enrichment law, can derive some valuable insights from it which can be of general application in the sphere of 'enrichments by performance'. They fall back on the reference to the 'result' or 'purpose' of a transaction in § 812 I 2 to interpret the phrase 'without legal cause' as meaning 'for a purpose which has failed'. This is a positive ground for restitution, almost on the same level as an English 'unjust factor', although, as will be seen in Chapter 11, the typology of relevant purposes adopted does mean that 'failure of purpose' cannot simply be equated with, for instance, 'failure of basis' in English law.[52] These arguments will be pursued further below.[53] For the present, it suffices to point out that even in German law a wholly abstract law of unjust enrichment has caused some unease.

2.5.4 The restitutionary claim

It is in accordance with the general preference of the *BGB* for the specific performance of all obligations that the subject matter of a restitutionary claim is the benefit itself, in so far as this is possible. § 812 I itself makes it quite clear that restitution is to be *in specie*, and this is amplified by § 818 II, which provides that only where specific restitution is not possible can there be restitution of the value in money. This will apply where the restitutionary claim is in respect of services rendered, or where the benefit has been consumed.

§ 818 I provides that the claim for restitution includes a claim for profits derived from the benefit. Thus, if the defendant has rented out the house which is the subject of the restitutionary claim, the claimant will be entitled to the rent he achieved.

---

51 See Arens, 1971, p 355. This example is not as uncomplicated as it might appear at first blush. The agreement between the parties might indeed be a contract, which might, however, be void under § 134 because it is illegal (contrary to § 257 of the penal code, prohibiting bribery) or under § 138 because it is immoral. In these cases, § 812 I 1, the *condictio indebiti*, might apply. However, the special feature of this case is that it is not possible to describe the defendant's undertaking not to report the crime as an obligation (analogous to § 888 of the Code of Civil Procedure), and it is generally agreed that on this basis the *condictio ob rem* will be available, possibly alongside the rules governing contractual *Rücktritt*.

52 The view that the *condictio indebiti* is based on failure of purpose is controversial in the German debate, but it does probably represent the dominant view. This purpose doctrine will adequately explain most cases, although some examples can be found which cause it difficulty: see below, pp 218 ff. For the purposes of the argument of this book it is not necessary to prove that the purpose doctrine is correct – attention is drawn to the debate in order to demonstrate that there are a significant number of writers in Germany who perceive a distinct need to identify positive reasons for restitution.

53 See below, p 218.

The measure of restitution is very much dependent on the state of mind of the defendant. Thus, if he knew of the restitutionary claim, or if he was *in bad faith* for some other reason, § 819 provides that he is liable 'according to the general rules'. This cross-reference has been discussed above.[54] It will be recalled that it takes us, via § 292, to the rules that govern the relationship between owner and possessor. The effect of these rules, as we have seen, is that the *mala fide* defendant has to compensate the claimant if he unreasonably failed to use the benefit which is the subject of the claim in such a way as to generate profits for the claimant. Thus, if he left a house which he knew was subject to a restitutionary claim deliberately empty, he will have to compensate the claimant for the rent which he would otherwise have received.[55] The *mala fide* defendant will also lose his right to rely on the defence of change of position, which we will turn to now.

2.5.5 The disenrichment defence: 'Wegfall der Bereicherung'

On any view, § 812 I 1 is a very broad provision. It is thus not surprising that it is counter-balanced by a strong defence of change of position or, more accurately, disenrichment.[56] In English law, this defence has also become necessary with the widening of the grounds for restitution: the 'liability mistake' rule was dispensed with in *Barclays Bank v Simms*,[57] the mistake of law bar has followed it in *Kleinwort Benson v Lincoln*,[58] and it now appears that the 'total failure' requirement in the law of failure of consideration is also about to go, if it has not gone already.[59] § 812 I was intended to be much wider still, and it was appreciated that the innocent defendant's interest in the security of his receipt needed to be safeguarded.

The German law of unjust enrichment is aimed at the reversal of an enrichment on the part of the defendant, not at the claimant's disenrichment. Liability should not, therefore, entail a decrease in the defendant's assets over and above the enrichment itself. § 818 III therefore provides that 'the obligation to make restitution *in specie* or in money is excluded, in so far as the recipient is no longer enriched'. The precise scope of this provision is, as much else in the law of restitution, the subject of intense debate. In particular, as will be seen in Chapter 15, there have always been those who have argued that § 818 III is simply too wide and ought to be restrictively interpreted.

2.6 CONCLUSION

This chapter, very much like the *BGB* itself, has proceeded from the general to the specific. It has aimed to provide a general framework, giving the reader some idea of the basics. It has also pointed out some of the differences in approach between a civilian code and the common law. These are of great importance to the subject matter of this book, as they

---

54 See above, pp 19 f.
55 §§ 292, 987. Cf Brox, 1993b, p 294.
56 'Wegfall der Bereicherung' means 'the falling away of enrichment'. In most cases a defendant's obligation is restricted to the extent that his assets remain swollen when the claim is made.
57 *Barclays Bank Ltd v WJ Simms Son & Cooke (Southern) Ltd* [1980] QB 677.
58 *Kleinwort Benson Ltd v Lincoln City Council* [1999] 2 AC 349.
59 See below, pp 117 f.

provide some very good reasons why a provision contained in a civilian code should not, without very careful scrutiny, be adopted by a common law country.

It was explained how German law, to the present day, is very heavily influenced by Roman law. It was outlined how the development of Roman law in Germany culminated in the codification of the *BGB* in 1900. If the *BGB* can be described as a code 'by lawyers for lawyers', this can be largely explained by three drafting techniques employed by the drafting commissions: the use of a 'general part', widespread cross-referencing and a fair number of general clauses stating wide principles which subsequently had to be filled with substance by judges and academics.

It is only against this background that it is possible to understand the substantive areas of German law with which this book will be concerned, namely the law of contract and the law of unjust enrichment. In this chapter, an attempt was made to equip the reader with the knowledge required to understand the more detailed discussion of these areas of German law which is to follow.

PART II
MISTAKE

CHAPTER 3

THE BASIS OF RESTITUTION FOR MISTAKE

'Mistake' is arguably the most important 'unjust factor' in the English law of unjust enrichment. In German law, as we shall see, it plays a similarly crucial role. Any legal system must decide to what extent it will allow restitution of benefits mistakenly transferred. It is thus surprising that, when one asks the crucial question why there should be restitution for mistake in the first place, the textbooks on the law of restitution do not even attempt to give an answer. The reason for this may be that Birks's proposition that when 'I didn't mean you to have it' I should be entitled to get it back seems so clear and obvious that it does not require further elaboration or critical analysis. Yet if we are to decide what limits, if any, should be placed on recovery for mistake, the question why restitution for mistake should be awarded is of great importance.

The word 'restitution' is normally employed to refer to the restoration of a gain already received. In this chapter, as indeed in this book generally, it is used in a wider sense. The prospect of a gain which can be obtained by enforcement of a contractual obligation must be considered a benefit in the same way as a gain already realised. After all, a contractual obligation can be sold or charged in very much the same way as a tangible object. As George Palmer wrote in 1961, 'there are analogous processes by which the prospect of unjust gain is eliminated from a contract not yet performed, either through cancellation of the contract (usually called rescission) or through reformation. The problems are much the same in each case, whether the gain has been realised or is only prospective – it seems best, therefore, to treat them together'.[1] In this book, I will do the same.

3.1 WHY DO MISTAKES TRIGGER RESTITUTION?

A person can acquire assets in one of two ways: he may originally acquire them, or he can receive them from another. Any theory of justice must therefore contain principles which determine in what way assets may be originally acquired, and in what way they may be transferred. Where an asset is acquired in a way which is neither original acquisition nor transfer, the acquisition must be reversed as the holder is not entitled to the asset.[2] The focus in the present context must be on the transfer of assets or entitlements. The law must provide rules which allow us to distinguish between valid and invalid transfers, and hence between 'just' and 'unjust' enrichments of the transferee. The important difference between rights obtained by transfer and rights originally acquired is that the former were already vested in someone.[3] In a liberal society, legitimate rights-holders should not without good reason be deprived of their rights without their consent: freedom of action would otherwise be seriously impeded. Consent can thus be identified

---

1 Palmer, 1962, p 3. The more modern English term for 'reformation' is, of course, 'rectification'.
2 Cf Nozick, 1974, pp 150–53.
3 Barnett, 1991, p 140.

as one moral basis of a valid transfer of an entitlement.[4] It is where that consent is vitiated that a presumption in favour of mistake-based restitution arises.

The Digest contains the maxim that *'errantis voluntas nulla est'* – the will of a mistaken party is null and void.[5] A mistake can thus be said to vitiate a right-holder's consent in a way which destroys the moral basis of his transfer.[6] As Hanoch Dagan writes in a recent article:

> A mistaken transfer is not derived from an autonomous decision of the actor, but rather subverts her control over her resources. Validating a wealth transfer based on such vitiated judgement would offend the liberal commitment for individual free choice; it would violate the maxim that the exercise of (subjective) free will should be the prerequisite to any legitimate transfer of, or interference with, resources. Therefore, absent conflicting considerations, a liberal law must prescribe restitution, that would reverse the mistake by nullifying the unintended consequences of the mistaken transfer and reinstating the *status quo ante*.[7]

It should be made clear from the start that this presumption in favour of restitution will be triggered by any mistake, whether it be of fact or law, and whether it could have been avoided by taking better care or not.[8] There is no reason to distinguish between these categories as far as the moral case for restitution is concerned.

3.2 CHANGES OF MIND: MANUFACTURED AND 'SPENT' MISTAKES

A mere change of mind does not trigger the presumption in favour of restitution. The transfer has been made in accordance with the transferor's unfettered will. Subsequently, the asset in question has passed to the transferee, who has now assumed the right to transfer the asset in his turn. If a change of mind on the part of the original transferor were to trigger the presumption, that right would vest in more than one person at a time. One difficulty with restitution for mistake is that mistakes are easily manufactured *ex post* in circumstances in which what has really happened is that the transferor has changed his mind. This is a matter of evidence, of course, and therefore not a real objection to restitution based on mistake in general. It will be for the claimant to convince a judge on the balance of probabilities that he was labouring under a mistake when making the transfer, and that he would not have made the transfer but for the mistake. The more unlikely and apparently contrived his story, the greater the likelihood that the desire to have restitution is based on a change of mind or on a risk realised, the more difficult it will be to convince the judge of the genuine nature of the claimant's case.

A much more difficult problem arises where the mistake itself is real enough, but where the mistake has not directly caused the transferor any prejudice. A company enters into a long term contract with a supplier. It believes the supplier to be a thoroughly

---

4   *Ibid*, p 141.
5   D 50.17.116.2.
6   Cf Savigny, 1841, who argues that since 'juridical facts' consist of free acts or omissions, the validity of a juridical fact which is based on a mistake is put in question.
7   Dagan, 2000, p 4.
8   *Kelly v Solari* (1841) 9 M & W 54, 152 ER 24.

solvent business. In fact, it is mistaken in this belief. The supplier is on the brink of insolvent liquidation. Had the company known this, it would never have entered into the contract. The supplier, however, manages to comply with its contractual obligations. The contract having run its course, the company discovers the true facts. It has also by then realised that the whole transaction represented a very bad bargain indeed. Do these facts raise the presumption in favour of restitution? I would suggest that they do not. This is because the reason why the company wants restitution is *not* its mistake, but the fact that it has changed its mind. The mistake itself never caused the company any prejudice. For this reason, it should not raise the presumption in favour of restitution.[9]

3.3 WHAT IS A MISTAKE?

Before we can go on with discussing the different ways in which mistakes can be categorised, we need to discuss what we mean by the term 'mistake'. In other words: in what circumstances can the will of the transferor be said to be vitiated so as to give rise to the liberal presumption in favour of restitution? By defining 'mistake' restrictively, the availability of restitution can be curtailed whether or not it would undermine a bargain or the recipient's security of receipts. There are three issues here which merit discussion:

(1) Does a mistake presuppose a conscious belief, or is a complete absence of knowledge of a relevant fact sufficient?

(2) Is the presumption triggered in circumstances in which the transferor entertains doubts as to the true position of affairs?

(3) Is there a difference between mistakes and mispredictions as far as the moral case for restitution is concerned?

3.3.1 Mistake and absence of knowledge

The obvious heading to use here would be 'ignorance', seeking to describe the situation where a person makes a transfer because he is wholly unaware of a fact which, had he been aware of it, would have caused him not to make the transfer. The term 'ignorance' is already used in a rather different sense, however. Birks uses it to refer to a situation where a person is wholly unaware of a shift of wealth from him to the defendant. It is important not to confuse these two scenarios. If the term is used in the sense Birks uses it, it describes the total absence of consent to the shift of wealth, while in this section we are dealing with a conscious transfer made under a disability, namely the absence of knowledge of a fact which would have had an impact on the decision whether or not the transfer should be made. I describe this idea by using the rather clumsy phrase 'absence of knowledge'.[10]

---

9 The problem was first identified by Birks, 1993, p 230, n 137, and gave rise to the doctrine of 'spent mistake'. Birks has since formulated the same idea as a sub-category of the defence of change of position (see below, pp 82, 304–05). In other words, to Birks the fact that the mistake is spent rebuts the presumption in favour of restitution. I would argue, along with his original view, that on such facts the presumption is never even raised.

10 Sheehan, 2000, pp 541–45, does not draw this distinction. To him, whether or not the transfer has been a conscious one is wholly irrelevant. In neither case, he argues, can the claimant be said to have been 'mistaken'.

We find an early comprehensive discussion of what constitutes a mistake in Savigny's *System des heutigen römischen Rechts*. Savigny points out that it would be more correct not to talk about mistake but about a '*Mangel an richtiger Vorstellung*' (lack of correct conception), which might be equated with 'absence of knowledge' or 'ignorance' in the non-Birksian sense. Savigny argues that the two kinds of 'defective intention', namely mistake and absence of knowledge, call for an identical legal response, and that the term 'mistake' should be preferred because of its empirically greater frequency.[11] Savigny finds some support for this in Roman law (which he was, after all, writing about), which never distinguished between 'error' and 'ignorantia'.[12]

In a recent article,[13] Duncan Sheehan argues that it would be incorrect to equate mistake and absence of knowledge. He writes:

> When one is ignorant, one has no view at all about the matter on which one is ignorant. One has no belief at all. Let us take some examples. I have no belief or knowledge at all about the existence of quarks. I have no knowledge of quantum physics and have never thought about it. My complete lack of any belief on the subject can be contrasted with the case where I believe I can mathematically prove that quarks do not exist. In fact my proof is flawed as any competent mathematician can see. There is a definite distinction between the two. In the former case, if asked if quarks exist, I shrug my shoulders and say that I do not know. In the latter I give an answer that turns out to be an incorrect one. It is true to say that in both cases I do not know the correct answer. However, in the latter case I have a definite belief as to the answer to the question that I do not have in the former. Only in the latter case can I be said to be mistaken.[14]

According to Sheehan, there is no way in which absence of knowledge can be described as a mistake. He does concede, however, that frequently it is possible to identify an actual mistake which is based upon the absence of relevant knowledge. He gives the example of *David Securities v Commonwealth Bank of Australia*.[15] In that case, the defendant bank had inserted a clause in a loan contract requiring the claimant borrower to make additional payments in respect of the bank's withholding tax liability. The clause was void under statute, and when this was discovered, the claimant sought restitution of moneys paid pursuant to the clause. The High Court of Australia held that he could recover the payments as money paid under a mistake of law. Sheehan finds it difficult to accept that the claimant's mistake in *David Securities* was his lack of knowledge of the existence of the statute. In other words, this lack of knowledge of the statute's existence cannot be translated into a mistaken belief into its non-existence.[16] Nevertheless, the result of the case can be salvaged, according to Sheehan, by arguing that the operative mistake was not a belief in the statute's non-existence, but a belief in the enforceability and validity of the clause.

In her book *Irrtum und Zweckverfehlung*, Meier gives the following example of what she calls a 'causative mistake', arguing that it should not lead to restitution: a person makes a donation to an environmental organisation, not knowing that it opposes and

---

11 Savigny, 1841, pp 111, 326.
12 Cf D. I.2.a.
13 Sheehan, 2000.
14 *Ibid*, p 542.
15 (1992) 175 CLR 353.
16 Sheehan, 2000, p 543.

lobbies against extending the runway of the local airport. He is much in favour of extending the runway and now wants his donation back.[17] Before we discuss the question whether he can succeed, we have to ask: did he make a mistake in the first place? Sheehan would regard this as a prime example of 'ignorance': it is impossible to translate the donor's lack of knowledge into a positive mistake. It is not that he laboured under the mistake that the donee charity approved the runway extension; he just did not think about the question at all. The next question we have to consider, however, is whether this changes the underlying moral case for restitution.

We have seen that a mistake triggers the presumption in favour of restitution because, absent tortious conduct, a liberal legal system recognises transfers of benefits only if they are based on the owner's consent. Thus, if that consent is vitiated, denying restitution would be contrary to the principle of private autonomy. The question now is whether the complete absence of knowledge of a given fact can vitiate consent in the same way as mistake. The answer must be clearly in the affirmative. This can be demonstrated using a simple 'but for' analysis: had the transferor been in possession of all the relevant facts, would he have made the transfer? If not, he clearly did not really mean the transferee to have the benefit. His consent to the transfer, and thereby the basis of the transfer, is vitiated. Restitution is justified. I thus do not accept Sheehan's argument that cases of mistake and absence of knowledge call for separate treatment. Fortified in the knowledge that I am adopting the same strategy as the great Savigny, I will therefore confine myself to referring to 'mistake' as encompassing both mistakes properly so-called and cases of 'absence of knowledge'.[18]

3.3.2 Mistake and doubt

The problem with a payment made under doubt as to the true position is that the payer can be said to have accepted the risk of being wrong. It could be argued that when I am in doubt, my judgment is not impaired by a mistake at all: a danger recognised is a danger forestalled. A person who doubts whether his view is correct can make inquiries to eliminate his doubts. If he fails to do this and pays anyway, he must be said to have accepted the risk of being wrong. Sue Arrowsmith argues, accordingly, that in such circumstances 'the payee's interest in the security of his receipt should outweigh those of the payer who was aware of the opportunity of avoiding the creation of false expectations'.[19] This may not be the end of the story, of course. There may be other reasons why he should be entitled to restitution: he may have succumbed to the payee's illegitimate pressure to pay. Or there may be policy reasons why he should have restitution, as was the case in *Woolwich*.[20] Finally, he might have made it clear to the other party that he was paying under reserve, namely on condition that his view of matters would not later turn out to be incorrect. It is possible to interpret this kind of case as

---

17   Meier, 1999a, p 87.

18   For the contrary view, namely that a person who has no view at all is less worthy of protection than someone who directs his mind to an issue but reaches a mistaken conclusion, see Mayer-Maly, 1970, pp 138 ff.

19   Arrowsmith, 1991, p 27.

20   *Woolwich Equitable Building Society v Inland Revenue Commissioners (No 2)* [1993] AC 70. See pp 191 f, below.

belonging to the category 'failure of consideration', or, as it should rather be called in modern times, 'failure of basis'. It is equally possible, of course, to argue that a contract came into existence between the parties to the effect that restitution should follow in such circumstances.[21]

This view derives additional support from the more recent American case of *Kansas Farm Bureau Life Insurance Co v Farmway Credit Union*.[22] The claimant insurance company paid out under a life policy where the insured had been missing for some time and was presumed dead. When it later turned out that he was alive, it sought to recover its payment. Although the Supreme Court of Kansas refused restitution on the basis that the payment had been made by way of compromise as demonstrated by the 'in full settlement of all claims' boilerplate on the claimant's cheques,[23] it appears that the court would have reached the same result even if there had been no evidence of a compromise between the parties. The alternative basis of the judgment is that the claimant 'assumed the risk that [the insured] was not dead'.[24] In other words, even though the insured was presumed dead, the insurance company was under no obligation to pay as long as the insured's death was not established. By paying, it assumed the risk that it might be wrong.

This approach may well impose too great a burden on a party in doubt. Thus, Tettenborn argues that 'it would be unfortunate were the law to penalise those who sought to be reasonable and accommodating in their disputes with others'.[25] The *Kansas Farm* case tends to confirm these reservations, given that the result of the case must be that insurance companies will become more reluctant to pay out in doubtful cases, the ultimate losers thus being beneficiaries of life insurance policies.

Thus, the argument that a doubter who resolves his doubts in just the wrong way is not mistaken would appear to be flawed, as it would prefer the reckless to the careful. Arrowsmith appears to accept this. She does not argue that there was no mistake in such a case – her argument is defendant-sided. To her, the liberal presumption of restitution is indeed triggered but rebutted by the defendant's interest in the security of his receipt. It is difficult to see, however, why the defendant should be so privileged. After all, there is little to distinguish him from a defendant who was enriched because of the claimant's straightforward mistake.

According to Ewan McKendrick the problem is best solved by a simple application of the 'but for' test of causation:[26] a party who is not sure whether or not he is obliged to pay may decide that, on balance, he is more likely than not to be so obliged, and, being unable to put the question beyond doubt, may decide to pay on that basis. If he can show that this was the reason he paid, he should be held to have been mistaken and be able to recover: but for the 'mistake', he would not have paid. According to McKendrick, the

---

21 *Banque de l'Indochine et de Suez v JH Rayner (Mincing Lane) Ltd* [1983] QB 711; cf Arrowsmith, 1991, pp 28–29.

22 P 2d 784 (1996).

23 *Ibid*, at 785.

24 *Ibid*, at 789.

25 Tettenborn, 1996, p 65.

26 McKendrick, 1997, pp 232–33.

question must therefore be: 'Did the bank enter into the transaction as a result of its mistake or as a result of some wider, commercial considerations?'[27]

The approach advocated by McKendrick finds support in the German law:[28] doubt as such is not fatal to a restitutionary claim, but a claimant who waives all inquiry and pays irrespective of the truth or falsity of the underlying assumption will find that restitution is denied to him.[29] Thus, in a case decided by the *Reichsgericht* in 1909, the creditor of joint debtors had received part of the latter's indebtedness from the wife of one of the joint debtors – against the will of the husband. When the husband went bankrupt and the trustee in bankruptcy demanded repayment of the money, the creditor began to doubt whether he was entitled to keep the money and paid it back into the insolvent estate. His subsequent action to recover the money was successful. The trustee had not been entitled to the money, and mere doubts did not exclude liability to make restitution under § 814, as the Reichsgericht explained.[30]

This must be contrasted with the situation in which somebody doubts his liability but then pays in order to avoid further disputes, that is, for a reason other than a belief in liability.[31] In a 1919 decision of the *Reichsgericht*,[32] a maritime insurer had issued a policy containing 'war and restraint of princes' as an excepted peril. The ship sank with all hands and the entire cargo was lost while travelling from Lübeck to Königsberg during the First World War. Initially, it was impossible to ascertain whether the ship had sank because of general perils of the sea or because of enemy action. Correspondence was exchanged between insurer and insured for several months, the insurer insisting that it could not pay until the cause of the loss was known. In the end, however, it paid out, 'so that the matter be resolved as soon as possible'.[33] When evidence emerged that the loss of the ship was war-related, it sought restitution and failed. The reasoning of the *Reichsgericht* is not particularly lucid, and it is difficult to extract the basis of this decision.[34] I would suggest that the best explanation can be found in McKendrick's analysis: the insurer knew that it was in no position to ascertain whether it was liable or not. It knew that it could not be compelled to pay until there was some evidence of the cause of the loss, but paid nevertheless after months of negotiations. The true cause of the payment was thus not any kind of mistake (there was no mistake), but a desire not to become known as a difficult payer in the market and to avoid further expense in carrying on complex negotiations.

---

27 *Ibid*, p 233
28 Cf § 814.
29 The paucity of case law in English law is explained by the presence of the mistake of law bar – doubt as to the legal position is much more common than doubt as to facts – in particular, facts are usually more easily checked. This must be the reason why the issue was settled in Germany (where the Roman mistake of law bar was rejected) very early on following the RG enactment of the *BGB*.
30 RGZ 72, 192 (12.9.1909), 199.
31 It is interesting to note that Kaehler, 1972, p 287, justifies this result in the same way as Arrowsmith, namely by reference to the expectations of the recipient, which according to both writers merit greater protection than the payer's interest in restitution in this scenario.
32 RGZ 97, 140 (3.5.1919).
33 *Ibid*, 141.
34 There is some mention of § 242, suggesting a form of estoppel – the use of § 242 by German courts is almost always indicative of an inability to find express reasons for an intuitively correct result.

3.3.3 Mistakes and mispredictions

Sheehan defines a mistake 'as a belief in something that can, at the time it is acted upon, be proven not to be the case'.[35] To him, a misprediction differs from a mistake because 'a misprediction cannot be proven to be correct or incorrect at the time it was acted upon'. Birks also thinks that a misprediction is generally different from a mistake: 'A mistake as to the future, a misprediction, does not show that the claimant's judgment was vitiated, only that as things turned out it was incorrectly exercised. A prediction is an exercise of judgment. To act on the basis of a prediction is to accept the risk of disappointment.'[36] To Birks, the difference between a mistaken person and a person who acted on the basis of a misprediction is that the latter is a risk-taker whereas the former is not. He gives examples illustrating this point: A looks after B hoping that B will leave him money when he dies, or an architect spends time and effort on preparing plans for a building which he hopes he will be awarded a contract to develop.[37]

It is, however, not altogether clear whether the point is valid for all mispredictions: for some future events, it can be proven that they will happen with about as much precision as anything can be proven. This point is made by Peter Jaffey in his recent book *The Nature and Scope of Restitution*:[38]

> As an exception that proves the rule, consider a mistake over some future event with respect to which there is no uncertainty, for example, the date of an eclipse or the next leap year. There is no reason why such a mistake should not generate a claim, if for some reason a mistake on such a matter were relevant to a payment.

This argument can also account for the doctrine of frustration of contract. Where a contract is frustrated, the parties are discharged from further performance and can recover payments already made. What is the reason for restitution? It is generally said to be failure of consideration. However, failure of consideration can only account for restitution of benefits following the discharge of the contract, it cannot explain why the contract is discharged in the first place. It might be argued that a frustrated contract is made on a basis which subsequently fails (namely that the frustrating event will not happen), but this is an entirely artificial way of looking at frustration which is, furthermore, contradicted by the doctrine itself: it is the essence of frustration that unforeseen events have occurred which render performance of the contract 'a thing radically different from that which was undertaken by the contract'.[39] By definition, there is no agreement between the parties that the contract is not to stand in the event of a radical change of circumstances. The ground for restitution can therefore not be 'failure of basis'. It must be something else. It cannot be mistake properly so-called – the essence of frustration is that circumstances have *changed* from what they were when the contract was entered into.[40] It must therefore be a misprediction that circumstances would not change

---

35   Sheehan, 2000, p 538.
36   Birks, 1989, p 147.
37   *Ibid.*
38   Jaffey, 2000, pp 173–74.
39   *Davis Contractors Ltd v Fareham Urban District Council* [1956] AC 696, 729 (*per* Lord Radcliffe)
40   This is true for English law, but not for German law, which would categorise mistakes such as the mistake in *Smith v Hughes* (1871) LR 6 QB 597 as frustration.

in the way in which they have changed.[41] The reason why the law affords relief is that, again by definition, the contract has failed to allocate the risk of a radical change of circumstances to one party or the other. Neither party can therefore be described as a risk-taker. Birks's objection to restitution for mispredictions has therefore fallen away.

Birks himself says that a misprediction properly so-called 'cannot be falsified at the time when it is made'.[42] It must follow from this that a misprediction which can be falsified at the time it is made is not the kind of misprediction he is talking about, namely a misprediction which renders consent defective. The point is that there is nothing inherently objectionable about restitution for mispredictions – it is, however, necessary to show that the transferor was in fact impaired by a misprediction, and that he was not just a disappointed risk-taker.[43] We will have to come back to this point when discussing the problem of restitution for mistake of law.[44]

3.4 RESTRICTIONS ON MISTAKE-BASED RESTITUTION

There are essentially two conflicting considerations which may militate against restitution for mistake. The first is that the recipient may, if he were required to make restitution, be prejudiced in that he would end up worse off than he was before the transfer was made. Another way to put this is that restitution would undermine the recipient's security of receipt. The second is that restitution for mistake may undermine a bargain. There are additional considerations which may militate against restitution where the mistake in question is not a mistake of fact but a mistake of law. These will also be briefly examined.

3.4.1 Undermining the security of receipts

Recipients will not always notice that a transfer was induced by the transferor's mistake. In such circumstances, they may come to harm in broadly two ways: they might dispose of the benefit received, or spend their own money believing to have been permanently enriched by the mistaken transfer. If recipients had to be permanently on their guard, permanently afraid of potential restitutionary claims in such circumstances, the stability of their affairs would be severely threatened. As Birks argues, they would have to maintain a 'contingency fund' in order to insure themselves against future restitutionary liabilities. In other words, the stability of their affairs would be jeopardised.[45]

---

41 Sheehan, of course, would not accept this. To him, this would at best be a case of 'ignorance' – the parties never thought about the question at all.

42 Birks, 2000a, p 224.

43 This view gains further support from the fact that German law does not draw the distinction at all: cf Flume, 1979, p 425; Titze, 1940, p 86. This is also reflected in the fact that the German law of frustration is concerned not just with the future, but also with the present – it just encompasses the English category of 'common mistake': cf MünchKomm/Roth, § 242, No 517. Also, see *Kommission zur Überarbeitung des Schuldrechts*, 1992, p 150, § 3306 (2).

44 See below, pp 43 f, 55 and 82 ff.

45 Birks, 1996a, p 62.

The law of unjust enrichment deals with this objection through the defence of change of position which, in theory, ensures that the recipient will never be worse off in financial terms than if the mistaken transfer had never been made.[46]

What, however, is the position where a party has changed his position in reliance on an executory contract which later turns out to be void or voidable on the basis of the other party's mistake? The logic of the change of position defence ought to apply here as well. Thus, in the American case of *Murray State Normal School v Cole*[47] the claimant had won a contract which had been awarded after a tendering procedure. He had miscalculated in preparing his bid and sought to avoid the contract on the ground of mistake. The court allowed him to rescind, but only on condition that he pay the costs incurred in running a second round of bidding (in which he had again been successful, this time on correct data). The same idea finds expression in § 122 *BGB*, which allows the other party to recover his 'negative interest', that is,ie his reliance interest in the contract, so long as this does not exceed his 'positive interest', that is,ie his expectation interest. Both the *Murray State* case and § 122 *BGB* protect the same interest as the change of position defence – given that a contract can be rescinded or a restitutionary claim be made on the basis of a mistake, even if that mistake is caused by the claimant's negligence, the *defendant's* interest in the security of the transaction and/or the receipt warrants protection, at least to the extent that he should not be worse off than before as a result of the transaction.

The remaining question, however, is whether it cannot be argued that, in spite of the availability of the change of position defence, the recipient/defendant might be harmed by the restitutionary claim in ways which cannot be measured financially. This raises the question whether the recipient's expectation to be allowed to retain the benefit is itself an interest worthy of protection. Is it possible to harm a person by conferring a benefit on him which he is later required to return? A child is given a bar of chocolate. It is then taken away from her again. She might well be crying now where she was not crying before. Likewise, if I were told that I had won the lottery and paid £1 m, only to be required to return the money a week later, I would probably feel considerably worse than I felt before. However, the situation would not be all that different if I had merely been *told* that I had won the lottery. In this case, the law would not afford me a remedy, because my expectation, however reasonable, was not based on a bargain. Patrick Atiyah has argued that even where bargained-for expectations are concerned, the above argument is not altogether convincing:

> To disappoint expectations is to 'let the promisee down', to dash his hopes, and many people would say that it actually makes the promisee worse off than he would have been if no promise had been given. I do not think this is self-evidently true; it is an empirical question whether a disappointed promisee feels worse off than he would have felt if there had never been a promise. And a utilitarian would be entitled to argue that the pleasurable anticipation of the promise being performed must itself be brought into the scales against this subsequent disappointment.[48]

The argument is much weaker still where there is no danger of undermining a bargain, but where the expectation is merely aroused by the receipt of a mistaken transfer.

---

46   See Chapter 11.
47   273 SW 508 (1925).
48   Atiyah, 1981, p 43.

It is for this reason that the objection from security of receipts is only accepted by the law where the recipient can show a relevant change of position.

3.4.2. Undermining bargains

Exchange economies depend on the facilitative institution 'contract'. As Palmer writes, 'in a world filled with error and uncertainty we all must act on the basis of approximate truth. To set aside a transaction for every relevant false assumption would make contract much too precarious to serve the ends it needs to serve'.[49] The natural lawyers put this in Latin: *error nocet erranti* – a declaration mistakenly made is nevertheless valid.[50] The boundaries of protected spheres must be ascertainable. This is not possible if entitlements can be affected by subjectively held and unexpressed intentions. Contract law thus requires that a party's consent to be bound must be manifested in a manner which can be objectively interpreted and understood.[51] The liberal presumption in favour of restitution will therefore have to be severely curtailed if stability in dealings is not to be jeopardised. Different legal systems have developed different strategies in carrying out this restriction exercise, none of which have been altogether successful.

It is important to make a clear distinction between exchanges and gratuitous promises and transfers. A gratuitous promise does nothing to rebut the presumption in favour of restitution. Nevertheless, it appears that both English and German law are reluctant to allow the reversal of gifts for a merely causal mistake. This is in spite of the fact that English law, unlike German law, has never perceived of a gift as a contract. In the presence of a strong change of position defence there is, it is suggested, nothing to rebut the presumption in favour of restitution in a mistaken gift situation.[52]

3.4.3 Mistakes of law

Both of these restrictions on the availability of restitution for mistake apply whether the mistake in question is a mistake of fact or law. The question thus arises whether there is any reason militating against restitution which is peculiar to mistakes of law. Birks has argued that there are indeed differences between mistakes of law and fact which explain why mistakes of law have generally been discriminated against.[53] He identifies three in particular. First, the very concept of a mistake of law is very difficult to grasp. As a result, the courts may become involved in impossible inquiries, from which, according to Birks, it would be better to protect them.

---

49 Palmer, 1962, p 17.
50 Cf Luig, 1980, pp 153–66.
51 Barnett, 1991, p 144. The objective theory of contract can be traced back to Grotius, who argued that a person cannot escape from the consequences of his declarations simply by saying that he meant something different from what he said: '... *quod sufficienter indicatum est, pro vero habetur adversus eum qui indicavit*', Grotius, 1689, p 222 (liber II, caput XVIII, III). For English law, see *Smith v Hughes* (1871) LR 6 QB 597, p 607, *per* Blackburn J.
52 Cf Pufendorf's different treatment of gift promises and contracts in *De iure naturae et gentium* III, VI, §§ 6, 7 (Pufendorf, 1672). He accepted any causal mistake to render a gift promise null and void, and by implication extended this to executed gifts. Where contracts were concerned, he carefully distinguished between executed and executory contracts.
53 Birks, 2000a, p 215.

Secondly, there is the need to provide for finality of transactions, in particular for finality of settlements 'to which recovery for mistake of law seems to pose a greater threat than recovery for mistake of fact'.[54]

Birks's final difference is that allowing restitution for mistakes of law poses a threat to the freedom of judicial reasoning, because judges will have to be mindful that if they change the law this may lead to a flood of restitutionary claims based on the claimants' prior 'mistaken' view of the law. Birks nevertheless concludes that none of these considerations is strong enough to rebut the presumption in favour of restitution, provided that the concept 'mistake' is correctly understood.[55]

3.5 CATEGORISING MISTAKES

The first part of this chapter sought to identify the reasons why the law should intervene to reverse mistaken transfers. We have seen that these are to be found in the principle of private autonomy. If a transfer is valid only if it is sanctioned by the will of the transferor, the law cannot just ignore it if that will is vitiated. However, we have also seen that this 'liberal presumption in favour of restitution' can be rebutted if a bargain would otherwise be undermined. Where that is the case, mistakes will be have to be treated with extreme caution if we are to avoid reverting to the 'will theory' of contract law. The danger cuts both ways, however: devices designed to protect bargains by limiting the availability of restitution for mistake should not be applied to cases in which there is no danger of undermining a bargain at all. These are typically cases involving unilateral transfers, over- or double-payments, and, crucially, gifts. It will become clear that this danger is in fact the more serious danger: where the presumption in favour of restitution is rebutted to avoid undermining a bargain which is wholly imaginary, the result must be injustice to the mistaken transferor.

We will now turn to examine some of the ways in which mistakes can be classified. As Palmer wrote in 1961:

> Any attempt to bring order into the law of mistake should observe two quite fundamental distinctions. One is the difference between a mistake in the expression of a transaction and a mistake that relates only to the reasons for entering into the transaction. The distinction parallels that between the statements 'I did not intend to say this' and 'I did intend to say this, but it was because I mistakenly believed the facts were thus and so'.[56]

In the following, this distinction is translated into the categories 'communication mistakes' and 'mistakes in underlying assumptions'.

3.5.1 Communication mistakes

The attitude displayed by legal systems to communication mistakes or, as we might call them equally well, misunderstandings, will be informed by the system's underlying

---

54   *Ibid.*
55   *Ibid*, p 216.
56   Palmer, 1962, p 6.

approach to contractual obligations. The starting point is determined by whether a legal system recognises contractual promises because the promisor intends to be bound (subjective theory or 'will-theory'), or because he has expressed an intention to be bound (objective theory or 'declaratory theory'). The law of contract cannot be explained on the basis of either theory alone,[57] but it is inevitable that different legal systems will have more objective or subjective elements than others. It is this which explains their different approaches to the law of mistakes generally, and to communication mistakes in particular.[58]

A contract only comes into existence if offer and acceptance, objectively interpreted, correspond. If an objective interpretation is simply not possible, there will be no contract. Thus, in *Raffles v Wichelhaus*,[59] the claimant had agreed to sell to the defendant 125 bales of cotton to arrive ex 'Peerless' from Bombay. The problem was that there were, rather ironically, two ships of that name, the first travelling from Bombay to England in October, the second in December. It was simply not possible to ascertain objectively which of the two vessels the parties were talking about. The court held that there was no contract, unfortunately without giving reasons. It is thus not clear whether the judges felt that, for a binding contract to be formed, there must be agreement *in fact* (the so-called 'will-theory' or subjective theory of contract law), or whether they decided, subscribing to the objective theory of contract law, that, although only agreement *in expression* was required, there had been no such agreement: there was no way by which the court could prefer the buyer's or the seller's interpretation of the phrase 'ex Peerless'.

Where one party intends to say one thing, but, on an objective interpretation of his statement, in fact says another, the question will arise to what extent he will be held to what his statement objectively meant. If contracts are enforced because 'the legal order recognises that people are free to arrange their affairs autonomously in accordance with their intentions', then there is no reason to uphold an 'agreement' which is based on a communication mistake.[60] Thus, where a person intends to sell his car for $10,000, but because of a 'slip of the pen' actually offers to sell it for $1,000, his intention does not provide a sufficient reason for enforcing a contract based on the offer as communicated.[61] If such a contract is enforced, the reason must lie elsewhere, namely in the value attached to upholding apparent bargains.[62]

Werner Flume has characterised this kind of mistake as 'mechanical'[63] and argues that the same characterisation is apt for the kind of mistake in which the offeror intends to use the words he then actually uses, but mistakenly attaches an incorrect meaning to them. In other words, he uses the wrong signs to convey his real meaning. In a case

---

57 Cf Corbin, 1993, p 627.
58 Cf Zweigert and Kötz, 1998, p 419.
59 (1864) 2 H & C 906, 159 ER 375.
60 Flume, 1979, p 415.
61 One question will, of course, be whether the offeree was justified in understanding the offer as being for the lesser sum, in circumstances where the actual value of the car was clearly much greater.
62 This attitude is reflected in Steyn J's speech in *Associated Japanese Bank v Crédit du Nord SA* [1989] 1 WLR 255: 'The first imperative must be that the law ought to uphold rather than destroy apparent contracts.'
63 *'Bei einem Erklärungsirrtum handelt es sich um einen Fehler hinsichtlich der Abgabe der Erklärung, der gewissermaßen technischer Natur ist'*, Flume, 1979, p 432.

decided by the *Landgericht Hanau* in 1979,[64] the deputy headmistress of a girl's secondary school intended to order 25 rolls of toilet paper on behalf of the school. She expressed this intention by ordering '25 *Gros Rollen*'; the word '*Gros*', she thought, referred to a kind of packaging. In this she was badly mistaken, as the word '*Gros*' is an old-fashioned expression for 12 dozen, so that the unfortunate teacher was in for a surprise when 3600 rolls of toilet paper were duly delivered to the school. Under the relevant rules of German law, namely § 119 I, she was allowed to rescind the contract; her mistake had been of a 'mechanical' kind – the words she had used had incorrectly expressed her intentions.

This result reflects an underlying view that contract law is concerned with the true intentions of the parties. Where the law is geared more towards the security and finality of transactions, subscribing to the declaratory theory of contract, it will not be as forgiving, as demonstrated by the leading English case of *Smith v Hughes*.[65] The claimant, a farmer, agreed to sell the defendant, a race horse trainer, a quantity of oats. Now, race horses are not too keen on new oats, for some reason. The oats which the farmer intended to sell were, however, new oats, and as such unsuitable for the race horse trainer's purposes. There was a conflict of evidence as to what was said in the negotiations, the defendant contending that he had clearly heard the claimant referring to 'good old oats', while the claimant maintained that the word 'old' had never passed his lips. The jury were directed that (a) if the word 'old' had been used by either party, they should return a verdict for the defendant. If, however, the word 'old' had not been used (and the judge himself was inclined to this view), they should (b) consider whether the claimant believed that the defendant believed to be buying old oats. In that case, they should also find for the defendant. The jury did find for the defendant, but they failed to specify whether on ground (a) or on ground (b). The claimant's appeal was allowed and a new trial ordered. The ratio of the case is neatly summed up in the speech of Hannen J:

> In order to relieve the defendant it was necessary that the jury should find not merely that the plaintiff believed the defendant to believe that he was buying old oats, but that he believed the defendant to believe that he, the plaintiff, was contracting to sell old oats.[66]

The catchwords in the Law Reports sum this up rather neatly: 'Passive Acquiescence of a Seller in the self-deception of the Buyer does not entitle the latter to avoid the Contract'. In other words, absent misrepresentation, the buyer could only resist the seller's action for the price if it could be argued that the seller knew that the buyer believed the seller to be warranting that the oats were old oats. We thus end up with the following mix of objective and subjective elements:

(a) Objective construction of the words used suggests agreement between the parties;

(b) Subjectively, neither party knew that the other did not mean to agree to his terms.[67]

Smith v Hughes has long been regarded as an unsatisfactory case. As Lord Wright wrote, extra-judicially, in 1943:

---

64 LG Hanau NJW 1979 (30.6.1978), 721.
65 (1871) LR 6 QB 597.
66 *Smith v Hughes* (1871) LR 6 QB 597, 611.
67 Cf Cartwright, 1991, p 8.

The maxim that a vendor may passively take advantage of the self-deception of the buyer (for which the case is generally cited) is calculated to encourage people to say that law is a mean and sordid business. Like *'caveat emptor'* it has a certain truth in some applications, but it needs to be substantially qualified and circumscribed.[68]

A legal system more influenced by the will-theory of contract law will reach rather different results. If contracts are recognised only because the promisor intends to be bound, a contractual communication which fails to express the true intention of the person who makes it may not be given full effect. It is this idea which underlies § 119 I *BGB*, which will be discussed in greater detail below.[69] The deputy headmistress in the 'toilet roll case' discussed above could, it will be remembered, rescind the contract on the basis of her mistaken understanding of the word 'gros'. In England, she would have been held to the bargain: interpreted objectively, she had ordered 3600 rolls of toilet paper. Her mistake was not readily apparent to the seller, and even if it had been, *Smith v Hughes* suggests that the seller was under no obligation to disabuse her of her misunderstanding of the term 'gros'. It should be borne in mind, however, that German law protects the reliance interest of the other party in § 122.[70]

Where one party is labouring under a mistake as to the identity of the other, the mistake is properly categorised as a communication mistake of the same kind as in *Smith v Hughes*. I need to renovate my flat. A friend recommends a firm of painters called 'Jones & Son'. I look for a firm by that name in the phonebook and place the order with 'Jones & Sons', without realising that this is an altogether different firm. My subjective intention is to contract with 'Jones & Son', but objectively I fail to get that meaning across. The difficulty for the law is to distinguish such 'identity mistakes' from 'mistakes as to attributes': what if I engage the correct 'Jones & Son', but do not realise that they are close to bankruptcy? This distinction represents the borderline between communication mistakes and mistakes in assumption, to which we now turn.

3.5.2 Mistakes in assumptions

While misunderstandings are mistakes as to the terms of a contract, a mistake in an underlying assumption might be described as a mistake as to the context of a contract, a mistake as to the surrounding circumstances and facts. I book a Caribbean cruise because I think I have won the lottery. I buy a flat in London because I think my employer will transfer me there. I buy an oil painting because I think it was painted by Picasso. The transfer of a benefit by a person labouring under a mistake of this kind does trigger the liberal presumption in favour of restitution. After all, he would not have made the transfer, he would not have made or accepted the offer, had he not been subject to a mistaken view of the surrounding circumstances. In the context of bargaining, however, the presumption is more easily rebutted where the mistake is a mistake in assumptions than where it is a communication mistake. This is because the mistaken party did form the intention to book the cruise, buy the flat or the painting. He successfully

---

68 Wright, 1943, p 127.
69 See below, pp 55 ff.
70 See below, p 59.

communicated that intention to the other party. How that intention was motivated is relevant, but the line has to be drawn somewhere to protect the security of transactions.

The first to draw the distinction between mistakes in expression and mistakes in motive this sharply was Savigny.[71] The distinction is strongly influenced by the will-theory, to which Savigny was committed. Where a person made a declaration which he did not want to make, or at least not in this form, the will-theory dictated that no contract could be based on this: he did not really consent at all. Where, however, he formed the intention to make a declaration and then went on to make it, the factors that led him to form that intention did not concern the other party. As Savigny wrote:

> If we say that the error determined the will, this should not be taken literally. It was always the actor himself who accorded the error such determinative force. The freedom of his choice between different decisions was unfettered; whatever advantages the error might have promised him, he could dismiss them, and thus the influence of the error does not negate the presence of a free declaration of his will. The correct understanding of this question depends on a sharp distinction of the will itself from that which was happening in the soul of the person who exercised that will; the will is an independent fact, which alone is relevant to the creation of legal relations. Linking that fact to that preparatory process, as if the latter were an essential part of it, would be arbitrary, not to say groundless.[72]

The distinction, which subsequently found its way into the *BGB*, can lead to apparently arbitrary results. If a person offering certain goods for sale misplaces a decimal point so that the price appears ten times lower than intended, and this offer is accepted, the contract might be voidable because the mistake is a mistake in expression. If, however, he miscalculates the cost of the goods to himself and bases his offer on that mistaken calculation, with the result that he would make a substantial loss if held to the contract, he will nevertheless be bound: his mistake is an error in motive only. It might be suggested that the law should refuse to draw such fine distinctions, and that the two cases should be treated no differently. The problem with this criticism is that lines need to be drawn somewhere: if the line between mistake in expression and mistake in motive were collapsed in this borderline case, the relevance of mistakes in motive would be extended from borderline case to borderline case, until it would disappear completely.[73]

Some have, of course, argued that this would not be a bad thing. The Swiss contract theorist August Simonius, writing in 1935, criticised the distinction as being based on the will-theory, by then thoroughly discredited. He could see no reason at all why an offeror who writes 1,000 rather than 1,500 is allowed to rescind, whereas an offeror who erroneously assumes his own overheads to be lower than they actually are is not.[74] Simonius praises French law for rejecting the distinction, and English law for having rejected it 'as a matter of course'.[75]

---

71 Although Savigny was not the first to draw the distinction: cf eg, Thibaut, 1817, Vol 2, p 105.

72 Savigny, 1841, p 113.

73 See Flume, 1979, p 451. It is equally possible, of course, that all kinds of mistake become irrelevant, contracts being generally enforced irrespective of them.

74 Simonius, 1935, p 252.

75 *Ibid*, p 253.

Heinrich Titze, writing in 1940, bases his criticism of the distinction on the argument that 'legal and economic purposes of a contracting party must be taken as a whole'.[76] The distinction between mistakes in expression and mistakes in motive, however, only focuses on the former, ignoring the latter. This, according to Titze, cannot be justified. He gives the example of a person buying a wedding present when unbeknown to him the engagement has already been broken off. Here, it cannot be seriously argued that will and declaration are congruent: they are, on the contrary, as divergent as they can be.[77]

Walter Schmidt-Rimpler defends the distinction against such attacks. While he acknowledges that it is based on the since repudiated will-theory, he provides a new rationale for the distinction which is in keeping with the objective theory. He admits that both mistakes in expression and mistakes in motive trigger the presumption in favour of restitution. It is therefore necessary to justify the non-availability of restitution rather than its availability. The justification is to be found in security of transactions. However, mistakes in expression are a less serious threat to security of transactions than mistakes in motive. For one thing, he argues, they are much less common. Moreover, where a person makes a mistake in expression, he does not assess the legal consequences of his declaration. He had no chance at all to exercise his judgment, and for that reason restitution should be more easily available. On the other hand, where a person falls victim to a mistake in motive, he will have considered the pros and cons of entering into the contract. His decision will be based on many factors, some of greater, some of lesser importance. If he gets this judgment wrong, he is, according to Schmidt-Rimpler, less worthy of protection than the person making a error in expression: after all, if his motive was of such importance to him, he could have made it a condition of his transfer.[78]

In conclusion, while it cannot be claimed that the distinction between errors in expression and errors in motive is the correct solution, it can be described as a possible solution.[79] If it is accepted that, on the one hand, a causal mistake triggers the presumption in favour of restitution which is, on the other, rebuttable if it is demonstrated that the mistake would undermine a bargain, a balance must be struck between the security of transactions on the one hand and the transferor's interest in restitution on the other. This can be achieved by either ruling out the rescission of contracts for mistake altogether, of course. But where this is not desired, it will be difficult to find perfect criteria for distinguishing relevant from irrelevant mistakes.

3.5.3 Mistakes in performance

So far, we have assumed that restitution for mistake depended on the avoidance of some underlying legal transaction, typically a contract. When the law puts obstacles in the way of restitution it is because the sanctity of contract is to be preserved – people are to be held to their bargains. There is, however, a danger that the restrictive attitude to restitution depending on the avoidance of a contract is carried over to what Palmer calls 'mistakes in performance', that is, 'restitution that does not require avoidance of any transaction

---

76 Titze, 1940, p 94.

77 *Ibid*, p 95.

78 Cf Schmidt-Rimpler, 1941, pp 188 ff; 1955, pp 9 ff; 1956, p 215.

79 Cf Flume, 1979, p 434.

except the transfer itself'.[80] Here, restitution can be made more difficult by insisting that the mistake in question be 'fundamental', that it be 'shared' or that it be a mistake as to a supposed liability. The result is that the rules relating to mistakes in performance are aligned with the rules relating to mistakes in contracting. The availability of restitution for mistake is restricted by insisting first that non-liability mistakes, that is, mistakes by which the transferors deceives himself to be under a liability to make the payment, are not sufficiently 'fundamental' to warrant restitution.[81] In the leading English case on this question, *Norwich Union v Price*[82] the holder of a bill of lading for a cargo of lemons claimed on the insurance when it believed that the lemons had been lost in transit. In fact, the lemons had been sold by the master because they were ripening – this did not constitute an insured risk. When the insurance company discovered the mistake, it sued the bill of lading holder for return of the money and succeeded. However, Lord Wright's speech gives the distinct impression that restitution was only available because first, the insurer's mistake of fact was of a kind that was 'fundamental or basic',[83] and, secondly, because it was shared by both parties.[84]

There are, in fact, cases in which restitution of money paid under a mistake in performance was denied because only the transferor was labouring under a mistake. In *Sellman v American National Life Insurance*, decided in Texas in 1955,[85] a wife claimed on an insurance policy on her divorced husband's life when a man killed in a train crash was identified by relatives as her husband. Within weeks of payment, the insurance company obtained information that he was still alive and sought restitution from the wife. This was denied for the bizarre reason that the wife did not know whether her husband was dead or alive at the time of the payment. As such, she was not mistaken, only the insurance company was. According to the court, however, 'money paid under a unilateral mistake cannot be recovered'.[86]

The Texas court clearly missed the importance of distinguishing between mistakes in performance and mistakes in contracting. It applied a device used to protect bargained for expectations of contractual parties, namely that both parties must share the mistake, to a case in which there was no threat to contractual expectations at all. The case demonstrates particularly clearly how this approach can lead to absurd results. On the facts of the case itself, had the wife shared the insurance company's belief that her husband was dead, she would have had to return the money. Had she known, on the other hand, that her husband was still alive, she would, on the court's reasoning, have been entitled to it.[87] In truth, however, there are no reasons present in the facts of *Sellman* to rebut the presumption in favour of restitution which is triggered when a benefit is transferred mistakenly. Where restitution threatens to upset a contract, the presumption may be rebutted because contracts are risk-allocation devices, and the risks allocated by a

---

80   Palmer, 1962, p 8.
81   Cf *Morgan v Ashcroft* [1938] 1 KB 49, 65–66; interpreting *Aiken v Short* (1856) 1 H & N 210, 215.
82   [1934] AC 455.
83   *Ibid*, at 463.
84   *Ibid*, at 460–61, quoting from Street CJ's judgment in the Supreme Court of New South Wales.
85   *Sellman v American National Life Ins Co* 281 SW 2d 150 (1955).
86   *Ibid*, at 154. More recently, the Kansas Supreme Court appeared to endorse this: see *Kansas Farm Bureau Life Insurance Company, Inc v Farmway Credit Union* 889 P 2d 784 (1996), 785.
87   Cf Palmer, 1962, p 70.

contract may include the risk that one or the other of the parties might be mistaken.[88] For this reason, limiting restitution for mistakes in performance by requirements that the mistake be fundamental or shared by both parties cannot be justified.[89]

The same is true of the requirement that a mistake, in order to be relevant, must be a mistake as to a supposed liability. Thus, in *Aiken v Short*,[90] the claimant bank thought it had acquired property which was subject to an equitable charge. It had agreed with the supposed grantor, who was personally liable for the debt secured by the charge, that it would pay off the debt and thus release the charge. It did so, but it turned out that the grantor had never had any title to the property. The bank had redeemed a charge on property belonging to somebody else. The bank's action against the holder of the charge was unsuccessful. Bramwell B refused restitution, because the bank's mistake had not been a liability mistake:

> In order to entitle a person to recover back money paid under a mistake of fact, the mistake must be as to a fact, which, if true, would make the person paying liable to pay the money; not where, if true, it would merely make it desirable that he should pay the money.

The irony of insisting on a liability mistake of this kind is that liability mistakes cannot be distinguished from mistakes which 'would merely make it desirable' to pay on the basis that only the latter are mistakes in motive: liability mistakes, after all, are mistakes in motive, too:[91] the supposed liability is the reason for the payment – the payment does not wrongly express the payer's intentions. The explanation for restricting restitution to liability mistakes, as will be further explained below,[92] lies not in the fear of undermining bargains, but in the fear of too much restitution in the sense that the defendant might end worse off as a result of the claim than he was before he ever received the benefit in question. It is for this reason that the arguments for retaining this particular restriction are very weak indeed if a system allows for a disenrichment defence or defence of change of position.

3.6 CONCLUSION

This chapter set out to identify why a mistaken transfer should be reversed, and in what circumstances restitution for mistake can be legitimately restricted. It has been argued that, on the basis of the principle of private autonomy, any causal mistake, be it of fact or law, be it more or less fundamental, be it a mistake 'in motive' or a mistake 'in expression', gives rise to a presumption in favour of restitution.

In answering the question what constitutes a 'mistake' we reached the following conclusions: first, there is no reason to differentiate between cases in which a benefit is conferred because the transferor is mistaken as to a relevant matter, and cases in which he is wholly unaware of a relevant matter. Secondly, the fact that the transferor was in doubt

---

88 Cf Burrows, 1993a, p 107.
89 This point is pursued further below, pp 72, 76 ff.
90 *Aiken v Short* (1856) 1 H & N 210.
91 Cf von Tuhr, 1979, p 483.
92 See below, pp 73 ff.

whether his view on a relevant matter was correct, does not by itself mean that he was not mistaken. Thirdly, in general mispredictions differ from mistakes, and do not raise the presumption in favour of restitution, because a prediction cannot be verified or falsified at the time it is made.

Having explained the meaning of the term 'mistake', the chapter went on to outline the ways in which the presumption against restitution can be rebutted. It was argued that the two main considerations militating against restitution for mistake were that it might undermine either the recipient's security of receipt or a contract freely entered into between the parties. While the recipient's security of receipt is safeguarded mainly by a defence of change of position or disenrichment, the law seeks to avoid undermining bargains by restricting the availability of restitution more or less drastically whenever exchanges made under a valid contract are involved. The problem of distinguishing between mistakes which lead to a contract being set aside and mistakes which leave a contract intact has never been solved satisfactorily. One possible approach is based on the distinction between mistakes 'in motive' or 'in assumptions', and mistakes in communicating an intention after it has been formed. Another is to allow 'fundamental' mistakes to destroy the contract, while 'lesser' mistakes leave it intact. There is a danger, however, that these categorisations are carried over to cases which do not involve contracts at all. It was therefore argued that 'mistakes in performance' should always trigger restitution (absent change of position), whether they be fundamental or not, and whether they be in expression or in motive.

In the following two chapters, the relevant rules of German and English law can now be examined in a little more detail.

CHAPTER 4

MISTAKE IN GERMAN LAW

Mistake plays a fundamental role in the German law of unjust enrichment. It is as true for German law as it is for English law that a mistaken payment or transfer can be recovered back. If the role of mistake in German enrichment law is sometimes underestimated, this is mainly for two reasons. First, § 119 *BGB*, which is the central provision relating to mistake in the code, appears to be concerned exclusively with contracts. Secondly, the law of unjust enrichment is structured in such a way that the true reason for restitution, be it mistake, duress, failure of consideration or some other reason, is hidden behind the abstraction 'without legal ground'. Nevertheless, mistake is relevant in the context of unjust enrichment in the following ways:

First and most obviously, where a contract is avoided because of a mistake under § 119 *BGB*, any performances which have already been rendered in accordance with the contract will be recoverable under §§ 812 ff *BGB*: the contract is now void, the 'legal ground' of the enrichment has thus fallen away and restitution will follow. The true reason for restitution is nevertheless the mistake: without the mistake, the contract would have continued to subsist. § 812 *BGB* would have had nothing to say. It is thus not surprising that most cases turning on the application of § 119 are in reality unjust enrichment cases, the claimant seeking restitution of a benefit transferred pursuant to a contract. In order to decide whether restitution is available under § 812 I, the court will first have to decide whether or not to set aside the contract on the basis of § 119. Thus, a case decided in 1980,[1] which shall serve as one example out of many, involved the sale of a harvester. The buyer argued that he had been mistaken about the age of the machine, and asked for his money back. The action was based on § 812 I, but before that provision could be applied, the court first had to consider the question whether a mistake as to the year of manufacture of goods bought was a relevant mistake under § 119 II. Having answered this question in the affirmative, the court worked out the restitutionary consequences of the buyer's successful rescission of the contract of sale.

Secondly, mistake is relevant, albeit in a more indirect way, where § 119 cannot be invoked because it is specifically geared towards *Willenserklärungen*, declarations of intent. Take the case of an overpayment. The mistake lies in the fact that the payer mistakenly thought to be obliged to pay more than was actually the case. The underlying contract remains valid, § 119 is irrelevant. Nevertheless, the overpayment can be recovered because it lacks a 'legal ground': the supposed liability to pay the surplus amount never existed. The fact that the true reason for restitution is mistake, whether of fact or law, is reflected in § 814: if the payer knew that he was not liable to make the payment, this provision says that he will lose his *prima facie* entitlement to restitution.

Thirdly, it is strongly arguable that even where § 119 does nothing more than enable the mistaken party to get out of an executory contract, the right to rescind the contract itself must be described as restitutionary. Say the declaration which is avoided under § 119 is a contractual acceptance. By accepting the offeror's offer, the offeree obtained

---

1   BGHZ 78, 216 (9.10.1980).

rights and became subject to obligations. Those obligations constituted a benefit to the offeror, which is wiped out, in effect returned, to the offeree when he avoids his acceptance. Given that an enforceable right to a performance is just as much a benefit as the performance itself, it is possible to characterise the rescission of a declaration under § 119 as restitutionary, even though the *BGB* does not categorise it as such.

It was pointed out in the previous chapter that a liberal legal system has to draw a distinction between cases where restitution involves the unwinding of a contract, and cases where it does not. The reason for this lies in the importance of bargains in an exchange economy. Where a benefit is transferred under a contract, the recipient's interest is not limited to his interest in the security of his receipt – his interest in the security of his transaction, his expectation interest, will also be entitled to protection. The law affords transactions which are the result of mutual bargaining and exchange a greater protection than mere transfers. Where a contract is involved, the law cannot simply allow one party to avoid the contract on the basis of a wholly subjective mistake, which the other party did not know about and could not have known about. All bargains would otherwise be undermined. In §§ 119 ff *BGB*, German law is therefore concerned with restricting the right of a mistaken party to rescind. German law goes about this in a way which is very different from English law. For one thing, German law does not draw a distinction between spontaneous mistakes and misrepresentations (although fraudulent misrepresentations are provided for separately in § 123). Then, in determining which mistakes are relevant and may allow a party to get out of a contract, German law does not ask how 'fundamental' a mistake may be, or whether the mistake could and should have been realised by the other contracting party.[2] German law is more interested in the nature of the mistake. Thus it distinguishes mistakes according to whether they arise 'in the transaction',[3] by using the wrong words,[4] or by saying or writing or typing words that were not intended to be said, written or typed.[5] Other mistakes are referred to as mistakes in motive,[6] and these are dismissed as irrelevant unless they fall within the special category of § 119 II.[7]

The two systems diverge even more sharply where a transfer is made gratuitously, in other words, by way of gift. Given that German law regards gifts as contracts, the restrictive regime of §§ 119 ff *BGB* applies to them as well. In English law, in contrast, it appears that a gift can be revoked on the basis of a mere causative mistake, whether of fact or law. This stark contrast between the two solutions is tempered to some extent by special rules in the German law, which allow a donor to rescind a gift in certain defined circumstances.

This chapter will first examine the regime which applies to contractual mistakes in §§ 119 ff. We will then be in a position to examine the special rules governing gifts. The

---

2   English law regards this latter point as raising questions of contractual construction: what was the (objective) content of the contractual communication? It is for this reason that the question whether the other party ought to have realised the mistake assumes such importance: see *Hartog v Colin & Shields* [1939] 3 All ER 566.

3   To adopt the terminology of Markesinis, 1997, p 198.

4   '*Inhaltsirrtum*', see below, p 56.

5   '*Erklärungsirrtum*', see below, p 56.

6   '*Motivirrtum*', see below, p 56.

7   See below, pp 57 f.

chapter will close with some concluding considerations about the true role of mistake in the German law of unjust enrichment.

4.1 MISTAKES OF LAW AND FACT

It was pointed out in the previous chapter that the presumption in favour of restitution will be triggered whether a mistake be a mistake of fact or law.[8] Nevertheless, recovery for mistakes of law has, from Roman times onwards, always been restricted.[9] Savigny explained this on the basis that a failure to know the law was presumed to be negligent, whereas the same could not be said of a failure to know facts, but sought to limit the mistake of law bar as far as possible against the background of the Roman sources, which to him, after all, constituted valid law.[10] The drafters of the BGB decided to drop the distinction between mistakes of law and fact altogether. The first commission thought that a special rule was required to put this beyond doubt.[11] This was not uncontroversial. A fairly large number of writers thought that the distinction between mistakes of law and fact was well founded and necessary.[12] The second commission finally decided to drop the provision, but not because it was persuaded by the adherents to the old bar, but because it thought a special provision unnecessary. That mistakes of law and fact were to be treated the same way was simply taken for granted.[13] Thus it is generally not significant in the modern German law whether a mistake is to be classified as a mistake of fact or law.

4.2 THE ROLE OF MISTAKE IN THE LAW OF CONTRACT GENERALLY

If the attitude of the German law of contract to mistakes is rather more liberal than the attitude of English law, this is explicable on two grounds: first, contrary to their own statements, the drafters of the BGB were still very much committed to the will theory of contract law.[14] Secondly, the BGB does not allow a party to rescind where his, otherwise irrelevant, mistake is induced by an innocent or negligent misrepresentation by the other party. Rescission for misrepresentations is restricted, in § 123, to intentional misrepresentations, in other words, to deceit.

Given the underlying acceptance of the will theory, it is not surprising that the drafters of the BGB accepted Savigny's distinction between misunderstandings and mistakes in motive. Communication mistakes are sub-divided into 'mistakes in expression' ('*Erklärungsirrtum*') and mistakes as to the content of a declaration

---

8   See pp 43 f, above.
9   Zimmermann, 1996, p 608. Cf Pomponius D 41, 3, 32, 1; ALR, § 12; AGBG, § 2.
10   Savigny, 1841, Vol III, p 336.
11   § 146 of the first draft.
12   See Siméon, 1901, p 585; Gebhard, 1888, p 261; Hatschek, 1922, p 125.
13   Mayer-Maly, 1970, p 147.
14   Cf Flume, 1979, p 448.

('*Inhaltsirrtum*') in § 119 I, the relevance of mistakes in assumptions is dealt with in § 119 II, while mistakes in performance are not dealt with in § 119 at all, but, albeit indirectly, in the law of unjust enrichment proper, in § 814.[15]

§ 119 reads:

(1) Wer bei der Abgabe einer Willenserklärung über deren Inhalt im Irrtume war oder eine Erklärung dieses Inhalts überhaupt nicht abgeben wollte, kann die Erklärung anfechten, wenn anzunehmen ist, daß er sie bei Kenntnis der Sachlage und bei verständiger Würdigung des Falles nicht abgegeben haben würde. [(1) He who, when making a declaration of will, is mistaken about the content of that declaration or did not mean to make such a declaration at all, can avoid the declaration if it can be assumed that he would not have made it had he had full knowledge of the facts and an opportunity reasonably to appreciate the situation.]

(2) Als Irrtum über den Inhalt der Erklärung gilt auch der Irrtum über solche Eigenschaften der Person oder der Sache, die im Verkehr als wesentlich angesehen werden. [(2) A mistake about such qualities of a person or a thing which are generally considered relevant is to be treated as a mistake about the content of a declaration.]

4.2.1 The main categories of mistake in German law

§ 119 thus categorises mistakes on the basis of the stage in the contracting process at which they occur. The provision is based on the following 'timetable' of contract making:

First, the parties form the intention to enter into the contract. This will be influenced by a complex array of considerations, ranging from an assessment of each party's own financial position, his own desires and preferences, to an estimation of the values of the contractual performances, fiscal consequences of the transaction and so on. Any mistake which occurs at this stage is referred to as a 'motivation mistake' (*Motivirrtum*), a mistake in assumptions. Mistakes in motive are dismissed by § 119 I as generally irrelevant,[16] subject to the important exception in § 119 II which equates some mistakes in motive to mistakes as to the content of a declaration.

The next stage in the contracting process consists of determining the best way of expressing the intention formed at the first stage. Any mistake which occurs at this stage will be relevant as a so-called *Inhaltsirrtum* or *Bedeutungsirrtum* (mistake as to the content or meaning of a declaration).[17]

Assuming, however, that the party has decided to use words which correctly convey the intended meaning, the next stage of contracting will be the expression of these words. Any mistakes which occur at this stage, be it by a slip of the tongue, the pen or the word processor, will be relevant. Such a mistake will be referred to as an error in the declaration (*Erklärungsirrtum*). Thus, if the wrong price is written down by omitting or adding a zero, the party making the declaration will be able to rescind his declaration under § 119: he 'did not mean to make such a declaration at all'. § 120 goes on to provide for the same consequences for mistakes in transmitting a message, say by telex or messenger.

---

15 See pp 64 f, below.
16 Medicus, 1997, p 284.
17 For an example, see p 46 above.

4.2.2 Other mistakes

A number of mistakes do not fit easily into the above typology. I will focus on two of these, namely mistakes as to the legal consequences of juridical acts, and mistakes as to the relevant quality of a person or thing.

Mistake of law with regard to the legal consequences of a juridical act

A seller of goods might reasonably believe that the maxim 'let the buyer beware' still holds good, and so he may not realise that as a seller he will be liable for defects in the quality of the goods. It is an unresolved controversy in the German debate how this kind of mistake is to be categorised. There are basically two possibilities: the seller might argue that he was mistaken as to the meaning of his declaration: he did not realise that by making an offer to sell, he was incurring potential liabilities over and above the liability to make delivery of the goods. As such, the mistake will be a relevant mistake which will allow the seller to rescind. The buyer, on the other hand, might argue that the seller's mistake was nothing more than an irrelevant motivation mistake: the seller's motive in offering to the sell the goods was to get them off his hands without incurring any liability in connection with them, and so he should not be able to rescind.

It is clear that were the seller's argument to prevail in the above example, the whole law of product liability could be undermined. Larenz therefore argues that, in the interests of legal certainty, rescission for mistake has to be kept within bounds.[18] It is, however, far from clear where the line is to be drawn.[19]

Mistake as to essential characteristics or identity of a person or thing

An identity mistake is generally accepted to be relevant under § 119 I: the declaration is made in respect of a different person or thing than the party making it intended. Medicus gives the following examples: a passer-by wants to give a beggar DM 1.00, but gives him a DM 5.00 piece by accident. A customer in a supermarket takes the wrong item to the check-out, and only realises his mistake after he has paid. Finally, a buyer of furniture gets the address wrong and places his order with the wrong furniture store, because this happens to have the same name.[20] Although such mistakes are in practice very rare they will be of particular relevance when we look at the topic of mistaken gifts.[21]

A mistake as to a quality of a person or thing must be distinguished from an identity mistake, as in the former the declaration is aimed at the correct person or relates to the correct object, it is just that these have different attributes or qualities than the person making the declaration thought. The distinction becomes blurred, however, once the attributes or qualities as to which a person is mistaken serve to identify the person or thing in question. Thus, if a man pays money to a child whom he mistakenly assumes to be his illegitimate daughter, does the fact that she is not in fact his daughter mean that he is mistaken as to her identity? While in any event a mistake as to a quality or an attribute

---

18   Larenz, 1989, p 376.
19   Medicus, 1997, p 288.
20   *Ibid*, p 291.
21   See below, pp 60 ff.

is made relevant by § 119 II, the instability of that provision makes it desirable to keep the two kinds of mistake separate.[22] As the above example shows, this is not always easy.

§ 119 II was added by the second drafting commission, who thought that without such a provision the law of mistake would simply be too narrow. It is today generally agreed that § 119 II is badly drafted,[23] mainly because it leaves the decision whether a mistake is relevant or not to be made by reference to custom and general practice. The dominant view holds that § 119 II constitutes a sub-category of motivation mistake which, exceptionally, allows the mistaken party to rescind: the quality which the mistaken party believes to exist is one of his motives for entering into the contract.[24]

It is striking that in seeking to control § 119 II, academics and courts have gone their different ways: while academics are still searching for a way to limit the provision in a predictable and coherent way,[25] the courts have long given up the attempt and are content to lay down different groups of cases according to criteria which are not always readily intelligible.

The academic debate is too extensive and the point not relevant enough to the subject-matter of this book to justify referring to it in any detail. The most interesting and influential contribution has come from Flume,[26] who wants to limit the applicability of § 119 II to characteristics of the person or thing to which the contract relates. While this approach has much to recommend it, its primary problem is that it simply does not reflect the wording of § 119 II, although, to quote Kramer, given that 'the wording in question is so meaningless', this might not be a particularly weighty objection.[27]

Some examples of mistakes which the courts have considered relevant are: material and size,[28] identity of the painter of a piece of art,[29] and the year of manufacture.[30] Not relevant are: value or market price,[31] who has the property in a thing or a piece of land,[32] or its economic usefulness.[33]

4.2.3 Consequences of mistake

Before a mistaken party can rescind a contract for mistake, he has to overcome some additional obstacles.

---

22 Medicus, 1997, p 292.
23 MünchKomm/Kramer § 119, No 10.
24 See Larenz, 1989, p 377.
25 See Müller, 1988, p 381.
26 Flume, 1948
27 MünchKomm/Kramer, 947, § 119, No 92.
28 RGZ 101, 68 (7.12.1920).
29 BGH NJW 88, 2598 (8.6.1988).
30 BGHZ 78, 216 (9.10.1980).
31 BGHZ 16, 54 (18.12.1954).
32 BGHZ 34, 32 (14 12.1960).
33 *Ibid.*

'Reasonable causality'

The first can be described as 'reasonable causality'. The wording of § 119 I suggests that mere causation is not enough: the mistaken party can only rescind 'if it can be assumed that he would not have made [the declaration] had he had full knowledge of the facts and an opportunity reasonably to appreciate the situation'. This is generally understood to mean that subjective causation is not enough.[34] It is not open to the mistaken party to argue that, given his own idiosyncratic preferences, he would not have made the declaration if he had had all the necessary information. Whether the mistake is serious enough to permit rescission will thus be determined on the basis of objective criteria. This requirement, however, has not played a significant role in reported decisions.

Promptness

§ 121 requires rescission to be declared 'without culpable hesitation', in other words, immediately upon realising the mistake. If rescission is delayed, it is ineffective.

The innocent party's reliance interest

Where a contracting party avoids the contract on the basis of his own mistake, whether it occurred 'in the transaction' or related to the identity or characteristics of a person or thing, this may cause reliance losses to the other party who may, for instance, have incurred costs in preparing his own counter-performance, or in packing and shipping goods sold. He will be compensated for such losses under § 122 I, although only to the extent that the now rescinded contract did not represent a bad bargain for him: the expectation interest represents a ceiling for the recoverable reliance loss.

Given that the question whether the mistake was induced by the other party to the contract is one which German law largely ignores, § 122 II provides that, where the other party knew or should have known about the facts leading to rescission, he will not be able to recover at all. This will include cases of negligent misrepresentation – as for wholly innocent misrepresentation, the courts have developed the law on an analogy with contributory negligence: the mistaken party will only be liable for a proportion of the other party's reliance losses in such a case.[35]

Rescission

Rescission (*Anfechtung*) of a contract, in German as in English law, is not tied to any specific form. § 143 I merely requires that it be communicated to the other party, although it is not clear whether the rescinding party is obliged to specify the reasons on which the rescission of the contract is to be based.[36] § 142 I provides that the effect of rescission is that the legal transaction is to be regarded as void *ab initio*. This will then be the point at which §§ 812 ff, the part of the German civil code devoted to unjust enrichment, will come into play.

---

34 Medicus, 1997, p 295.
35 BGH NJW 69, 1380 (14.3.1969).
36 Cf MünchKomm/Mayer-Maly, § 143, No 7, p 1214.

4.3 MISTAKEN GIFTS

The donation contract is one of several gratuitous contracts recognised by German law. Other gratuitous contracts include gratuitous loan of property (§ 598) and interest-free loan of money (§§ 607, 609 III), gratuitous service contracts (§ 662) or gratuitous bailment contracts (§ 688). All of these contracts raise similar problems when they are affected by the mistake of the performing party. These problems, however, are hardly discussed at all in the literature;[37] the general rules, in this case §§ 119 ff, are supposed to deal with them adequately.

The problem is that § 119 treats the majority of mistakes in motive as irrelevant. As we have seen in the previous chapter, however, it is inherently problematical to treat 'voluntary' transfers on a par with contractual transfers: only in the latter case is the presumption in favour of restitution, triggered by the mistake, rebutted by the presence of contractual risk-allocation. German law recognises this in the context of testamentary dispositions: a provision in a will can be avoided if it can be shown that it was made under a mistake, any mistake in motive being relevant: § 2078 II. There is, however, no such provision relating to gifts generally. *Prima facie*, therefore, the provisions in § 119 will apply. The drafters of the *BGB* did, however, consider it necessary to depart from these general rules in a number of respects. First, it is possible for the donor to make his gift subject to a condition (*Auflage*). This is similar to the English purpose trust: the donee has to use part or the whole of the gift in a certain manner.[38] This *Schenkung unter Auflage* gives the donor an enforceable claim against the donee. If the donee has put it out of his power to perform, or if he has so delayed his performance that it has become worthless to the donor, the donor will have a restitutionary claim in respect of so much of the gift as would have been required to fulfil the condition. Secondly, § 528 allows the donor to revoke the gift if he has fallen on hard times, more precisely 'if after execution of the gift he is unable to maintain a reasonable living or to discharge his maintenance obligations in respect of relatives, current or former spouses'. The gift can then be recovered following the rules of the law of unjust enrichment.[39] Thirdly, §§ 530 ff give the donor the right to revoke his gift should the donee prove himself 'grossly ungrateful' either towards the donor himself or a near relative. Again, the law of unjust enrichment will provide the rules governing this restitutionary claim.

The drafters of the *BGB* thought that these qualifications of the donee's right to keep the gift were sufficient. The first drafting commission thought that, although there was much to be said for relaxing the rules relating to mistake in the case of gratuitous contracts, the difficulties of distinguishing gratuitous from non-gratuitous contracts were simply too great, so that differentiated treatment would prejudice legal certainty.[40] This

---

37 Thus, MünchKomm/Kollhosser, § 516, No 11, p 990, discusses the applicability of the general rules in §§ 104–84 to donation contracts. He focuses on capacity issues (gifts by parents to their children) and whether gifts can be void because '*contra bonos mores*' under § 117. No mention is made of §§ 119 ff.

38 The *Schenkung unter Auflage* may be distinguished from a bilateral contract (under which the counter-performance must derive from the other part's general assets) and from the so-called Zweckschenkung, which makes the gift contingent on the attainment of a certain collateral purpose.

39 This is yet another example of the use of the cross reference in the *BGB*: see above, pp 19 f.

40 Motive I, p 201.

decision was particularly momentous given that the first commission proposed to draw the distinction between mistakes in expression and mistakes in assumption much more sharply than was finally done in the code, with no right to rescind at all for mistakes in motive.

In the first few years following the enactment of the code, it was felt not to be at all obvious that the view of the first drafting commission was to prevail. It is interesting to note that commentators who bemoaned the width and uncertain scope of § 119 II go on to argue that, applied to gifts, it is in fact not wide enough. Lenel, writing in 1902, notes that the application of the provision to gifts 'causes serious difficulties'.[41] His argument hinges on the phrase: '... qualities which are generally considered relevant in practice'.[42] He argues that this phrase must mean something different if applied to a gratuitous contract such as a gift because, while the important elements of a contract of exchange can be more or less objectively determined, this does not hold true for gifts:

> A person making a gift does not pursue purposes which could provide a objective point of reference for the evaluation of the different qualities of the thing ... The decision to give depends on subjective considerations, greater or lesser generosity, greater or lesser affluence and so on.[43]

He therefore arrives at the following 're-interpretation' of § 119 II in its application to gifts: every quality is to be considered relevant which the donor, had he been able to consider his gift properly, would have considered relevant. The objective test is turned into a highly subjective one.[44]

The next significant contribution to the debate came from Siegmund Schloßmann in 1903. He sees § 119 II as an open invitation to judges to dispense palm tree justice. He writes:

> If our judges are to be given the same powers which were always claimed by the Roman *praetor*, to act *iuris civilis corrigendi*, this should be openly stated: a law which bears such fruit is indefensible, no matter whether the 'legislator' intended these consequences or not: the law is not to be applied.[45]

Following such strong words, it is particularly interesting that he goes on to argue that, applied to gratuitous contracts, the provision is more likely too narrow than too broad:

> For some transactions, however, such a wide provision does no harm, on the contrary, it must be appropriate to give as many escape routes as possible to the mistaken party, by which he can reverse the consequences of a transaction because of a mistake as to the attributes of the object in question.[46]

---

41 Lenel, 1902, p 24.
42 This is an inadequate translation of '*Eigenschaften, die im Verkehr als wesentlich angesehen werden*'. '*Verkehr*' cannot be translated. The provision is meant to refer to those characteristics which are considered relevant in practice, in everyday exchanges between contracting parties generally.
43 Lenel, 1902, p 25.
44 *Ibid.*
45 Schloßmann, 1902, p 64.
46 *Ibid*, p 67.

The defendant's interest in retention is qualified by the fact that he would only be returning something which he received gratuitously – it should therefore be appropriate to require him to make restitution.[47] He gives examples: a gift of supposedly fake jewellery – the diamonds turn out to be genuine. A coin received by way of payment is made a gift of to another person. It then transpires that the coin is very rare and highly valued by collectors. A field on the outskirts of a town is given away. Unknown to the transferor, the planning authority has designated it for development and it is 20 times its supposed value in consequence.[48] In all these cases, Schloßmann argues, the donor should be able to rescind the gift. As this involves merely the putting aside of the underlying contract of donation, and not a rescission of the gift with *in rem* effect, there is, according to Schloßmann, nothing wrong with this: the restitutionary consequences of rescission are for the law of unjust enrichment, with its strong disenrichment defence, to sort out, and this will sufficiently protect the donee.[49] Like Lenel, he therefore advocates a more flexible interpretation of § 119 II which allows for a gift's value to be taken into account. However, Schloßmann goes no further than this. If it cannot be said that the quality in question is generally considered relevant, but that it is only relevant to this particular donor, the gift must stand in spite of a mistake which would have caused the donor not to make the gift. Otherwise the donor would always be able to reverse his gift by inventing mistakes of this very subjective kind *ex post*. Examples given include: the donor does not know that the picture he has just given away was painted by his late father – the gift stands. It would have been otherwise had the painting been by Picasso. He gives away his dog, little knowing that the animal once saved his child from drowning, or an old chest, not knowing it is a family heirloom. The gifts cannot be avoided given the wording of § 119 II. Schloßmann does, however, go on to say that it may well be possible for a judge to stretch the literal meaning of the provision in such cases. This comment is again to be taken seriously given that Schloßmann, in light of his earlier comments, is no friend of palm tree justice. This does not, of course, make the suggested solution any more attractive.

Leo Lippmann, writing in 1907, wants to exclude gifts completely from the ambit of § 119 II. To him, a gift is not a '*Verkehrsgeschäft*', because it is not a transaction *do ut des*.[50] The word '*Verkehr*', notoriously difficult to translate, can indeed be said to include the idea of exchange. Lippmann argues that therefore § 119 II should be confined to exchange transactions, and not to gratuitous transfers. On the analogy with § 2078 in the law of probate, he argues that all causal mistakes, including mistakes in motive, should allow the donor to claim restitution of the gift:

> [I]n the same way as in the case of last wills, in the case of gifts the free, unfettered will of the testator/donor is *suprema lex* and therefore any mistake which was determinative of the declaration will render the latter voidable ...[51]

Lippmann finds it quite difficult to reconcile this result with the wording of the *BGB*. Particularly, he finds it hard to account for the fact that § 2078 expressly provides that

---

47 *Ibid*, p 69.
48 *Ibid*.
49 *Ibid*, p 70.
50 Lippmann, 1907, p 377.
51 *Ibid*, p 379.

mistakes in motive render a will voidable, while there is no such provision in §§ 516 ff.[52] This is not surprising given the clear decision by the drafters of the *BGB* to make gifts subject to the general rules.[53]

Lenel's, Schloßmann's and Lippmann's work demonstrates, however, that, apart from all its other problems, the provision in § 119 is unsatisfactory if applied to gratuitous transfers. It is therefore surprising that, from 1907 onwards, the debate just went to sleep. The standard commentaries of today, in a way similar to the *travaux préparatoires* of the *BGB*, simply assume that §§ 119 ff will apply to gifts. The notable exception in the more recent literature is Flume's momentous work on the general part of the *BGB*.[54] Having outlined why the drafters of the *BGB* were correct in considering errors in motive to be generally irrelevant, he draws attention to the exception to this general rule in § 2078 and argues that a similar exception should apply to gifts *inter vivos*.[55] He dismisses the objection that this would undermine the donee's security of receipt. The consequences of a mistake in motive can be very serious indeed. Given the absence of a counter-performance, the donor's motive must form part of the *causa* or 'legal ground' of the gift. The donee is protected by § 122 which enables him to recover his reliance interest. This provision may indeed, depending on one's interpretation of § 818 III, be rather wider than the defence of change of position. Unfortunately Flume's argument has found few if any followers. On the contrary, most commentators do not even realise the problem. It is certainly true that nobody has as yet proven Flume wrong: nobody has even attempted to controvert his views.

There are surprisingly few cases involving mistaken gifts in German courts. This may well be because many donees will feel honour-bound to return mistaken gifts, or because mistaken donors are advised that their chances of success are extremely limited. All the reported cases involve the tax implications of gifts. In a case decided by the *Bundesfinanzhof*, the highest German fiscal court, in 1989, the claimant had made a gift of his share of a piece of land to his wife – this 'gift' was motivated by tax considerations. The manoeuvre backfired and his taxable income went up from DM 16,536 to DM 463,730. He sought to rescind the contract of donation, based on his mistake as to the fiscal consequences of the gift. The court held that he was unable to do so: the mistake was a mistake as to motive only, and as such irrelevant.[56]

In conclusion, it would appear that in German law as it stands, a mistake in motive will not give the donor a right to rescind, unless he can bring himself within § 119 II. This state of the law is unsatisfactory. To apply a rule which is primarily intended for executory bilateral transactions[57] to gifts, executed or otherwise, is taking the 'General Part' ideology[58] a step too far. In a mistaken gift scenario, the only considerations which might rebut the liberal presumption in favour of restitution are taken care of by the

---

52 *Ibid*, pp 381–82.
53 See pp 60 f, above.
54 Flume, 1979.
55 *Ibid*, p 426.
56 BFH DB 1990, 22 (20.9.1989); see, also, BFH/NV 1986, 21 (30.4.1985).
57 For evidence that it is these which the drafters of the *BGB* had in mind, see Prot I, p 107.
58 See above, pp 17 ff.

change of position defence.[59] A gift cannot realistically be described as a 'bargain'. When German law treats gifts as contracts, this is only giving expression to the truism that nobody can be forced to accept a gift – to that extent, offer and acceptance are necessary. Yet gifts lack, by definition, the element of exchange which gives contracts their special status in liberal legal systems. Thus, where the donee is not harmed by the reversal of the gift, there are no reasons for upholding it.

4.4 MISTAKE AND THE LAW OF UNJUST ENRICHMENT

As was pointed out in the introduction to this chapter, mistake plays a fundamental role in the law of unjust enrichment, although German lawyers may not always be aware of this. First of all, as was discussed above,[60] the rescission of a contract can always be analysed as restitution of a benefit: the rescinding party gets back his promise, his obligation to perform. Thus all cases of contractual rescission for mistake are also cases of restitution for mistake. Secondly, where an executed contract is rescinded for mistake, restitution in German law of any benefits transferred under the contract will not happen automatically. Nor will rescission have any effect *in rem*. As was explained in Chapter 2, the *BGB* refers the restitution creditor to § 812 I: the contract having been declared void *ab initio*, the transfer now lacks a 'legal ground': restitution will be the consequence. This abstraction, so well beloved by German lawyers, should not, however, deceive us into believing that the mistake which rendered the contract voidable is irrelevant to the restitutionary claim. On the contrary, it provides the reason for restitution – but for the mistake, there would be no unjust enrichment claim at all.[61] Thirdly, mistake is of immediate relevance to the German law of unjust enrichment in that § 814 excludes restitution where 'the performing party knew that he was not obliged to perform'. Thus, if a person thinks he is obliged to pay money to another under a contract, but that contract never existed, say because he forgot that he never got the expected letter of acceptance, he will be entitled to restitution. The reason for restitution must be mistake. It does not matter whether the mistake in question is one of law or fact.

The mistake in question will normally be a liability mistake, but this is not necessarily so,[62] because some legal transactions only come into existence at the point of performance. The classic example is the gift. This, as exhaustively discussed above,[63] is categorised as a contract in German law. An unexecuted gift promise requires notarisation to be binding[64] – in the same way as in English law a gift promise will only be binding if made by deed. An executed gift does not require any formalities (again, both legal systems agree in the result[65]) – the lack of form is 'healed' by delivery. Where a person gives more than he was supposed to give under the 'gift contract', he will be able to

---

59 This point was in fact raised in discussion during the liberations of the second commission: Prot I, p 107.
60 Above, p 33.
61 Cf below, p 213.
62 Cf Reuter and Martinek, 1983, pp 126 ff.
63 See pp 60 ff, above.
64 § 518 I 1 *BGB*.
65 § 518 II *BGB*; *Cochrane v Moore* (1890) 25 QBD 57.

recover the overpayment even though his mistake was not a mistake as to an existing liability. Meier has called this kind of mistake 'causa mistake'.[66] The idea is that, underlying the payment, there is the transaction 'gift contract'. If the payment exceeds the payment covered by the underlying transaction, the mistake will nevertheless give rise to a restitutionary claim:[67] the basis of the transfer, its 'legal ground' is lacking.

Of course, as pointed out in Chapter 2, the German law of unjust enrichment does not work with mistake in this way: if at all, the requirement of a mistake is implicit in §§ 812 ff. The closest German law gets to requiring a mistake is in § 814: it excludes a restitutionary claim where the transferor knew that there was no basis of the transfer. Thus, if you demand I pay you under a supposed contract and I, knowing full well that the contract is void, pay you anyway, I cannot then turn round and ask you to make restitution. This suggests that the mistake requirement does exist in German law, albeit in a negative way, and with a reversed burden of proof. Another twist of § 814 is that it does not confine restitution to mistake: it only requires absence of knowledge of non-liability.[68] Thus, a person who doubts that his liability exists, but nevertheless pays, will in most cases be able to recover.[69]

4.5 CONCLUSION

German lawyers do not think of their law of unjust enrichment as being based on mistake. Indeed, positive unjust factors are alien to them. As we have seen in this chapter, however, mistake does play a crucial role in the German law of unjust enrichment. The position can be summed up as follows:

First, because German law does not distinguish between spontaneous and non-fraudulently induced mistakes, and because it is more subjective in its attitude to the law of contract than the common law, its regime governing mistakes in the formation of contracts is more liberal than the common law regime (which forms the subject-matter of the next chapter). The German regime is based on a distinction between mistakes in the transaction and mistakes in motive. German law has been forced, however, to relax this distinction in the controversial provision of § 119 II, making restitution available for some mistakes in motive notwithstanding the valid formation of a contract.

Secondly, German law has a problem when it comes to gifts. This problem is caused by an exaggerated enthusiasm for the 'general part' technique of codification outlined in Chapter 2.[70] Because a gift is characterised as a contract, the general rules relating to all contracts are brought to bear on mistaken gifts. These problems are mitigated to some extent by special rules governing the revocability of gifts, but it has been argued that this is not sufficient. A causal mistake vitiates a gift and raises the presumption in favour of

---

66 Meier, 1999a, p 46.

67 Of course, if there is no preceding gift promise, the transfer itself might be construed as an offer of a gift which would become binding by acceptance of the transfer. It would then be necessary to rescind the gift contract under § 119 I – the mistake would be a mistake in expression.

68 Cf MünchKomm/Lieb, p 1305.

69 See the cases referred to above, p 39.

70 See pp 17 ff, above.

restitution. Whether a gift is characterised as a contract or not, there is nothing in a gratuitous transfer to rebut that presumption.

Thirdly, it has been explained how in German law the real reasons for restitution only play a role in the background. As § 814 demonstrates, however, they do have a role to play. The danger of the German approach is that the real reasons for restitution are overlooked. This makes it more difficult to appreciate in what circumstances the presumption in favour of restitution is rebutted by a change of circumstances. This will be further explained in Chapter 15. For now, it is enough to appreciate the fact that there are reasons for restitution in German law, and that they operate 'automatically' in a system of inter-related provisions.

CHAPTER 5

MISTAKE IN ENGLISH LAW

5.1 MISTAKES IN CONTRACT AND UNJUST ENRICHMENT

5.1.1 Mistakes affecting bargains

English law rejected the will theory more quickly than continental legal systems. This is reflected in its attitude to mistake. Bargains are sacrosanct. Although there are cases in which contracts will be set aside for mistake, such cases constitute the exception rather than the rule. This attitude is summed up rather neatly in Steyn J's words in *Associated Japanese Bank v Crédit du Nord SA*:

> The first imperative must be that the law ought to uphold rather than destroy apparent contracts. Secondly, the common law rules as to a mistake regarding the quality of the subject matter, like the common law rules regarding commercial frustration, are designed to cope with the impact of unexpected and wholly exceptional circumstances on apparent contracts.[1]

While the distinction between mistakes in expression and mistakes in underlying assumption is indeed drawn, both kinds of mistake are treated equally harshly.

Mistakes as to terms

We have already discussed the leading case of *Smith v Hughes*.[2] In that case it was held that even where the seller realised that the buyer did not want to buy that which, objectively speaking, he was ordering, the seller was not obliged to disabuse the buyer of his 'self-deception'. In German law, this case would have been decided the other way: the mistake would have been treated as a mistake in expression which renders a contract voidable under § 119 I BGB. In *Tamplin v James*[3] a public house was sold at auction. The defendant buyer knew that the adjoining gardens were occupied along with the public house. He assumed that they were included in the sale of the house and offered £750. This offer was accepted, and he signed the memorandum of agreement. When it later turned out that the adjoining land was not included, he refused to complete. The Court of Appeal dismissed the appeal from an order of specific performance made by Baggallay LJ at first instance. The court stressed that there had been no misrepresentation and that the mistake alone was not enough. In German law, as we have seen, this mistake would clearly have entitled the buyer to rescind the contract, although it should again be stressed that German law has no separate regime for cases of innocent misrepresentation.

1   [1989] 1 WLR 255, 268.
2   (1871) LR 6 QB 597.
3   (1880) 15 Ch D 215, CA.

Identity mistakes

Mistakes as to the identity of the other party to the contract can also be categorised as 'mistakes in expression'.[4] English law has been more generous in setting aside contracts on the basis of identity mistakes than it has been for other mistakes in expression. These cases almost all involve the same fact pattern:[5] a seller of goods gives credit to a rogue believing the rogue to be someone else more creditworthy. The rogue sells on the goods before the mistake is discovered, and the contest is between the *bona fide* purchaser of the goods and the seller.[6] In these cases, the mistake as to the rogue's identity may prevent the formation of a contract. It is possible that the court's approach to identity mistakes is more generous because different considerations are in play. The question is normally not whether the contract should be enforced, but whether relief should be given against fraud, and whether a third party should be protected.

Mistakes in assumptions

It is exceedingly difficult to get a contract set aside on the basis of a mistake in assumptions. There is no equivalent of § 119 II – the general rule is that a party to a contract accepts the risk of his own mistake. The only relaxation of this general rule, if relaxation is the word, is in cases of mistakes which are (a) fundamental and (b) shared by both parties. In effect, the scope of mistakes in assumption to vitiate contracts is thus confined to cases which would have been treated as cases of frustration had the mistake not been to present or past but to the future.[7]

The law in this area is complicated by a supposed difference in treatment of mistakes at law and in equity. Steyn J, in the *Associated Japanese Bank* case, expressed the view that the state of the law with a narrow doctrine of common law mistake supplemented by a more flexible equitable doctrine was 'entirely sensible and satisfactory',[8] but it is difficult to see how treating mistakes differently at law and in equity can be justified.[9]

In the well-known case of *Bell v Lever Brothers*,[10] employees of a company were given a golden handshake in circumstances where they could have been summarily dismissed because they had previously committed breaches of their contracts of employment. It was considered important that neither of the parties had been aware of that fact, making the mistake a so-called mutual mistake. It is clear that the company would never have entered into the compensation contract had it known of the previous breaches of duty.

---

4   German writers agree: see p 57, above.

5   One exception is the well known case of *Boulton v Jones* (1857) 27 LJ Ex 117, in which a buyer was able to extricate himself from contract of sale. He thought he had contracted with a trader against whom he had a set-off, but that trader's business had in the meantime been assigned to the claimant. The claimant did not even obtain restitution in respect of the use the defendant had had of the goods. As Atiyah, 1979, p 376, points out: Bramwell, B 'disliked the whole law of quasi-contract, for he could not understand how a man could be forced to pay for a benefit which he had received but which he had not agreed to pay for'.

6   Cf, eg, *Cundy v Lindsay* (1878) 3 App Cas 459; *Ingram v Little* [1961] 1 QB 31; *Car and Universal Finance Co Ltd v Caldwell* [1965] 1 QB 525; *Lewis v Averay* [1972] 1 QB 198.

7   *Bell v Lever Brothers Ltd* [1932] AC 161; *Solle v Butcher* [1950] 1 KB 671; *Associated Japanese Bank v Crédit du Nord SA* [1989] 1 WLR 255.

8   *Associated Japanese Bank v Crédit du Nord SA* [1989] 1 WLR 255, 267–68.

9   Cf Beatson, 1998, p 295.

10 *Bell v Lever Brothers Ltd* [1932] AC 161.

Nevertheless, the House of Lords, by a bare majority, allowed the contract to stand. The parties had got precisely what they had bargained for. The mistake was not fundamental enough.

It is difficult to see, however, how it could have been more fundamental than on these facts,[11] which has led Denning LJ (as he then was) to express his view in *Solle v Butcher*[12] that contracts will only be void for mistake at law if they concern 'some condition on which the existence of the contract depends'. Denning LJ thus sought a way in which relief for mistake could be made available if this was justified 'on the merits'. He held that some mistakes rendered a contract not void at law, but merely voidable in equity. This 'mistake in equity' Denning LJ based on 'the great case of *Cooper v Phibbs*'.[13] In that case, the appellant had rented a fishery which had in fact belonged to him all along. The House of Lords were reluctant to hold that the tenancy agreement was a nullity, given that the respondents had expended significant sums on the improvement of the fishery. They therefore held that the tenancy agreement was 'not in equity binding upon the Appellant and Respondents, but ought to be set aside' on terms.[14] In *Solle v Butcher*, Denning LJ reasoned that there must therefore exist a separate doctrine of mistake in equity. *Solle v Butcher* itself concerned a tenancy agreement. Both parties thought that the tenancy was subject to rent control, but in this they were mistaken. The landlord was allowed to avoid the tenancy agreement for mistake. Denning LJ stressed that, in order to rescind a contract for mistake, three conditions had to be satisfied: first, the mistake had to be fundamental; secondly, it must be inequitable for the party seeking to uphold the contract to rely on it; and thirdly, the party seeking to set the contract aside must not himself have been at fault, although what precise degree of fault will disqualify him is unclear. In any event, even this supposedly 'more flexible' approach to mistake in equity is therefore considerably narrower than § 119 II, although it is probably no more stable.[15]

The only clear case of mistake which might allow a contract to be set aside is where the subject-matter of the contract does not exist, but only in circumstances where neither party has accepted that risk.[16] As such, mistake can be regarded as a kind of 'pre-contractual frustration'.[17] English law is able to adopt this unforgiving attitude to mistakes because it has separated off all those cases in which the mistake is induced by the other party. The regime of the Misrepresentation Act 1967 represents a compromise between the interests of the parties which is similar to § 122 *BGB*, only that it is not the mistaken party who is required to make good the other's reliance loss, but the party who induced the mistake.

---

11 One problem with *Bell v Lever Bros* is that the House of Lords had to proceed on findings of fact which are hardly credible (an extract of the jury's finding can be found in Lord Blanesburgh's judgment at pp 185 ff), namely that the appellants had forgotten their earlier breaches of duty. This led Lord Blanesburgh to comment that if the contracts had been void for mistake, 'the appellants would have been left exposed to the same consequences as if the charges [of dishonesty and fraud] had all been true' (see p 200).

12 *Solle v Butcher* [1950] 1 KB 671, 691.

13 *Cooper v Phibbs* (1876) LR 2 HL 149.

14 *Ibid*, at 167.

15 Cf Cartwright, 1987, who argues that *Solle v Butcher* is based on misconceived reasoning.

16 But see Treitel, 1988a, pp 504 ff, who seeks to distinguish the *Associated Japanese Bank* case from *Bell v Lever Bros* 'on the merits'.

17 Cf Beatson, 1998, p 299; *Associated Japanese Bank Ltd v Crédit du Nord SA* [1989] 1 WLR 255, 268; Adams and Brownsword, 1987, pp 109–13.

5.1.2 Voluntary dispositions by way of deed

It was argued above that there is nothing to rebut the presumption in favour of restitution where the mistaken transfer involved no bargain and the recipient has not changed his position. This view is not supported by the English law relating to gifts transferred under a deed. While there is an equitable jurisdiction to set aside voluntary dispositions where the settlor or donor has acted under a mistake, this jurisdiction is certainly not exercised on the basis of a merely causal mistake. Indeed, Millett J (as he then was), in summarising the relevant authorities in *Gibbon v Mitchell*[18] supports the view that only mistakes in expression will suffice:

> [The voluntary disposition] will be set aside if the court is satisfied that the disponor did not intend the transaction to have the effect that it did. It will be set aside for mistake whether the mistake is a mistake of law or fact, so long as the mistake is as to the effect of the transaction itself and not merely as to its consequences or the advantages to be gained by entering into it.

Andrew Burrows, although he supports the inclusion of some mistakes of law, expresses doubt whether a precise line can be drawn 'between a mistake as to the effect and the consequences of a transaction'.[19] However, the distinction appears clearly to reflect the distinction between mistakes in expression and mistakes in motive.

The authorities show, however, that some mistakes in motive will suffice nevertheless. In *Lady Hood of Avalon v Mackinnon*[20] the donor made an appointment by deed poll in 'utter forgetfulness' of an earlier appointment. The appointment was set aside. Goff and Jones take the view that in this case the *onus probandi* set out in *Gibbon v Mitchell* was satisfied, but it is difficult to see how this is so. In fact, it appears clear that the mistake is a mistake in motive, a mistake 'as to the consequences or the advantages' to be gained by making the appointment, namely to make equal gifts to both her daughters. Meier takes the case as evidence that 'a mistake in making a gift will be more easily held to be relevant than a mistake in entering into a contract', but argues that this does not mean that any mistake in motive will suffice.[21] True, the mistake still has to be a serious mistake, and this is difficult to explain against the background of our analysis of mistaken gifts in Chapter 3. It is possible that the formality involved in making a gift under deed makes it desirable that the gift is upheld in spite of the donor's mistake in motive. Many such gifts are made in order to achieve a desired tax outcome. Often the Inland Revenue will therefore be joined as a party where such gifts are sought to be set aside, although a case decided by the Manx High Court in 2000 indicates that where the tax objective of a gift is not achieved, this will in itself be grounds of rescission.[22]

---

18 [1990] 1 WLR 1304, 1309.

19 Burrows, 1993a, p 113.

20 [1909] 1 Ch 476.

21 Meier, 1999a, pp 88–89.

22 *Orwell* (2000, precise date of judgment not known). The deemster had no difficulty in setting a company's gifts aside on the basis that it was labouring under a mistake as to the fiscal consequences of the gift. Nobody could complain because the recipients were *ex hypothesi* volunteers. The decision was based on the authority of *Phillips v Mullings* (1871) 7 Ch App 244. It will be remembered that the German *Bundesfinanzhof* has refused to rescind a gift in a similar case on the basis that the mistake was a mistake in motive only: BFH DB 1990, 22 (20.9.1989). See above, p 63.

5.1.3 Mistakes and unjust enrichment

The requirement that a mistake must be 'fundamental' and shared between the parties has in the past been insisted upon even where the mistake in question was a mistake in performance.[23] This approach has now been discredited.[24] On one view, all that is required now is that the mistake in question caused the defendant's enrichment.[25] If this view is accepted, and we will discuss this question below, it is subject to one important qualification, namely that a causal mistake will not trigger restitution in circumstances in which value was transferred pursuant to a contract which is not itself voidable or void because of the mistake.[26] This has been implicit in the whole of the preceding discussion, and can be explained on the basis that the liberal presumption in favour of restitution, triggered by the mistake, is rebutted by the contractual allocation of risks between the parties.[27] Meier has argued that a subsisting contract is one example of a 'legal ground' recognised by English law.[28] She writes:

> A performance which discharges a subsisting obligation can be caused by a mistake of the performing party. The performing party may discharge a claim because he does not know that his contractual partner is in economic difficulty, so that he is not sure if he will ever receive his counter-performance; had he known the true facts, he would not have performed. Or he does not know about conduct of the recipient which would have caused him to refuse to perform and wait for a law suit. If the mistake analysis is taken seriously, every such mistake would have to be examined in order to ascertain if it qualified as an unjust factor for an enrichment claim, because the intention to transfer was not exercised correctly, so that Birks's sentence 'I did not mean you to have it' should apply.[29]

She cites a number of authorities in support of the proposition that contractual payments are irrecoverable on the ground of mistake, unless the contract is first set aside,[30] and argues that 'this restriction is not easily reconciled with a system which bases the enrichment claim primarily on the mistake'.[31] Her 'proof' that the contractual obligation constitutes a 'legal ground' then runs along the following lines:

(1) If a mistaken payment which is covered by an existing contractual obligation does not give rise to an 'unjust' enrichment, the reason for this can only be the fact that the law allocates the benefit to the recipient.

(2) This adds an objective element to the requirements of an enrichment claim, namely the absence of an underlying obligation.

---

23   *Norwich Union Fire Insurance Society v WH Price Ltd* [1934] AC 455; *Sellman v American National Life Ins Co* (1955) 281 SW 2d 150; cf above, pp 50 ff.

24   Cf *Barclays Bank Ltd v WJ Simms* [1980] QB 677, 696–99, *per* Robert Goff J; approved by Dillon LJ in *Rover International v Cannon Film Sales (No 3)* [1989] 1 WLR 912, 933.

25   Cf Burrows, 1993a, pp 104–07; Goff and Jones, 1998, p 180.

26   *Barclays Bank Ltd v WJ Simms Son & Cooke (Southern) Ltd* [1980] QB 677, 695, *per* Goff J; cf Tettenborn, 1996, 28, pp 65–66; Burrows, 1993a, p 126; Goff and Jones, 1998, p 48.

27   See above, p 43.

28   Meier, 1999a, pp 99–103.

29   *Ibid*, pp 99–100.

30   *Steam Saw Mills v Baring Brothers* [1922] 1 Ch 244; *Works and Public Buildings Commissioners v Pontypridd Masonic Hall* [1920] 89 LJ QB 607.

31   Meier, 1999a, p 101.

(3) The enrichment claim thus requires not just a mistake, but also the absence of an obligation.

(4) The underlying obligation is therefore nothing but a 'legal ground'.[32]

The fallacy of this analysis is that it assumes that, because a valid obligation prevents a restitutionary claim, the absence of a valid obligation must be a requirement of a restitutionary claim based on mistake. The negative requirement 'absence of consideration' is not something which the claimant has to prove, however. One might as well say that 'non-expiration of the limitation period' constituted an element of any enrichment claim, given that a claim can no longer be brought once the limitation period has expired. The fact of the matter is that the English law of unjust enrichment will not undermine bargains. There is no need for English law to refer to this as a 'legal ground', because it is the presence, rather than the absence of a valid contract which has legal consequences. Absence of consideration, without more, does not have any legal consequences whatsoever, or at least that was the position prior to the *Westdeutsche* case.

In the following, we will examine the English law relating to mistake in unjust enrichment cases. We will return to Meier's argument towards the end of this chapter, when we come to discuss the question whether restitution for mistake should be limited in English law.[33]

5.2 RELEVANT MISTAKES IN THE LAW OF UNJUST ENRICHMENT

Restitution for mistake has traditionally been restricted in two main ways: first, recovery was restricted to cases where the mistake in question was as to a supposed liability to transfer the benefit; and secondly, there was traditionally no recovery in cases where the only possible reason for restitution was a mistake of law. It is suggested that these limitations were in place for at least two reasons:

(1) It was not until the middle of the 20th century that the principle against unjust enrichment was properly recognised by legal scholars in England, notably Robert Goff and Gareth Jones, and not until 1991 that the courts endorsed this recognition formally. The principle being unrecognised, it was easy to miss the fact that all causal mistakes trigger the presumption in favour of restitution.

(2) Related to the failure to recognise the principle against unjust enrichment is the lack of a change of position defence in English law. Without such a defence, the law was unable to respond to circumstances, other than the existence of a bargain, which rebutted the liberal presumption in a sensitive manner. The only way to avoid too much restitution, that is, restitution which placed the innocent defendant in a position which was worse than the position he was in before receiving the benefit, was to limit the incidence of restitutionary claims at the liability stage.

There was an additional factor which militated against allowing restitution for mistakes of law. The common law operates on judicial precedent. A decision of the Court of Appeal

---

32 *Ibid*, pp 101–02.
33 See below, pp 76 ff.

or the House of Lords can change the common law. The question whether in such circumstances a transfer made under the previous law should be recoverable on the ground of mistake of law was one which the law instinctively avoided, with good reason as it now turns out.[34]

5.2.1 Liability mistakes

The leading case on restitutionary liability for mistake is still *Kelly v Solari*.[35] An insurance company paid out under a life insurance policy. It missed the fact that the last premium had not been paid, and that therefore the policy had lapsed. It could recover the money from the widow of the insured. Parke B said:

> I think where money is paid to another under the influence of a mistake, that is, upon the supposition that a specific fact is true, which would entitle the other to the money, but which fact is untrue, and the money would not have been paid if it had been known to the payer that the fact was untrue, an action will lie to recover it back, and it is against conscience to retain it.[36]

The fateful words are 'which would entitle the other to the money', of course. This has been picked up in later cases to deny restitution to mistaken payers whose mistakes were not as to a supposed liability. It will be remembered that in *Aiken v Short*[37] the claimant bank had never believed to be *liable* to make the payment – it merely did so in order to redeem a charge which encumbered a property the bank mistakenly believed to have acquired. The payment was therefore a payment for its own benefit. Bramwell B's *dictum* now finally laid down the 'liability mistake rule':

> In order to entitle a person to recover back money paid under a mistake of fact, the mistake must be as to a fact which, if true, would make the person paying liable to pay the money; not where, if true, it would merely make it desirable that he should pay the money. Here, if the fact was true, the bankers were at liberty to pay or not, as they pleased.[38]

Birks has identified four reasons why recovery for liability mistake has troubled the courts less than recovery for other kinds of mistake.[39] First, he explains that it represents no threat to bargains. By definition, the liability did not exist, and therefore no bargain can be undermined. Secondly, Birks argues that there will be fewer problems with counter-restitution as the transfer will generally have been made solely to discharge the supposed liability. Birks's third reason is the one given above, namely that by limiting the availability of restitution in whatever way, the danger of too much restitution is kept in check. He elaborates this idea by arguing that, apart from limiting restitution to a single category, there can be no danger of a claimant adducing 'trivial or collateral errors' which might or might not have been critical. In other words, evidential problems are reduced to a minimum. Birks's fourth reason is particularly apposite in the present context. He writes:

---

34   See below, pp 82 ff.
35   (1841) 9 M & W 54, 152 ER 24.
36   *Ibid*, at 58.
37   (1856) 1 H & N 210, 156 ER 1180; see above, p 50.
38   *Ibid*, at 215.
39   Birks, 1989, p 152–53.

Behind all this there is comfort of another kind against the fear of floodgates: Roman jurisprudence was known to have worked with this category. When the Roman action of debt (the condictio) was divided and explained according to the causes of indebtedness, 'money and other performances not owed' became a prominent category. In fact 'debt for liability mistakes' is as good a translation as any for the Latin *'condictio indebiti'*.[40]

To Birks, this is just one way of explaining the 'magic' of liability mistakes, as a special comfort against the fear of floodgates.[41] Meier seizes upon this idea and turns it into the mainstay of her argument. To her, the existence of the 'liability mistake rule' is compelling evidence for English law having in the past operated a 'legal ground' system. She argues that restitution of money paid under a liability mistake and restitution of a performance for which there was no legal ground have two things in common: first, the performance is made in response to an obligation which does not exist; secondly, the performing party did not know this.[42] The second requirement limits the scope of § 812 I in German law,[43] while *Kelly v Solari*[44] makes it the foremost requirement of the claim in English law. Meier's argument is that in limiting restitution for mistake to liability mistakes, the common law was on the right track and that a legal ground analysis is necessary in order – and this is where Birks's third reason for the liability mistake rule comes in – to distinguish between trivial and important mistakes. We will examine this argument below.[45] For now, it will be necessary to outline briefly how the liability mistake rule fared once the law of unjust enrichment had been discovered as a subject in its own right.

The first serious attack on the liability mistake rule was made in *Larner v London County Council*.[46] In that case, the Council passed a resolution to make up the difference in pay between service pay and civil pay of its employees who had been called up to war. It was incumbent on the servicemen to keep the council informed of changes in their service pay. The claimant, an ambulance driver who had been called up to join the Royal Air Force, failed to do this and was accordingly overpaid by the Council. When this was discovered after the war, the Council deducted the overpayments from the claimant's wages, and the claimant sought to recover the deductions under his contract of employment. His main argument was that the Council had never been *bound* to make the payments to him – they could have revoked their resolution at any time. As such, their mistake had not been one as to a supposed liability, and on the authority of *Aiken v Short* they would have been unable to recover. As such, they had had no right to deduct the overpayments from the claimant's wages. Denning LJ, reading the judgment of the Court of Appeal, said:

> But it is said that they were voluntary payments, which were not made in discharge of any legal liability, and cannot therefore be recovered back. For this proposition reliance was placed on the dictum of Bramwell B in *Aiken v Short*; but that *dictum*, as Scott LJ pointed out in *Morgan v Ashcroft*, cannot be regarded as an exhaustive statement of the law. Take this case. The London County Council, by their resolution, for good reasons of national policy,

---

40 *Ibid*, p 153.
41 *Ibid*.
42 Meier, 1999a, p 33.
43 § 814 I *BGB*.
44 (1841) 9 M & W 54, 152 ER 24.
45 See below, pp 76 ff.
46 [1949] 1 KB 683.

made a promise to the men which they were in honour bound to fulfil. The payments made under that promise were not mere gratuities. They were made as a matter of duty ... Indeed that is how both sides regarded them. They spoke of them as sums 'due' to the men, that is, as sums the men were entitled to under the promise contained in the resolution. If then, owing to a mistake of fact, the council paid one of the men more than he was entitled to under the promise, why should he not repay the excess, at any rate if he has not changed his position for the worse? It is not necessary to inquire whether there was any consideration for the promise so as to enable it to be enforced in a court of law. It may be that, because the men were legally bound to go to war, there was in strictness no consideration for the promise. But that does not matter. It is not a question here of enforcing the promise by action. It is a question of recovering overpayments made in the belief that they were due under the promise, but in fact not due. They were sums which the council never promised Mr Larner and which they would never have paid him had they known the true facts. They were paid under a mistake of fact, and he is bound to repay them unless he has changed his position for the worse because of them.[47]

For a time, *Larner* represented an exception to the liability mistake rule: if the payment was made pursuant to a moral rather than a legal duty, the liability mistake rule no longer stood in the way of restitution.

In *Barclays Bank v Simms*,[48] Goff J (as he then was) launched a frontal attack on the liability mistake rule. The claimant bank had honoured a cheque because it had overlooked the fact that it had been stopped by the drawer. When it sought to recover the payment, the defendant argued that its action should fail because the mistake had not been a liability mistake. Goff J reviewed the authorities and concluded that the liability mistake rule did not form part of English law. To him, the main criterion was whether the mistake caused the payment. He gave a number of examples to show that the liability mistake rule was indeed indefensible:

(1) A man, forgetting that he has already paid his subscription to the National Trust, pays it a second time.

(2) A substantial charity uses a computer for the purpose of distributing small benefactions. The computer runs mad, and pays one beneficiary the same gift one hundred times over.

(3) A shipowner and a charterer enter into a sterling charterparty for a period of years. Sterling depreciates against other currencies; and the charterer decides, to maintain the goodwill of the shipowner but without obligation, to increase the monthly hire payments. Owing to a mistake in his office, the increase in one monthly hire payment is paid twice over.

(4) A Lloyd's syndicate gets into financial difficulties. To maintain the reputation of Lloyd's, other underwriting syndicates decide to make gifts of money to assist the syndicate in difficulties. Due to a mistake, one syndicate makes its gift twice over.[49]

---

47 *Ibid*, at 687–88.
48 [1980] 1 QB 677.
49 *Ibid*, at 697.

Against this background, Robert Goff J therefore laid down the following test:

(1) If a person pays money to another under a mistake of fact which causes him to make the payment, he is *prima facie* entitled to recover it as money paid under a mistake of fact.

(2) His claim may, however, fail if:

(a) the payer intends that the payee shall have the money at all events, whether the fact be true or false, or is deemed in law so to intend; or

(b) the payment is made for good consideration, in particular if the money is paid to discharge, and does discharge, a debt owed to the payee (or a principal on whose behalf he is authorised to receive the payment) by the payer or by a third party by whom he is authorised to discharge the debt; or

(c) the payee has changed his position in good faith, or is deemed in law to have done so.[50]

The above statement reflects quite well the argument so far presented here: a causal mistake triggers the liberal presumption in favour of restitution (Goff J's rule (1)). This will be rebutted if the defendant can show that (a) restitution would undermine a bargain (Goff J's rule (2)(b)) or (b) that his security of receipt would be undermined (Goff J's rule (2)(c)), in the sense that he would be worse off following restitution than he had been before the transfer was made. What remains to be discussed is Goff J's rule (2)(a), namely that the claimant intended the defendant to have the benefit at all events, whether the fact in question was true or false, or is 'deemed' in law so to have intended. This suggests that Goff J contemplates that in some circumstances his test might lead to inequitable results – in other words, restitution for all causal mistakes might be too liberal.

5.2.2 Limiting recovery for mistake?

Andrew Tettenborn argues that allowing restitution for all causal mistakes of fact may be going too far. He writes:

Assume I give £1,000 to my niece as a birthday present, not realising that she has just married a man I privately detest. It seems instinctively odd that a footling or idiosyncratic error like that should entitle me to repent of my generosity and recover my money, even if I can prove by impeccable evidence that had I known the relevant facts I would not have made the gift in the first place – that is, that the mistake caused the gift.[51]

He goes on to suggest that mistake should be seen as 'a variant of failure of assumptions, looking to the intentions of both claimant and defendant as understood by a reasonable person'.[52] Tettenborn's approach takes restitution for mistake dangerously close to failure of consideration:

Now, with failure of assumptions it is incontrovertible that a mere disappointment will not do, however causative of the defendant's benefit. Suppose I give you £500, secretly hoping you will invite me for a shooting weekend. No one suggests that I can or should recover it if the invitation is not forthcoming, even if I can prove that had I known you would not invite

---

50 *Ibid*, at 695.
51 Tettenborn, 1996, p 64.
52 *Ibid*.

me I would not have given you anything. My only chance of restitution is by showing that you ought to have known, from the circumstances or otherwise, that my gift was made on that assumption; in other words, my right of recovery is based not on any supposed vitiation of my intent to give you £500 but on the assumption shared by both of us, as shown by agreement or the objective circumstances surrounding my action. But if so, it is difficult to see why it ought to make any difference if my payment was made in the erroneous belief that you had already posted an invitation to me. Yet on the pure 'causation' approach, this is precisely what happens. This surely cannot be right.[53]

It is suggested that it can be. The two examples given by Tettenborn are, in fact, fundamentally different. In the second example, I am of the opinion that my friend has invited me on a shooting weekend. I want to make it up to him. In effect, I want to 'pay' for the time I will be spending on his manor, I do not want to accept such a generous gift without making some payment. I am mistaken – no invitation has ever been issued. I paid for something which I am not going to get. Why should I not be entitled to ask for restitution? My mistake triggers the presumption in favour of restitution, and there is nothing to rebut it.

In the first example, on the other hand, I do not make a mistake at all. If anything, it is a misprediction. Now, it has been argued above that some mispredictions can be dealt with on the same footing as mistakes.[54] This is not one of those. The risk that no invitation will follow is squarely on me. The only way in which I can avoid that risk is by making it clear to my friend that the payment is made in anticipation of a forthcoming invitation to a shooting party. In that way I will have specified the basis of my giving, and that basis failing, I will be able to recover. The reason for restitution is failure of basis, or in traditional terms, failure of consideration.[55]

This takes us back to Tettenborn's original case: the gift of money to my niece who, unbeknown to me, has just married a thoroughly unpleasant man. Tettenborn's distaste at giving me a restitutionary claim for mistake is shared by German law, as we have seen above. It is also shared by Meier. Meier suggests an arguably more sophisticated way of dealing with the problem. She proposes a legal ground analysis which would draw a sharp line between *transaction* mistakes and *execution* mistakes. The distinction mirrors the distinction we drew in Chapter 3 between mistakes in performance and other mistakes.

To Meier, the *Larner* case discussed above[56] is a very good example of this distinction. In that case, the Council was not mistaken about Larner's previous record as an ambulance driver, or about Larner's service record as an RAF pilot. Such mistakes could, given appropriate facts, have caused them easily to have reconsidered making the *ex gratia* payments to Larner. Nevertheless, Meier would argue, such mistakes, albeit causal for the payments, would and should not have been sufficient grounds for restitution once the payments had been made. She points out that, by German law, on the facts in *Larner* the *condictio indebiti* would be available without any question at all. She bases this on the

---

53 Tettenborn, 1996, p 65.
54 See above, pp 40 ff.
55 For the issue whether failure of consideration is available in non-contractual cases, see Chapter 9 below.
56 See above, pp 74 f.

argument that under German law unilateral promises of an employer form part of the contract of employment and are binding.[57] According to Meier, English law's insistence on the consideration requirement thus makes the case for restitution in such a case stronger rather than weaker.[58] Even absent these employment law considerations, however, under German law a gift contract would have come into existence between Larner and the Council, and this would not have covered the portion of the payments by which Larner was overpaid.

Meier's argument is that English law should not allow restitution where a mistake occurs in forming the intention to make a payment, but only where the mistake occurs in putting that intention into practice. This would take care of Tettenborn's example referred to above, but also of a number of examples supplied by Meier herself: a man makes a donation to the Red Cross in the mistaken belief that the mayor and the vicar have made donations too. Somebody gives money to Friends of the Earth, not knowing that they are opposed to the additional runway at Heathrow, which he supports. A charterer decides, to maintain the goodwill of the shipowner, to increase his monthly hire payments. He has overestimated his own financial position, however, or did not realise that the shipowner is best friends with his archenemy.[59] All these mistakes, as in Tettenborn's example, were causal for the enrichment, and the enrichments are not underpinned by a contractual obligation as in *Bell v Lever Bros*. Meier finds this hard to stomach. She points out that none of the examples given by Robert Goff J in *Barclays Bank v Simms* in support of general recoverability for causal mistakes concerns mistakes in forming the intention to make a payment. The examples therefore lend no support to the thesis that 'any performance can be demanded back based on any mistake in motive'.[60] To her, this is evidence that English law would not easily allow restitution in such cases. English law, she argues, is still free to replace the category 'liability mistake' with a category entitled '*causa* mistake'.

These arguments really concern the recoverability of gifts. To what extent should the law protect the expectation of donees to be entitled to keep gifts? We have seen above that German law finds it difficult to cope with the problem that, although there are some special rules in place in respect of gifts, the general rule that mistakes in motive are normally irrelevant applies to gifts in the same way as it applies to all contracts.[61] The argument that in German law the gifts in Meier's examples would stand is thus to be treated with a certain amount of caution.

It will be useful to look at the examples given by Tettenborn and Meier and see (1) to what extent restitution would be undesirable in such cases and (2) how, if that is the case, restitution can be avoided on English law principles. Let us first take Tettenborn's example of the gift I make to my niece little knowing she has just entered into an alliance which I, to say the least, consider unfortunate. Tettenborn argues that in this case right

---

57 It is doubtful, of course, whether Larner was in fact an employee of the Council: on being called up, he probably ceased to be a Council employee and became a serviceman: cf *National Association of Local Government Officers v Bolton Corporation* [1943] AC 166, 193, *per* Lord Porter.

58 Meier, 1999a, p 45.

59 *Ibid*, p 87.

60 *Ibid*, p 87.

61 See above, pp 60 ff.

thinking people have an 'instinctive objection' to restitution, but fails to explain what this objection is based on. The mistake in question here is a 'passive' mistake in that I did not even consider the possibility of my niece marrying when I made the gift. Sheehan would use the word 'ignorance', I have preferred to call it 'absence of knowledge'. It is assumed that, had I known of my niece's marriage, I would not have made the gift. That is the kind of Dickensian character that I am. It is, however, difficult to see why, evidential difficulties having been overcome, I should not be able to recover. Absent change of position, no factor is present which would serve to rebut the presumption in favour of restitution. If the presumption were rebutted on these facts, English law would be raising the status of gifts onto a higher plane which would be almost contractual. The German example shows that this is not a very good idea. If we were to insist on some kind of objective test ('would a reasonable person have considered the fact in question relevant?') we would be negating the very freedom which is behind the liberal presumption in favour of restitution. The point is that people are, within limits, free to dispose of their assets in any way they choose. The consequence must be that, where that choice is exercised in a way which is defective, any transfer which is made as a result should be reversible. Moreover, while the 'reasonable man' sometimes needs to be employed as a guiding light by judicial decision makers, using him also poses considerable dangers. Who is to say whether the uncle in Tettenborn's example is 'reasonable' in demanding his gift back? What is the reason for the enmity he bears towards his niece's husband? Can it not be imagined that he would be deeply offended by the thought that his hard earned money should benefit a man for whom he has nothing but contempt?

Similar considerations apply to the examples given by Meier. All of these examples (a donation to a charity motivated by a desire to emulate local dignitaries, to a charity opposing a project the donor supports, or to an organisation the donor's archenemy is deeply involved with) involve donations which we feel the donor should have made in any event. We disapprove of his motives and this suggests the conclusion that those motives should not be relied upon in a restitutionary claim. Yet that is the price of liberty.

Gifts and other gratuitous transfers do not allocate risks. It is understandable that the German code has lumped them together with contracts of exchange for the sake of a well ordered regime relating to all transfers. English law has no reason to follow the example of German law here.

Even if we were to agree with Meier that the above examples show that restitution following on from mistaken gifts should be somewhat curtailed, Meier does not offer a viable yardstick by which relevant mistakes are distinguished from irrelevant ones. By describing the decision to make a gift as a 'legal ground' we have not even begun to answer the question which gifts should be reversible on the basis of what mistakes. The danger would be that English law, like German law, would simply use the same criteria as it uses for contracts. As we have seen, it is much more difficult to rescind a contract for mistake in England than it is in Germany, so that this solution would be even less desirable.

Certainly the distinction between 'mistakes in motive' and other mistakes which Meier likes to draw does not provide a suitable frame of reference: even a mistaken belief in an existing liability is, after all, a 'mistake in motive' – the motive being to discharge the liability.[62] It should also be borne in mind that German law provides a regime which

---

62 Cf von Tuhr, 1979, p 483.

governs the recoverability of gifts on grounds which would not even be contemplated by English law, such as gross ingratitude or impoverishment of the donor.[63] Calling a gift a legal ground helps us only in so far as we can separate off those mistakes which occur in execution of a donative intent. It does not tell us anything whatsoever about the kinds of mistake which destroy this 'legal ground'. We are only adding one layer of abstraction where it simply is not needed.

One strong argument which Meier puts forward is that English law as it stands does not appear to subscribe to Goff J's causal mistake approach, at least not in cases involving voluntary dispositions made by deed. As was argued above,[64] restrictions based on restitution in such cases may well be explained on the basis that the formality of the transaction and the underlying fiscal considerations lend dispositions by way of deed a quality similar to bargained-for exchanges.

Meier's argument does derive some support from the recent draft of the next American *Restatement of the Law of Restitution and Unjust Enrichment*.[65] § 11 of the draft is devoted especially to 'Mistake in gifts *inter vivos*', and the provision distinguishes between 'unintended enrichment' (§ 11(1)) and 'mistake in inducement' (§ 11(2)). The first category is roughly the equivalent of Meier's 'causa' mistake, in that it governs the case in which the donor transfers 'something more than or different from the property intended to be transferred'.[66] The second category could be said to refer to mistakes in motive:

> (2) A donor whose gift is induced by invalidating mistake has a claim in restitution as necessary to prevent the unintended enrichment of the recipient.

The draft thus follows Meier in distinguishing between 'causa' mistakes and mistakes in motive – restitution for the former is always available, while it is restricted for the latter: a mistake in motive must have induced the transfer and it must be 'invalidating' if restitution is to follow. However, the present commentary to the provision treats any causal mistake as 'invalidating'. It reads:

> The mistake that will invalidate a gift under the rule stated in subsection (2) is a misapprehension of existing circumstances that is the cause in fact of the resulting transfer ... The donor's mistake must have induced the gift; it is not sufficient that the donor was mistaken about relevant circumstances ... Invalidating mistakes of this type must be distinguished from various kinds of 'mistake', apparent in hindsight, that may reveal a gift to have been an error of judgment on the part of the donor. Neither improvidence nor disappointed expectation will serve as the basis of a claim under the rules of this section.[67]

What does the draft mean by saying that 'it is not sufficient that the donor was mistaken about relevant circumstances'? Does it mean that even where the donor can prove that he would not have made the transfer had he known about the relevant circumstances, he will nevertheless not be entitled to restitution? The answer is not altogether clear, and nor

---

63 This puts a question mark over Meier's variation of Goff J's example of the charterer who makes *ex gratia* payments to a shipowner because he overestimates his own financial position: see Meier, 1999a, p 87.

64 See p 70, above.

65 American Law Institute, 2001. I am most grateful to Professor Andrew Kull of Emory University, for sending me a copy of the draft.

66 *Ibid*, p 135.

67 *Ibid*, pp 140 f.

do the examples given in the draft shed any real light on the question. Two cases are contrasted. In the first,[68] a man conveys property to his supposed wife so as to provide for her in her old age. It turns out that she was married to another all along, and that therefore their marriage was never valid. According to the draft, he is entitled to restitution. The facts are then changed slightly,[69] in that the transfer is made to the wife's son toward whom the claimant has acted as father for 10 years. Again it turns out that the marriage was bigamous. Crucially, the draft adds a finding of fact: 'The court finds that A's mistake about his legal relationship to B and C did not induce the gift to C; rather the cause was A's affection for C based on their life together. A has no claim in restitution against C.' The question thus remains unanswered: had the court found that the gift would not have been made if the claimant had known about the true state of affairs, would he still have been denied restitution? Probably not. The question is one of causality, and the question whether restitution should follow or not is relegated to the court's factual inquiry. None of the other examples given in the draft is as extreme as the examples given by Tettenborn and Meier. The line is not, however, drawn between mistakes in motive and other mistakes. Thus, in one of the examples a son pays his father's final medical bill, wrongly believing that the estate has no resources. A clear mistake in motive, but the draft nevertheless proposes that he should be entitled to restitution.[70]

The answer for English law will no doubt be similarly pragmatic. As Zweigert and Kötz sum up the attitude of English law: 'We will cross that bridge when we come to it'.[71] In most cases the evidential difficulties will be almost insurmountable. Any practitioner will appreciate that convincing a judge on the examples given by Meier that the donor was really mistaken and has not merely concocted a mistake because he has changed his mind will be an uphill task. If evidential difficulties of this kind are overcome, it will give us some indication that maybe restitution is a result which the judge feels able to contemplate. If not, it is still open to English law to restrict the reversibility of mistakes. Goff J in *Simms* left the door ajar to such developments by adding his rule (2)](a): did the donor intend (or even, is he 'deemed' to have intended) that the donee should be able to keep the gift in any event? This is certainly an intention which can be imputed to the uncle in Tettenborn's example, and it would also present a convenient way out for any judge called upon to decide Meier's own examples. This is just another way to kill that particular cat, of course, given that such an intention negatives causation. The 'deeming' exercise hints at the kind of reasonableness test which German law has put in place. Whether that is a good thing or a bad thing (and I suggest the latter), English law would be free to choose this route. While these 'piecemeal' solutions may appear unsatisfactory, they are, it is suggested, far preferable to changing the whole approach of English law to restitution for mistakes.

---

68 *Ibid*, p 141, example 8.

69 *Ibid*, example 9.

70 *Ibid*, p 143, example 14.

71 Zweigert and Kötz, 1998, p 70.

5.2.3 'Spent' mistakes

One limitation on restitutionary liability for mistakes has already been referred to in Chapter 3. Where a causal mistake does not prejudice the claimant in any way, the presumption in favour of restitution is not triggered at all. English law has refused to accept this. In the *Lincoln* case, the banks relied on their 'mistaken' belief in the enforceability of the claims against them. That belief, however, had not caused them any prejudice whatsoever. The prejudice was caused by the fact that the interest rate swaps they entered into lost the banks money. The mistake, if any, had nothing to do with that. It was not the mistake which caused the losses, it was the setting of interest rates in a way which the bank had betted against. As Birks puts this:

> The swap contract was void. But, as events worked out, it was fully performed despite its nullity. Thus, the facts which happened after the mistake was made had the effect of depriving the mistake of all adverse effect, in that the disappointment inherent in the mistake never materialized and could never do so.[72]

The House of Lords effectively rejected this argument on the basis that the cause of action was complete at the time of the mistaken payment.[73] This overly formalistic argument totally ignores the moral case for restitution, which, as was pointed out above, is no stronger in a case of a spent mistake as in a case in which the transferor subsequently changes his mind.[74]

5.2.4 Mistakes of law

There is nothing to distinguish mistakes of law from mistakes of fact when it comes to triggering the liberal presumption in favour of restitution. Under both kinds of mistake, in other words, the claimant 'did not mean' the defendant to have the benefit in question. The traditional bar against restitution must therefore be explained on different grounds. The explanation which is normally given is that the bar was in place to compensate for the absence of a defence of change of position.[75] By not allowing restitution for mistakes of law, a whole category of cases was eliminated and the danger of too much restitution reduced accordingly. If this method was crude, it was undoubtedly effective.

One rationale for the rule, namely that everyone must be assumed to be cognisant of the law, was never particularly convincing. Taken from its original context in criminal law, this rationale really comes down to this: everyone has a duty to keep himself up to date with legal developments. If they fail to do so, they must be deemed to have been negligent and can, for that reason, not have restitution. As Tettenborn rightly points out, this argument lost its force when it was realised that negligence on the part of the claimant does not prevent restitution based on mistake of fact.[76]

---

72 Birks, 2000a, p 220.
73 *Kleinwort Benson v Lincoln* [1999] 2 AC 349, 386 (Lord Goff, Lord Hoffmann concurring, relying on *Baker v Courage* [1910] 1 KB 56), 416 (Lord Hope).
74 See pp 34 f, above.
75 See p 271, below.
76 Tettenborn, 1996, pp 60–61; cf *Kelly v Solari* (1841) 9 M & W 54, 152 ER 24.

Against the background of the recognition of change of position in *Lipkin Gorman*, it was generally felt only to be a matter of time before the mistake of law bar would come down in England. As Birks explains in a recent article, however, it was thought unlikely that a suitable case would ever reach the House of Lords: given that the demise of the mistake of law bar was a foregone conclusion, who would spend good money on defending such a case? The swaps saga, however, did provide the House of Lords with the opportunity to abolish the bar in *Kleinwort Benson v Lincoln*, though in a way which could not have been foreseen. The majority of the bank's claims in *Lincoln*, if pursued on the basis of failure or absence of consideration, were time-barred: the transactions in question had been fully performed more than six years before the writ was issued. The only hope was to ground restitution on mistake, as this would allow the bank to rely on s 32(1)(c) of the Limitation Act 1980. Under this provision, time only begins to run from the moment at which the mistake on which the claim is founded could reasonably have been discovered. This moment was the House of Lords' decision in *Hazell v Hammersmith and Fulham*.[77] Only because of this limitation point did the question ever end up before the House of Lords. Because it was clear that only that court could resolve the issue, the appeal was allowed to leapfrog the Court of Appeal, which meant that the members of the House of Lords found themselves in the unusual position to have to decide a case without the benefit of any reasoned judgments in the Court of Appeal below.

Curiously enough, both parties before the House of Lords were agreed that the mistake of law bar could no longer be maintained. The dispute focused on the question whether the bank was in fact labouring under a mistake at all when it made the payments to the local authority. At the time the payments were made, the prevailing view amongst lawyers, bankers and those involved in local government was that local authorities were perfectly able to enter into interest rate swaps under their general authority to raise money by borrowing. On one view, therefore, the House of Lords in *Hazell* changed the law. Before that case, interest swaps were valid, after that case, they were void. If that is the right way of looking at it, then it is difficult to argue that at the time the bank made the relevant payments it was mistaken as to the legal position. Granted, it did not realise that the law was about to be changed by the House of Lords. That 'mistake', however, should be classified as a misprediction. It was argued above that mispredictions can, contrary to Birks's argument, sometimes trigger restitution. This only applies to mispredictions, however, which can be proved to be true or false at the time that they are made. For other mispredictions, the transferor takes the risk that he may turn out to be wrong.[78]

As Lord Lloyd points out in his judgment, the local authority started 'more than half way home':[79] the bank had conceded that where the House of Lords overrules a prior Court of Appeal decision on the basis of which a payment is recoverable, there could be no question of restitution based on mistake of law, the reason being that the payer had not made a mistake.

Lords Browne-Wilkinson and Lloyd thought that the concession was rightly made. They argued that the bank could not be described as having paid the money under a

---

77   [1992] 2 AC 1.

78   See above, pp 40 f.

79   See *Kleinwort Benson v Lincoln* [1999] 2 AC 349, 391.

mistake at all: at the time the payment was made the law was indeed what they thought it was, and most lawyers would have advised them that they were liable to pay. It was only later, when the Divisional Court declared swap transactions *ultra vires* local authorities, that the law was changed. While both Law Lords accepted that the decision of an English court was to some extent retrospective, they both felt that 'retrospection cannot falsify history'.[80] The 'paradigm case' which they relied on is one in which the House of Lords overrules a line of Court of Appeal authority. In that situation, according to Lord Lloyd,[81] prior to the House of Lords ruling, the law was as the Court of Appeal had said. The House of Lords is unable to change this. 'The House of Lords can say that the Court of Appeal took a wrong turning. It can say what the law should have been. But it cannot say that the law actually applied by the Court of Appeal was other than what it was.'[82]

The majority, however, refused to accept the concession. They took the view that the declaratory theory of judicial decision meant that the law applicable at the time of the payment indeed had been what the House of Lords now declared it to be. It followed from this that at the time of the payment the payer was labouring under a mistake of law. Along with Lord Browne-Wilkinson one might think it surprising that the House found 'the law to be that which neither of the parties contended for'.[83]

One of the few defenders of the result reached by the majority is Sheehan. His argument is based on Dworkinian theory. Starting from his definition of mistake as 'a belief in something that can, at the time at which it is acted upon, be proven not to be correct',[84] he argues that, according to Dworkin's theory of legal interpretation, there is a right answer to every question of law.[85] If that is true, then there must be a sense in which a given case, say a case decided by the Court of Appeal or indeed the House of Lords, can be said to be wrong. Sheehan uses Dworkin's superhuman judge Hercules to demonstrate this. It will be remembered that Hercules devises a theory of law on the basis of which a single political official can reach most or all decisions reported in the cases. He does this on the basis of two criteria: first, how can any given case be best accommodated against the background of the existing precedents? Secondly, how good is the theory in terms of the substantive political morality of the society in question? If a precedent does not fit the theory developed on this basis, it is incorrect and must be overruled. Thus, if a payment is made on the basis of a decision of the Court of Appeal or House of Lords which does not fit into the Herculean theory, then the payment is made under a mistaken view of the law because, says Sheehan, 'at the very least, Hercules, the super judge, can show that at the time that one forms the mistaken view that it is mistaken'.[86]

Sheehan's argument may sound convincing in theory, but it suffers from the fact that it is based on a fairytale in the same way as the declaratory theory of judicial decision making, albeit a somewhat more sophisticated fairytale. The problem is that Hercules does not exist in the real world. By definition, he is a 'superhuman' judge, and, with

---

80   *Ibid*, at 517 (Lord Browne-Wilkinson), at 548 (Lord Lloyd).
81   *Ibid*, at 548.
82   *Ibid*.
83   *Ibid*, at 362.
84   Sheehan, 2000, p 539.
85   Dworkin, 1978, p 113.
86   Sheehan, 2000, p 548.

respect, superhuman judges sadly do not exist. There is something distinctly unreal about an argument that the 'correct' legal result in a personal injury case is that a severed arm is worth £50,000 as opposed to £55,000. As Reinhard Zimmermann explains, the assumption made by Dworkin and the declaratory theory that there is a right answer to any question of law is 'distinctly implausible'.[87] Court decisions, such as in the above example, clearly contain a 'constitutive element'.[88] Even if it is correct, argues Zimmermann, that legal decisions depend on arguments derived from general principles, these arguments have to be weighed against one another, which is a highly subjective exercise for which the legal order provides no precise or objective criteria.[89] As Lord Hoffmann, who changed his mind in the course of writing his judgment, admits, the 'common sense notion of mistake as to an existing state of affairs is that one has got it wrong when, if one had been better informed, one could have got it right'.[90] On the above argument, even the mythical judge Hercules could not have got it 'right' – and as such, the common sense view would dictate that in *Lincoln* there had been no mistake.

Thus, the main problem with the majority's conclusion is that, on any realistic view, a payer who pays in accordance with an existing Court of Appeal decision has, at that time, a correct view of the law. As such, he is not impaired at the time of paying. The reason for restitution, if restitution is to follow, must therefore be something other than his impairment.[91] Possible reasons for restitution, which might have been available but for the limitation problem, were failure of consideration, absence of consideration and policy. These alternatives will be examined below. Restitution in the *Lincoln* case was not based on any of them. Assuming that the bank did not make a mistake of law when it made the payment, what remains? As Birks has argued,[92] the House of Lords must be taken to have awarded restitution on the basis that the underlying transaction, the interest rate swap, was void. The focus shifts from the claimant's impairment at the time of paying to the validity or otherwise of the obligation which the payment was meant to discharge. In consequence, whenever a payment is now made under a void contract, a defendant will face an uphill struggle if he is to convince the court that the claimant was not labouring under a 'mistaken' belief in the validity of the contract. The result will be that in the overwhelming majority of cases nullity by itself will be sufficient to trigger restitution.

Lord Goff referred to comparative law in order to justify his reasoning. German law took pride of place in his analysis:

> It is of some interest that, in German law, recovery is not dependent on proof of mistake (whether of fact or law) by the claimant. Para 812(1) of the *BGB* (*Bürgerliches Gesetzbuch*) confers a right to recover benefits obtained without legal justification (*ohne rechtlichen Grund*) ... Para 814 of the *BGB* however provides that a person cannot reclaim a benefit conferred by him if he knew that he was not bound to confer it; but it seems that the burden rests on the recipient to prove the existence of such knowledge (a striking contrast with the common law, which requires the claimant to prove mistake). It is of some interest however

---

87   Zimmermann, 1999, p 722.
88   *Ibid.*
89   *Ibid.*
90   *Kleinwort Benson v Lincoln* [1999] 2 AC 349, 399.
91   This is elegantly demonstrated by Birks, 2000a.
92   *Ibid.*

that a number of these cases, in which it has been held that it is unnecessary for the plaintiff to prove that he was mistaken, have been concerned with the recovery of taxes: see in particular an early German case decided by the Reichsgericht in 1909 (29.10.1909, RGZ 72, 152) ... In such cases, as was recently held by this House in *Woolwich Equitable Building Society v Inland Revenue Commissioners (No 2)* [1993] AC 70, English law too dispenses with any requirement that the money should have been paid under a mistake and indeed goes further, allowing recovery even if the taxpayer pays in the belief that the money is not due. Here is food for thought for both German and English comparative lawyers. For present purposes, however, the importance of this comparative material is to reveal that, in civil law systems, a blanket exclusion of recovery of money paid under a mistake of law is not regarded as necessary. In particular, the experience of these systems assists to dispel the fears expressed in the early English cases that a right of recovery on the ground of mistake of law may lead to a flood of litigation, while at the same time it shows that in some cases a right of recovery, which has in the past been denied by application of the mistake of law rule, may likewise be denied in civil law countries on the basis of a narrower ground of principle or policy.[93]

While Lord Goff thus insists that the common law requires the claimant to prove mistake, the tenor of this passage is that there is no reason why nullity should not trigger restitution. This question will be discussed in detail below. At this point, it suffices to point out that Lord Goff is fully aware of the fact that he is moving the common law closer towards civilian legal systems, and that his emphasis is not so much on an impairment of the claimant's mind, but on the nullity of the swap transaction.

If anything, Lord Hope's speech takes English law even closer to civilian learning. In a comparative overview of unjust enrichment, he argues that restitution in both civil law and common law is based on the principle against unjust enrichment, the essence of which he sees to be 'that it is unjust for a person to retain a benefit which he has received at the expense of another, without any legal ground to justify its retention, which that other person did not intend him to receive'.[94] Although he then goes on to point out that English law does require an unjust factor over and above the lack of legal ground, he concludes his discussion by saying:

My impression is that the common law tends to place more emphasis on the need for proof of a mistake. But the underlying principle in both systems is that of unjust enrichment. The purpose of the principle is to provide a remedy for recovery of the enrichment where no legal ground exists to justify its retention.[95]

Two things need to be observed. First, Lord Hope freely uses legal ground terminology, not just for the civil law, but also for the common law. To this extent, his speech vindicates the approach adopted by Meier, who, as we saw above, regards an existing obligation as a 'legal ground' of an enrichment. Secondly, Lord Hope uses the comparative material to argue, impliedly, that the requirement of a mistake is not actually all that important. One gets the distinct impression that he feels that 'lack of legal ground' alone might be sufficient. Given this starting position, it is then not surprising that he finds that the bank

---

93 *Kleinwort Benson v Lincoln* [1999] 2 AC 349, 374–75.
94 *Ibid*, at 408.
95 *Ibid*, at 409.

was indeed mistaken as to the legal position when it made the payment, a conclusion which, as has been argued above, is most difficult to accept.

The conclusion drawn from this by civilians is that English law is inexorably drawn towards a system based on legal ground thinking.[96] Zimmermann, having explained why there was no mistake in *Lincoln*, continues:

> The payer was therefore at the time of payment in fact not labouring under a mistake about the legal position. It follows that he is not entitled to recover. A strange result.[97]

Zimmermann regards the result as strange because a true mistake of law can be avoided by taking decent legal advice, while a change of the law by the judicature is usually not foreseeable.[98] He argues that the result could only be avoided in one of four ways:

(1) by applying the declaratory theory of judicial decision making (which the House of Lords said it would not do!);

(2) by allowing restitution for mistake only if the mistake in question could not have been avoided by taking reasonable care (which would be contrary to *Kelly v Solari*);

(3) by equating mispredictions about the future legal position with mistakes about the current legal position (which would clearly lead to too much restitution);

(4) by dispensing with mistake as a relevant unjust factor altogether.[99]

According to Zimmermann only the fourth option, therefore, represents a viable way forward. He describes the question whether the transfer was based on the transferor's defective intent ('I did not mean you to have it') as an 'exceptionally formalistic criterion' (!!):

> What should be decisive is whether there is a justification for the shift of wealth or not. If there is no reason to keep the benefit for the transferee, the enrichment must be reversed, irrespective of the intentions of the transferor at the time of the transfer. The problem of lack of consent should, in other words, be separated off from restitution.[100]

Zimmermann concludes his article by expressing the hope that, whatever its faults, the decision in *Lincoln* might mean that the system of unjust factors will have to be jettisoned altogether, with the consequence that English law would have to succumb to a 'civilian embrace'[101] by adopting a legal ground analysis on the German model.[102]

As we have seen in the last chapter, however, German law cannot dispense with mistake as a reason for restitution. It just hides it behind an added layer of abstraction, the legal ground analysis. There are other reasons for restitution: failure of basis, as we will see below, is one. Frequently, restitution will be policy-motivated. In German law, the policy favouring restitution is expressed through a provision rendering a given transaction void. The effect of the word 'void' is then carried through to restitution. The

---

96 Cf Meier and Zimmermann, 1999, p 560; Meier, 1999b, pp 562–64; Zimmermann, 1999, pp 728–29.

97 Zimmermann, 1999, p 725.

98 AP Herbert goes as far as to suggest that 'no reasonable man can foresee a decision of the House of Lords', and that therefore a judgment of the House can be described as an 'Act of God': see Herbert, 1935, p 316, in the fictional case of *Dahlia Ltd v Yvonne* (Act of God), p 314.

99 *Ibid.*

100 Zimmermann, 1999, p 726.

101 Birks, 2000a, p 230.

102 Zimmerman, 1999, p 731.

fundamental criticism of the majority ruling in the Lincoln case is that it simply takes it for granted that a similar system will work in English law. It simply assumes that the policy leading to the nullity of swap transactions must automatically carry through to restitution. Zimmermann and Meier are guilty of the same error. Yet as Birks has pointed out, while a civil law system 'is set up to respond to nullity', the common law is not. If restitution for nullity is to work here, 'it would be necessary for us to put in some essential infrastructure'.[103] In Chapters 8 to 10, this book will examine this issue in much greater detail. For now, we can conclude that the Lincoln case dispenses with the requirement of a true mistake without putting anything in its place.

5.3 CONCLUSION

While the modern English law is slower than German law to set aside a contract on grounds of mistake, the cases of *Barclays Bank v Simms*[104] and *Kleinwort Benson v Lincoln*[105] suggest that its attitude towards mistakes in performance is much more liberal than the attitude adopted by German law.

There have been calls, however, to limit the availability of restitution for mistake even in cases not involving contracts. Meier in particular has argued that restitution for all causal mistakes is simply going too far. Given that, according to her, English law as it stands fails to distinguish between relevant and irrelevant mistakes, she regards the adoption of a legal ground model as the only way forward for English law. It has been argued in this chapter that such calls to restrict the availability of restitution for mistake should be resisted. As was established in Chapter 3, mistakes raise a presumption in favour of restitution. If there is nothing to rebut that presumption, restitution should therefore follow in such cases. On this basis, it is certainly not necessary for English law to adopt a legal ground model.

English law may nevertheless be moving in that direction. This is because the House of Lords in *Kleinwort Benson v Lincoln* held that a payment made in accordance with the law as laid down by the Court of Appeal is made under a mistake if that decision is subsequently overruled by the House of Lords. This approach emphasises the validity or otherwise of the underlying obligation, not the state of mind of the payer. It therefore moves English law much closer towards the continental model based on legal ground reasoning.

---

103 Birks, 2000a, p 232.
104 [1980] QB 677.
105 [1999] 2 AC 349.

PART III
FAILURE OF CONSIDERATION

CHAPTER 6

FAILURE OF CONSIDERATION IN CONTRACTUAL CASES IN GERMANY

The 'absence of consideration' doctrine, which will be discussed in Part IV of this book, only came into our law because Hobhouse J considered, in the *Westdeutsche* case, that failure of consideration was not available as a basis for restitution. In the following four chapters, we will therefore take a detailed look at that unjust factor. It will be argued that, properly understood, it would have led to the correct result without the need to resort to 'absence of consideration' at all.

Failure of consideration is a ground for restitution because, like mistake, it raises the liberal presumption in favour of restitution. The presumption is raised by a mistake, as we saw in Chapter 3, because under the principle of private autonomy an individual can decide for himself or herself whether or not to transfer part of his assets to another. If that decision is flawed by a mistake, upholding the transfer would negate the very freedom which a liberal legal system affords. Failure of consideration raises the presumption because an individual cannot just decide if he wishes to make a transfer, but also how and in what circumstances, in short, on what basis, he wishes to do so. The crucial difference between the two grounds for restitution is, however, that this basis must be communicated to the transferee. Otherwise a failure of the basis would be a mere misprediction which, as discussed in Chapter 3, does not normally raise the presumption at all.

As Lord Goff observes in *Westdeutsche*,[1] there are two problems with failure of consideration which lead to the perceived necessity of a ground for restitution entitled 'absence of consideration'. The first lies in the relationship between contract and restitution: can there be restitution for failure of consideration in cases that do not involve a contract? The second is the requirement that the failure of consideration must be total if restitution is to follow. In this part, both these problems are addressed in turn. The question will be asked whether there is a reason to treat contractual cases differently from non-contractual ones, and answers given to this both in England and in Germany will be discussed. If contractual cases *are* to be in a category of their own, the next question will concern non-contractual ones: we shall ask whether restitution should be denied in such cases, or what it should be based on. Should there be a separate category for such cases, similar to the Roman *condictio causa data causa non secuta*? Or do they become submerged in a general unjust enrichment claim, possibly one based on the negative requirement of 'absence of consideration'? The argument put forward here is that failure of consideration should not be restricted to contractual cases, and that, once the requirement that a relevant failure of consideration must be total is abandoned, this traditional unjust factor is a much better tool for the attainment of justice than a wide and as yet undefined negative ground for restitution based on 'absence of consideration'.

---

1   [1996] AC 669, 683.

6.1 *RÜCKTRITT* AND FAILURE OF CONSIDERATION

We have seen that in cases of failure of contractual reciprocation § 812 I is of limited applicability. These situations are generally seen as a matter of contract law, and § 346 governs the restitutionary liability of the parties. We are dealing with the termination of contracts. The German term for this is '*Rücktritt*'.

In a recent paper on *Rücktritt*, Dannemann writes: 'It may come as a surprise to English lawyers that there is no requirement of total failure of consideration in German law, or indeed of any failure of consideration'.[2] This reflects a widely held view in Germany that the law of *Rücktritt* is different from the law of unjust enrichment, and that restitution in cases of *Rücktritt* is not based on the injustice of the enrichment, but on the fact that the contract has been terminated. As Dannemann continues: 'If the innocent party does have the right to terminate the contract, it can, in principle, require restitution of all payments made under the contract, regardless of whether the other party has not performed at all, has performed badly, partially or completely.'[3] It will be argued in this book, however, that, in German as in English law, restitution is not required because of the effect of some abstract rule of law, but because the bargained-for counter-performance has failed. It becomes clear later on in Dannemann's paper that he would not disagree with this proposition. Let us recall in what situations the innocent party will have a right of *Rücktritt*. First, there is a right of Rücktritt which has been agreed in advance in the contract. In effect, this constitutes a contractual right on the part of the party entitled to declare *Rücktritt* to ask for his own performance back. This is conditional upon its returning any benefits it has received itself. Alternatively, one could say that, by claiming back its own performance, the first party has brought about an *ex post* failure of consideration, which in turn is the basis of the other party's restitutionary claim. On any analysis, the situation in English law would be exactly the same, if only as a matter of contract law.

The second situation in which a right of *Rücktritt* may arise is where the other party is unable to perform (*Unmöglichkeit*). This must therefore mean that the consideration for the first party's performance has failed. Similarly, where a buyer is entitled to reject faulty goods under § 465, he has not received what he has bargained for and can therefore claim that there has been a failure of consideration. It is this which underlies his right of restitution once he has declared *Wandelung*.[4] Finally, a right of *Rücktritt* may arise where the other party has delayed performance. Again, this gives the first party a right to reject the tardy performance and claim that the consideration has failed.

It is, of course, correct to say that the claimant does not have to show that there has been a failure of consideration as such: in showing that the counter-performance is impossible, faulty, or late, however, that is exactly what he is showing. Failure of consideration is thus implicit in the requirements of *Rücktritt*. Given that thus the law of *Rücktritt* seems to respond to a set of facts which, in England, have always seemed to trigger the general law of unjust enrichment, we have to ask why it was felt to be

2   Dannemann, 1997, p 132.
3   *Ibid*.
4   See above, p 26.

necessary to make separate provision for the restitutionary consequences of the termination of a contract. There are three possible answers:

First, the development of a separate contractual restitutionary regime might have been no more than a historical accident. We will see that in Roman law there was no general right to terminate a contract. When this limitation was overcome, the consequences of the exercise of the new right to terminate were specifically worked out, and it might simply not have been appreciated that the law of unjust enrichment was functionally similar and would have been able to provide adequate solutions.

Secondly, it can be argued that a general restitutionary regime such as provided by §§ 812 ff cannot adequately address the special problems that arise in contractual cases. Contractual performances are tied to one another, they are dependent on each other. In the case of services, for instance, the contract will be important evidence of the value attached to the service by its recipient. In other cases, the indiscriminate application of the defence of change of position might cause problems given the inter-dependency of the respective contractual obligations. To give each party an independent restitutionary claim based on the injustice of his enrichment, whatever that might mean, could thus be seen as an unhappy solution.

Thirdly, it is possible that there is something inherently different, from a doctrinal point of view, about an enrichment that has come about under a valid contract. In particular, much importance is usually attached by jurists to the question whether *Rücktritt* destroys a contract *ab initio*, or whether the contract survives, primary duties of performance being replaced by secondary duties to pay damages or to make restitution. Serious concerns may be voiced concerning the relationship between the law of contract and the law of restitution which do not apply in non-contractual cases. Thus, should a claimant be permitted to succeed in a restitutionary claim when he would fail in a claim for damages because he has made a bad bargain? Is there a danger that the law of restitution may undermine the law of contract? Separate treatment of restitutionary claims in contractual cases may thus be warranted, as it ensures that the problems that arise can be dealt with specifically.

In this chapter, we will examine all three arguments in turn. First, there will be an outline of the developments of the rules of *Rücktritt*, starting with their antecedents in Roman law and with reference to the minutes of the two drafting commissions. Secondly, we will address the tricky question of the availability and measure of restitution in situations where the transferred benefit has deteriorated or has been destroyed. Thirdly, we will, with reference both to historical development and modern doctrine, address the question of the juridical nature of the right of *Rücktritt*.

6.2 HISTORICAL DEVELOPMENT OF THE RULES

6.2.1 Roman law

Roman law, which was always the starting point for the deliberations of the drafting commissions, did not recognise a general right to terminate a contract. The only remedy of the disappointed claimant was the *actio venditi* to claim the price or damages. There was no unilateral right to withdrawal.[5]

The lex commissoria

It was, however, possible for the parties to enter into a collateral contract giving one or both of them the right to terminate the contract in certain circumstances. The most important of these contracts was the *lex commissoria*, which gave the seller the right to recover his goods if the buyer, for whatever reason, had failed to pay on a given date.[6] The term '*commissoria*' makes it clear that the exercise of the right to terminate the contract had proprietary effect: the buyer 'forfeited' his property, it fell back to the vendor. In the *ius commune* this proprietary effect was criticised and doubted, given that it did not allow a differentiated legal response to deteriorations in the goods which might have occurred in the meantime.[7]

The actio redhibitoria

Sale was exceptional. A contract of sale could be brought to an end if the sold goods were defective. This was the effect of the *actio redhibitoria*. To exercise his right to recover the price, the buyer had to return the goods first. If that was no longer possible, specific rules applied which had developed for typical dispute situations. If the buyer had been negligent in damaging or destroying the goods, he could only recover his price if he could make restitution of the value of the goods as he had received them.[8] If the goods had been damaged by accident, the buyer had a right to full restitution based on the rule of '*mortuus redhibetur*', that is, he simply returned the damaged goods (or, indeed, the dead slave), and obtained restitution of his price in return.

6.2.2   The *Allgemeine Deutsche Handelsgesetzbuch* of 1861

The first German code to contain a right of termination was the *Allgemeine Deutsche Handelsgesetzbuch* (ADHGB), a commercial code for the whole of Germany that had become law in 1861. In Arts 354–56, the ADHGB laid down a right of *Rücktritt* in cases of late delivery. It was to take effect 'as though the contract had never been entered into' (Arts 354, 355), and thus had destroyed the contract *ab initio*. This was, however, of limited importance, given that the right to terminate in the ADHGB was restricted to wholly executory commercial sales contracts, avoiding the tricky restitutionary problems of unwinding executed transactions.

6.2.3   The drafting commissions of the *BGB*

The first drafting commission of the *BGB* decided to drop these restrictions. There was to be a general right to terminate, either based on contractual agreement or by operation of

---

5   Zimmermann, 1996, p 738.
6   Leser, 1975, pp 16 ff.
7   *Ibid*, pp 18 ff.
8   von Staudinger/Kaiser, Introduction to §§ 346 ff, No 5.

law in cases of impossibility due to negligence or intention and in cases of delay. The restitutionary consequences of the termination of executed contracts were based upon a combination of the *lex commissoria* and the *actio redhibitoria*.[9] The second commission extended the new general right to contracts for services and hire in what is today § 346 2. It also equated the position of the debtor under § 346 to that of a possessor holding somebody else's property: if he damaged the goods negligently or intentionally, he was made liable in damages to the restitution creditor. This rule, now contained in § 347, was justified on the basis that he had to be aware of the possibility that he might come under a duty to make restitution, and that it was thus appropriate to impose a duty of care on him.

From a perusal of the minutes of the two drafting commissions it becomes clear that the argument that the restitutionary consequences of *Rücktritt* were given separate treatment was merely a historical accident is not sustainable. While the first commission found it difficult to overcome the binding nature of a contract in Roman law completely,[10] and was concerned that an *ab initio* effect of *Rücktritt* might have proprietary consequences, both of these objections were dismissed by the second commission. Nevertheless, the second commission refused to adopt a modification of the law of *Rücktritt* to the effect that 'the obligation based on the contract is extinguished', but there was nevertheless broad consensus for a view that the contract would be avoided *ab initio*. One took the view that, in the absence of special contractual rules, the law of unjust enrichment would govern the restitutionary consequences.[11]

The second commission retained the special contractual provisions therefore not because it considered the law of *Rücktritt* to be different from the law of unjust enrichment as a matter of doctrine, but because it sought to reflect the fact that the parties were in a synallagmatic relationship. It was thought that this should be taken into account in situations where normally the defence of change of position would apply. We will see in the next section of the chapter if this concern was justified, and whether it retains its justification in the present day.

6.3 THE AVAILABILITY AND MEASURE OF RESTITUTION

There are two types of case in which the giving and taking back required by § 346 1 may be difficult: the first involves benefits of a kind which cannot be returned *in specie*, such as labour, services, use of property etc. The second involves goods transferred under the terminated contract which have since been damaged or destroyed, and can therefore not be returned in the state in which they were received, if at all.

In the first of these two categories we encounter the possibility that the law of contract may be undermined by a solution which allows one party to evade the consequences of having made a bad bargain. In the second category, on the other hand, we are more concerned with giving expression to the reciprocity of the original performances, which should be reflected in the restitutionary solution adopted.

---

9   Leser, 1975, pp 29 ff, 60 ff.
10 Motive II, pp 280–81.
11 Prot VI, p 158.

6.3.1 Restitution for benefits that cannot be returned *in specie*

German law is still struggling to give expression to the concept of subjective devaluation in the law of unjust enrichment.[12] If I leave my car at the garage to be repaired, and the mechanic mistakenly gives it a full service and a new coat of paint, there is no reason why I should be required to pay for this. I did not ask for it, and, as Bowen LJ said in *Falcke v Scottish Imperial Insurance Co*,[13] 'liabilities are not to be forced upon people behind their backs'. The situation is otherwise, of course, where the benefit has been realised in money by the recipient (for example, by selling the car at a better price than would otherwise have been achieved), or where the benefit has saved the recipient a necessary expense. As Birks writes, the argument from subjective devaluation is 'based on the premise that benefits in kind have value to a particular individual only so far as he chooses to give them value'.[14]

In German law, there are very few cases which even touch on the issue, and § 818 II seems to demand that, if restitution *in specie* is not possible, the objective value of the benefit be made the subject of the restitutionary claim. Nevertheless, the problem of 'imposed enrichments' is generally regarded as an important one. Many writers agree with the English approach and attempt to fit the perceived correct solution into the framework of the *BGB*, reconciling it in some way with § 818 II.[15]

The same problem presents itself, in a slightly modified way, where one deals with failed contracts for services. While it is, in this context, not correct to speak of an 'imposed enrichment' of the defendant, it would clearly be contrary to the idea of subjective devaluation to allow the claimant to recover the market value of his services. The defendant had requested the service, and he had specified what he would be willing to pay for it. § 346 2 assumes that the value of the benefit to him should therefore be equated to the price he agreed to pay for it:

> *Für geleistete Dienste sowie für die Überlassung der Benutzung einer Sache ist der Wert zu vergüten oder, falls in dem Vertrag eine Gegenleistung in Geld bestimmt ist, diese zu entrichten.* [For services rendered as well as for the use of a thing the objective value has to be paid, or, if the contract makes provision for a counter-performance in money, this is to be paid.]

Hans Leser interprets this provision as a rebuttable presumption that the value specified by the contract does represent the market value.[16] Thus, if the market value of the service can be shown to be less than that agreed in the contract, § 346 2 is rebutted. This interpretation has, however, been rejected by most writers. Contrary to Leser's view, they see the provision as a reflection of the continued existence of the contract.[17]

---

12 Cf Markesinis, 1997, pp 760 f.

13 *Falcke v Scottish Imperial Insurance Co* [1886] 34 Ch 234, 248

14 Birks, 1989, p 109; see also his discussion of the argument, pp 109–32

15 Thus, Lieb regards it as a 'permissible extension of the law' to make an exception to the objective valuation envisaged by § 818 II, based on the principle of private autonomy: MünchKomm/Lieb § 812, No 262

16 Leser, 1975, p 170.

17 von Staudinger/Kaiser, § 346, No 54, 457. See further below, pp 106 ff.

However, as we have seen above,[18] the second drafting commission, which itself added the second sentence of § 346, took the view that *Rücktritt* would extinguish the contract *ab initio*. Why, then, was § 346 2 included? It is suggested that § 346 2 should be seen to give effect to the idea of subjective devaluation. The problem was appreciated in the context of terminated contracts, but not for the whole law of unjust enrichment, as § 818 II shows. § 346 2 is designed to prevent the restitutionary consequences of the termination of a contract from undermining the risk allocations of the law of contract as a whole. If the value of the rendered service is smaller than the agreed price, that is, if the party rendering the service has made a bad bargain, he will not be able to get out of it by terminating the contract.

Given the absence of a rule providing for subjective devaluation in enrichment law, § 346 2 provides an additional argument that it was indeed necessary to regulate the consequences of the termination of a contract separately. The contractual context is the one context in which there is clear evidence of the value put on the service by the recipient, and it thus might make sense to single it out.

However, this argument disappears if one appreciates that there is a need for a subjective devaluation concept throughout the law of unjust enrichment, and that attempts to correct § 818 II are indeed being made by very eminent writers. If the concept is indeed within interpretative reach, the argument for a separate treatment for contractual cases based on § 346 2 disappears.[19]

Similar problems arise where counter-restitution in respect of the user of the benefit is in issue. § 347 2 refers to the owner-possessor model in §§ 987 ff *BGB*, in particular to the regime which applies between the owner and the possessor of a chattel from the time at which the possessor has become aware of the owner's claim. § 987 provides that in such cases the owner has a claim against the possessor in respect of any benefits derived from the chattel. The code leaves open the question how such benefits are to be valued. There are essentially two possibilities: the owner might be entitled to the objective value of the user, that is, the relevant market rental, or he might claim the diminution in the value of the chattel. If the latter, the question will arise how the value of the chattel is to be determined. In a relatively recent case,[20] a hotel company had contracted with the State to accommodate a large number of asylum seekers. To be able to put them up, it had bought a large number of bunk beds. These were of unsatisfactory quality, but even though it sought to terminate the contract under § 462 *BGB* (*Wandelung*),[21] the seller resisted such termination and the beds were used by asylum seekers for some eight months before the court adjudged the beds to be of such bad quality as to entitle the claimant to reject them. The question arose what credit the claimant had to give for the use of the beds over eight months. The *Bundesgerichtshof* decided that the proper measure was the diminution of the value of the beds, taking into account the purchase price agreed between the parties as a starting point in assessing the original value of the beds. Thus the *Bundesgerichtshof* used an approach very similar to § 346 2 in tackling this problem. In reaching this result, the

---

18   See above, p 93.

19   In England, Birks's subjective devaluation approach has been expressly endorsed by the Court of Appeal in *Ministry of Defence v Ashman* [1993] 2 EGLR 102.

20   BGHZ 115, 47 (26.6.1991).

21   As to which, see below, p 126.

Bundesgerichtshof took principles of subjective devaluation into account. There is no reason why a similar approach cannot be adopted in the context of the general law of unjust enrichment.

Although § 347 appears to provide that the party in question will always be accountable for his own use of and profits derived from the chattel as though he had known all along that he was not entitled to use it, it is clear that up until he knows that he is entitled to terminate the contract, or that the other side is seeking to terminate himself, general enrichment rules will apply, which means that in such cases the change of position defence will be available.[22] This further strengthens the argument that a single restitutionary regime would have sufficed, and that there is no particular need for the specialised *Rücktritt* rules.

6.3.2 Destroyed or damaged goods

When the *BGB* was drafted, there was a fundamental difference between *Rücktritt* and unjust enrichment: the latter was subject to the very strong defence of change of position. Contractual relationships were seen to require a more differentiated treatment. A contract characteristically gives rise to an exchange of performances: *do ut des*. It was felt that this connection between performance and counter-performance had to be taken into account. §§ 812 ff failed to do this. § 812 I does not refer to the other side's counter-performance at all: as drafted, there would have been two independent restitutionary claims which could at best be set off against each other (§§ 387 ff). Serious problems would thus be caused by the defence of change of position ('*Wegfall der Bereicherung*') in contractual cases. An example may illustrate the problem:

> B buys a car from S. Unbeknown to him, the car has a hidden defect, entitling him to ask for *Wandelung*. One night, having become senselessly intoxicated, he crashes the car into a tree. When the accident is investigated by the police, the defect is discovered. Returned from his hospital bed or his prison cell, B now seeks *Wandelung*.

If there were no special rules for contractual cases, it is arguable that he could ask for restitution of the purchase price while himself relying on the change of position defence in answering S's counterclaim for return of the car. In other words, B would get his money back, while S would have to be content with the wrecked car, B being under no obligation to make restitution of the value of the car because of the effect of § 818 III. It is clear that this would not be an acceptable result. The return of the car must be the condition for restitution of the money: the two performances were dependent on one another, and so should be the two restitutionary claims. In the end, it comes down to risk allocation: B accepts the risk of loss when he accepts delivery of the car, and it is difficult to see how a hidden defect can shift the risk back to S. In contractual cases, it is therefore necessary to provide more differentiated rules. This was done in §§ 350 ff, though whether the result commends itself as an acceptable solution is a different question.

---

22   See, eg, BGH NJW 1992, 1965 (1.4.1992).

Contractually agreed right to terminate

§§ 346 ff are primarily drafted with a contractually agreed right to terminate in mind. It follows that the restitutionary rules provided by the law of *Rücktritt* are least objectionable in such cases. Nevertheless, particularly § 350, allowing the party entitled to terminate to exercise his right even though the benefit he has received has been accidentally damaged or destroyed, has caused problems even in this paradigm area.

Where both parties know that either of them is entitled to terminate the contract in certain circumstances, it is acceptable to impose a duty on them to take care that the benefits they have received do not come to harm while they are under their control. It is not quite so clear who is to bear the risk of loss in a situation in which the damage occurs wholly by chance, neither party being to blame. For the law of sales, the applicable rule is contained in § 446, which provides that the risk of loss passes to the buyer on delivery.[23] Why should the same not apply here? The problem becomes more obvious when it is not the party in whose custody the benefit has been damaged, but the other party, who terminates the contract. He is now obliged to return that which he has received, normally the contract price, but has to suffer that the other party returns nothing at all.[24] Having declared his *Rücktritt*, however, he may not be able to go back on his declaration, as the mistake made will be as to his motive, and such a mistake is not sufficient to avoid a declaration under § 119.[25]

The words of § 350 are unambiguous. However, at least as far as contractually agreed rights of *Rücktritt* are concerned, many writers have been most inventive in finding ways around the rule. Most of these attempts focus on the fact that both parties were or should have been aware of the possibility that the contract would be terminated by one of them. Thus, it is thought acceptable that the term '*Verschulden*', denoting the responsibility of the parties for negligence or intention, is given an extensive interpretation. Medicus, for instance, advocates that if a buyer exposes the goods to an increased risk of damage, for instance by using them for an unusual purpose or wholly unreasonably, he should bear the risk of loss under § 351.[26] For example, if B were to use the car he has bought in a cross-country race, this would constitute an extraordinary risk and if it was damaged, albeit not through his fault, he would not be able to shift the burden of that risk to S. B will thus no longer be able to terminate the contract: § 351. Other writers have gone even further, defining '*Verschulden*' as 'any free action' ('*jede freie Handlung*').[27] Thus, if B uses the car he has just bought to drive to the supermarket, and an accident happens on the way, but which cannot be said to have been his fault, he would be deprived of his right to terminate because he used the car in the first place. These writers would thus restrict § 350 to cases in which the goods have perished for a reason the other party is responsible for (the car had faulty brakes), or where the destruction or damage of the goods was due

---

23 This, for a change, is a rule that English law would do well to adopt. In English law, the principle *res perit domino* applies (s 20, of the Sale of Goods Act 1979), so that property, not possession or control is the decisive factor. Cf Goode, 1995, p 248.

24 Cf Medicus, 1996a, pp 250 f.

25 For a way round this conundrum, see Larenz, 1987, p 412.

26 Medicus, 1996a, p 250.

27 von Caemmerer, 1973, pp 621, 623 f; Leser, 1975, pp 197 f and 201 ff.

to *force majeure*. In view of the wording of § 350, these attempts to interpret it out of existence can at best be described as doubtful.[28]

It is suggested that the interpretation put forward by Medicus, based on whether or not the goods were put to their 'normal' use, is the preferable one. The undesirable consequences of § 350 are tempered a little by the fact that the person attempting to terminate the contract bears the burden to show that the destruction or damage of the benefit is not due to his fault.

Right to terminate arising by operation of law

We have seen that in practice rights to terminate arise most often by operation of law. It is thus unfortunate that the rules in §§ 346 ff are drafted with the contractually agreed *Rücktritt* in mind. This has caused two considerable problems. One concerns the use of the concept of 'fault' in determining the restitutionary liability of the parties, the other the question what rules are to govern the restitutionary liability of an innocent party who is not to blame for the circumstances which have brought about the right to terminate the contract.

Fault ('Verschulden') in §§ 351, 347

As pointed out above, in the case of a contractually agreed *Rücktritt* the parties can be expected to take reasonable care of the benefits they have received. This is otherwise in the case of a right to terminate arising by operation of law, for example, because the goods contain a defect entitling the buyer to reject them. The unconditional buyer of a car, having acquired absolute title, cannot be under a duty of care to the seller to treat the car with due care. That would be contrary to the very concept of property. What standard of care is therefore required? Can an owner be 'at fault' when he negligently damages his own property? Medicus uses the example of the buyer of a car who chooses to use the car to drive around by night, in an intoxicated state, failing to put on his headlights, and on the wrong side of the road. Could it have been the intention of the legislator to leave his right to terminate, possibly on the basis of a minor defect, intact?

The special kind of fault in § 351 must therefore be one which does not require a breach of duty, maybe akin to the concept of contributory negligence. How this is to be applied in practice is not altogether clear. The courts have so far been of little assistance. In a recent case that came before the *Bundesgerichtshof*,[29] the claimant, a Tunisian company, had ordered a quantity of plastic granules from the defendant company in Germany, and had paid by letter of credit once it had inspected a sample. When the granules were delivered, the claimant alleged that they were not in conformity with the sample, and asked the defendant to exchange them within three days. These having expired, it threw the granules away. It now sought to recover the price based on a right to *'Wandelung'* stemming from the non-correspondence of the goods with the sample. The court rejected the claim. By throwing away the granules, the claimant had been at fault and could not rely on § 350. On the contrary, under § 351 its right to terminate the contract had been lost. However, the court does not give us any hint as to what is meant by 'fault'

---

28 Cf Palandt/Heinrichs, § 351, No 3, 437.
29 BGHZ 115, 286 (9.10.1991).

in § 351. The case is not very helpful for present purposes because arguably the claimant was under a duty to treat the granules with due care as soon as it became aware of the alleged defect. It now knew that it intended to terminate the contract and to recover the price, and it knew that it would then be under a duty to return the goods. This duty was breached by throwing them away.

More difficult questions arise in situations in which the goods perish or are damaged before the party in question is aware of its right to terminate. It is in these situations that it is no longer possible to speak of a duty of care in any meaningful sense. The formula commonly used refers to the standard of care normally observed in looking after one's own affairs (*'eigenübliche Sorgfalt'* or, in Latin, *'diligentia quam in suis rebus adhibere solet'*). This will include using the goods for the purpose for which they are designed, and refraining from wilfully destroying them or exposing them to an extraordinary risk.[30]

As Zimmermann writes in a recent article, the relationship between §§ 350 and 351 'is largely determined by the soundness, or otherwise, of the policy underlying § 350 BGB'.[31] It is suggested, and Zimmermann would appear to agree with this assessment,[32] that German law would be better off without that rule, which in its turn is based on a Roman rule (*'Mortuus redhibetur'*) which itself has exercised the minds of Romanists all over the world for a considerable number of centuries.

Innocent party's liability to be determined by general enrichment rules? (§ 327 2)

The second great debate in the law of *Rücktritt* can again be blamed on the cross-referencing technique. § 327 is not itself part of the law of *Rücktritt*, but is the provision which refers to §§ 346 ff where a party is given a right to terminate for impossibility of performance or delay, provided the other side is at fault. The second sentence of § 327, however, refers not to the law of *Rücktritt*, but to the law of unjust enrichment:

> *Erfolgt der Rücktritt wegen eines Umstandes, den der andere Teil nicht zu vertreten hat, so haftet dieser nur nach den Vorschriften über die Herausgabe einer ungerechtfertigten Bereicherung.* [If the contract is terminated for a reason which the other party is not responsible for, he will only be liable according to the rules applying to the restitution of unjust enrichment.]

If the provision is interpreted literally, its field of application will be very small indeed, given that according to §§ 325 and 326 'the other party' will *always* be responsible for the reason of termination. Thus, if a party is given the right to terminate, this must be due to the other party's fault. The only possible field of application, if § 327 2 is interpreted literally, is § 636 I 1. This applies to construction contracts, and gives the person for whom the construction is carried out the right to terminate the contract if the construction is objectively late (normally he will be required to specify a further reasonable extension of time), notwithstanding the fact that the other party is not at fault. It is, however, doubtful that § 327 2 was intended for this – relatively rare – case. In particular, it would be contrary to the overall structure of the BGB to include a provision applicable only to one paragraph in the special law of obligations in the general part of the law of obligations.[33]

---

30 Palandt/Heinrichs, § 351, Nos 3 f; MünchKomm/Janssen, § 351, No 4.
31 Zimmermann, 1997, p 19.
32 *Ibid*, p 20.
33 Medicus, 1996a, p 256.

The courts have therefore adopted an expansive interpretation of § 327 2. In a case which came before the *Reichsgericht* in 1930,[34] a dockyard had agreed to build a freighter for the claimants for RM 8.5 m. The first instalment of RM 1.7 m was paid in 1919. When Germany was hit by inflation, the dockyard demanded that the price be adjusted accordingly, which it was able to do under the then current jurisprudence of the *Reichsgericht*. When the claimants refused, the dockyard terminated the contract. It was entitled to do so under the doctrine of frustration (*'clausula rebus sic stantibus'*), developed by the *Reichsgericht* for precisely this kind of case. The question was whether, in making restitution of the money received, the defendant was liable under the rules of contractual Rücktritt in §§ 346 ff, or under the rules governing enrichment claims in §§ 812 ff, including the defence of change of position. The money had become worthless due to inflation, it was literally worth no more than the paper it was printed on. It appears from the judgment that the parties themselves were not fully aware of the significance of the distinction. The claimants had pleaded their case in such a way as to indicate that if general enrichment rules applied, their claim would be reduced by RM 10,000. It seemed to be generally agreed between the parties that the claimant's claim was for restitution of the value of the money in gold, which came to some RM 300,000. Logically, however, the difference might have been huge, namely between nothing at all if enrichment law applied, and RM 1.7 m if the court applied the rules of *Rücktritt*. Even though the impact on the practical outcome was thus not as significant as it might have been, the court made it clear that the dockyard could rely on the defence of change of position. It was not to blame for the reasons of its termination, and could, by analogy to § 327 2, make restitution in accordance with the rules of enrichment law, rather than § 346. The court was well aware that this solution was not in accordance with the literal meaning of § 327 2, but was content to refer to the drafting minutes of the second commission to arrive at the conclusion that § 327 2 pursues the general aim of enabling the innocent party, who did not have to expect that the contract would be terminated, to take advantage of the more lenient liability under § 818. The formulation of § 327 2 was probably to be put down to a drafting error,[35] in any event it was clear that it could be applied by analogy to the case before the court.[36]

The *Bundesgerichtshof* has adopted the view of its predecessor. Thus, in 1970 the court affirmed that the *Landgericht* below had been correct in applying § 327 2 to the person himself terminating the contract: '... the meaning of the provision is that in all cases the innocent restitution debtor is liable only to the extent that he is still enriched.'[37] The case, which is in reality a pure enrichment case, will be discussed in detail below.[38]

Most commentators have adopted this interpretation.[39] They see it not as decisive who actually terminates the contract, but who is responsible for the reasons that lead to

---

34   RGZ 130, 119 (24.10.1930).

35   *Ibid*, 123.

36   *Ibid*, 124. Recent cases in which the application of enrichment rules makes any difference are rare or indeed non-existent, given the convergence of the rules determining the measure of restitution in both areas. The only other examples are thus fairly old decisions: RG JW 1928, 57 (11.10.1927); RG Warn Rechtspr 38, 140, No 60 (20.12.1937).

37   BGHZ 53, 144 (8.1.1970), 148 f.

38   See below, p 103.

39   For many, Medicus, 1996a, p 257; Palandt/Heinrichs, § 327, No 3; Walter, 1987, p 193. See also Zimmermann, 1997, p 15.

that termination.[40] Recently a literal meaning of § 327 2 has been gaining ground again, although the courts are still committed to its extensive interpretation. Many writers now, based on the drafting history, argue that the draftsmen of the BGB indeed intended § 327 2 to mean what it says, and that it was indeed meant to apply to § 636 I 1 only. They argue that § 818 III is far too lenient for the recipient of a money payment, and that it is thus appropriate to restrict § 327 2 to such an extremely limited field of application.[41]

The 'Saldotheorie'

The idea underlying the law of *Rücktritt* is that the restitutionary claims of the parties to a failed contract are dependent on one another. It is for this reason, as we have seen, that it was thought necessary to make specific provision for such contractual cases. The way in which this was put into practice, however, was less than satisfactory. This was due mainly to the model of the Roman *actio redhibitoria*, and to the unfortunate decision to use the law of contractually agreed termination as a blueprint for rights of termination arising by operation of law.

It is suggested that it would not have been necessary to make separate provision for failed contracts had it been realised that the law of unjust enrichment would be faced with very similar problems. Not all failed contracts fail because they are terminated under the provisions in §§ 346 ff. Many fail because either offer or acceptance are void *ab initio*, or are avoided with *ab initio* effect. As we have seen, a contract may be avoided (rather than terminated) for a number of reasons such as mistake, duress or fraudulent misrepresentation.[42] In such situations, the parties are in a contractual relationship no different in fact from the relationship of parties to a terminated contract. However, in the eyes of the law the contract has never existed. In drafting §§ 812 ff, the draftsmen failed to take account of this factual link of the two performances. The courts have therefore corrected enrichment law, in that they have taken the 'factual *synallagma*' between the two performances into account in assessing the measure of restitution. They now deny a party the right to rely on the defence of change of position in respect of the other party's performance, while at the same time claiming full restitution of his own performance. The purpose of the contract was the exchange of performances, and this is reflected in the respective duties to make restitution imposed on the parties.

The problem first arose in 1903, only three years after the BGB had passed into law.[43] The claimant had bought the defendant's manor and estates. Having lived in the manor for a few months, and having disposed of some of the inventory (apparently for far less than its true value), he claimed that the defendant had induced him to buy by fraudulent misrepresentation, and avoided the contract. He claimed full repayment of the price plus interest. The defendant resisted the claim on the ground that he would be entitled to set off the value of the things the claimant had disposed of, rent for a few months' occupancy of the castle and various other items. At first instance, the court had applied the so-called

---

40 Cf Medicus, 1996a, p 257.
41 Cf most recently Larenz, 1987, pp 410 ff, but also Leser, 1975, pp 204 ff.
42 See above, p 21.
43 RGZ 54, 137 (14.3.1903).

'*Zweikondiktionentheorie*', which assumes that, in accordance with the wording of §§ 812 ff, each party has an independent enrichment claim against the other. The *Reichsgericht* disagreed:

> As is apparent even from the heading 'Unjust Enrichment', and from § 818 III, which limits the duty to make restitution *in specie* or in money to the surviving enrichment, the 'something' which has to be returned under § 812 cannot be any single value which has passed from plaintiff to defendant, but only the totality of what has passed taking account of the values which were given in exchange and the encumbrances resting on what has been received.[44]

This was the birth of the so-called '*Saldotheorie*'. By '*Saldo*' the German language means the difference in value between the performances. In the case of bilateral contracts which have been avoided *ab initio*, performances having passed both ways, the subject of a restitutionary claim will be the difference in value between the performances. There is only one restitutionary claim, not two, with one being set-off against the other.

It is suggested that there is nothing special about the consequences of the *Rücktritt* of one party as long as the law of unjust enrichment provides a restitutionary regime which is designed for the unwinding of exchange transactions. There is thus nothing to justify a different restitutionary regime. Indeed, this is reflected in the case law of the *Bundesgerichtshof*. In adjudicating claims brought under §§ 812 ff, the court usually pays much attention to the question how the case would be decided under §§ 346 ff. Thus, in justifying the above decision of the *Reichsgericht* involving the void sale of the manor house, the analogy to § 351 is frequently relied upon.[45] The argument runs as follows: in exposing the received benefit to increased risks, or in treating it in such a way so as to damage it, the recipient takes the risk of decreasing his assets by the value of his own performance. Thus, if I buy a car and crash it into a tree while drink driving, I risk losing whatever I have paid for the car. I should not be allowed to transfer my loss to the seller, merely because the contract turns out to be void for some reason.

The question which is still more or less open is whether § 350 is also to be applied by analogy. Lorenz makes the following criticism of the *Saldotheorie*:[46] he assumes that a car with a latent defect is bought and accidentally destroyed after the buyer has taken delivery. § 67 1 icw[47] § 350 means that the risk of loss 'jumps back' to the seller: by returning the remains of the car, the buyer would be able to reclaim the price. If, however, the seller had known about the defect and had failed to inform the buyer about it, the contract could be avoided under §123 I. According to the older *Zwei-kon-diktion-en-theor-ie*, the buyer would be able to rely on the defence of change of position, which would lead to the same result as § 350. The *Saldotheorie*, however, would only allow the buyer to claim the difference in value between the price and the value of the car with the defect, as he is no longer in a position to return it. Its value must therefore be set off against the price. Lorenz sees this as a serious criticism of the *Saldotheorie*. Within his own parameters, he is, of course, right: there is no reason to treat the two cases differently, and since § 350 is valid

---

44 *Ibid*, p 141.
45 Eg, von Staudinger/Lorenz, § 818, No 42.
46 *Ibid*, § 818, No 41.
47 'icw' = 'in connection with'.

law, its solution should prevail.[48] For the comparative lawyer the question is a different one: which solution should be preferred?

The problem has more recently arisen before the *Bundesgerichtshof*, whose judgments have sparked the debate afresh. A number of cases concerned sales of used cars.[49] The seller had either made fraudulent misrepresentations as to the mileage or age of the cars, or the defect was so fundamental that the *Bundesgerichtshof* allowed the buyer to rescind the contract *ab initio* on the ground of mistake (§ 119 II). In all cases the cars had been destroyed or seriously damaged in accidents. If the *Saldotheorie* had been applied without reference to the law of *Rücktritt*, the respective claimants would not have been able to obtain full restitution of the price without making restitution of the value of the defective car. They would not have been able to rely on § 818 III. However, the *Bundesgerichtshof* sought to give effect to the principles of the law of *Rücktritt* in making the availability of the defence dependent upon the culpability of the parties.

In BGHZ 53, 144 (8.1.1970), the claimant had been deceived about the true mileage of the car. The defendant had tampered with the odometer. The car was badly damaged the day after delivery, but no fault could be proved on the part of the claimant, who discovered the fraud and avoided the contract. The defendant relied on the *Saldotheorie*, but the *Bundesgerichtshof* refused to apply it. It held that the *Saldotheorie* did not apply because a fraudster should not be placed in a better position than a seller answering restitutionary claims following the *Rücktritt* of the buyer. Had the restitutionary claim been based on §§ 346 ff, § 350 would have allocated the risk of accidental destruction to the seller, and this risk-allocation should be emulated by the law of unjust enrichment.

In BGHZ 57, 137 (14.10.1971), on the other hand, the buyer was solely to blame for the destruction of the car. He sought to rescind the contract because of the seller's fraudulent misrepresentation that the car had not been involved in any accidents. The *Bundesgerichtshof* again refused to apply the *Saldotheorie*, overruling the court below, which had only allowed the buyer to recover the difference in value between the actual car he bought and the car he thought he bought (that is, one that had not been involved in an accident). The main reason why the *Bundesgerichtshof* disagreed was that the seller was, in effect, a fraudster who did not deserve the protection of the law.[50] As a result, the buyer was allowed to drive the car at the seller's risk, because the seller had been fraudulent. The decision is generally criticised because it is inconsistent with § 351, and because fraudulent misrepresentation is not seen as a sufficient reason to deprive the fraudulent party of the benefit of the *Saldotheorie*.[51] These questions need not be discussed in detail. What is striking is that throughout the discussion it is generally assumed that the evaluations contained in §§ 350 ff are highly relevant. In effect, this can be seen as an acknowledgement that the functions of the law of *Rücktritt* and the law of unjust enrichment are identical, and that the question whether a contract has been avoided *ab initio* or merely terminated *de futuro* is of little restitutionary relevance. Again, the crucial

---

48 As Zimmermann points out, there is a general consensus 'that restitution under §§ 812 ff BGB should be governed by the same evaluations as restitution after termination of contract or *redhibition*': Zimmermann, 1997, pp 25 f.

49 BGHZ 53, 144 (8.1.1970); 57, 137 (14.10.1971); 72, 252 (26.10.1978); 78, 216 (9.10.1980).

50 BGHZ 57, 137 (14.10.1971), 148.

51 Reuter and Martinek, 1983, pp 608 ff.

question is therefore whether termination requires a different regime from rescission, which avoids the contract ab initio, so as to make way for the general law of unjust enrichment.

In some situations the innocent party will have a choice between rescission and termination, and it will not necessarily be clear from the words employed in calling off the contract which alternative he has chosen. Thus, in the case involving a misrepresentation by the seller that the car he wanted to sell had not been involved in an accident,[52] the buyer had a choice between rescinding the contract based on the fraudulent misrepresentation and termination on the ground of non-correspondence with description (under §§ 459 II, 462, 467 1). In the not unlikely event that the buyer is not an expert of German private law, he will be wholly unaware of the fact that there are these two possibilities to put an end to the contract. How his declaration (for example, 'You can keep your car!' or 'Here's your car back!') is to be construed will be almost impossible to determine, which again demonstrates that there is little difference in practice between restitution based on *Rücktritt* and restitution based on unjust enrichment. Zimmermann shares this view. He argues that 'it is rather difficult to see why different sets of restitution rules should be necessary for cases of termination and of rescission'.[53]

Conclusion

The rules provided by the law of *Rücktritt* for tackling problems of valuation of services (§ 346 2) and for distributing risks between the parties (§§ 350 ff) have been or are being overtaken by developments in the general law of unjust enrichment. While in the former case writers are struggling to extend § 818 II so as to give expression to the idea of subjective devaluation, the *Saldotheorie* has long since addressed many of the concerns which §§ 350 ff were based on. While it is still doubtful that subjective devaluation can be interpreted into § 818 II, and while the *Saldotheorie* is being heavily criticised, both developments demonstrate that the problems are identical for all cases involving the restitution of performances, and that therefore the need for separate contractual treatment becomes more questionable.

6.3.3 The juridical nature of *Rücktritt*

The remaining argument that needs to be answered is that there is a doctrinal difference between restitution following a contract that has been avoided and restitution following a terminated contract. In order to do this, it is first necessary to consider the nature and effect of *Rücktritt*. The English reader will find parts of the discussion familiar, and the parallels in the development of English law will be drawn in the next chapter.

Doctrinal development following the enactment of the Code

In the early years of the *BGB* it was generally thought that the *Rücktritt* of one party provided a permanent defence to a claim based on the contract and gave rise to new and

---

52 See above, p 103; BGHZ 57, 137 (14.10.1971).
53 Zimmermann, 1997, p 26.

independent restitutionary claims.[54] This 'indirect effect doctrine', mainly put forward by Crome and Dernburg, was based on structures in the *ius commune*, but did not survive for long. By 1904, Paul Oertmann felt justified in writing that, according to the general view, the exercise of a right of *Rücktritt* destroyed a contract *ab initio*.[55] His essay was most influential at the time, and deserves to be briefly examined.

Oertmann outlines three broad views that were being argued for in his day:

(1) the indirect effect doctrine as propounded by Crome and Dernburg;

(2) the 'rescission *ab initio*' view held by Oertmann himself;

(3) an intermediate view, holding that termination gives rise to restitutionary claims on the one hand, while freeing the parties of their contractual obligations for the future on the other. Hellwig[56] argued that termination would not destroy the transaction at all, the restitutionary claims were not based upon unjust enrichment but were, on the contrary, obligations based upon the contract itself.

Oertmann's main preoccupation was to attack the 'indirect effect' view held by Dernburg and Crome and he thus neglected slightly the intermediate theory put forward by Hellwig.

It is interesting that Oertmann admits freely that to prove or disprove any of these theories will be difficult if not impossible, given the second commission's deliberate choice to leave the matter open. His criticism of Dernburg and Crome's view, however, is convincing. He starts from the paradigm case of a contractually agreed termination clause. A mere defence against an action on the contract could not have been intended by the parties. They clearly intended to have the *status quo ante* restored, to be freed from all future obligations. To achieve this end by giving them a mere defence is rightly seen as inadequate.[57] Such a limitation is not necessary. The first commission only argued for the indirect solution because it feared proprietary consequences. Oertmann gives short shrift to those fears: the destruction *ab initio* of the contract only gives rise to obligations to make restitution, it does not undo the whole transaction automatically, with the consequent re-vesting of property. Oertmann's arguments were widely accepted, Dernburg's and Crome's theories largely discredited.[58]

However, having established that termination affected the contract directly rather than indirectly, the question whether it would destroy the contract *ab initio* remained unanswered. The intermediate view, put forward by Hellwig, argued that, while affecting the contract directly, termination took effect '*ex nunc*' and not '*ex tunc*'. To Oertmann, however, the destruction of the contract *ab initio* ('*ex tunc*') is the only possible alternative to the view put forward by Dernburg, and thus he fails to give serious consideration to the intermediate position. Some 20 years later, the intermediate view gained new prominence and was given more secure theoretical foundations in Heinrich Stoll's doctoral dissertation.[59]

54　Cf Dernburg, 1915, § 107; Crome, 1902, § 174.

55　Oertmann, 1904, pp 65, 69.

56　Hellwig, 1900, pp 21 f.

57　Oertmann, 1904, p 71.

58　Cf Wunner, 1968, p 433.

59　Stoll, 1921.

The survival of the contract

A contract will give rise to primary (performance) and secondary remedial obligations (damages). Stoll builds on this insight, and includes the claim for restitution following the termination of a contract amongst the category of 'secondary obligations'. The contract can totally change its aspect, it may appear in a wholly different form, but it is still the same contract.[60] The damages claim is based on the contract, and so is the claim for restitution under § 346. The reciprocal claims of the parties are redirected – what used to be rights to performance are turned into rights to restitution. These are not based on the destruction of the contract's 'juridical cause', but on the contract itself. To Stoll, therefore, the restitutionary regime consequent upon *Rücktritt* is as much part of the remedial machinery as any claim for damages.

As was pointed out above,[61] one important argument supporting this view is that under § 346 2 the contract continues to rule the relationship between the parties even though it has been terminated. Given that the *BGB* normally fails to take subjective devaluation considerations into account, this might indeed indicate that the contract must be taken to have survived. The counter-argument adopted above, however, holds that subjective devaluation arguments were seen as more important in the contractual context, at least where the valuation of services was concerned.[62] Nevertheless, it should be pointed out that Stoll can derive considerable support for his argument from § 346 2.

One important consequence of this view of the law of *Rücktritt* is that secondary duties under the contract will survive its termination. While damages for non-performance are excluded where *Rücktritt* has been declared (§ 325 I as well as all other sections giving the option to declare *Rücktritt* present the victim of a breach with the clear alternative between *Rücktritt* and damages), accrued damages for breaches of secondary duties can still be claimed.[63] Clauses in the contract designed to regulate the duties of the parties vis à vis each other remain in force,[64] and this will include arbitration as well as choice of forum clauses.

An example: S has delivered cattle feed of inferior quality to F, whose cattle have perished as a result of eating it. F withdraws from the contract, yet he will still be able to base his claim for compensation on S's positive breach of contract ('positive *Ver-trags-ver-letz-ung*') and will not have to rely on any wrong committed by S.

Equally, if the breach consists of late delivery, any damages flowing from that breach (and recoverable under § 286 I) can still be liquidated by the buyer.[65]

Modern opinions

Although Stoll's theory gathered support only slowly, today it can be said to represent the predominant academic view. The courts, however, have been reluctant to accept it. To put

---

60   *Ibid*, pp 21 ff.
61   See above, pp 94 ff.
62   Cf above, p 94.
63   Leser, 1975, p 164.
64   Jauernig/Vollkommer, § 346, No 4(a).
65   BGHZ 88, 46 (24.6.1983).

it at its highest, the courts have now taken up a neutral position. A relatively recent case[66] decided by the *Bundesgerichtshof* concerned the following fact situation: on 15 January 1980 the claimants had sold a flat to the defendants, who were to pay the purchase price of DM 70,000 by 29 February and were to go into possession the following day. The defendants also undertook to pay the ground rent from the day the contract was concluded to the day of completion. While the defendants paid the ground rent, albeit with some delay, they never paid the DM 70,000, until, in September 1980, the claimants terminated the contract under §§ 326 and 346. When the claimants claimed their costs and interest for late payment, they were met with the argument that the termination had destroyed not only primary, but also secondary obligations, such as the payment of damages for late payment and costs incurred in connection with the contract. Although the court expressly and repeatedly reserves its position as to the juridical nature of the claims arising under § 346, the defendants' argument was rejected by the *Bundesgerichtshof*. The defendants had to compensate the claimants for all costs arising from their late payment. While the termination had put an end to the parties' primary duties, this was not the case as far as secondary duties were concerned. It is difficult to see, however, how this result could be reached if the court continued to accept the old view as put forward by Oertmann in 1904. One way has been suggested by Canaris, who argues that secondary obligations might be derived from an independent duty of care, which parties contemplating contractual relations owe to each other.[67] The court further refers to a judgment by the *Reichsgericht*, which expressly subscribed to Oertmann's view, but nevertheless held that the claimants were entitled to damages for late delivery.[68]

If secondary obligations survive on either view, it is understandable that the court refuses to come down one way or another, as the dispute can have very little practical impact. This is also observed by Brox in a leading student text-book,[69] who writes: 'The legislator has left the question open; it need not be decided here; both views lead to identical results.'

For our purposes, however, the question is of some importance. The ascending view suggests that the restitutionary claims following termination of contract are based on the original contract, and not on the law of unjust enrichment; indeed, it suggests that the bases of the two claims are wholly different – that the reasons for restitution are different. The discussion, however, has become so abstract that nobody takes the trouble expressly to spell out these reasons for restitution. It is suggested that once one does this it becomes clear that they are identical in both cases: an exchange relationship has failed. Benefits have been transferred in order to obtain counter-performances which have failed. Restitution follows, in the final analysis, for this reason. There is very little room for differentiation.

This view is supported by von Caemmerer. He regards the claims under § 346 as modified enrichment claims. In other words, the post-*Rücktritt* regime is nothing but a specialised application of the general law of unjust enrichment. In laying down the structure for the modern law of unjust enrichment, he points out that the most important

---

66 *Ibid.*
67 Canaris, 1965, p 475.
68 RGZ 94, 203 (6.12.1918), 206.
69 Brox, 1993a, p 121.

enrichment claim, the *Leistungskondiktion*, which lies in situations where performances have failed, is in the same category as other restitutionary claims arising in the law of obligations. Thus, in the context of debt, loan, hire, bailment, *Rücktritt* and *Wandelung*, if the restitutionary claims were not provided for by special rules, they would simply be cases of the *condictio causa finita*.[70] He goes on to say that the fact that these claims are provided for separately does not indicate a fundamental difference to enrichment law, but is merely due to the different measure of restitution which is thought appropriate in these different situations. It is clear that von Caemmerer supports a view which states that the juridical nature of a claim based on *Rücktritt* is identical to the nature of a claim in unjust enrichment. His argument comes down to this: the conceptual structure of the general law of unjust enrichment as fixed in the *BGB* has the effect of separating the formal from the factual reasons for restitution. The factual reasons for restitution thus lie outside the law of unjust enrichment. Restitution follows for factual reasons, such as duress, mistake etc. It is only as a matter of legal technique that 'the law separates the inquiries'[71] and makes restitution immediately dependent on the absence of a 'legal cause'. We will return below to what the law is thought to mean by this phrase. It is sufficient for the moment that von Caemmerer clearly regards the nature of the claims under discussion as being substantially identical. The reason for restitution in each case is the failure of the expected counter-performance which would trigger a claim in the general law of unjust enrichment, but for the fact that §§ 346 ff are *leges speciales*.

Zimmermann goes further: '... this proposition [that the contract is void in one case and transformed in the other] is based neither on logic nor statutory authority. It is not intrinsically more convincing than the view maintained for many years after the enactment of the German Civil Code: namely that termination terminates the contract and renders applicable the law of unjustified enrichment.'[72] However, the effect of the original approach was, as we have seen, that 'there would no longer be a doctrinal basis for (contractual!) claims for damages arising from the infringement of an ancillary duty'.' Against this, Zimmermann argues, that 'it is not ... obvious why delictual protection should not be sufficient for these situations. Also, one could apply the rules relating to *culpa in contrahendo*'.[73] It may not be obvious why delictual protection should not be sufficient, but on reflection it will be appreciated that there are strong reasons for basing the relevant ancillary duties on the contract rather than the general law of delict. For one thing, certain kinds of loss, most prominently pure economic loss, will not be recoverable in delict, while there is nothing to prevent recovery if it is based on contract.[74]

There is, it is suggested, nothing to stop the law of unjust enrichment from applying in a situation in which a contract survives, albeit in modified form, as long as the contract itself is not opposed to the restitutionary claim, in other words, as long as the bargain between the parties is not undermined by restitution. This will, however, only hold true

---

70 von Caemmerer, 1954, p 342.

71 *Ibid*, p 343.

72 Zimmermann, 1997, p 26.

73 *Ibid*, p 18.

74 German law here suffers from the lack of a general concept of 'breach' of contract. An English lawyer would not need to turn to tort, given the 'wrong' of breach of contract. German law, in contrast, has had to develop devices such as *culpa in contrahendo* to fill the gap.

as long as the law of unjust enrichment is not based on the absence of an underlying obligation (which a terminated contract would represent), but on the purpose of the transfer.

Rücktritt *and damages*

It was briefly mentioned above that the *BGB* presents the innocent party with a choice: he can either terminate the contract under § 346 or ask for expectation damages.[75] Following Stoll's work on the subject, and this is where its true importance lies, it is now generally accepted that damages that have accrued before *Rücktritt* is declared are recoverable, as long as they are not aimed at the expectation interest. Thus damages for positive violation of the contract (that is, loss suffered as a result of the defendant's bad performance), damages for late performance and reliance damages remain recoverable in spite of *Rücktritt* having been declared.[76] German law assumes, however, that restitution and expectation interests are incompatible. Whether this assumption is well founded will now briefly be discussed, as such a discussion may provide valuable insights into the relationship between contract (normally aimed at fulfilling expectations) and unjust enrichment (aimed at restitution of benefits received).

By presenting the innocent party with the choice between restitution and damages, the practical importance of *Rücktritt* is in effect limited to two situations:

(1) If he asked for damages, the innocent party would have to prove his expectation loss, which may not always be easy. In such a case, half a loaf is better than no bread, and he will prefer to terminate the contract and recover his own performance rather than his reliance or even his expectation interest.

(2) The innocent party has made a bad bargain and has now spotted his chance to get out of it by asking for restitution. In these cases the restitution interest *exceeds* the expectation interest, and will therefore be the preferred measure of recovery.

There is the possibility that the innocent party may wish to recover his own performance because it is recoverable *in specie*. He may expect it to go up in value, or it may be of particular value to him. Nevertheless, he may not wish to forego the benefit of his bargain, and ask for damages alongside restitution. This course of action is not open to him, at least not under the regime laid down by the *BGB*.

The view that *Rücktritt* and damages, restitution and expectation interests are mutually exclusive does, of course, have a certain superficial attraction, in particular if one adopts the original view of the second drafting commission that *Rücktritt* destroys the contract *ab initio*. In these circumstances, there is no longer any basis for a claim in damages. However, as we have seen, this view is now largely discredited.

A second argument for the rule might run as follows: the innocent party has only acquired his expectation interest by investing his own performance. Why should he retain his right to expectation damages and at the same time recover his own stake? This objection is largely based on the concern to avoid double recovery. However, the problem is not insurmountable. It is quite possible to allow the innocent party to terminate, while

---

75 See above, p 24.
76 MünchKomm/Janßen, before § 346, Nos 31 ff.

reducing his claim to damages by the objective value of the benefit he seeks to recover. At the moment this is probably not to be reconciled with the wording of the code, but in principle it is difficult to see any objection to this solution.[77] This view finds some support in the Uniform Law of International Sale of Goods (ULIS), and the United Nations Convention on Contracts for the International Sale of Goods ('The Vienna Convention'). The Vienna Convention replaced ULIS in Germany on 1 January 1991. Both conventions allow damages and termination to be combined.[78] Both conventions are hailed as superior to the law of sales as contained in the *BGB*, and parts of ULIS are to serve as a blueprint for a reform of the German law of obligations.[79]

The practical question which faces the claimant is at what point he will be bound by his election. As long as both remedies are available to him, he would, in a perfect world, be able simply to choose the more advantageous one. Problems arise because it will not always be clear which remedy is more advantageous. Nevertheless, the courts do assume that as soon as *Rücktritt* is declared, the contract has been irrevocably transformed and damages and other remedies become unavailable forthwith.[80] The general academic view is opposed to this all or nothing approach adopted by the courts. To hold the claimant to a choice once made might well lead to inequitable results, for example, in situations in which it was impossible to assess the full expectation loss in advance. The view which is put forward, therefore, is that the claimant should only be held to his election once final settlement or satisfaction has been reached, and as long as, in the individual case, it would not be inequitable (that is, inconsistent with the general principle of good faith in § 242) to allow the claimant to choose a different remedy than the one he has chosen.[81]

6.4 CONCLUSION

This chapter examined the area of German law concerned restitutionary claims following the termination of a contract (§§ 346 ff). This is said to be strictly separate from the law of unjust enrichment. The discussion led to the conclusion, however, that the claim under § 346, arising from the termination of a contract, is nothing more than a modified enrichment claim. The following arguments are in favour of this view:

(1) The underlying reasons for restitution are identical to those under § 812 I.

(2) At the time the *BGB* was drafted, the generally accepted view was that Rücktritt would destroy the contract *ab initio*, which on any view would have triggered liability under § 812 I.

---

77 Leser, who is one of the few writers who seeks to give reasons for the rule, is largely critical of the exclusivity of *Rücktritt*, but does, in the end, support it as far as the expectation interest is concerned. His objection to a cumulation of remedies is as follows: the innocent party has chosen to opt for the simpler and quicker remedy, and he should now be confined to it: Leser, 1975, p 148.

78 ULIS, Arts 24, 41, 55, 63; Vienna Convention, Art 81.

79 See generally Bundesminister der Justiz, 1992.

80 BGH NJW 1979, 762 (17.1.1979); BGH NJW 1982, 1279 (10.2.1982). Also RGZ 85, 280 (23.9.1914), 282.

81 MünchKomm/Emmerich, § 325 No 21. This approach is surprisingly similar to that adopted by the Privy Council in the recent case of *Tang Man Sit v Capacious Investments* [1996] 1 All ER 193, as to which see below, p 135.

(3) The fundamentally sound argument that the contract (and the secondary duties thereunder) survives termination does not exclude the possibility of a restitutionary claim based on unjust enrichment. Under the modern view, restitution of failed performances follows because the purpose of the performance has failed. There is thus no reason to think that the survival of the contract in the way described by Stoll would exclude a claim in unjust enrichment.

(4) The measure of recovery in unjust enrichment has, in the context of failed contracts, moved very much in the direction of §§ 347 ff. The only difference between liability under § 346 and § 812 lies in § 350, which, as we have seen, is widely criticised. Any argument holding that the juridical natures of the two claims are radically different must thus be abstract, doctrinal and theoretical.

(5) Indeed, it is to be doubted that it would have been necessary to make special provision for the restitutionary consequences of the termination of a contract, if the importance of reciprocal performances had been realised sooner in the law of unjust enrichment. It would be quite possible to leave the consequences of termination to the law of unjust enrichment, while laying down clear rules in the law of contract in what circumstances termination would be possible.

FAILURE OF CONSIDERATION IN CONTRACTUAL CASES IN ENGLAND

7.1 INTRODUCTION

In the previous chapter, we examined the reasons which led the drafters of the *BGB* to provide separately for the restitutionary consequences of a breach of contract. In this chapter, we return to English law, asking very much the same questions. Hobhouse J took the view in the *Westdeutsche* case[1] that the phrase 'failure of consideration' always implied that there had at some stage been a valid contract, that it was in effect a 'contractual principle'. Are there any reasons to support this view? What is the relationship between the law of contract and the law of unjust enrichment in English law? Is there any need to keep them separate, so as to avoid the latter undermining the former?

In Chapter 9 we will turn to the operation of failure of consideration in non-contractual cases. As we shall see there, authority for the proposition that this cause of action does operate outside contract is still hard to find. On principle, however, the argument that failure of consideration extends beyond the contractual context is very strong. If there is a reluctance to see it as a broad concept, the difficulty stems from the confusion caused by the different meanings which the term 'consideration' bears in contract and unjust enrichment.[2]

The question which must be asked is whether the law of failure of consideration can apply to cases of extra-contractual failure of basis, for instance to cases in which money is paid in anticipation of a marriage which never happens, or a deposit made subject to a contract which is then never concluded. Burrows approaches the problem by treating the failure of a 'bargained-for counter performance'[3] as a matter 'that is primarily in mind' when discussing failure of consideration. While he acknowledges that Birks's broad approach, taking failure of consideration to mean 'failure of basis', is correct, he nonetheless asserts that:

> ... it is indisputable that the non-promissory meaning is much less familiar. It has rarely featured in the case law. To avoid needless confusion this book treats 'failure of consideration' and 'failure of promised performance' as synonymous subject to rare instances where the contrary is stated.[4]

While he recognises that 'failure of an unpromised future event' should be an unjust factor in the law of restitution, he treats it, to a certain extent, as separate from failure of consideration. While this approach evades the confusion based on the ambiguity of 'consideration', it takes us back to the question whether contractual cases merit special treatment. By restricting failure of consideration to contractual cases, leaving other cases

---

1   *Westdeutsche Landesbank Girozentrale v Islington London Borough Council Council; Kleinwort Benson Ltd v Sandwell Borough Council* [1994] 4 All ER 890.

1   *Westdeutsche Landesbank Girozentrale v Islington London Borough Council Council; Kleinwort Benson Ltd v Sandwell Borough Council* [1994] 4 All ER 890.

2   Cf pp 4 f, above.

3   Burrows, 1993a, p 251.

4   *Ibid*, pp 252 ff.

of failure of basis, so to speak, 'out in the cold', Burrows does not, it is suggested, clarify matters, but, on the contrary, he compounds the already considerable confusion.

The problems that can arise can be demonstrated by reference to McHugh J's judgment in a recent Australian case, *The Mikhail Lermontov*.[5] The case concerned a passenger's claim against the owner of a cruise ship which had sunk off New Zealand. She claimed restitution of her full fare on the grounds of failure of consideration. McHugh J, perhaps influenced by Burrows's approach, distinguished between two grounds of recovery, namely failure of consideration and failure of condition. The first was to be confined to contractual payments. It could not help Mrs Dillon because, according to the unanimous view of the court, there had been no 'total' failure because she had enjoyed part of the cruise.[6] McHugh J then went on to explain a number of cases in which restitution had apparently been granted even though the claimant had enjoyed some benefit, such as *Rowland v Divall*[7] and *Butterworth v Kingsway Motors*.[8] In both these cases the claimant had had the use of a car for some time, but when it turned out that the seller had not been able to pass good title, or that the car was so defective that the claimant could reject it, the claimant was entitled to claim restitution of his purchase money, notwithstanding the fact that the failure of consideration the claimant had suffered had not been strictly 'total' in the sense that he had obtained no benefit at all. McHugh J explains these cases on the ground that the sellers 'cannot retain the purchase moneys because their retention is conditional upon the vendor making good his or her promise to transfer the title of the vehicle to the purchaser'.[9] McHugh J thus purports to identify a whole new category of restitutionary claims based on the conditionality of a contractual payment. In attempting to resolve the semantic tension inherent in the phrase 'failure of consideration', he thus seems to suggest that there are two distinct causes of action, one which uses the word 'consideration' and one which expresses the idea of failure of basis in the language of conditionality.

On the one hand it is relatively easy to see the tendency to confine failure of consideration to the contractual context as a semantic accident. On the other the common law often proceeds on the assumption that its accidents express an intuition as to an underlying necessity. What seems to be an error or unreason can turn out to be sound sense. Is that the case here? Is there in reality some good reason why failure of contractual reciprocation should be separated and equipped with its own regime? I shall consider two arguments in favour of that separation. The first is based on the danger, already encountered in the previous chapter, that the law of restitution might not be able to take account of the fact that in a contractual case we are dealing with benefits which pass both ways. As we have seen in German law, there is a strong argument that this reciprocity should be reflected in making restitutionary awards, in particular when it comes to

---

5   (1992–93) 176 CLR 344.

6   It should be noted that she had already received a *pro rata* refund of the fare by way of a voluntary payment to all passengers – she went to Court claiming the whole fare. She had thus already received restitution for partial failure of consideration, but was claiming that, because of the disastrous end of the voyage, the benefit she had received had been negated and she had in fact suffered a total failure – hence to Court's preoccupation with the 'total' failure problem. As to that problem, see below, pp 117 ff.

7   [1923] 2 KB 500.

8   [1954] 1 WLR 1286.

9   *Baltic Shipping Co v Dillon 'The Mikhail Lermontov'* (1992–93) 76 CLR 344, 389.

applying the new defence of change of position. This, we have seen, was the main reason why the *BGB* chose to treat contractual claims differently from non-contractual ones.

The second is based on the fear that enrichment law might undermine the law of contract. Again, the problems are similar to those encountered in German law: does the terminated contract survive or is it destroyed *ab initio*? If the former, should its continued existence block a restitutionary claim, and, if so, why? It should be emphasised even at this stage that on any view restitution on the basis of failure of consideration will only be allowed where any contract between the parties has been discharged.[10] However, this does not mean that the contract must be rescinded *ab initio* before restitution can follow. That was the mistake in *Chandler v Webster*,[11] which could only be corrected almost half a century later in the *Fibrosa*[12] decision. Given that the contract survives, although it has been discharged *de futuro*, the question will be to what extent it should continue to govern the relationship between the parties, and what impact it should have on their restitutionary liabilities.

Both these problems have in the past been suppressed because of the operation of the 'total failure' requirement. Problems of counter-restitution and change of position did not even arise because, if there had been reciprocal payments, there would be no restitution at all. Whether this was a just solution is a different question, but it certainly simplified things. As to the second fear, one of the arguments relied upon to support the requirement has been that it served to avoid conflict between the law of unjust enrichment and the law of contract. This possible conflict could be one argument for a distinct treatment of cases involving contracts. As Birks points out, however, the 'total failure' requirement never really addressed this problem: 'The most that could be said would be that the requirement of total failure served as a blunt instrument to reduce the incidence of conflict between the two causes of action.'[13] The 'primacy of contract' argument has therefore rarely been addressed independently.

7.2 THE RECIPROCITY OF CONTRACTUAL PERFORMANCES AND 'TOTAL FAILURE'

In *Westdeutsche Landesbank v Islington*,[14] Hobhouse J, having pointed out that he did not believe failure of consideration to apply at all in non-contractual cases, went on to say that in the case before him there could be no question of recovery on that basis because the failure had not been total:

> If the opposite party has at least partially performed his obligations under the contract so as to confer some benefit upon the plaintiff, then the plaintiff cannot rely upon the principle.[15]

---

10 Cf Friedmann, 1991, p 247.
11 [1904] 1 KB 493.
12 [1943] AC 32.
13 Birks, 1996c, pp 179, 189.
14 [1994] 4 All ER 890.
15 *Ibid*, at 925.

The principle that a failure of consideration must be total is of respectable antiquity.[16] In *Whincup v Hughes*[17] the claimant had apprenticed his son to a watchmaker for six years, and had paid a premium of £25 in respect of board and lodging as well as instruction in the art of making watches. The watchmaker died after less than a year. The claimant sought to recover part of the premium from the executrix and failed. While the death of the master frustrated the contract, the failure of consideration was only partial, and in the words of Bovill CJ, 'where a contract has been in part performed no part of the money paid under such contract can be recovered back'.[18]

The 'total failure' requirement has long been subjected to severe academic criticism.[19] First, it has been argued that the moral case for restitution is just as strong where the consideration has partially failed as where it has totally failed: in both cases the claimant qualified his giving by specifying a basis for the transfer, and in both cases that basis has failed, thus rendering the defendant's enrichment unjust.[20]

Moreover, the courts have reacted against this element of arbitrariness by watering down the requirement by not taking 'total' literally.[21] Thus, in *Rowland v Divall*,[22] the claimant had bought a car from the defendant which turned out to be stolen property. He recovered from the defendant the price he had paid on the ground of total failure of consideration, even though he had received a perfectly good car and was able to use it for two months. He succeeded on the narrow ground that he had not received title to the car, and since title was what he wanted and what he had paid for, there had been a total failure of consideration.[23]

The third argument put forward concerns the increasing incoherence of the law in this area, with different results being reached depending either on the type of benefit conferred on the defendant (the 'total failure' requirement has never applied to *quantum meruit* and *quantum valebat* claims, but only to claims for the recovery of money),[24] or on the label attached to the action brought by the claimant. Thus, in the sale of goods, in the context of the rejection of unmerchantable (or unsatisfactory) goods, the requirement has never caused any problems: the buyer is given the remedy of rejection, and as long as that

---

16 Cf *Cutter v Powell* (1795) 6 Term Rep 320, 101 ER 573; *Hunt v Silk* (1804) 5 East 449, 102 ER 1142.

17 (1871) LR 6 CP 78.

18 *Ibid*, at 81.

19 Cf Burrows, 1993a, pp 259 ff; Birks, 1989, p 242; Birks, 1996c, p 177. It was a 'major disappointment' (Burrows) that the Law Commission came down on the other side of the argument, deciding not to endorse its provisional recommendation to scrap the requirement: 'Pecuniary Restitution on Breach of Contract', Report No 121 (1983).

20 Burrows, 1993a, p 260.

21 Birks, 1996c, p 198; Burrows, 1993a, p 260.

22 [1923] 2 KB 500.

23 Cf also *Rover International Ltd v Cannon Film Sales Ltd (No 3)* [1989] 1 WLR 912. The best example of manipulation of the 'total failure' requirement is arguably *DO Ferguson & Associates v Sohl*, obscurely reported in (1992) 62 BLR 95. In that case a building contract had been repudiated by the claimant builder. The defendant counter-claimed in restitution because it had paid for more work than had actually been carried out. It was successful in a claim based on 'total' failure of consideration, even though the majority of the work had been carried out and it had thus received a substantial benefit. Hirst LJ said that 'for the £4,673 there was indeed a total failure of consideration because £4,673 was paid by the defendant for which that was never done at all'. This all but abrogates the 'total failure' requirement.

24 Burrows, 1993a, p 260.

is still available to him he can bring about a total failure of consideration.[25] It is also clear in the sale of goods that a buyer who accepts short delivery having already paid is entitled to sue for the balance of the price as on a failure of consideration.[26] Similarly, where a contract is rescinded *ab initio*, the emphasis is not on total failure of consideration, but on the requirement that the claimant must make counter-restitution,[27] and where a contract is frustrated, restitution now follows, subject to counter-restitution, whether the claimant received part of what he bargained for or not.[28]

7.2.1 Total failure requirement and counter-restitution: a success story

It is interesting that Hobhouse J in *Westdeutsche*, while basing himself on 'absence of consideration' as a ground of recovery, goes on to set off payments made and received by the parties against each other, allowing the 'loser' to claim the balance. Thus, as under one swap Westdeutsche had paid Islington £2,500,000 while Islington had paid Westdeutsche merely £1,354,474.07, Hobhouse J ordered that Islington make restitution of the difference. Westdeutsche's claim in restitution was thus not for all it had paid, but took into account the counter-performance it had received from Islington.

If it is possible to set off the payments made by parties against each other, the consideration for the balance must have totally failed. In effect, it is possible to apportion payments in such a way as to create a 'total' failure. The Court of Appeal accepted this.[29] As we have seen, it is not quite clear whether the Court of Appeal decided the case on the ground of absence or failure of consideration. On balance, their Lordships seem to say that the decision can be explained on either ground. If that is correct, their Lordships must be taken to have accepted that partial failure of consideration is sufficient as long as counter-restitution is merely a matter of arithmetic.[30]

This next step was recently taken, albeit by the Privy Council, in *Goss v Chilcott*.[31] In that case a company director wished to borrow money from his own company. Being unable to do so himself (due to his office), he persuaded his brother-in-law, the defendant, to take out the loan and grant the company a mortgage over his business. The money, however, was paid directly to the director. Two interest payments were made before things went horribly wrong. The company went into liquidation, the director had no assets and the liquidator sought to enforce the loan agreement against the defendant. At the trial it emerged, however, that the mortgage deed had been altered by the company, which rendered it absolutely void.[32] The only viable basis for the claim against the

---

25   See *Rogers v Parish (Scarborough) Ltd* [1987] QB 933; Birks, 1996c, p 198.
26   *Biggerstaff v Rowatt's Wharf Ltd* [1896] 2 Ch 93; *Behrend & Co Ltd v Produce Brokers Co* [1920] 3 KB 530; *Ebrahim Dawood Ltd v Heath Ltd* [1961] 2 Lloyd's Rep 512.
27   Cf Burrows, 1993a, p 32.
28   Law Reform (Frustrated Contracts) Act 1943. The Act, by s 2(5), does not apply to contracts for the carriage of goods by sea, many charterparties, insurance contracts and in the sale of goods where the goods have perished, bringing into play s 7 of the Sale of Goods Act 1979. It is not clear why these exclusions were considered necessary.
29   *Westdeutsche* [1994] 4 All ER 890, 958, *per* Dillon LJ.
30   See, also, Birks, 1996c, p 184.
31   [1996] 3 WLR 180.
32   *Pigot's case* (1614) 11 Co Rep 266, 77 ER 1177.

defendant was therefore in restitution, for money paid on a failure of consideration. At first instance it had been held that the claim in restitution failed because there had been consideration for the advance in the form of a valid mortgage. The New Zealand Court of Appeal had allowed the claimant's appeal, holding that the invalidity of the mortgage instrument did not preclude him from relying on the advance itself and the agreement to repay it in three months, which gave rise to a debt independent of the mortgage instrument. The Privy Council, however, was clear that the latter argument was not sustainable, as the original oral agreement had become merged in the mortgage instrument and could therefore no longer be relied upon, given the latter's invalidity. The Judicial Committee also disagreed with the judge at first instance that the mortgage instrument had furnished consideration for the loan. The only factor that stood in the way of recovery for 'total' failure of consideration was that the defendants had paid two instalments of interest. Did this preclude recovery?

Lord Goff, giving the advice of the Privy Council, thought not: '... since no part of the capital sum had been repaid, the failure of consideration for the capital sum would plainly have been total,'[33] and it was 'both legitimate and appropriate' to consider separately interest payments, whose function it was 'to pay for the use of the capital sum' and the repayment of the capital sum.[34] However, it was not even necessary to do so, as 'even if part of the capital sum had been repaid, the law would not hesitate to hold that the balance of the loan outstanding would be recoverable on the ground of failure of consideration, *for at least in those cases in which apportionment can be carried out without difficulty, the law will allow partial recovery on this ground*' (emphasis added).[35] His Lordship referred to *Westdeutsche* to demonstrate that, where both parties have restitutionary claims against each other, 'judgment would, in the event, be given for the balance'.[36]

The advice has since been commented on in two notes, one by John Carter and GJ Tolhurst,[37] one by Charles Rickett.[38] Neither note appears to appreciate the full significance of the case. Rickett devotes much space to the question whether the Privy Council was right to hold that there could be no remedy in contract because the underlying contract of debt had become merged in the (void) mortgage instrument. As to the claim in restitution, Lord Goff's emphasis on apportionment 'may open up the prospect of a shift from total failure to substantial failure of consideration'.[39] It is submitted that such a shift would be most unwelcome. It would introduce those problems into the law of restitution that the law of contract has encountered in the context of substantial performance. Where is the cut-off point to be? The injustice of denying restitution to one claimant where he has only received marginally more than another, which is the main criticism that can be levelled at the total failure requirement, would merely be shifted back a little if the law were to adopt a substantial failure requirement. The law of restitution would have jumped out of the fire into the frying pan.

---

33 *Goss v Chilcott* [1996] 3 WLR 180, 188.
34 *Ibid*, at 187 ff.
35 *Ibid*, at 188.
36 *Ibid*; reliance was also placed on *David Securities Pty Ltd v Commonwealth Bank of Australia* (1992) 175 CLR 353, 385.
37 Carter and Tolhurst, 1997, p 162.
38 Rickett, CEF, 1996, p 263.
39 *Ibid*, p 265.

Carter and Tolhurst give a careful account of the facts of *Goss v Chilcott*. Their discussion of the case concentrates, however, mainly on the impact of *Pigot's case*[40] and the relationship between contract and restitution as expressed in *Fibrosa v Fairbairn*,[41] putting it into historical context and suggesting that 'failure of consideration was, as a concept, as much contract as restitution'.[42] While these are important arguments, and while it is true that *Goss v Chilcott* confirms the line taken in *Fibrosa* that enrichment claims are independent of contract, the true importance of the case is not discussed until the conclusion. The authors refer, as does Lord Goff, to a passage in *David Securities* where Their Honours had said that 'where consideration can be apportioned or where counter-restitution is relatively simple, insistence on total failure of consideration can be misleading or confusing'.[43] In the view of the authors, the 'real importance of *Goss v Chilcott* lies in the willingness of the Privy Council to adopt the first of the two ways of relaxing the concept, namely, apportionment'.[44] Rickett argues, however, that apportionment may not always be so easy as it was in *Goss v Chilcott*, where the Privy Council was able to distinguish between capital repayments (of which none were made) and interest payments.[45] 'Apportionment' is here used to denote the divisibility of the contract into several 'sub-contracts'. Thus, in the case of a sale of goods, if S sells B 100 widgets, at £1 per widget, and B, having paid £100, receives only 50 widgets, the court will divide the contract into 100 contracts for the sale of one widget at a time, or into two contracts for the sale of 50 widgets. The result will be the same: while the 50 widgets that have been delivered have been paid for, there has been a total failure of consideration as far as the other half of the contract is concerned. As Birks remarks, 'the exercise of construction to discover an implied agreement to divide up the consideration is unlikely to be other than a difficult and obscure vehicle for manipulating the notion of divisibility.'[46] Apportionment has always been a convenient way for the courts to avoid the total failure requirement.[47] In some cases it is not quite so clear whether apportionment is indeed relied upon, or whether they are simply examples of recovery on the basis of a partial failure of consideration. Thus, in *Devaux v Conolly*[48] the buyers of goods recovered an overpayment on the basis of 'failure of consideration', with no mention of apportionment or the 'total failure' requirement anywhere in the judgment. Indeed, Counsel for the buyers had argued that this was 'a simple case of partial failure of consideration'.[49] That case was relied upon in *Behrend & Co Ltd v Produce Brokers Co*,[50] which can, it is submitted, only be explained as a case of partial failure of consideration. The buyers had entered into two contracts for the supply of cotton seed to be delivered in London. On the arrival of the ship the buyers paid for the goods, and some seed was

---

40 (1614) 11 Co Rep 266, 77 ER 1177.
41 [1943] AC 32.
42 Carter and Tolhurst, 1997, p 169.
43 *David Securities Pty Ltd v Commonwealth Bank of Australia* (1992) 175 CLR 353, 383, *per* Mason CJ, Deane, Toohey, Gaudron and McHugh JJ.
44 Carter and Tolhurst, 1997, p 170.
45 Rickett, 1996, p 265.
46 Birks, 1996c, p 199.
47 Cf *Biggerstaff v Rowatt's Wharf Ltd* [1896] 2 Ch 93.
48 *Devaux v Conolly* (1849) 8 CB 640, 137 ER 658.
49 *Ibid*, at 666 (CB).
50 *Behrend & Co Ltd v Produce Brokers Co* [1920] 3 KB 530.

discharged. Because of the way in which the goods had been stowed, the carrier was able to discharge only fifteen tons of one contractual parcel and 22 tons of the other. The remaining quantities were stowed under other cargo that had first to be discharged in Hull before the vessel returned to London two weeks later to discharge the balance of the contract goods. Prior to the vessel's return, the buyers notified the sellers that they would reject the balance of the goods under s 30 of the Sale of Goods Act 1893, and sought to recover their overpayment. The special twist of this case is that the buyers were only entitled to reject the balance of the goods if they could show that the contract did not provide for delivery by instalments (which would have triggered s 31 of the Sale of Goods Act 1893), in other words, that each contractual parcel was indivisible. In a short considered judgment, this was held to be the case by Bailhache J:

> ... in the absence of any stipulation to the contrary the buyer, being ready with his craft, is entitled to delivery of the whole of an indivisible parcel of goods sold to him for delivery from a vessel which has begun delivery to him before she leaves the port to deliver goods elsewhere.[51]

However, did this mean that the buyers could recover their overpayment? Bailhache J held that it did:

> If this is so the rest of the case is covered by s 30 of the Sale of Goods Act, and the buyer can either reject the whole of the goods, including those actually delivered, in which case he can recover the whole of his money; or he may keep the goods actually delivered and reject the rest, in which case he must pay for the goods kept at the contract price, and he can recover the price paid for the undelivered portion: see *Devaux v Conolly*.[52]

The case cannot be explained on the grounds of apportionment, as it involves an express finding that the contracts were indivisible. Michael Bridge, in his book on domestic sales, suggests that if the buyer accepts short delivery, this should be regarded as under a new contract, 'whether implied in fact or on a restitutionary basis'.[53] He resorts to this analysis because he cannot explain *Behrend v Produce Brokers* in any other way compliant with the 'total failure' requirement. His analysis thus becomes rather more complicated than it would have to be:

> ... the result is acceptable if the buyer's partial recovery of the price paid is seen as a recovery in full of the price paid under the original contract subject to a set-off of the lesser price owed to the seller for the goods accepted under the new contract.[54]

These attempts to revive the implied contract heresy must not be allowed to succeed. It can only be hoped that the view adopted in this book is widely accepted, and that *Goss v Chilcott* will not be explained away as an example of apportionment.

To return to our discussion of that case, Rickett's argument that apportionment in *Goss v Chilcott* was 'easy', is hard to sustain. It will often be difficult to decide whether a payment in respect of a loan was made as a capital repayment or as an interest payment. Moreover, the argument can be advanced that the payment of interest was itself the

---

51 *Ibid*, at 534 ff.
52 *Ibid*, at 535.
53 Bridge, 1997, p 227.
54 *Ibid*, p 228.

consideration for the loan, and thus part of the basis on which the money was advanced. *Goss v Chilcott* is far removed from the paradigm sales case, the construction exercise appears strained. It is this which leads Lord Goff to say that it would not have been necessary for the contract to have been divisible. Herein lies the true significance of the case. Lord Goff is willing to treat any repayment of principal as merely reducing the restitutionary claim. Technically, his remarks on this subject are obiter. It is suggested, however, that the case should, for the above reasons, nevertheless be treated as abandoning the total failure requirement.

7.2.2 Working out the implications of counter-restitution

The main argument that led to the fall of the 'total' requirement was that its work could be much better done by insisting on counter-restitution. A question that has remained open, however, is whether counter-restitution will be based on an independent restitutionary claim (itself based on failure of consideration),[55] or whether we are dealing with just one claim for the balance between restitution and counter-restitution. We have seen in our discussion of the German law on the subject that this question is not just one of semantics, and it is not just an interesting technical point of law. It may have repercussions for limitation periods, but most importantly it can affect the outcome of cases involving the new defence of change of position.[56]

If, in a case such as *Westdeutsche* itself, one party has, in reliance on receipt of the money, changed its position in good faith, it might seek to rely on the new defence. In such a case, would it be just to require the other party to make full restitution, given that it will not receive full counter-restitution? Does the requirement of counter-restitution in some way 'trump' the defence? An example may illustrate how the problem that led to the development of the *Saldotheorie* in German law might arise against the background of English law:[57]

> S is in financial difficulties. To restore his liquidity, he sells a virtually new crane (worth £82,000) to B for £75,000. After four months a cable snaps, the crane collapses and is seriously damaged. S goes into compulsory liquidation. The liquidator claims that the sale of the crane was a transaction at an undervalue and demands restitution of the crane. The value of the crane has been reduced by £25,000. There is no evidence that the crane was in any way of unsatisfactory quality. The user of the crane over four months is worth £5,000.

For present purposes we can assume that the restitutionary claim of the liquidator is a good one, and that accidental damage is taken into account when assessing the extent to which a defendant can rely on the defence of change of position.[58] If we take the view

---

55 This seems to be suggested by Burrows, 1993a, pp 133 ff.

56 This defence has now been recognised to be part of the English law of restitution: *Lipkin Gorman v Karpnale* [1991] 2 AC 548. It corresponds closely to the defence in § 818 III *BGB* (*'Wegfall der Bereicherung'*), although it is difficult to compare the two given the embryonic state of the English defence.

57 The fact situation is based on BGHZ 53, 144 (8.1.1970).

58 Birks now accepts this: see Birks, 1995, p 330. His argument is based on the protection of security of receipts, which would not be complete if accidental losses did not count for the defence of change of position. He also mentions that accidental loss is the paradigm case of *Wegfall der Bereicherung* under § 818 III *BGB*. See Chapter 15, below.

that we are dealing with two independent restitutionary claims (the liquidator's claim being policy-based, the buyer's claim being for failure of consideration), the following picture emerges:

The liquidator's claim for the value of the crane (originally £82,000) is met with the defence of change of position. The crane is now worth £57,000. The buyer thus has to pay £57,000 to the liquidator. In the alternative, he may give back the crane in its damaged condition. Further, he will have to make restitution of the value of the user (£5,000).

Having given back the crane, the buyer has in effect 'created' an *ex post* failure of consideration entitling him to restitution. He can therefore demand repayment of the full £75,000, and will be jolly grateful to the liquidator for bringing the claim under s 138 of the Insolvency Act 1976. The buyer will get full restitution, while the liquidator, due to the defence of change of position, will not.

It is hoped that the example demonstrates effectively that now the 'total failure' requirement is all but gone, the problem can quite possibly occur in English law, and that the above solution would be just as unpalatable here as it was to the *Reichsgericht* back in 1903. For one thing, it is clear that such a result would wholly undermine the policy of the bankruptcy laws. However, there would still be problems in non-bankruptcy situations, for example, where a contract of sale is terminated for some reason, or where it is vitiated by mistake or misrepresentation. The problem arises because the two performances were intrinsically linked. The claimant only delivered the crane because he would receive the purchase price; the defendant only paid the purchase price because he received the crane. Moreover, the normal rule in English sales law is that risk passes with property: s 20(1) of the Sale of Goods Act 1979. In German law, it passes with possession: § 446 *BGB*. To allow the one to avoid his restitutionary obligations by relying on change of position, while the other has to give up everything he received will thus lead to injustice

The requirement that a failure of consideration must be total avoided this problem. Having abandoned the 'bright line' of the 'total failure' requirement, we now need to face up to this problem, and the *Saldotheorie*[59] may assist us in doing so. In the above example, the buyer has only received the crane because he paid for it, and the seller has only received the payment because he made delivery of the crane. When things go wrong, it would thus be misconceived to disregard the factual link between the two.

In Germany, the *Saldotheorie* is applied only to cases in which a contract is avoided *ab initio*, and not to those contractual cases which are the subject matter of this chapter. We have seen that the special rules for contractual failure of consideration, part of the law of contract, specifically exclude the *Saldotheorie* in § 350, and this has sparked much criticism of the theory on the one hand, and of § 350 on the other. We have seen, however, that there is no convincing reason in German law why a single restitutionary regime should not apply to all cases of reciprocal performances. The only arguments, which are, of course, formidable ones in the context of German jurisprudence, are based on the wording and system of the *BGB*. English law, however, is not shackled by the words of a codification, and it is free to adapt to changes in other areas of the law. The step taken by Hobhouse J, in allowing a claim for restitution of the balance, is thus to be applauded, but

---

59 See above, pp 101 ff.

there is no need to confine it either to cases which he calls 'non-contractual', or to contractual cases.

7.3 THE RELATIONSHIP BETWEEN CONTRACT AND RESTITUTION

As was said at the beginning of this chapter, the total failure requirement was sometimes supported by arguing that to allow recovery for partial failure of consideration would undermine the law of contract in general and the allocation of risks by the parties in particular. It is clear that this argument was unsound. It could just as well be used to attack recovery on the ground of total failure. However, now that the total failure requirement has gone, it is possible to examine the argument on its own merits. This is particularly important now because, even though the contract must still be discharged before a restitutionary claim can be brought, the removal of the total failure requirement will lead to more instances of restitution for failure of consideration. If the restitutionary claim does subvert the law of contract, much more damage can be done now than before.[60]

The argument that restitution subverts the law of contract is based on the view that the two measures of recovery (expectation loss and restitution) achieve contradictory goals: the one moves the parties forward, fulfilling their expectations, the other returns them to the *status quo ante*; the one maintains the bargain, the other allows escape from a bad bargain. The counter-argument is that there can be no question of contradictory remedies, but that we are dealing with alternative and distinct causes of action. If different causes of action give different measures, so be it. Further, the restitutionary cause of action is only available once the contract has been discharged. So if the contract itself says that the risks are off, what objection can there be to giving free rein to a cause of action which is capable of reversing the contractual risks? This again can be answered by the objection that termination does not destroy the contract *ab initio*, but merely suspends the parties outstanding obligations *de futuro*.

These arguments have not been rehearsed to the same extent when we were discussing the German law, primarily for the simple reason that the law of contract itself provides for restitution, setting up its very own restitutionary regime. However, some of the problems have been encountered in the preceding chapter: the juridical nature of termination and its effect on the restitutionary claim in the general law of unjust enrichment,[61] the problem of valuing intangible benefits,[62] and the question whether a restitutionary award can be combined with an award of damages (above, pp 109 f).

In the following we will look at two ways in which contracts can be discharged in English law: frustration and breach. We will then ask the vital question whether it is or should be possible to combine a damages claim with a claim for restitution.

---

60 But, as was mentioned above, the total failure requirement had already been removed in relation to frustrated contracts by the Law Reform (Frustrated Contracts) Act 1943. The exclusion of important contract categories, including the sale of goods, in s 2(5) have meant that only one case has been reported under the 1943 Act: *BP Exploration Co (Libya) Ltd v Hunt (No 2)* [1983] 2 AC 352. The lifting of the requirement for cases of discharge by breach will thus be of great practical significance.

61 Above, pp 104 ff.

62 Above, pp 94 ff.

7.3.1 Contracts discharged by frustration

The obvious starting point is the infamous case of *Chandler v Webster*.[63] The claimant had rented a room in Pall Mall with the express purpose of viewing King Edward VI's coronation procession. He paid £100 up front, leaving a balance of £41 15s. The contract provided for the whole sum to be paid well in advance of the procession, and the claimant was thus technically in arrears. The King became ill, and the coronation was cancelled. The Court of Appeal not only dismissed the claimant's claim for the £100 he paid in advance, it also allowed the defendant's counterclaim and held that Chandler was liable to pay the balance as well. Their Lordships' judgments are incisive, eminently logical, and fundamentally flawed.

Collins MR deals with the counterclaim first. He places much emphasis on the fact that the full amount had become payable before the performance of the contract became impossible. The defendant thus had an accrued right to be paid, and that right survived the subsequent frustration of the contract. Frustration, says Collins MR, excuses the parties from further performance, each party bearing his own loss. It does not, however, upset accrued rights. All depended therefore on Chandler's main claim for restitution of money paid as on a total failure of consideration. After all, he had not received anything of what he had bargained for. However, Chandler's claim was rejected. Collins MR said:

> ... where, from causes outside the volition of the parties, something which was the basis of, or essential to the fulfilment of, the contract, has become impossible, so that, from the time when the fact of that impossibility has been ascertained, the contract can no further be performed by either party, it remains a perfectly good contract up to that point, and everything previously done in pursuance of it must be treated as rightly done, but the parties are both discharged from further performance of it. If the effect were that the contract were wiped out altogether, no doubt the result would be that money paid under it would have to be repaid as on a failure of consideration. But that is not the effect of the doctrine; it only releases the parties from further performance of the contract. Therefore the doctrine of failure of consideration does not apply.[64]

His Lordship thus effectively said that the coming into existence of a valid contract will once and for all exclude an action for unjust enrichment, or at least an action for restitution of money paid as on a total failure of consideration.

The rules of contract often appear to take precedence over the rules of enrichment law. Thus, if money has been paid under the influence of a causative mistake sufficient to satisfy the conditions laid down by Goff J in *Barclays Bank v Simms*,[65] restitution will only follow if the mistake is sufficiently fundamental to destroy the contract under which the money changed hands.[66] This rule ensures that the law of contract is not subverted by the law of unjust enrichment. As long as a contract is in place, it falls to that contract to allocate the risks between the parties. While the contract is fully effective (as it was shown to be, for instance, in *Bell v Lever Bros*), the law of restitution thus should have nothing to say. It is only when the contract is ineffective for some reason, in *Chandler v Webster*

---

63 [1904] 1 KB 493.
64 *Ibid*, at 499.
65 [1980] QB 677.
66 *Bell v Lever Brothers Ltd* [1932] AC 161; see above, pp 68 f, 71 f.

through frustration, that restitutionary questions may arise. Herein lies the fallacy of *Chandler v Webster*. The Court of Appeal, pointing out (rightly) that frustration does not 'wipe out' the contract completely, fails to consider whether it should leave the contractual allocation of risks intact.

In the *Fibrosa* case[67] the House of Lords overruled *Chandler v Webster*. The case involved a contract by which English suppliers were to deliver certain machinery to buyers in Poland. The buyers paid £1,000 in advance. The outbreak of the World War made delivery to Poland impossible, and the buyers asked for their money back. The House of Lords held that the buyers were entitled to restitution of the advance payment as money paid upon a consideration which had wholly failed.

Viscount Simon LC's speech contains two main criticisms of Collins MR's speech in *Chandler v Webster*. First, says his Lordship, the claim for restitution on the ground of failure of consideration is not based on the contract itself, but on the action of *assumpsit* for money had and received. That must be right. His Lordship's statement is particularly helpful in refuting Hobhouse J's view in *Westdeutsche* that there can be no recovery for failure of consideration outside of contract. However, as a criticism of Collins MR in *Chandler v Webster* it misses the point. While there is considerable discussion in *Chandler v Webster* as to what the terms of the contract were, Collins MR does not in fact say that an action for failure of consideration has to be founded on a term in the contract. As we have seen, his argument centred on the continued existence of the contract, which, as he rightly pointed out, had not been wiped out altogether by the frustrating event. As the contract survived, it had to govern and there was no room for an action for money had and received. A right to restitution had to be found in the terms of the contract or not at all.

The second criticism offered by Viscount Simon LC is directed at a misunderstanding: Collins MR had said that the doctrine of failure of consideration did not apply where the contract remained a perfectly good contract up to the date of frustration. To Viscount Simon LC, this suggests that Collins MR thought that where a contract is validly formed (that is, for good consideration), and is then not 'wiped out altogether', the consideration can never fail. However, Viscount Simon LC said:

> In English law, an enforceable contract may be formed by an exchange of a promise for a promise, or by the exchange of a promise for an act – I am excluding contracts under seal – and thus, in the law relating to the formation of contract, the promise to do a thing may often be the consideration; but, when one is considering the case of failure of consideration and of the quasi-contractual right to recover money on that ground, it is, generally speaking, not the promise which is referred to as the consideration, but the performance of the promise. The money was paid to secure performance and, if performance fails, the inducement which brought about the payment is not fulfilled.[68]

Again, this *dictum* is of fundamental importance. It is almost, but not quite, strong enough to provide a sound basis for challenge of Hobhouse J's view that there can be no failure of consideration outside contract at all. However, it is not quite a fair criticism of Collins MR in *Chandler v Webster*. His conclusion that failure of consideration cannot apply where the contract has not been fully wiped away, while possibly derived from the above

---

67 [1943] AC 32.
68 *Ibid*, at 48.

misunderstanding, might be based on the concern that restitution should not subvert the law of contract. As long as the contract remains in existence, the provisions of contract law should govern.

It is difficult to see, on the other hand, how restitution can undermine a contract that has been frustrated. By definition, the risk of a frustrating event happening has been left unallocated by the contract. That does not mean, however, that losses and benefits should now lie where they fall. On the contrary, what is required is a default rule combining the virtues of certainty and equity. The law of contract does not supply such a rule, but there is no reason why the general law (including the law of unjust enrichment) should not fill the gap. There is no rule of contract law that could thereby be subverted (unless the parties have expressly or impliedly contracted out of restitution). The existence of the (discharged) contract does not have any impact at all on the moral case for restitution, which is that the claimant has conferred a benefit on the defendant which he did not mean him to have as circumstances have turned out. *Chandler v Webster* was wrong not because it confused contract and unjust enrichment as categories, but because it upheld the primacy of contract without asking whether the imposition of enrichment liability was in any way likely to subvert a bargain.

More difficult questions arise where a contract has not been discharged by frustration, but by the breach of one of the parties. Discharge for breach is different from frustration because the law of contract does provide a remedy, and it is that remedy that might be in danger of being subverted by the alternative remedy in unjust enrichment.

7.3.2 Contracts discharged by breach

Where a contract is discharged by breach, the problem of a conflict between restitution and contract can become acute. This could be thought to be particularly so where the claimant is himself in breach of contract. This was the position in *Dies v British and International Mining*.[69] A buyer had paid in advance for arms which he no longer wanted. He was able to recover the prepayment. Does this undermine the law of contract? It is suggested that the difficulty here is more apparent than real. First, it is clear that there can be no question of restitution if the other party refuses to accept the repudiation of the contract. Secondly, where the contract has been discharged, the innocent party will have a claim in damages. That claim is to put him back in the position he would have been in had the contract been duly performed, but it may also exceed the value of the pre-payment or other advance performance. In that case damages are going to be reduced by way of set-off. If, however, the pre-payment is in excess of the innocent party's expectation interest, there is no reason why the contract breaker should not be able to recover the excess. In fact, the rules of contract law demand such a result. It is, of course, possible for the parties to agree that the pre-payment is to be regarded as a non-refundable deposit. Such a term will survive the discharge of the contract and the law of unjust enrichment will have nothing to say. Effectively, it will have been contracted out of.

The real problems arise where the claimant, as the innocent party, has made a losing bargain. If he obtains full restitution, does this undermine the law of contract? An

---

69 [1939] 1 KB 724.

examination of the law relating to reliance damages would suggest that there is a problem here. In *CCC Films v Impact Quadrant Films*,[70] for instance, Hutchison J held that where a party chose to claim reliance rather than expectation damages following a breach of contract, that choice was unfettered unless the contract breaker could prove that the innocent party had in fact made a losing bargain. Although this rule makes things considerably easier for the innocent party by shifting the burden of proof to the defendant, the general rule that contract damages are to put the innocent party in the position it would have been in had the contract been performed is upheld. The question is, therefore, whether similar considerations should apply to restitutionary claims, given that restitutionary damages may often be co-extensive with reliance damages.

The paradigm case is the US case of *Bush v Canfield*.[71] The claimant contracted to buy 2,000 barrels of flour at $7 a barrel. He paid $5,000 upfront. The price of flour dropped to $5.50 at the time of delivery, yet, inexplicably, the defendant failed to deliver the flour. Had the contract been performed, the claimant would have made a loss of $3,000. Had he sued for expectation damages, therefore, he could have recovered $2,000. The buyer brought an action on the case for the breach and not in *indebitatus assumpsit*, that is, in contract rather than in unjust enrichment. The court, Hosmer J dissenting, allowed the buyer to recover the full amount of his payment, $5,000, notwithstanding the seller's objection that recovery should be reduced by the buyer's loss: 'The defendant has violated his contract; and it is not for him to say that if he had fulfilled it, the plaintiffs would have sustained a great loss, and that this ought to be deducted from the money advanced.'[72] Hosmer J, dissenting, took the view that the buyer would only have recovered had he framed his action in *indebitatus assumpsit*.

Another important US decision is *Boomer v Muir*.[73] In that case a dispute arose between a subcontractor and a main contractor on a hydroelectric dam project. The main contractor had failed to deliver certain materials and the subcontractor walked away from the site. The jury found that he had been entitled to do so, as the main contractor had been in breach. The subcontractor sought restitutionary, not compensatory damages. This led to the strange result that he was awarded the market value of his performance on a quantum meruit, $258,000, even though the balance due under the contract for full performance by the subcontractor would have been only $20,000.

The only difference between these two cases is that *Bush v Canfield* involved a contract of sale, whereas *Boomer v Muir* involved a construction contract. In *Bush v Canfield* the claimant asked for his money back, while in *Boomer v Muir* the claimant asked for the value of his services. This distinction is traditionally of importance in the law of restitution: failure of consideration is traditionally only available to recover money paid; to recover the value of goods and services the appropriate action is a *quantum valebat* or a *quantum meruit* respectively.[74] This distinction is the legacy of the common counts, and writers in the law of restitution are almost unanimous that the ground for restitution

---

70 [1985] QB 16.
71 (1818) 2 Conn 485.
72 *Ibid*, at 488.
73 24 P 2d 570 (1933).
74 Cf Goff and Jones, 1998, pp 517 f.

should be the same, that is, failure of consideration.[75] However, as Goff and Jones are careful to point out, only the House of Lords is free to adopt these proposals.[76]

Nevertheless, the distinction will always retain some importance because services received can be subjectively devalued. If the market value of the service is greater than the contract price, the defendant can use the subjective devaluation argument to limit his restitutionary liability to the contract price. The 'contract ceiling' is replaced with a 'valuation ceiling'. On this analysis, *Bush v Canfield* is right while *Boomer v Muir* is wrong.[77] The contract price is used as an indicator of the value the defendant subjectively ascribes to the benefit he received. The subjective devaluation argument can only apply to services and to goods that are not readily or not any longer realisable by the defendant. Thus the subversion of the law of contract by the law of unjust enrichment is avoided in such cases, but not in cases in which the benefit conferred was money, as in *Bush v Canfield*. However, the reason for imposing a 'valuation ceiling' is not the concern that the parties' allocation of risk, their bargain, may be undermined, but the concern that the defendant should not incur liabilities 'behind his back'. The 'valuation ceiling' thus does not answer the question whether restitution should give way to contract at all – it avoids the conflict, but for wholly unrelated reasons.

We have to face the question: irrespective of whether the benefit conferred consisted of a service, goods, or money, should the law of unjust enrichment give way to the law of contract?

Until relatively recently it was not at all clear what happens when a contract is terminated on the ground of breach: does the termination operate retrospectively or prospectively? This question is of fundamental importance not just as regards the survival of exclusion clauses, liquidated damages clauses and contractual duties of care, but also insofar as it may have a considerable impact on the restitutionary claim. A contract that is wiped out *ab initio* has nothing more to say about the allocation of risk between the parties. Enrichment law can thus freely occupy the ground vacated by the law of contract. If the effect of termination is, however, that the parties are merely excused from further performance, the position might be otherwise.

As recently as 1967 Lord Reid said in the infamous *Suisse Atlantique*[78] case:

> I do not think that there is generally much difficulty where the innocent party has elected to treat the breach as a repudiation, bring the contract to an end and sue for damages. Then the whole contract has ceased to exist.[79]

This view was comprehensively rejected in *Photo Production Ltd v Securicor Transport Ltd*.[80] In that case, the claimants' factory was burned down by a night-watchman employed by the defendants. The contract between the defendants and the claimants excluded

---

75 Burrows, 1988, p 576; Birks, 1989, p 226; Goff and Jones, 1998, p 414. But see Jaffey, 2000, pp 9, 39.

76 Goff and Jones, 1998, p 517.

77 The contract price has since assumed some significance in American law as *evidence of reasonable value*. Cf *US v Western Casualty & Surety Co* 498 F 2d 335 (1974) ('The contract price, while evidence of reasonable value, is neither the final determinant of the value of the performance nor does it limit recovery'). For additional cases in the same vein, see Palmer, 1978, Cum Suppl 1997, p 161.

78 [1967] 1 AC 361.

79 *Ibid*, at 398.

80 [1980] AC 827.

vicarious liability. The Court of Appeal had held that that clause could not be relied upon because the fundamental breach by the defendants had wiped out the contract, including the exemption clause. The House of Lords reversed that decision, rejecting the view that the breach of one party, accepted by the other as discharging him from further performance of the contract, brought the contract to an end. The discharge operated *prospectively*. Lord Diplock was adamant that 'breaches of primary obligations give rise to substituted or secondary obligations on the part of the party in default, and, in some cases, may entitle the other party to be relieved from further performance of his obligations. ... The contract, however, is just as much the source of secondary obligations as it is of primary obligations; and like primary obligations that are implied by law, secondary obligations too can be modified by agreement between the parties'.[81]

The crucial difference between contracts discharged by frustration and contracts discharged by breach is thus that in the latter the law of contract provides for the consequences: the party in breach is to put the innocent party in the position he would have been in had the contract been performed.[82] The question is whether this secondary obligation should take precedence over the obligation imposed by the general law, viz. that benefits received have to be returned if the consideration for them fails. It will be attempted to answer this question by reference to principle and policy.

In a recent article, McKendrick discusses the primacy of contract argument at some length, albeit in the context of an attack on the total failure requirement. Now that that requirement has gone, it is possible to re-examine the arguments. First, he says, it can be argued that the continued existence of the secondary obligation prevents there being a failure of consideration.[83] This argument receives some support from the High Court of Australia in the leading case of *The Mikhail Lermontov*,[84] although the situation Their Honours referred to was one in which the compensatory award had already been made. In such a situation, according to Their Honours, 'the damages are awarded and received as full compensation for non-performance or breach of the promise and represent the indirect fruits of the promise. ... In such a case, the promise has been indirectly enforced and the award of compensation has, as a matter of substance, been received in substitution for the promised consideration. In those circumstances, the promisee, having received full compensation for non-performance of the promise, is not entitled to a refund of the price upon payment of which the performance of the promise was conditioned'.[85]

The argument is also put by Andrew Kull in an article in the Southern California Law Review.[86] He criticises *Boomer v Muir*, arguing that that the contract breaker in a *Boomer v Muir* scenario cannot be said to be unjustly enriched: 'Because the seller who holds the buyer's money remains liable for the promised performance or its monetary equivalent, the seller has not been enriched in any economic sense beyond the benefit of the

---

81 *Ibid*, at 848 ff.

82 Note that at the time *Chandler v Webster* was decided this was not at all clear, and the general view seems to have been that a fundamental breach would lead to the rescission *ab initio* of the contract. Thus, the exception made in that case for contracts rescinded *ab initio* probably conceded more than would appear to the modern lawyer. Cf Birks, 1989, p 222; Carter, 1997, p 132.

83 McKendrick, 1995a, pp 217, 223.

84 (1993) 111 ALR 289. For a brief account of the facts, see above, p 114.

85 *Ibid*, at 316, *per* Deane, and Dawson JJ.

86 Kull, 1994, p 1465.

bargain.'[87] The view of enrichment taken by Kull is an economic one (his whole article is strongly influenced by law and economics reasoning). However, though the matter is disputed, that is not the view of enrichment usually taken in the law of restitution. The market value of an enrichment can be nil, without preventing it being an enrichment. Thus, in *Planché v Colburn*,[88] the defendant had commissioned the claimant to write a work on 'Ancient Armour' to be published in the defendant's series 'The Juvenile Library'. The price was £100, payable upon submission of the manuscript. Half the work completed, the defendant abandoned the series. The claimant was able to recover £50 in quasi-contract, based on the value of the work he had done, even though the claimant could not be said, in any meaningful economic sense, to have been enriched by that work. He had bargained for it, and from that it could be inferred that he valued it.[89]

Kull's argument focuses on the enrichment of the defendant. However, it can be extended to encompass not just enrichment but also the ground for restitution itself: the buyer, in return for his payment, has received the right to be compensated in damages. The consideration thus has not failed, there is no unjust enrichment. McKendrick dismisses this argument as being 'based on a Holmesian perspective of contract law, namely that a contracting party does not accept a duty to perform his promise, rather he has a choice either to perform or to pay damages for not performing'.[90] His objection is that 'the innocent party did not bargain for a right of action for damages and that it cannot be said that damages is an alternative to performance so as to prevent there being a failure of consideration'.[91] That must be correct. The argument is one from an unjust enrichment perspective. If it is to stand up, it must be possible to argue that the claimant, when he conferred the benefit, did so on the basis that either he would get his counter-performance or he would get damages. Such an argument would be very strained indeed. In reality, the claimant conferred the benefit in order to get his counter-performance, and nothing else.

Another argument that can be made in favour of primacy of contract is that the parties must be taken to have contracted out of restitution by the very making of the contract. *Securicor* tells us that the contract is the source not only of primary, but also of secondary obligations. As Lord Diplock observed in that case, the parties are free to agree what their respective obligations are to be in case of breach (as long as they do not fall foul of the rule against penalties). As long as the parties have made no such agreement, the law implies a secondary obligation to pay damages into the contract. The parties are taken to have agreed to this, as though they had included a liquidated damages clause into the contract. McKendrick counters this argument by referring to *Henderson v Merrett Syndicates Ltd*.[92] In that case, the House of Lords made it clear that the general law (in

---

87   *Ibid*, p 1479.
88   (1831) 8 Bing 14, 131 ER 305.
89   Some commentators do not accept that *Planché v Colburn* is an unjust enrichment case at all. They see it as an example of contractual compensation, the measure of compensation being determined by reference to the contract price. Beatson argues that there is now no need to resort to unjust enrichment reasoning, because reliance-based compensation is now firmly established. He also remarks that if there was an independent restitutionary claim, the contract price would be irrelevant. See Beatson, 1991, pp 39 ff. Cf also Burrows, 1993a, pp 8 ff, p 267.
90   McKendrick, 1995a, p 223.
91   *Ibid*.
92   [1995] 2 AC 145.

Henderson, the law of torts) will apply unless it can be shown that the parties have agreed to exclude it in their contract. In other words, in English law there can be concurrent liability with the claimant being free to choose the most advantageous claim open to him. *Fibrosa* established, says McKendrick, that restitution for failure of consideration is part of the general law, and does not arise because it is one of the stipulated conditions of the contract. Thus, 'the mere fact that the parties have entered into a contract should not preclude resort to the law of restitution'.[93]

However, the analogy with the law of tort, while superficially attractive, might be misconceived in the context of a claim for failure of consideration. Tortious liability is generally imposed by the general law without reference to the intention of the parties. Liability for failure of consideration might be different. The difference might lie in the fact that the basis of the transfer must be agreed between the parties, if not expressly then by implication. In Birks's words, the essence of failure of consideration is 'that the plaintiff specified the basis of his giving'.[94] In accepting the benefit, the recipient must therefore be taken to have accepted that basis. The precise nature of this 'agreement' has never been fully worked out in English law.[95] Within the contractual context, however, it seems clear that normal contractual rules will apply. We thus have an agreement between the parties to the effect that the benefit is to be returned if the specified basis of the transfer fails. The difference between tort and failure of consideration might be that, in the case of tort, liability is imposed purely by operation of law, while in the case of failure of consideration there is an element of consent, and, therefore, it is arguable that contractual rules should govern. However, just as the law of contract will trump the law of tort where the contract expressly and within the confines permitted by policy as expressed in the Unfair Contract Terms Act 1977 excludes tortious liability, so the law of contract will only exclude liability for failure of consideration where this has become part of the deal between the parties.

It thus becomes clear that it is difficult to argue for the absolute primacy of contract from legal principle. It appears that there is no reason in law why the claims should not be allowed to be concurrent. However, if a strong case could be made out in terms of policy, it would, of course, be possible to block the restitutionary claim. The policy argument has recently been put forward by Kull. He objects that the result of allowing recovery in unjust enrichment would invert a party's normal interest regarding the other side's performance:

> A performing party's ordinary objective – the secure anticipation of timely counter-performance – will yield to the perception that the other party's material breach or repudiation would in fact be a more desirable outcome. Because the other party will presumably share this assessment of the situation, both parties acquire an incentive to expend resources, not in performance or the negotiation of appropriate contract modifications, but in strategic behavior intended to enhance their position in potential litigation.[96]

---

93   McKendrick, 1995a, p 225.
94   Birks, 1989, p 219.
95   For the position in German law see below, pp 144 ff.
96   Kull, 1994, p 1472.

There are a number of answers to this argument. First, even from within a law and economics framework, Kull's assumptions are flawed. As Gordon and Frankel point out in a reply to Kull's article,[97] it is wrong to assume that contracts which will cause a given party a loss in the short term are 'losing contracts' in the long term. They put forward an alternative view, namely that 'many ostensibly losing contracts are in fact beneficial to both parties'.[98] If a party enters into a losing contract, this may 'indicate that something else compensates her for the under-priced performance'.[99] Such intangible benefits may include the continuation of a longer-term business relationship or the prestige value of undertaking an important and well-publicised venture (such as, for instance, in *Boomer v Muir*). The calculations of such intangible benefits for the purposes of assessing expectation losses are notoriously difficult, if not impossible. Thus, argue Gordon and Frankel, 'it is *desirable* for courts to give suppliers the option of receiving a restitutionary award even if it exceeds the contract price'.[100]

Another possible answer to Kull's argument is that it is unrealistic to expect contracting parties to engage in strategic behaviour of the kind he envisages. It is difficult to imagine situations in which one party can influence the other party's behaviour in such a way as to induce it to commit a fundamental breach of contract. Equally, if the performing party takes care to avoid breaching its contract that is only right and proper. A breach of contract is a civil wrong and as such *prima facie* unlawful. There is no room in English law for the doctrine of 'efficient' breach.

In fact, it is possible to argue that policy in fact dictates that a breaching party should not benefit from the contract it has breached. Palmer, in discussing *Bush v Canfield*, points out that in that case 'the seller gave nothing in exchange for the $3,000 except a broken promise, and the principle of unjust enrichment is applicable. If the buyer had made no payment and had been the party who repudiated the contract, the seller could have recovered $3000 damages for loss of his bargain. It would be curious indeed for the seller to obtain the same advantage when he is the one guilty of breach'.[101] This would appear entirely correct. If a defendant breaches a winning contract, he has only himself to blame, and there is no reason in policy to allow him to benefit from the contract he has breached. As long as the benefit received is incontrovertible (as it was in *Bush v Canfield*, a case concerning the payment of money), there is thus no reason to insist on the contract price as a limit to recovery. Difficulties will only arise where it is impossible to return the benefit in specie. Kull impliedly acknowledges this by recognising that the result in *Bush v Canfield* is correct. He disputes, however, that the claimant recovered $5,000 to prevent the defendant's unjust enrichment, arguing that he won 'because judges since the 18th century have identified circumstances of breach or repudiation in which a plaintiff is entitled, as an alternative to suing for damages, to call off the deal'.[102] As a matter of contract law, however, there is no difference between the termination in *Bush v Canfield* and the termination in *Boomer v Muir*. The difficulty with the latter case arises because the

---

97 Gordon and Frankel, 1994, p 1519.
98 *Ibid*, p 1523.
99 *Ibid*, p 1524.
100 *Ibid*, p 1525 (original emphasis).
101 Palmer, 1978, p 393.
102 Kull, 1994, p 1484.

court is forced to put a value on the claimant's performance. This value is not readily realisable by the defendant. As was argued above, the law of restitution is thus right to insist on the contract price as a limit to recovery, but not because the law of contract would otherwise be subverted, but because, up to that limit, the claimant will have to meet the subjective devaluation argument.

We can conclude that there is little danger of the law of unjust enrichment undermining the law of contract. The enrichment claim is an independent claim, part of the general law, and as long as the parties have not expressly or impliedly contracted out of restitution, a claim for failure of consideration (total or partial) will lie.

7.3.3 A combination of claims?

In Germany, it is clear that there can never be any combination of restitutionary and expectation damages, as the code presents the claimant with a clear choice between the two. The explanation for this is to be found in legal history: as in England, the claimant's choice to put an end to a contract was perceived to destroy the contract completely, retrospectively rather than prospectively.[103] In English law it is worth asking the question: does the claimant have to choose between restitution and compensation?

The High Court of Australia has given a positive answer to this question. In *The Mikhail Lermontov*[104] it made it quite clear that a restitutionary claim could not be combined with a compensatory award of damages for breach of contract.[105] It will be remembered that Mrs Dillon's claim against the defendant shipowners included a claim for restitution of the fare as well as a claim for 'compensation for disappointment and distress at the loss of entertainment'. The question for the High Court was whether there could be a combination of the two claims. The English and Australian authorities favoured a combination of claims,[106] and so did the American Uniform Commercial Code (s 2-711 (1)), while general American law seemed to have its face set against combining the remedies.[107] The High Court decided, however, that no such combination was possible. A number of reasons were given. First, it was argued that 'restitution of the contractual consideration removes, at least notionally, the basis on which the plaintiff is entitled to call on the defendant to perform his or her contractual obligations'[108] In other words, since Mrs Dillon's right to the cruise, and her right to expect that the captain would refrain from sinking the ship, depended on her fare, restitution of the fare removed her entitlement to contractual performance. Kit Barker criticises this argument. To him, it would lead to ludicrous consequences: '... the recovery of a 50p bus fare would automatically preclude a passenger from suing in contract for spinal injuries caused to her by the driver's culpable negligence.'[109]

---

103 See above, pp 109 f.
104 (1993) 111 ALR 289.
105 For the facts, see above, p 114.
106 *Heywood v Wellers* [1976] QB 446, 458; *Millar's Machinery Co Ltd v David Way and Son* (1935) 40 Com Cas 204.
107 Cf, eg, *Balon v Hotel and Restaurant Supplies Inc* 433 P 2d 661 (1967).
108 *Baltic v Dillon* (1993) 111 ALR 289, 300, *per* Mason CJ.
109 Barker, 1993, p 295.

A second argument relied on by the High Court has been referred to above, when we were discussing whether the law of contract should in some way trump the law of unjust enrichment in cases of discharge for breach.[110] It was to the effect that in a case in which a compensatory award has been made, there has been no failure of consideration at all because the award of compensation is to be regarded as a 'substitute performance'. As Barker formulates the view he opposes: 'She has received something for her money – namely, damages.'[111] As we have dismissed this argument above, we can also dismiss it here: Mrs Dillon did not bargain for damages, she bargained for a cruise.

On the whole, it is possible to agree with Barker that there is no reason in logic or policy to restrict a combination of restitutionary and compensatory claims, based on the same breach of contract. It is, however, important to note that there is an important qualification to this: there must be no double recovery. This was recognised in *Heywood v Wellers*.[112] In that case a woman's claim for an injunction restraining her former lover from pestering her had been more than incompetently handled by her solicitors. Her claim against them succeeded in part: she was able to recover restitution of £175 which she had paid on account of costs, but the trial judge held that she should not recover any damages for the solicitors' negligence. On appeal, Lord Denning MR held that she should recover both: 'Take this instance. If you engage a driver to take you to the station to catch a train for a day trip to the sea, you pay him £2 – and then the car breaks down owing to his negligence. So that you miss your holiday. In that case you can recover not only your £2 back but also damages for the disappointment, upset and mental distress which you suffered.'[113] In assessing the damages payable for the solicitors' negligence, however, he qualified this: 'Some reduction should be made for the fact that if the solicitors had done their duty (and saved her from molestation) it would have cost her something.'[114] This is clearly right. The same point is stressed by Treitel: 'Obviously a buyer of defective goods cannot both keep them and claim restitution of the price: if he wants to keep the goods his only claim is for damages. Similarly a buyer who has paid in advance for goods which are not delivered cannot recover both his payment and the value of the goods.'[115]

The question is, however: 'What difference does it make?' Apart from Treitel's first example, that of the buyer who wishes to retain the faulty goods rather than reject them, in English law we are dealing exclusively with awards in money. A claimant who claims restitution and compensation will, on the above analysis, receive exactly the same as one who restricts himself to a claim for either compensation *or* restitution: in assessing compensatory damages, the law will take into account the restitutionary award, and the compensation will thereby be reduced accordingly. In granting restitution, any compensatory award received to date will also be taken into account, at least in so far as it relates to losses connected to the defendant's gain The claimant will thus lose on the swings what he has gained on the roundabouts.

---

110 See above, pp 123 ff.
111 Barker, 1993, p 295.
112 [1976] 1 QB 446.
113 *Ibid*, p 458.
114 *Ibid*, p 459.
115 Treitel, 1988b, p 99.

We have seen in our discussion of the German law on the subject that it tends to focus on the question whether a claimant should be obliged to make a choice between the different remedies available to him, and whether he should be bound to that choice once it is made.[116] In English law, this is also the one area in which the question assumes great practical importance. This became clear in the recent Privy Council case of *Tang Man Sit v Capacious Investments Ltd*.[117] The case did not concern a choice between contract and restitution, but a choice between two alternative remedies available for a breach of trust: an account of profits on the one hand, damages on the other. The defendant had, in breach of trust, rented out 16 houses which, in equity, belonged to the claimant. The claimant claimed an account of profits and damages. At the summary trial, it did not occur to anyone that an election might have to be made, and judgment was entered for both remedies. The claimant accepted part of the sums due under the account of profits, and then discovered that his claim for damages far exceeded his restitutionary claim. The defendant claimed that, by accepting part of the account of profits, the claimant had once and for all chosen to pursue his restitutionary remedy, a choice he could now not go back on. Lord Nicholls, giving the advice of the Privy Council, accepted an earlier *dictum* by Lightman J in *Island Records Ltd v Tring International plc*,[118] in which Lightman J laid down that in intellectual property disputes, where the trial is usually divided into separate inquiries into liability and damages, the claimant did not have to choose between remedies (damages or account of profits) until he was in possession of all material facts so as to enable him to make an informed choice.[119] Applying these principles to the facts in *Tang Man Sit v Capacious Investments*, the Privy Council held that, while an election had to be made, the claimant had not made it simply by accepting the money. He would be allowed to postpone his election until he was in possession of all the facts.

It can be argued that to talk of election is wholly unnecessary: the court could have ascertained the relevant facts, determined which award would be the greater and made it accordingly, deducting any payments which had been received by the claimant before trial. Thus, in *Mahesan v Malaysia Government Officers Co-operative Housing Association Ltd*,[120] the claimant housing association had sued its agent for loss caused by his having corruptly induced it to pay far too much for a parcel of land, he himself accepting a bribe of $122,000 for this 'service'. The loss suffered by the claimant, however, was far greater and amounted to $443,000. It could clearly not recover both, as that would have led to double recovery, and the Privy Council chose for it, allowing the judgment for the loss alone to stand.

We can conclude this discussion by stating that a combination of restitutionary and compensatory claims is conceptually possible, and that this is an important insight from a doctrinal point of view. Practically it will be important only insofar as the claimant is required to choose between remedies, or in the case of breach of contract, between the causes of action.

---

116 See above, p 109.
117 [1996] 1 All ER 193.
118 [1995] 3 All ER 444, 447.
119 See also Birks, 1996d, p 375.
120 [1979] AC 374.

Having analysed the relationship between the causes of action for breach and unjust enrichment for failure of consideration, we can now turn to the question whether in fact a claim for restitution based on failure of consideration is a separate cause of action at all, or whether it is, as Hobhouse J seems to suggest, just another remedial response that the law provides for breach of contract.

7.4 FAILURE OF CONSIDERATION AS A CONTRACTUAL PRINCIPLE?

We asked at the beginning of this chapter whether Hobhouse J was correct in taking the view that failure of consideration is a contractual principle. At its most extreme, it might be argued that the duty to make restitution for failure of consideration is a secondary duty imposed by the law of contract, in the same way as the duty to compensate the claimant for loss.

In we looked at the German law of *Rücktritt*, and at Stoll's now widely accepted idea of restitution as a secondary duty. It was argued, however, that the link with contract was merely *contextual*, not *causative*. In other words, the underlying reason for restitution was not the failure of the contract, but the failure of the expected counter-performance. Rücktritt thus appeared to be a contractual remedy, but turned out to be little more than a slightly modified enrichment claim. In English law, claims for failure of consideration are most frequently made in a contractual context. However, the action for money had and received is no longer classified as part of the law of contract. The 'implied contract' heresy has been overcome, and so we can assume that a claim for failure of consideration is a claim in unjust enrichment, and not in contract. Or so it would seem. However, as we will see in Chapter 9, which will discuss whether there can ever be restitution for failure of consideration in non-contractual cases, the repercussions of the initial error of the implied contract idea are still to be felt today, in that it is very difficult to find cases to support the argument that there can be a failure of consideration not involving a contract. Seeing failure of consideration claims as contractual remedies goes one step further, back to the bad old days when all restitutionary claims were regarded as based on implied contracts.

On this view, the law of *Rücktritt* and the law of failure of consideration are not all that different: both are placed in a contractual context in their respective legal systems, and yet neither is, it is argued here, responding to the failure of a contract, but rather to the failure of the expected counter-performance, or, indeed, to the failure of the basis of a transfer. This argument will be developed in the following two chapters.

7.5 CONCLUSION

In this chapter we have looked at the relationship between contract damages and restitutionary damages for failure of consideration, both in order to provide an overview of failure of contractual reciprocation, and to provide an answer to the question whether there is any good reason why the law of failure of consideration should be separated off and equipped with its own regime.

First, we looked at the 'total failure' requirement. It was argued that that requirement is about to be dropped, if that has not already happened. However, it was also observed that, following the demise of the 'total failure' requirement and the development of a change of position defence, it will be necessary to follow the German law in developing something resembling the *Saldotheorie*. This is because English law will then increasingly have to deal with cases involving contractual exchanges in which value has passed both ways. These cases were previously taken out from the start because neither failure of consideration had been 'total'. The *Saldotheorie* is the device currently used by German law to deal with restitutionary claims following exchanges, 'disapplying' the disenrichment defence in § 818 III where one party seeks restitution but is refusing to make counter-restitution on the basis that he has changed his position. If English law does develop a comparable mechanism, the question will have to be asked again: is there something special about contractual reciprocation? The answer appears to be that there is something special about reciprocation in general, about performances made in the expectation of counter-performances, whether under a contract or not. As in German law, there appears to be little justification for separate treatment on the mere ground that the parties have entered into a contract.

The second argument in favour of special treatment as a sub-category of the law of contract is that failure of consideration might undermine the contractual allocation of risks if it is not controlled within a contractual framework. However, an analysis of the present law shows that there is little danger of this, given both the attitude taken generally by English law to concurrent remedies and causes of action, and the fact that a contract will always have to be discharged, and hence rendered ineffective *de futuro*, before restitution for failure of consideration can follow.

The question which now remains to be addressed is whether there can ever be restitution for non-contractual failure of basis, or, more narrowly, for non-contractual failure of reciprocation. Both in German and in English law this question is hotly debated: in German law the continued applicability of the *condictio causa data causa non secuta* in a system which appears to be based on the absence of an underlying obligation is questioned by many jurists, and this debate will be gone into in the next chapter. In English law there has always been great reluctance on the part of the judiciary to use the language of failure of consideration in cases not involving a contract. The reasons for that reluctance, and the question how such cases are dealt with by English law, will be gone into in Chapter 9.

CHAPTER 8

NON-CONTRACTUAL FAILURE OF
CONSIDERATION IN GERMANY

It will be recalled that in German law, problems of failure of contractual counter-performance generally belong to the law of *Rücktritt*. However, we have seen that if a contract has been avoided *ab initio*, the restitutionary consequences will be governed by the general law of unjust enrichment in §§ 812 ff. In these cases the contract is treated as though it had never existed. Performances made *causa solvendi*, for the purpose of discharging it, have not in the event achieved that purpose. The 'legal ground' of the enrichment has thus fallen away. Whether a contract is void *ab initio* or merely ineffective therefore determines whether the general enrichment claim in § 812 I or the more specialised enrichment claim in § 346 will lie under the name of *Rücktritt*.

It is possible to discern a certain parallel to what Hobhouse J attempts in *Westdeutsche*. On the one hand, there is what he calls 'the contractual principle': failure of consideration. While he does not unequivocally detach this from the general law of unjust enrichment, his terminology at times suggests that he regards this as a principle within the law of *contract*, a contractual response to termination, rather than the response of the general enrichment law to a failure of counter-performance. On the other hand, there is the claim for 'absence' of consideration, which we will consider in Chapter 12. Hobhouse J clearly regards that claim as belonging to the general law of unjust enrichment. Superficially, at least, the similarities to German law are striking. German lawyers would generally regard cases of *Rücktritt* as contractual, while cases under § 812 would be categorised as 'pure' enrichment claims. Within the general law of unjust enrichment in § 812 I there is one figure which is indisputably a case of failure of consideration operating outside the context of contract. In the literature this figure retains the old Latin names '*condictio ob rem*' or '*condictio causa data causa non secuta*'. In the code it appears in § 812 I 2, 2nd alt:

> *Diese Verpflichtung [zur Herausgabe] besteht auch dann, wenn ... der mit einer Leistung nach dem Inhalt des Rechtsgeschäfts bezweckte Erfolg nicht eintritt.* [This obligation [to make restitution] arises also where ... the result contemplated by the legal transaction is not attained.]

This provision must be read in the context of the whole of § 812 I, which, it will be remembered, is in the following terms:

> *Wer durch die Leistung eines anderen oder in sonstiger Weise auf dessen Kosten etwas ohne rechtlichen Grund erlangt, ist ihm zur Herausgabe verpflichtet. Diese Verpflichtung besteht auch dann, wenn der rechtliche Grund später wegfällt oder der mit einer Leistung nach dem Inhalt des Rechtsgeschäfts bezweckte Erfolg nicht eintritt.* [He who obtains something through somebody else's performance or in another way at his expense without a legal cause, is obliged to make restitution to the other. This obligation arises also where the legal cause falls away later or where the result contemplated by the legal transaction is not attained.]

As we will see, this figure was included in § 812 I because it was felt that there might be a field of application for it even where there had never been any 'legal cause' at all, in other words, where there had never been a legal obligation on the claimant to render his performance. In particular, it was felt necessary to make doubly clear that there would be no 'legal ground' where an underlying obligation which existed at the time of the transfer was later avoided *ab initio*, the so-called *condictio ob causam finitam*.

However, in making sure that no category of claims was left out, the draftsmen included a claim which, on one reading, is broad enough to swallow up the whole of the law of unjust enrichment, at least as far as enrichments by performance are concerned. The final half of the second sentence in § 812 I makes restitution dependent on the result, the outcome of a transaction. Apart from telling us that this outcome must be 'contemplated by the legal transaction', the provision does not define what it means by the word '*Erfolg*'. All sorts of mistakes and mispredictions, not normally relevant in the law of contracts, could suddenly be relied on as a ground for restitution, notwithstanding the fact that to grant restitution would upset a bargain. How the provision can be limited in scope has thus been the subject of intense debate. Opinions vary from a total rejection of the *condictio ob rem* as a mere residue of legal history,[1] to its endorsement as a 'general part of the law relating to the unwinding of transactions'.[2]

It is impossible to understand the above provision without some reference to history. I will thus attempt to give a brief account of the historical development of the *condictio ob rem*, starting with its roots in Roman law, its reception into the *ius commune* and its ultimate adoption by the draftsmen of the *BGB*.

8.1 ROMAN ROOTS OF THE *CONDICTIO OB REM*

8.1.1 The *numerus clausus* of enforceable contracts

Roman law, unlike English law, did not recognise a general law of contract. In English law, once there is an agreement supported by some form of consideration, the promisor will be *prima facie* liable. While specific contracts, such as the second volume of *Chitty on Contracts* is devoted to, may amplify or restrict this general liability, the claimant will normally not be required to show that a given contract is a contract of sale to bring an action for breach. However, even in English law this is a relatively modern development.[3] The English law of torts has not yet reached this stage. The forms of action still rule us from the index of any textbook on the subject, where the ancient names of trespass, assault and battery, conversion, libel and nuisance can still be found to the present day. No general principle of tortious liability has yet replaced them, and a claimant will have to bring his claim under one of these heads if he wants to succeed. While the Judicature Act of 1873 eliminated the risk of a claimant being non-suited because he failed to specify the proper basis for his claim, and while the law of negligence seems to become more and more all embracing, the example of the English 'law of torts' is useful to illustrate the dilemma of the Roman litigant faced with a *numerus clausus* of contracts. If an agreement could not be subsumed under one of the accepted heads of contract, it was not enforceable. If one party had already performed under such an agreement, some

---

1   Batsch, 1973, pp 1639, 1640.
2   Liebs, 1978, pp 697, 701.
3   Cf Simpson, 1987, p 6.

mechanism was needed to avoid the injustice which would otherwise flow from the absence of a general contractual principle based on agreement.

We can imagine the classical Roman law of contracts as a number of institutional islands in an ocean of invalidity. The first group of islands were the so-called contracts *re*: the loan for consumption (*mutuum*) or for use (*commodatum*), pledge and deposit. These had in common that the obligation only came into existence as the money or the goods were handed over – they could not be created by informal agreement. Birks and McLeod argue that the four contracts *re* have in common that 'they become binding by conduct, that is to say by the performance of the act identified by their names, which in each case is the delivery of a thing'. The Latin *'res'* is thus translated by 'conduct', not by 'thing'.[4] A second important group of islands were the contracts *consensu*: sale, hire, partnership and agency. Zimmermann calls the development of these contracts 'one of the most remarkable achievements of Roman jurisprudence'.[5] They were truly based on agreement, on consent. Not all agreements, of course, could be described as sale, hire, partnership or agency, and agreements that fell outside these categories were in danger of falling into the sea of unenforceability surrounding the contractual islands. Roman law enabled the parties, however, to make *any* agreement enforceable by following the formalities of the *stipulatio*. This was the most important of the *contracti verbis*. Characteristically, it consisted of a verbal exchange of question and answer: *'dari spondes?'* – *'spondeo'*, *'facies?'* – *'faciam'*.[6]

In effect, the *stipulatio* enabled the parties to construct themselves a raft to keep their contractual obligations afloat. However, the construction of a raft is a burdensome exercise, and while the system ensured ultimate contractual certainty, it proved to have serious problems as the Roman economy developed, some of which were never overcome. Most importantly, the *stipulatio* was *stricti iuris*, and left little or no room for implied terms of any kind. Its usefulness as a commercial tool was therefore limited, and the danger that some *bona fide* agreements might fall into the non-contractual sea surrounding the recognised contractual islands was increased.

8.1.2 Innominate contracts and the *condictio ob rem*

Agreements outside the definitions of the nominate transactions thus had no place in the Roman contractual system. One such case was the *datio ob rem*, consisting of a transfer (*datio*) and the promise of a counter-performance (*res*). Again, the translation of *'res'* by 'conduct' makes the meaning of the phrase clearer. Thus, the claimant might have given a horse for a cow or for the service of ploughing, or paid money in order that a slave be liberated or an action discontinued,[7] only to find that he had no way to enforce the counter-performance: the *datio ob rem* successfully transferred the property in the money he had paid, but did not give rise to an obligation to render the promised counter-performance. Here the disappointed transferor did however have a non-contractual response, for it had been established that the action of debt (the *condictio*) would lie to

---

4   Birks and McLeod, 1987, p 13.
5   Zimmermann, 1996, p 230.
6   Gai III, 92.
7   Ulpianus D 12.4.1: *'ut filius emanciparetur vel servus manumitteretur vel a lite discedatur'*.

recover, not the value of the performance which the other had failed to make, but the value of the transferor's own performance. Paul puts it in this way: '*ob rem datum ita repeti potest, si res, propter quam datum est, secuta non est*'.[8] Hence the classical name for the action used to recover one's own performance: *condictio ob rem datorum*. The classical *condictio ob rem* envisaged a failed counter-performance, and was thus probably narrower in scope than Birks's vision of 'failure of basis'. Some time before Justinian's codification the terminology changed, however. The *condictio ob rem datorum* became the *condictio causa data causa non secuta*. Some try to explain this terminological shift by etymological accident and changing fashion.[9] An alternative explanation might be that this is an example of unstable terminology and taxonomy. If '*res*' means 'conduct' in this context, the *condictio ob rem* could only be relied on where the claimant's performance was made in order to induce the defendant to pursue a certain conduct, to elicit a counter-performance. The shift of terminology might indicate an attempt to widen the scope of the action to situations in which things simply failed to turn out as planned. The *causa data* thus not only encompassed a transfer made to elicit a counter-performance, but, in the words of Liebs, also 'a performance made to satisfy a condition which later became unnecessary'.[10] An example might be the payment of a dowry by a bride's father. The marriage then falls through. Even though the marriage can hardly be described as 'counter-performance', he can demand restitution.[11]

For a time the *condictio ob rem* filled the gap which arose because not all agreements were enforceable, and thus played a most important role. In time a general doctrine was developed allowing innominate contracts to be enforced: whenever under a bilateral agreement one party had completed his part, he could enforce the other's unexecuted reciprocation. 'Innominate' contracts thus filled the gaps between the contractual islands of the classical law, and this somewhat reduced the importance of the *condictio*, which did, however, remain the only remedy in some cases. One question which has so far remained unanswered is whether Roman law always allowed reliance on the *condictio ob rem* even where the transaction did fit within a nominate contract, as where the buyer had paid for goods which were then never delivered. The usual answer is that it did not allow recourse to the *condictio* in such cases, but this is very difficult to prove.

It is, however, clear that in Justinian's code the *condictio causa data causa non secuta* was retained, even where the claimant could rely on the *actio praescriptis verbis* to enforce the contract itself.[12] The claimant who had performed his side of the bargain was thus put in the enviable position of being able to choose between claiming the agreed counter-performance and asking for the value of his own performance (if he had made a bad bargain), but only as long as the defendant had not yet performed (giving the latter a strong incentive to perform as quickly as possible).

In the *ius commune* the *condictio causa data causa non secuta* became rare. Well before the 18th century it was possible to state with confidence that '*ex nudo pacto oritur actio*',[13] and

---

8   Paul D 12.5.1.1.
9   Cf Schwarz, 1952, pp 120 ff.
10   Liebs, 1986, p 163.
11   D 12.4. 6–10.
12   Paulus D 19.5.5.
13   Stryk, 1717, Lib II, Tit XIV, § 1

the *numerus clausus* of contractual actions, along with the *actio praescriptis verbis*, had become obsolete. Zimmermann explains that 'if someone performs in order to receive a counter-performance, the parties will usually have concluded a contract. The first performance can then not be classified as a *datio ob rem* but occurs *solvendi causa*'.[14] This statement explains Birks's ironic inversion:[15] the *condictio ob rem* cannot lie in contractual cases, because if a contract is involved the first performance will invariably be made in order to discharge an obligation, *solvendi causa*, which will lead to the applicability of the *condictio indebiti* rather than the *condictio ob rem*.

For now we should note that the *condictio causa data causa non secuta* remained part of the *ius commune*, ready to be used in those unusual cases where there was a right, but no obvious remedy.

8.2 THE DRAFTING OF THE *BGB*

When it came to deciding whether this *condictio* should be included in the *BGB*, opinions were divided. Objections were raised that 'it should be considered that the *condictio ob causam datorum*, which developed alongside the Roman innominate real contracts, has lost its essential significance with the decline of that legal institution'.[16] However, these objections were rejected. The crucial argument which was put forward was that 'the *condictio ob causam datorum*, while its scope had been reduced compared to Roman law, had not lost its significance for the modern law'.[17] The commission freely accepted that this *condictio* could not trespass within the field of contract, and relied on a number of non-contractual examples, one of which was the payment of a sum of money to be used as a dowry, where the marriage was subsequently never celebrated, another the advance making of an acknowledgement of indebtedness where the supposed lender never made the loan.[18] The *condictio ob rem*[19] was thus retained even though the commission was fully aware of its relationship to the – now defunct – Roman innominate real contracts. It was envisaged that this *condictio* should retain an albeit diminished area of application.

8.3 MODERN VIEWS OF THE *CONDICTIO OB REM*

Josef Esser complained almost 40 years ago that 'no enrichment claim under §§ 812 ff is so misunderstood both in terms of its character and its significance as frequently by both judges and commentators as § 812 I 2, 2nd alt'.[20] Even today we find that amongst academic jurists there is a myriad of contradictory opinions. There are a number of propositions, however, that can be made in the knowledge that they enjoy general

---

14 Zimmermann, 1996, p 861

15 Cf Birks, 1993, p 209

16 Prot II, p 692.

17 Prot II, p 693.

18 *Ibid.*

19 German writers generally prefer the name *condictio ob rem* to *condictio causa data causa non secuta*. See below, p 148.

20 Esser, 1960, p 793.

support. Beyond these, nothing is quite certain and the main disputes will be outlined. The remainder of this chapter will examine those cases in which it is generally agreed that this *condictio* is applicable, and these will be illustrated using concrete examples. The chapter will close with a look at some writers who argue that the *condictio ob rem* does not fit into the system of the *BGB* at all, and should be of mere historical significance.

8.3.1 The general view

Doctrinal background

There is general agreement in the German literature that the *condictio ob rem* still has some role to play. Most commentators agree, however, that its area of application is limited to *non-contractual* cases: as we have seen, cases of *contractual* non-reciprocation will be governed by the law of *Rücktritt*, which is found in a contractual rather than an unjust enrichment context in the *BGB*. If contrasted with English law, this is Birks's ironic inversion: where the English case law suggests that failure of consideration is confined to contractual cases, the German *condictio ob rem* excludes contractual cases altogether, and that is one limit on the ambit of this *condictio*.

Where a performance is made in order to discharge a legal liability we have seen that the *condictio indebiti* will lie if it turns out that that liability never existed, or that it has been destroyed subsequently by rescission *ab initio*. Thus, where a car is sold and paid for by the buyer, and it later turns out that the seller was guilty of serious misrepresentations, the buyer will be able to rescind the contract. To avoid duplication of inquiries, the German law of unjust enrichment will make restitution available on the basis of the invalidity of the supposed contract, in other words, the buyer will be able to recover the price he paid for the car on the basis of a *condictio indebiti*. His purpose in making the payment was the discharge of his liabilities under the contract of sale. That purpose, as it turns out, has failed and restitution follows. The *condictio ob rem*, given its wide formulation, could well apply to this situation. The disappointed buyer could argue that he did not get what he bargained for, that the 'result contemplated' by the contract was not attained and that therefore he should have restitution. It is generally agreed that this would be incorrect. The elegant interlocking of different parts of the *BGB* (in this case contract and unjust enrichment) is only achieved by focusing on the discharge of the underlying obligation as the primary purpose of a performance. It is only where no such primary purpose can be identified, in other words, where there is no supposed underlying obligation, that actual substantive purposes such as the acquisition of a car can become relevant.

The *condictio ob rem* can thus only apply to *non-contractual* cases in which the parties never intended to give rise to or discharge mutual obligations. Restitution will follow where the 'result of the legal transaction', which cannot be a fully fledged contract, is not attained. The question remains what kind of legal transaction is left, once all legal obligations are eliminated. It cannot refer to a fully formed and binding contract, but must refer to something rather less. However, it is generally agreed that it must be more than the mere unilateral motive of one party.[21] There must be some sort of agreement –

---

21 Reuter and Martinek, 1983, p 149.

short of a fully fledged contract – between the parties, to the effect that the performance is rendered for a certain purpose, and that the benefit may be retained by the recipient in order that this purpose be attained.[22] In most cases, however, it will not be difficult to identify such an agreement, as it can be conclusively formed by the mere acceptance of the performance, always supposing that the transferor clearly spells out the basis of his giving.[23]

One problem, which leads some commentators to deny the existence of the *condictio ob rem* altogether, is that whenever there is a transfer of wealth in German law it will normally not be difficult to find some kind of contract. On this basis, it is argued that the proper basis for any claim for failure of basis or counter-performance will be the law of frustration rather than the law of unjust enrichment. Thus, if a gift is made in order to induce an, albeit non-enforceable, counter-performance, the gift itself will constitute a contract, carrying with it a number of obligations. On this view, there can be no 'non-contractual' cases at all. While it is possible to take this view, the danger is that it will lead to an overburdening of the (largely discretionary) law of frustration, which furthermore is merely a judicial creation with no firm basis in the *BGB*. On the other hand, the *condictio ob rem* arguably provides the legal machinery to handle cases of this kind adequately.[24] The difference might thus not strictly be between *contractual* and *non-contractual* cases, but between what German law calls synallagmatic ('*gegenseitige*') and non-synallagmatic ('*nicht gegenseitige*') contracts.

Some examples

One of the paradigm cases relied on by the second drafting commission was that of an IOU ('*abstraktes Schuldanerkenntnis*')[25] or a pledge granted in the expectation of a loan. The claimant might have given the defendant possession of a valuable painting, on the understanding that a loan would later be agreed upon. When it all falls through, the claimant can ask for his painting back. He has no legally enforceable right to the loan, as the relevant contract was never concluded. However, he parted with his painting on the (possibly tacit) understanding that it was to be pledged as security for a loan, and in such circumstances § 812 I 2, 2nd alt gives him the right to ask for restitution.[26] The transfer of possession in the painting is similar to a pre-contractual deposit. Where such a deposit is made, say during negotiations intended to lead to the sale of a house, it can also be recovered on the basis of the *condictio ob rem*.[27] Such deposits are made in the expectation that the other side will in due course be bound to make the desired counter-performance, once the formalities required by the law have been complied with. The promise of a contract is thus definitely in the air, although it has not yet been concluded at the time of the claimant's performance.

---

22 BGH NJW 1973, 612 (19.1.1973), 613.

23 BGHZ 44, 321 (29.1.1965).

24 See below, p 152.

25 This is not to be confused with the case in which an IOU is granted by A to B in order to recognise the former's obligation under eg a previous contract. This case would, if the obligation did not in fact exist, be covered by the special *condictio indebiti* in § 812 II.

26 In practice, it would be preferable to rely on the much stronger proprietary claim, the *rei vindicatio* in § 985.

27 BGHZ LM § 820, No 1 = JZ 1961, 699 (10.7.1961).

There are cases, however, in which no contract is even contemplated by the parties, be it because the other side cannot or will not agree be bound. The *Reichsgericht* had to decide the following case back in 1927:[28] a bank clerk had helped himself to a 'loan' from the funds of the bank. When the shortfall was noticed he applied to the bank to have the 'loan' retrospectively ratified. His application was accompanied by a guarantee signed by the defendant, his father-in-law, who sought to avert the shame of summary dismissal or disciplinary or even criminal proceedings by guaranteeing to pay the relevant amount himself. The application to have the loan ratified was not successful and disciplinary proceedings were initiated against the son-in-law which led to his summary dismissal and loss of pension rights. The bank then sought to recover the lost money from the defendant, suing him on the guarantee. His defence was based on mistake and misrepresentation. However, the judge dismissed the claim on the basis of § 812 I, and this decision was upheld by the *Reichsgericht*. Even though the guarantee had been validly granted, the court held that 'the defendant had the right, according to § 812 *BGB*, to demand restitution of his performance, the guarantee promise, if the goal of the *Leistung* inherent in the legal transaction was not attained'.[29] It is interesting to note that this case did not involve restitution of money, but restitution of a promise. Indeed, this is generally seen to be the most significant point of the case, and not the general availability of restitution in such situations.

A very similar case came before the *Bundesgerichtshof* as recently as 1990.[30] Here, a dishonest bank clerk's husband had granted the bank a mortgage on his house to secure the sum she had embezzled. When the theft was nevertheless reported to the police and criminal proceedings taken, he sought to avoid the mortgage on the grounds of mistake and misrepresentation. Again, the *Bundesgerichtshof*, as the *Reichsgericht* before it, decided the case on the basis of § 812 I instead: 'The purpose of the mortgage, according to the finding of fact at first instance, was to avoid criminal proceedings against the wife. ... According to § 812 I 2, 2nd alt *BGB* the purpose pursued by the plaintiff has failed.'[31] The claimant was thus entitled to restitution of the mortgage.

A case not involving criminal or disciplinary proceedings, but which nevertheless belongs in the same category, came before the *Reichsgericht* in 1927.[32] The claimant's house had been threatened with requisition in the post-war years, because it was larger than was deemed necessary for his family. When the decision was finally made to requisition the house, he appealed and entered into negotiations with the relevant authority. It was agreed that he should promise to pay RM 5,000. When he had paid RM 2,000, the requisitioning order had still not been lifted, and in view of this he decided to suspend further payments. He brought an action for a negative declaration, claiming that the purpose of making the promise to pay (that is, the lifting of the requisitioning order) had not been attained and that he was therefore not obliged to pay any more. Having failed at first instance, the action was successful before the *Oberlandesgericht* Kiel and the *Reichsgericht*. Both based their decision on the *condictio ob rem*.

---

28 RGZ 118, 358 (7.11.1927).
29 *Ibid*, p 360.
30 BGH WM 1990, 819 (23.2.1990).
31 *Ibid*, p 819.
32 RGZ 116, 336 (29.3.1927).

A paradigm example of the *condictio ob rem* is a decision of the *Reichsgericht* in 1924.[33] It is a rather pathetic case. A farmer was heartbroken because his wife had left him. In order to induce her to return to him, he transferred to her all his lands, his house and farm buildings. She failed to return. Undeterred, he also gave her his farm animals and machinery. Both donations were made in the proper form before a notary. On the second occasion, when asked by the notary whether she accepted the gifts, the wife said that she did, in view of the fact that they had now decided to move back in together. However, move back in she did not. On the contrary, she sued the husband when he failed to deliver the animals, asking for one cow and compensation in the amount of RM 2,000! This proved a bad move on her part, as her husband counter-claimed for the return of all his gifts and succeeded on the basis of the *condictio ob rem*. It had been agreed between the parties, albeit impliedly rather than expressly, that in return for the gifts the wife would move back in. She failed to do so, and thus the goal of the transfer had not been achieved. The husband was entitled to restitution. The deal between the parties had not been a bilateral contract, although it had not been wholly gratuitous. At the time of the gifts, the wife had been in no position to refuse to move in with her husband anyway. Both spouses were under a duty to live together under § 1353 *BGB*. The proper basis for the husband's claim was therefore § 812 I 2, 2nd alt.

We have thus identified two firmly established categories in which restitution for failure of consideration is granted in non-contractual cases: the first involves performances made in anticipation of a binding contract which is then not formed; and the second concerns situations in which the claimant has tried to induce the defendant to act in a certain way, that is, to do something or to refrain from doing something in circumstances which fall short of putting him under any legal obligation. If he does not reciprocate, however, he is obliged to return the performance. That the *condictio ob rem* is the correct basis for restitution is such cases is generally accepted.[34]

A possible third category of cases is more controversial. Here the *condictio ob rem* is used to deal with *Quistclose*[35] situations: money is paid over or property transferred on condition that it be used in a certain way. When the condition is not complied with, a restitutionary claim arises. Thus in a case decided by the *Bundesgerichtshof* in 1983,[36] the defendant was given a house to live in by his family. When he moved out a year later and proceeded to let the house, family members brought a claim under § 812 I and succeeded before the *Bundesgerichtshof*. The courts below had held that, for lack of the proper formalities, any agreement not to let the house to third parties was not binding on the defendant, and that therefore the claimants' claim had to fail. The *Bundesgerichtshof* disagreed. This was a donation for a purpose (*'Zweckschenkung'*): the house had been given to the defendant for the purpose that he should live there, the intention being that the house should remain 'in the family'. It had been made clear at the time that he was expected to live in the house, and that he would not let it to anyone else. That had been the purpose and the basis (*'Geschäftsgrundlage'*) of the donation. That purpose had now

---

33   SeuffA 78, 1924, No 124 (18.1.1923).
34   Cf Reuter and Martinek, 1983, pp 151 ff; Koppensteiner and Kramer, 1988, p 57; Jauernig/Schlechtriem §§ 812, 944 to name but a few.
35   *Barclays Bank Ltd v Quistclose Investments Ltd* [1970] AC 567.
36   BGH NJW 1984, 233 (23.9.1983).

failed, and in principle the claimants were entitled to have the house transferred back to them. Although the court refers to the purpose as the *Geschäftsgrundlage* of the contract of donation, implying that the contract of donation has been frustrated by its failure, it does base its decision, not on the *condictio ob rem*, but on the *condictio causa data causa non secuta*. Its language is remarkably close to Birks's terminology.

Birks, as we have seen, argues that 'failure of consideration' could be expressed by 'failure of basis': the performance has been made on a basis which has failed, and restitution must therefore follow.[37] Suppose an uncle gives money to his niece and her fiancé. The wedding then falls through. Can the uncle recover the money under § 812 I? Some writers,[38] and, as the above case shows, the *Bundesgerichtshof*, argue that he can. Esser argues that these cases are paradigm cases of the *condictio ob rem*, which is, according to him, designed to protect the reliance of the claimant on certain circumstances (which must not consists of a legally enforceable obligation), on the basis of which he has rendered his performance. While the *Bundesgerichtshof*, as we have seen, agrees with Esser, most other writers[39] take a different view. Reuter and Martinek argue that 'the *condictio ob rem* would be totally removed from its historical background, as the intended goal – in contrast to [the other two categories] – cannot be regarded as an equivalent counter-performance for the performance rendered'.[40]

If the historical background of the *condictio ob rem* is seen in classical Roman law this is indeed correct: as we have seen, the focus of the *condictio ob rem* was here the other party's conduct, his counter-performance. As Liebs explains, however, *the usage had changed* even before Justinian's compilation.[41] The new name *condictio causa data causa non secuta* was intended to convey the idea that the first performance could not only be recovered if made to elicit a unenforceable counter-performance, but also if made to satisfy a condition which turned out to be unnecessary.[42] It is this shift of emphasis which German law arguably never followed. Possibly this is one reason, apart from a general preference for the purity of classical Roman law, for the insistence by most German commentators to refer to § 812 I 2, 2nd alt as *condictio ob rem*, rather than *condictio causa data causa non secuta*.

However, it is not obvious that the second drafting commission intended to restrict this *condictio* in this way. One example relied on by that commission was that of a dowry paid with the wedding subsequently not taking place.[43] In this example, we have the same difficulties in regarding the celebration of a wedding as a counter-performance as we will encounter in discussing the English law on the subject.[44] What all are agreed on, however, is that the claimant in these examples must have some remedy – the disagreement is limited to the question whether the remedy should be provided by the *condictio ob rem*. The device most academic writers fall back on is the law of frustration.

---

37 Birks, 1989, pp 219 ff.
38 Esser and Weyers, 1991, p 455.
39 Reuter and Martinek, 1983, p 154; Koppensteiner and Kramer, 1988, p 58; MünchKomm/Lieb, No 175 etc.
40 Reuter and Martinek, 1983, p 154.
41 Liebs, 1986, p 173.
42 See above, p 142.
43 Cf fn 17, above.
44 Cf below, pp 162 ff.

This appears not to be limited to contractual situations, but can include 'legal transactions' of the kind contemplated by § 812 I 2, 2nd alt. Thus, in RGZ 169, 249, the *Reichsgericht* was faced with the following scenario: the claimant had transferred his business to his wife in order to defraud his creditors in his bankruptcy. Subsequently a certain Gottfried N became a partner in the firm. The wife committed adultery with N, which led to the divorce of the parties. The claimant husband demanded that the defendant wife re-transfer the undertaking to him. The *Reichsgericht* held that the transaction between the parties had been frustrated by the divorce, and that therefore the wife had to make restitution in money to the husband. The re-transfer of the business itself, which would have been the proper remedy under § 812, was refused. This was possible under the very wide and discretionary § 242, on which the doctrine of frustration is based. This may well have been the reason for basing the decision on § 242 rather than § 812, as the consequence of a re-transfer would have been that the claimant would have ended up in a partnership with the very man who cuckolded him!

The argument is essentially one about terminology and taxonomy. The fact that the court is resorting to frustration is all the more remarkable in that frustration is not expressly provided for in the *BGB*. The approach followed by the *Reichsgericht* will lead to a number of legal remedies based on some form of 'failure of basis', and differentiated according to whether the basis consisted in an expected counter-performance or other condition for the payment.

On the whole, it is thought that the *condictio ob rem* will only lie where the 'goal' of the performance was some sort of counter-performance. While in *Quistclose* situations the courts grant restitution, they are doing so in the face of strong academic opposition. Where the underlying basis of the transfer has failed, both courts and commentators prefer to apply the law of frustration rather than the law of unjust enrichment. As remarked above, at bottom the argument is about terminology and taxonomy, and it boils down to the question how many different forms of 'failure of basis' a legal system should have, and how these different forms should be categorised.

8.3.2 The '*Anstaffelungslehre*'

The room for the *condictio ob rem* has to be found between those cases which are referred to as *Rücktritt* (and thus fall notionally within the law of contractual remedies) and the *condictio indebiti*. In other words, the facts must not reveal a valid contract which has been terminated or rescinded *ab initio*, or a void contract creating the impression of a debt which had to be paid.

Difficult problems arise when the parties to a contract agree to pursue additional purposes. The payer thus pays not merely to discharge the obligation under the contract, but for an additional purpose which has not, however, become part of the contract itself. Thus the *Reichsgericht*, in the deserted husband case discussed above,[45] expressed the view that even in cases involving bilateral contracts there was some, albeit limited scope for the *condictio ob rem* to apply, namely in cases in which 'a result over and above the counter-performance was contemplated'.[46]

---

45 SeuffA 78, 1924, No 124 (18.1.1923), discussed above, p 147.
46 *Ibid*, 205.

Suppose, for instance, a niece looks after her elderly aunt for many years for not more than pocket money. She expects to inherit the bulk of her aunt's property. This expectation is well known to the aunt, but when she dies, there is no will. Can the niece recover the true value of her services from the estate? While the German Federal Industrial Court (*Bundesarbeitsgericht*) does not refer to enrichment law but to the so-called 'factual contract' doctrine,[47] the case raises fundamental issues. What if two counter-performances are envisaged, one enforceable under a contract, the other unenforceable? There are any number of different views of how this problem is to be solved, and we shall now examine the three main strands of discernible opinion. The debate may be of some relevance for English law, which has not yet had to face the problem given that it was only recently that the requirement that a failure of consideration must be total was dispensed with. As long as the actual contract was performed, there could thus be no 'total' failure and additional purposes could never enter into it. The question is whether this should now change.

The German courts even today assume that it is possible to array additional purposes behind the typical purpose of discharging a contractual obligation. This view is referred to as '*Anstaffelungslehre*' (from '*anstaffeln*' = to array).[48] In the academic literature, opinions range from a full acceptance of the relevance of the additional purpose to its complete rejection. Those who reject the '*Anstaffelungslehre*' argue that enrichment law is here dealing with questions that should properly be dealt with by the law of contract. Contracts, they argue, allocate risks. It is only in extraordinary circumstances that a contract will be re-written by the courts where the basis of the transaction has been destroyed by events that neither party could foresee. This is the so-called '*Wegfall der Geschäftsgrundlage*', or in English, the doctrine of frustration.

Originally, the German courts adopted the view that the parties to a contract can agree that the contract should be regarded as pursuing more than the purpose of exchanging performances. This view was first expressed in an *obiter dictum*,[49] but quickly became entrenched case law.[50] After the war, the *Bundesgerichtshof* did not hesitate to adopt the *Anstaffelungslehre*. In one case, a piece of land had a pig farm on it. The land was sold in 1942. The parties made a collateral agreement by which the seller was to relocate the pig farm in order to improve the amenity of the land sold. In 1952, the pig farm still was where it had been. The buyer sought to recover the purchase price paid under § 812 and succeeded before the *Bundesgerichtshof*. While the collateral agreement could not be enforced as a contract (for what precise reason does not become clear), it gave expression to a common additional purpose behind the payment of the purchase price. When that purpose had failed, the defendant seller was no longer entitled to retain the money and had to make restitution.

---

47 Cf BAG NJW 1963, 2188 (5.8.1963).

48 The word '*Anstaffelung*' is not in everyday use in German, and it is most difficult to express the same idea in English. A '*Staffellauf*' is a relay race, staggered working-time is '*gestaffelte Arbeitszeit*'.

49 Cf RGZ 66, 132 (5.4.1907).

50 RGZ 106, 93 (20.12.1922), 98.

In four cases between 1970 and 1977,[51] criticised by Liebs in an article published in 1978,[52] the *Bundesgerichtshof* made some concessions to the critics of the *Anstaffelungslehre*, but continued to adhere to the idea that it is possible to pursue additional, unenforceable, but restitution-yielding purposes by entering into a contract. The first of these cases concerned a divorce settlement. Husband and wife had acquired their home together, and they both were liable under the mortgage instrument. The husband formally undertook to relieve the wife from her obligations vis à vis the bank. In order to avoid various taxes, the parties informally agreed that the house was to be transferred to the husband at a date to be agreed. Predictably, the wife later refused to do this, but took the husband to court in order to obtain a declaration that he was liable under the mortgage. At first instance such a declaration had been refused on the grounds that the husband could rely on the *condictio ob rem* as a defence: it had been a collateral purpose of his undertaking to take over the wife's liabilities that the house would be transferred to him. That purpose had now failed. The *Bundesgerichtshof* agreed that no declaration should be granted, but differed in its reasoning. It based the decision on § 242, the 'catch all' good faith provision of the *BGB*, which is the provision that German lawyers relied upon to develop the doctrine of frustration:

> *Der Schuldner ist verpflichtet, die Leistung so zu bewirken, wie Treu und Glauben mit Rücksicht auf die Verkehrssitte es erfordern.* [The debtor is obliged to render his performance according to the standards of good faith, having regard to established custom and practice.]

The second case criticised by Liebs concerned a transaction between mother and son. The son had rented parts of a plot of land belonging to his mother, at a very advantageous rent. In return, he undertook to pay interest and make capital repayments to a bank which held a mortgage over the land. There was an informal but serious agreement between mother and son that the son would be granted proprietary rights over the land in question. Nine years later the mother went back on that agreement. The rent was adjusted upwards, and the son stopped feeding the mortgage. The son now re-claimed the instalments he had paid under the mortgage. At first instance he succeeded on the basis that the collateral purpose of paying the instalments had been the ultimate acquisition of a proprietary interest. The *Bundesgerichtshof*, however, adopted a more differentiated approach, taking into account the fact that, while he had fed the mortgage, he had paid a much reduced rent. This correct result was achieved, however, not through an unjust enrichment analysis, but primarily by means of amending the contract to reflect the new circumstances, applying the principles guiding the law of frustration derived from § 242, and with reference to the doctrine of good faith itself. Enrichment law was accorded merely a subsidiary role. In this way, the court argued, it was possible to come to differentiated, case by case decisions, and to amend the contract agreed between the parties in such a way as to reflect the doctrine of good faith. Liebs, while agreeing with this result, deplores the reasoning. Enrichment law might have provided the court with the analytical machinery to tackle the problem. Enrichment principles ought to have been applied in order to arrive at a principled decision. To Liebs, 'the appeal to the doctrine of

---

51   BGH WM 1971, 276 (26.11.1970); BGH WM 1972, 888 (4.5.1972), BGH WM 1975, 366 = NJW 1975, 776 (17.1.1975); BGH WM 1977, 535 = NJW 1977, 950 (9.2.1977).
52   Liebs, 1978, p 697.

good faith is no substitute for the development of realistic guidelines with a claim to universal applicability'.[53]

It appears, therefore, that the *Bundesgerichtshof* now gives precedence to contractual remedies, in particular the doctrine of frustration and related doctrines based on the doctrine of good faith.[54]

Liebs argues against this that additional purposes become part of contractual arrangements, even though they be not enforceable. On this basis alone, the doctrine of frustration should have no role to play, given that it is the very essence of frustration that an allocation of risks has *not* taken place, that is, that the frustrating event has not been averted to and its consequences have thus not become part of the contract.[55] Restitution is the correct response, as it draws the consequences from the fact that one purpose of the performance, as agreed on by the parties, has not been achieved. As seen above, Liebs attacks the doctrine of frustration further on the basis that it would lead to unpredictable case by case decisions. He argues that, despite its great age, it is still preferable to work with the *condictio ob rem* 'rather than on a *tabula rasa*, which would be the consequence of an uncontrolled extension of the doctrine of frustration', however helpful that doctrine might otherwise be.[56] Liebs draws attention to a further problem of extending the ambit of frustration. It might indeed be possible to sweep the whole of enrichment law aside and replace it with frustration, 'for every lack or failure of the legal cause would also be a frustrating event if frustration were this widely interpreted'. The consequence would be '*Kadijustiz*' or palm tree justice,[57] the first signs of which are arguably detectable in the second *Bundesgerichtshof* decision involving the mother and son.

The third of the four cases illustrates a different point: how ignoring enrichment principles can lead to positively unjust results. There the landlady of a pub had sold some land behind her pub at a ridiculously low price. It had been agreed that the buyers would construct and maintain a crazy golf course on the land (which was expected to benefit the pub). Planning permission for the development was subsequently refused. The buyers got over this 'setback' rather quickly and started using the land for their own purposes. The *Bundesgerichtshof* held that the landlady could not have her land back: 'The inadequacy of the agreed consideration for the performance cannot justify the rescission of the contractual agreement.' The court thus, according to Liebs, completely ignored the real problem of the case, ie the failure of an additional purpose agreed between the parties. The doctrine of frustration was not applicable, said the court, and that disposed of the case. Enrichment law did not enter into it. The result did not only produce injustice in that the buyers received a windfall, it was, says Liebs, clearly contrary to the code. A judicial creation, the doctrine of frustration, loosely based, as we have seen, on § 242 and the doctrine of good faith, took precedence over § 812 I 2, 2nd alt, arguably put into the code to provide for this very type of case.

To give precedence to contractual principles in this way might well lead to the total demise of the *condictio ob rem* as a cause of action in unjust enrichment, argues Liebs. This

53   *Ibid*, p 702.
54   Cf BGHZ 84, 1, 10 (29.4.1982).
55   Liebs, 1978, p 702.
56   *Ibid*, p 703.
57   *Ibid*, p 701.

is illustrated by the fourth *Bundesgerichtshof* decision he criticises, a paradigm failure of basis case: the testator owned 25% of the shares in a family company. His two daughters and his wife owned the rest in equal proportions. His son owned no part of the company. On the understanding that all three children would inherit one third of the company on the death of the surviving parent, the two daughters each transferred 15% of their shares to their father. However, the father disinherited them and left all the shares to his wife and his son. One of the daughters brought a claim in respect of the value of the 15% stake in the company which she had gratuitously transferred to the father. As Liebs says, 'a classical case of an enrichment claim based on failure of purpose'.[58] The court, however, applied purely contractual reasoning and, rightly on that reasoning, dismissed the action. Contractual thinking had grown so dominant as to displace the *condictio ob rem* in as clear a case as one could wish for.[59]

While Liebs puts forward a strong argument in favour of the *Anstaffelungslehre*, restitution lawyers should always tread extremely warily when there is a danger of undermining bargains, particularly since the doctrine of frustration in German law is now fully developed – the danger of palm tree justice has thus been diminished considerably. While Liebs is thus probably right in saying that the above case was wrongly decided, that is not to say that the case should necessarily have been decided on the basis of the *condictio ob rem*. The first question must surely be whether contract law cannot produce a satisfactory answer. If, in the first example, it is indeed true that the agreement to construct a crazy golf course had become part of the 'legal transaction' between the parties, it is difficult to see why it was not incorporated into the contract. If it was not, it must surely be for the law on frustration to decide whether the intention to construct the course was so central to the contract that the refusal of planning permission led to frustration.

Most academic writers endorse this view, and would indeed go further than the *Bundesgerichtshof*. They argue that purposes additional to the exchange of contractual performances are irrelevant if they have not been made a condition of the contract. The failure of such a purpose can, in extreme circumstances, cause the contract to be frustrated, but can never trigger a *condictio ob rem* which should be confined to purely non-contractual cases.

One of the first to put forward this view, and probably the most influential, was von Caemmerer. His essay[60] will be discussed in great detail below,[61] as it was instrumental in persuading most German jurists of the necessity for the distinction between enrichments by performance and enrichments 'in another way'. In pointing out the advantages of the German system, which, according to him, lie mainly in keeping apart contractual and restitutionary inquiries, he argues strongly that an intermingling of the categories should be avoided. Referring to some examples where the courts have applied the *condictio ob rem* to additional purposes, he writes that 'all the cases in which the courts

---

58 *Ibid*, p 703.

59 It should be said that the parties had argued the case in contract, not in unjust enrichment, the daughter claiming that she had made a conditional gift to the father (which would be seen as a contract in German law). However, unlike English courts, the German court would have been free to decide the case on the basis of enrichment principles on its own initiative.

60 von Caemmerer, 1954, p 333.

61 See below, pp 211 ff.

have proceeded in this way involve problems of frustration of contract, which should be solved according to the principles developed for that purpose'.[62] The view put forward has found many backers.[63] The arguments put forward are persuasive. The starting point of the critics is the question why a purpose, if it has truly become part of the contract, should not be enforceable. The proponents of the *Anstaffelungstheorie* argue that the additional agreement is placed in the 'grey area' between irrelevant motive and contractually binding condition. Given freedom of contract, any irrelevant motive can be elevated to a contractual condition, with the consequence that it becomes part of the contract, and its breach thus a matter for the law of contract. If it remains a motive, the consequence will be that it is immaterial for the relations between the parties. It is irrelevant, and cannot be relied on to support a restitutionary claim. Thus an additional purpose can be either motive or condition and, as Batsch points out, '*tertium non datur*'.[64] There can be no isolated 'grey area', which can only be imagined for purposes agreed for performances wholly independent of contracts.[65] As Reuter and Martinek argue, contractual parties will 'almost always pursue additional purposes'.[66] It is for the law of contract to determine whether these purposes have become part of the contract, or whether the contract has become frustrated by its failure. When Liebs argues that parties, in a system based upon freedom of contract, should be free to agree upon additional purposes that have, however, no obligatory effects, he fails to see that nobody denies that the parties are indeed free to do so: there is nothing to stop them from including a right to withdraw in the contract if an additional and otherwise unenforceable purpose fails. Thus, the claimant in the case discussed by Liebs could have insisted on a clause protecting her interest in the construction of a crazy golf course by providing in the contract that if planning permission was refused or the scheme aborted for some other reason, she would have a right to withdraw from the contract and claim restitution of the land. Even if such a clause was missing from the contract, the court may be able to find an implied term to the same effect, using the principles of 'supplementary contractual construction' ('*ergänzende Vertragsauslegung*') which are found in § 157 BGB.[67]

The courts, by giving general precedence to contractual remedies including the doctrine of frustration, are backing away from their original jurisprudence and may, before long, be in complete agreement with the majority of academic opinion. I would suggest that the problem is caused by the very wide formulation of § 812 I 2, 2nd alt, and its literal application by the Reichsgericht. It should further be noted that '*Wegfall der Geschäftsgrundlage*' was a relatively late development and was thus not at the disposal of the *Reichsgericht*, which was thus possibly right to fall back on the *condictio ob rem*.

In general, it seems that Birks is right when he draws attention to the irony that German enrichment law refuses to entertain a claim for failure of contractual reciprocation, while Hobhouse J argues that contractual reciprocation is the only 'consideration' that can fail. However, Hobhouse J's view does enjoy some limited

---

62 von Caemmerer, 1954, p 346.
63 Cf for many, Arens, 1971, pp 355, 358, fn 23; Esser and Weyers, 1971, § 49 II, p 456; Schlechtriem, 1995, p 653; Reuter and Martinek, 1983, pp 155 f.
64 Batsch, 1973, p 1640.
65 Reuter and Martinek, 1983, p 162.
66 *Ibid*.
67 Cf Larenz and Canaris, 1994, p 153.

support in Germany, namely by those who completely reject the *condictio ob rem* and who thus take the view that the only recovery for failure of consideration can be under §§ 346 ff. We will therefore now turn our attention to them.

8.3.3   Critics of the *condictio ob rem*

According to these critics, a disappointed transferor will either have a remedy in contract, or under the *condictio indebiti*, or not at all. If additional, non-contractual purposes have been agreed between the parties, then it will be a matter for contract law if they will be disregarded as irrelevant motives, or whether their failure will so fundamentally change the contractual structure that the contract can be effectively re-written under the doctrine of frustration. However, even if the agreed purpose is not collateral to a contract between the parties, but stands on its own, ie in the paradigm failure of non-contractual consideration case, they find it hard to see how such a purpose can be anything but an irrelevant motive. In the absence of a doctrine of consideration, the law will decide whether a promise is given contractual force. If it is not, then it should be disregarded. If it does amount to a contractual promise, there will be an enforceable contract. If that contract fails, the *condictio indebiti* will lie. There is thus no need at all for the *condictio ob rem*, which is simply not needed in a system based on freedom of contract.

While to von Caemmerer the *condictio ob rem* is no more than a 'historical relic',[68] he acknowledges that it is still applied to certain limited groups of cases.[69] Later writers, however, have built upon his criticism. In a recent article,[70] Martin Weber argues for further restrictions on the *condictio ob rem*. Having first outlined the historical background, he proceeds to condemn the acceptance by the courts of the relevance of purposes agreed in addition to a contract. However, he does not stop there.

His next target are the so-called '*Zweckverwendungsfälle*', that is, cases in which property is transferred in order to be used for a certain purpose. We likened these cases above to *Quistclose* scenarios in English law.[71] In Weber's argument, they are no different from cases involving contracts pursuing additional purposes, as here, too, a primary purpose (to make a gift) is combined with a secondary purpose (to induce a given behaviour). For this reason, he rejects this category and commends the courts' practice to tackle such situations predominately using the doctrine of frustration or indeed the general canon of contractual construction contained in §§ 133, 157. It is ironic that German law is argued to deny a remedy completely where English law, in the eponymous *Barclays Bank v Quistclose Investments*,[72] will give the strongest remedy imaginable: a proprietary claim. Again, the same arguments that were used above to support the *Bundesgerichtshof*'s jurisprudence can be relied on here. It should not matter that the 'hierarchy of relevant purposes' is upset in this way. What matters is that the parties have agreed that the transfer has a certain purpose. When that purpose fails, § 812 I 2, 2nd alt tells us that restitution should follow.

---

68   von Caemmerer, 1954, p 346.
69   *Ibid.*
70   Weber, 1989, p 25.
71   See above, pp 147 f.
72   [1970] AC 567.

Weber goes on to attack even those cases which are generally accepted as the secure remaining area of application for the *condictio ob rem*. These are, as we have seen, cases in which a transfer is made in anticipation of a contract, but before the contract is formed,[73] and cases in which the defendant was to be induced to act in a certain way.[74] The former he rejects absolutely, the latter subject to limited qualifications. As far as the former cases are concerned, Weber acknowledges that the fact that the agreed purpose takes the form of a counter-performance is suitable to distinguish this group of cases from the ones rejected before; however, he doubts that for this reason they are any more justified. The main danger, he argues, is that in cases where a transfer is made before a contract is formed the bar to restitution contained in § 814 can be circumvented by applying the *condictio ob rem*. § 814 excludes restitution where the claimant knew that he was not liable to perform, or where he performed to discharge a 'natural obligation' or moral duty. Weber's argument that the *condictio ob rem* would undermine this provision is, it is suggested, misconceived. § 814 is clearly intended to limit the negative formulation of § 812 I 1, so that restitution will only follow if a transfer is made in the mistaken belief thereby to be discharging a legal obligation, and not if it is made outright. The *condictio ob rem*, however, triggers restitution for a different reason: the failure of the purpose of the transfer above and beyond the purpose of discharging a legal obligation. It is often stressed, and indeed Weber does so himself,[75] that the *condictio ob rem* is the only enrichment claim in German law which formulates its own reason for restitution, and does not leave this task to the rest of the law. § 814 can thus not apply, and this is made clear in § 815 I, which limits the *condictio ob rem* to cases in which the transferor did not know from the start that the attainment of his purpose was not possible.

Weber goes on to argue that even the remaining category of cases, in which the claimant makes a transfer in order to induce the defendant to act in a certain way, should be narrowly confined. Other legal institutions, foremost amongst them the 'factual contract' and the doctrine of frustration, are to take precedence. According to him, the only cases that remain are cases in which the transfer is made in the expectation of a counter-performance which cannot be made enforceable for reasons of public policy or for the protection of certain vulnerable groups. This solution does have one great advantage: the *condictio ob rem* stays true to its classical roots in that it only lies in situations where it is not possible to make a binding promise of counter-performance. However, whether that alone is reason enough to accept the whole argument remains to be seen.

Weber is much influenced by a frequently quoted article[76] by Karl Ludwig Batsch, who criticises in particular that the *condictio ob rem* is argued to lie in a supposed 'grey area'[77] between contractual obligation and mere motive. According to Batsch, this grey area did indeed exist in classical Roman law and, less pronounced, in the *ius commune*, but ceased to exist with the enactment of the *BGB* whose central pillar is freedom of contract. He continues:

---

73 Cf above, pp 145 ff.
74 *Ibid.*
75 Weber, 1989, p 25.
76 Batsch, 1973.
77 *Ibid*, p 1640.

The whole concept of a purpose of a performance, which is elevated from an irrelevant subjective motive to 'the content of the legal transaction', is only possible and sensible in a legal order based on a '*numerus clausus*' of contracts.[78]

The *BGB*, he argues, is based on freedom of contract, and it is thus possible to elevate a mere motive to a term of the contract by simply stipulating to that effect. Thus, there can only be two categories of purpose in the system the *BGB* is based on: either the purpose has become a full term of the contract, or it has remained a mere motive.[79] Batsch thus rejects the *condictio ob rem* not only where additional purposes in a contractual situation are concerned, but totally, for all situations. In this, he overlooks a couple of important points. First, it was not the *BGB* that introduced freedom of contract – the *ius commune* had long since overcome the Roman *numerus clausus* of contracts,[80] retaining the *condictio ob rem*. Admittedly, its scope was significantly curtailed; yet it was never abolished. Secondly, when the *BGB* was drafted, a conscious decision was taken to retain the *condictio ob rem*. As far as legal history is concerned, and Batsch relies heavily on legal history and the Roman roots of the *condictio*, there is thus very little support for his assertions.

As Weber points out, the *condictio ob rem* differs from all other *condictiones* because *it contains its own reason for restitution*. It spells out clearly that if a benefit is conferred with a certain purpose in mind, and that purpose fails, restitution is to follow. The general law does not need to be referred to. Batsch who, as we shall see, is a fervent critic of the modern view of enrichment law based on positive reasons for restitution, cannot accommodate this *condictio* within his system based on the absence of an underlying legal obligation. It will be argued below that the experiment basing the law of unjust enrichment on one all-embracing general cause of action has failed. Batsch is one of those jurists who insist that it has not, and continue to argue that a unified cause of action in unjust enrichment, based on the lack of an underlying obligation, is feasible.

We thus see the *condictio ob rem* in a new light: the issue is not confined to whether or not there should be restitution in those very few cases where there has been a failure of purpose between parties that have not entered into contractual relations. It becomes much more significant. At issue is a fundamental decision: should the law look for individual, positive reasons for restitution, or should it be content with negative requirements such as absence of consideration? A system based on the latter will not tolerate recovery for failure of consideration outside contract. Thus the implications of Hobhouse J's *dictum* at the beginning of this book[81] go well beyond the relatively limited question it appears to address. It turns out that it is closely related to his proposed solution: recovery for absence of consideration.

The kind of abstract legal reasoning practised in Germany finds it difficult to accommodate the *condictio ob rem*. We encountered similar problems above when discussing the law of *Rücktritt*: a reluctance to acknowledge positive, concrete reasons for restitution.

---

78 *Ibid.*
79 *Ibid.*
80 Cf Zimmermann, 1996, p 537.
81 *Westdeutsche* [1994] 4 All ER 890, 924; discussed above, p 7.

8.4 CONCLUSION

In this chapter the reader's attention was drawn to the curious fact that, while in England it is hotly debated whether restitution for failure of consideration is available at all in non-contractual cases, in Germany it appears to be the only area of application for the so-called *condictio ob rem*, the German equivalent of failure of consideration. This claim is based on the failure of an agreed counter-performance, and is expressly restricted to non-contractual cases.

The anomaly disappears, however, if one places the German claim into context. First, we highlighted the Roman origins of the claim and its close connection with the Roman *numerus clausus* of enforceable contracts. It was then seen how, given that German law has long subscribed to the maxim that *pacta sunt servanda*, the modern *condictio ob rem* in § 812 I 2, 2nd alt is now being criticised as superfluous. Indeed, it is seen as a positive danger, given that the courts at times resort to the provision in cases in which the parties agreed to pursue additional purposes over and above the purposes explicit in a contract agreed between them. We have seen how this '*Anstaffelungslehre*' may have led to just results, but has threatened to undermine the neat and elegant mechanism of German enrichment law.

Finally, it was pointed out how it is precisely those commentators who favour an abstract law of unjust enrichment, divorced from positive reasons for restitution, who find the *condictio ob rem* in its different permutations particularly obnoxious. It was argued in this chapter, however, that this *condictio* shows that German law does require positive reasons for restitution. It is, after all, part of the German law of unjust enrichment, whatever its critics may say, and it is certainly arguable that it has an important role to play.

CHAPTER 9

NON-CONTRACTUAL FAILURE
OF CONSIDERATION IN ENGLAND

9.1 INTRODUCTION

Most, if not all, cases on failure of consideration are contractual in the sense that they involve a contract. One party has failed to perform his side of the bargain and has thus breached the contract. As we have seen, it will sometimes be more advantageous to the innocent party to ask for restitution of his own performance rather than rely on his remedy in damages.

The courts are reluctant to use the language of failure of consideration in cases not involving a contract. This may, of course, be nothing more than a historical accident. The English law of unjust enrichment has only recently been separated from the law of contract, which would explain the strong bias in the authorities towards contractual cases. Indeed, this might pose a problem to those who are sceptical of the availability of non-contractual claims, as they might be open to the charge that they have succumbed to the old implied contract heresy, which can by now be said to be comprehensively discredited.

On the other hand, their scepticism may well be justified. We have seen that in German law there is a strong school of thought which contends that the *condictio causa data causa non secuta* (generally known by the classical name *condictio ob rem*) should be abolished or at least of limited application. This would confine restitution for failure of basis to cases involving contracts, dealt with in the context of the law of contract. This school of thought relies on the argument that where a party seeks to qualify his giving in such a way as to enable him to recover his stake if things fail to turn out as expected, he should secure his position by entering into a contract. This view is so strongly held that it is put forward even though the BGB appears to be saying the very opposite.[1]

English law, however, with its doctrine of consideration (here used in the contractual sense, of course), makes it more difficult than German law to enter into contracts, and on this basis ought perhaps to be more inclined to allow non-contractual claims for failure of basis. Furthermore, the above argument has never been put forward in any English case to refuse restitution in a non-contractual case. On the contrary, the courts usually bend over backwards in order to give a deserving claimant some other remedy,[2] or they allow the claimant's claim without making reference to failure of consideration.[3]

The reluctance of the courts to allow claims for failure of consideration in non-contractual cases can thus, as will be seen, cause unexpected problems in areas of the law which on the surface appear to have little or nothing to do with the subject matter of this discussion. The common law remedy being supposedly unavailable, parties and judges take refuge in equity, and attempt to do justice by imposing resulting or constructive trusts. Claims behind trusts have proprietary effects, and thus they are capable of affecting third parties. In an insolvency situation it is vital, however, to preserve the *status*

---

1   See above, pp 155 ff.
2   Eg, *Hussey v Palmer* [1972] 1 WLR 1286.
3   *Chillingworth v Esche* [1924] 1 Ch 97, discussed at pp 163 ff, below.

quo so as to facilitate *pari passu* distribution, and to avoid the displacement of existing security interests. The granting of proprietary remedies must be strictly warranted and justified, and there is little to commend a legal system which grants a proprietary remedy incidentally, merely because the corresponding personal claim appears to be unavailable. Moreover, the terminology of implied, constructive and resulting trusts is inherently unstable, which does nothing to promote the rational treatment of proprietary remedies. It will be necessary to discuss some of the problems in this area later in this chapter.

9.2 HOBHOUSE J'S VIEW OF FAILURE OF CONSIDERATION

A legal rule can belong to the law of contract because it is the response to the causative event 'contract', or, more neutrally, because it responds to the causative event 'consent'. 'Contract' and 'consent' are here seen as causative categories. On the other hand, a rule can be included in books on the law of contract because it happens to be frequently applied in contractual cases. Thus Treitel's leading textbook on the law of contract includes a section on the law of restitution,[4] even though restitution is not triggered by the parties' consent but by the unjust enrichment of one of the parties. 'Unjust enrichment' is the causative category, restitution the response. However, when contracts fail, the unjust enrichment of one of the parties is often the incidental consequence, and for this reason it makes sense to include some reference to the law of restitution in a book on contract. If at all, it belongs to the law of contract seen as a *contextual* category.

It will be recalled that Hobhouse J expressed his view of the cause of action in failure of consideration as follows:

> The phrase 'failure of consideration' is one which in its terminology presupposes that there has been at some stage a valid contract which has been partially performed by one party. It is essentially a concept for use in the law of contract and provides a common law remedy governed by rigid rules granted as of right where the contract becomes ineffective through breach or otherwise.[5]

The question is whether his Lordship here refers to the law of contract as a causative or as a contextual category.

The law of *Rücktritt* is seen by many German jurists, as discussed in Chapter 3, as belonging to the law of contract as a causative category: restitution is seen as one of the remedial responses of contract law. By entering into a contract, the parties agree to be subject to that remedial regime. There are some indications in his *Westdeutsche* judgment that Hobhouse J shares this view where the English law of failure of consideration is concerned. He refers to it as 'the contractual approach'[6] and 'the contractual principle'.[7] These may, however, be merely slips of the judicial pen. It cannot be doubted that unjust enrichment, and not consent, is the causative event. Its affinity to contract is merely

---

4   Treitel, 1999, p 976.
5   *Ibid*, p 924.
6   *Ibid*.
7   *Ibid*, p 925.

contextual, not causative. Hobhouse J himself places the heading 'Total failure of consideration' under the general heading 'Money had and received'.

A second interpretation of what Hobhouse J means is far more difficult to disprove: while failure of consideration is an unjust factor in the law of unjust enrichment, one of its requirements may be that there has at some stage been a valid contract. Judges have often used concepts from the law of trusts to achieve the same results that the common law would have reached in a contractual case. This device may often lead to cases of 'proprietary overkill', as the finding of a resulting or constructive trust will have proprietary consequences which may not always be welcome, or at least may go further than necessary to reach the desired outcome.[8]

9.3 FAILURE OF BASIS: A PRINCIPLED APPROACH

To Birks, failure of consideration is an 'unjust factor', a ground for restitution, belonging to the 'I didn't mean it' category of events encompassing mistake, duress etc, with the difference that the enrichment is considered unjust not because the consent of the claimant was vitiated, but because it was 'qualified and never purified'. That is to say, the claimant specified the basis of his giving, and that basis subsequently failed. Much trouble would have been saved had this ground for restitution been christened 'failure of basis', rather than failure of consideration, with all its contractual undertones. As Birks explains, the term 'consideration' here bears the same meaning as it did when it first came into the common law. 'A "consideration" was once no more than a "matter considered", and the consideration for doing something was the matter considered in forming the decision to do it.'[9] It was only much later that the law of contract insisted that the only permissible 'matter considered' could be some sort of reciprocation. Outside the law of contract, the original meaning remained.

One great irony, says Birks,[10] of Hobhouse J's approach is that it mirrors an earlier error, committed by Collins MR in *Chandler v Webster*.[11] In that case, the Master of the Rolls was discussing the effect of frustration on a contract. In pointing out that a frustrated contract 'remains a good contract' up to the frustrating event, his Lordship observed that therefore 'the doctrine of failure of consideration [did] not apply'.[12] As long as there was 'consideration' (in the contractual, and indeed, according to Collins MR, only possible sense) sufficient to form a contract, that consideration had not failed and indeed could not fail. In other words, as long as there was a valid contract at some point, there could be no failure of consideration – exactly the opposite of what Hobhouse J says in *Westdeutsche*, but based on exactly the same misunderstanding of the term 'consideration'.

As pointed out above, the difficulties start when one sets out to try and back up these arguments by reference to the English case law, given that (1) most cases of failure of basis

---

8   *Hussey v Palmer* [1972] 1 WLR 1286.
9   Birks, 1989, p 223, referring to Simpson, 1975, p 321. See also above, pp 4 f.
10 Birks, 1993, p 209, fn 39.
11 [1904] 1 KB 493.
12 *Ibid*, at 499.

will involve a contract of some form and (2) the reluctance of judges to use the terminology of consideration in non-contractual cases.

9.4 CASES AT LAW: FAILURE OF CONSIDERATION

First, it should be pointed out that Hobhouse J's view of what constitutes a contractual case appears to be narrower than that of judges before him. There has never been any problem in bringing an action for restitution where a contract has been rescinded *ab initio*, even though, according to the logic of retroactive extinction, it is deemed to have never existed in the eyes of the law. Restitution follows either because it is an inherent part of the remedy of rescission, itself part of the law of contract (as a causative category), or because in the law of unjust enrichment the reasons that allow a party to rescind a contract (that is, mistake, misrepresentation, duress and undue influence) also allow him to obtain restitution of benefits conferred.[13] This latter analysis gains some support from a leading case on duress, namely *Universe Tankships v ITF ('The Universe Sentinel')*,[14] in which a contract was avoided for duress, restitution following on the basis of a claim for money had and received. Lord Diplock thought that it was settled law that duress was 'a ground for treating contracts as voidable and obtaining restitution of money paid under economic duress as money had and received to the plaintiff's use'.[15] Given Hobhouse J's new approach to the law of unjust enrichment, it is now doubtful if recovery in all cases of rescission could not simply be based upon the absence of consideration established by the very avoidance of the contract. As we have seen, this is the approach adopted by German law.[16]

In *Rover v Cannon*[17] the fact that the contract was void did not prevent the claimant from relying on failure of consideration. Even though there had never been a valid contract, failure of consideration was successfully relied on as a ground for restitution. Though the voidness of the contract was instrumental in bringing about the failure of consideration, it was not relied on as a reason for restitution, and thus Hobhouse J is surely wrong when he says that 'the analysis of Kerr LJ is essentially contractual'.[18] What Kerr LJ is saying is not that restitution follows because the contract is void, but because the consideration has failed. If Kerr LJ's analysis appears contractual, this is because of the unwholesome effects of the 'total failure' requirement: Kerr LJ has to find a way to discount the collateral benefit of having the use of the films, and for this he refers to the terms of the contract, arguing that it was not the use of the films, but the possibility of sharing the films' profits, which had been the condition of the payment.

---

13 There is a third possibility: rescission can be seen as itself a response of enrichment law to an unjust enrichment, the benefit conferred being the contract itself. The defendant has been enriched by having the benefit of the claimant's obligations under the contract, and because this enrichment was unjust, the contract has to be unravelled. This approach is favoured by Birks (Birks, 1996b, p 1), and is most attractive from a taxonomical point of view, but has nevertheless not been adopted in any reported case. See, also, p 33, above.

14 [1983] AC 366.

15 *Ibid*, at 383.

16 See above, p 21, and further below, pp 207.

17 [1989] 1 WLR 912.

18 *Westdeutsche Landesbank Girozentrale v Islington London Borough Council* [1994] 4 All ER 890, 929.

It is more difficult to prove Hobhouse J wrong where there has never been any kind of contract, not even a supposed one. However, this is necessary if we want to show that it is indeed the failure of basis, rather than the failure of a contract, which lies at the heart of the cause of action, that what matters is the *qualification of the will* of the claimant.

Chillingworth v Esche[19] is a classic case of failure of basis. It concerned the planned purchase of freehold land. The parties had entered into a preliminary agreement, 'subject to a proper contract to be prepared by the vendor's solicitors'. The prospective purchasers paid £240 'as deposit and in part payment of the said purchase money'. When the negotiations broke down, they sought to recover the money they had paid. Having held that there would be no agreement at all until a proper contract had been prepared, Pollock MR ordered restitution. However, his judgment fails to specify on what precise ground he did so. Counsel for the claimant had suggested that the money was recoverable 'on the ground that there never was a contract' and Pollock MR thought that *prima facie* he was right.[20] Basing himself on *Baylis v Bishop of London*,[21] Pollock MR argues that it is for the vendor to point to reasons why he should be entitled to keep the money, and not for the purchaser to show the opposite. The speeches of Warrington and Sargant LJJ are no more illuminating. Their Lordships appear to proceed on the basis that, since both parties were fully entitled to break off negotiations at any time, it would be unfair to punish the purchaser by the loss of his deposit if he chose not to proceed.

On this basis, *Chillingworth v Esche* can, in fact, be taken to support Hobhouse J's approach based on absence of consideration. The focus is very much on the fact that the parties never entered into a binding agreement. The defendant is required to justify his retention of the deposit. That is very close to saying that, given the absence of an underlying contract, there is a presumption that the enriched party's enrichment is unjust unless he can point to a 'just factor' a reason why he should be entitled to keep it: restitution for 'absence of consideration', in other words.

However, Pollock MR does go on to discuss circumstances in which a deposit would be held to be non-returnable, and this part of his speech can indeed be analysed as expressing a failure of basis. Having cited from Bowen LJ's speech in *Howe v Smith*,[22] to the effect that 'persons may make exactly what bargain they please as to what is to be done with the money deposited', he goes on to 'consider what in fact was the effect of the document',[23] which he previously held not to constitute a binding contract. The court's task was 'to ask ... whether this deposit was by those documents intended to pass irrevocably to the vendor if the purchasers did not carry out the transaction'. In the circumstances, his Lordship concludes that the deposit is recoverable because '[t]here was no provision made in the documents which would justify the vendor in declining to return it; though if it had, by appropriate words, made provision for that in the document, such a provision could have been upheld'.[24] In other words, the parties are free to agree a basis on which a payment is made. One such basis could be the successful

---

19 [1924] 1 Ch 97.
20 *Ibid*, at 106.
21 [1913] 1 Ch 127.
22 27 Ch D 89, 97.
23 *Ibid*, at 108.
24 *Ibid*.

completion of a sale, the failure of the sale causing the basis to fail and entitling the payer to restitution. Another possible basis would be that the prospective vendor would not break off negotiations (this would trigger restitution), while the prospective purchaser would forfeit the payment if he chose not to proceed with the sale.

The picture that emerges is confused: on the one hand, there is Pollock MR's focus on the absence of a binding contract, placing the onus on the defendant to prove that he is entitled to retain the payment. On the other, there is his Lordship's acceptance that it would have been possible for the parties to agree on a 'basis' on which the payment was made, which the defendant could point to as a 'ground of retention'. It should be borne in mind, however, that the English law of unjust enrichment is a very young subject. The judges in *Chillingworth v Esche* were still trapped by the implied contract theory. Since restitution still had to be explained in terms of contract, the link between the term 'consideration' and contract was almost irresistible. There was no independent law of unjust enrichment which deserved the name. It would thus have been quite impossible to decide the case on what we would today regard as a satisfactory basis.

However, the contractual connotations of the term 'consideration' prevent the judges in *Chillingworth* from specifying the precise ground of recovery. This reluctance to use 'failure of consideration' in its original sense prevails to the present day. In the more recent case of *Guardian Ocean Cargoes Ltd v Banco do Brasil SA*,[25] *Chillingworth* came to be applied in a major shipping case. The facts were rather complicated. In a simplified form they came down to this: the claimants had hired a ship on hire purchase. The building of the ship had been financed by the defendant bank. At the time of the completion of the vessel the bank was given security interests in it. The owners of the ship subsequently defaulted in their repayments to the bank. Anxious not to lose its interest in the vessel (to obtain full property rights by exercising its option to purchase at the end of the hire - purchase term), the claimant sought to refinance the deal with the bank. To encourage the bank to agree to its proposals, it paid in total $600,000 to the bank. When negotiations failed, the claimant sought to recover that sum, a claim resisted by the bank which claimed that the payments had been voluntary payments intended to discharge the ship-owners liability under the original financing agreement. The ship having been arrested, the claimants were thus in danger of losing both the ship and the money. Hirst J (as he then was) found as a fact that the payments were conditional upon the ultimate success of the negotiations and a successful re-financing deal. His Lordship then observed:

> In *Chillingworth v Esche* the question arose whether a pre-contractual deposit was recoverable by the prospective purchaser from the prospective vendor after the former had refused to sign a contract prepared by the prospective vendor's solicitors, and had declined to proceed with the proposed transaction for the sale of land. The Court of Appeal held that the question which had to be asked was whether on the evidence (which in that case was entirely documentary) the deposit was intended to pass irrevocably to the vendor if the purchaser did not carry out the transaction (*per* Pollock MR at p 108 and *per* Lord Justice Warrington at p 111). The Court of Appeal held that on the evidence it was not so intended, and gave judgment in the prospective purchaser's favour for the return of the deposit.

> It follows from my above finding of fact that the answer to the same question *mutatis mutandis* in the present case is that it was not intended that the payments should pass

25   [1991] 2 Lloyd's Rep 68.

outright and irrevocably to the bank whatever the outcome of the negotiations, but only if those negotiations resulted in a concluded refinancing deal. The claimants thus succeed on the main point, and are, as in *Chillingworth v Esche*, entitled to a judgment simpliciter for the return of their money.

This is the only part of the judgment which discusses the actual cause of action on which the case is based, and his Lordship contrives to do this without calling it by its name: failure of consideration. Indeed, that phrase does not appear in the judgment at all. Nor does it appear in the judgment delivered at a subsequent hearing to resolve a dispute over interest,[26] nor is there any mention of it in the Court of Appeal, which upheld Hirst J's judgment on liability, but varied it on interest.[27]

The cause of action is thus merely based on the authority of *Chillingworth v Esche*, and can thus be no more informative than that case. What is striking, again, is the reluctance of the judges to call a spade a spade, and to use the phrase 'failure of consideration' out of the contractual context.

In *Re Ames' Settlement*[28] we do find the phrase 'failure of consideration' in a seemingly non-contractual context. The settlor covenanted to pay £10,000 to the trustees of a settlement made in contemplation of his son's marriage 'in case the intended marriage shall be solemnised'. He paid the money to the trustees when the ceremony had taken place. Subsequently the marriage was annulled. The question arose who should receive the capital of the settlement fund. It was held that the money should be paid to the executors of the settlor, and not to the next of kin of the son, who would have been entitled under the terms of the settlement. Vaisey J said: 'I think that this is a simple case of money paid upon a consideration which failed'.[29] Lord Browne-Wilkinson, discussing the case in *Westdeutsche*,[30] describes the judgment as 'very confused', and concludes that 'the fund was vested in trustees on trusts which had failed. Therefore the moneys were held on a resulting trust'.[31] Equally, Jill Martin writes that 'Vaisey J decided ... that the property was held on a resulting trust for the executors of the settlor'.[32] However, this finds no support in the text of the judgment in *Re Ames*. The case is an example of 'common law in the Chancery Division'; the decision was based on failure of consideration.

Re Ames involved a marriage settlement (which is, of course, a trust and not a contract). It was directly concerned with a disposition made by way of deed between the settlor and the trustees, by which he had appointed to pay the sum of £10,000 to the trustees within one year of the date of solemnisation of the marriage. Thus, *Re Ames* cannot be said, in any meaningful sense, to involve the failure of contractual counter-performance: the trustees were not meant to render any performance at all. There was no need for consideration in the contractual sense, and no such consideration could thus fail.

---

26 *Guardian Ocean Cargoes Ltd v Banco do Brasil SA* [1992] 2 Lloyd's Rep 193.
27 *Guardian Ocean Cargoes Ltd v Banco do Brasil SA* [1994] 2 Lloyd's Rep 152, CA.
28 [1946] Ch 217.
29 *Ibid*, at 223.
30 [1996] AC 669, 715.
31 *Ibid*.
32 Martin, 1997, p 232.

What failed was the marriage; the being and remaining married was not a contractual obligation.

P v P[33] is a decision of the Irish High Court and the Court of Appeal. It concerned a marriage voidable at the option of the wife whose brother had paid some £475 to the husband 'in consideration of the marriage'. When the marriage was declared void *ab initio* the wife was able to recover £400 in an action for money had and received on a failure of consideration. In the modern world it is rare to regard a marriage promise in the light of contractual consideration. This is due to a profound change in attitude both to the role of women and the value attached to the institution of marriage. However, there is no doubt that not so many years ago marriage was regarded as the ultimate goal of the English young woman.[34] Any reader of PG Wodehouse is familiar with that scourge of the young British aristocracy, the breach of promise action.[35] In fact, the very first examples of consideration in the common law of *assumpsit* concern marriage as consideration.[36] Informal promises of marriage gifts had long been enforced in the Chancery, and this practice may well have influenced the developing law of *assumpsit*.[37] There was a problem to explain theoretically why a marriage was good consideration to support a promise to endow the marriage, and the most common way to do this was to argue that the promisor (usually the bride's father) derived a benefit from the marriage, the daughter being taken off his hands.[38] The problem with this analysis in *P v P* is that it was the claimant's brother, and not the claimant, who had given the consideration, and who should thus have been the only one who could rely on the contract. However, the same problem arises if the case is analysed (as we would like to do) as a case of failure of basis in unjust enrichment: the husband was enriched at the claimant's brother's and not the claimant's expense.

P v P can be analysed as a case of failure of basis or the failure of non-contractual counter-performance. However, in the view of different attitudes to marriage prevailing in Ireland in the earlier decades of this century, it has to be treated with caution. It is only of limited assistance in proving Hobhouse J's judgment wrong.

9.5 CASES IN EQUITY: RESULTING TRUSTS – FAILURE OF PURPOSE

The idea of restitution for 'failure of basis' or, indeed, 'failure of purpose', is, of course, familiar to trust lawyers as terminology often used when judges are trying to justify the imposition of a resulting trust. Chambers has convincingly demonstrated that the

---

33 [1916] IR 400.

34 If Jane Austen is to be believed, of course, this is equally true of eligible bachelors.

35 This action was only relatively recently abolished: Law Reform (Miscellaneous Provisions) Act 1970 (c 33).

36 Cf *Joscelin v Shelton* (1557) 3 Leonard 4, 74 ER 503; *Hunt v Bate* (1568) Dyer 272a, 73 ER 605.

37 Cf Simpson, 1987, p 420.

38 Cf the claimant's argument in *Sharington v Strotton* (1566) Plowden 298, 301, 75 ER 454: '... as if I promise and agree with another that if he will marry my Daughter, he shall have my Land from thenceforth, and he does so, there he shall have a Use of my Land, and I shall be seized to his Use, because a Thing is done whereby I have Benefit, viz the other has married my Daughter, whose Advancement in the World is a Satisfaction and Comfort to me, and therefore this is a good Consideration to make him have a Use in my Land.'

resulting trust is equity's main contribution to the law of unjust enrichment.[39] Just like the action for money had and received at common law, the resulting trust responds to the transferor's vitiated or qualified intention. Chambers's work will be considered in some detail below.[40]

There are four main ways in which a resulting trust can be imposed where the purpose of a transfer has failed:

(1) S transfers money to T to hold it on express trust for B. That was the purpose of the transfer. However, for any of a number of reasons, foremost amongst them the certainties and formalities, this has failed. The beneficial interest 'results' to S: T holds on resulting trust for him. The resulting trust is here used as a corrective device where an intended express trust has failed.[41]

(2) An express trust may fail because the purpose for which it was set up has not, cannot or will not be achieved. Again, equity imposes a resulting trust in favour of the settlor. It should be remembered, however, that non-charitable purpose trusts are of course void (and fall under the first category) unless they satisfy the test laid down in *Re Denley*,[42] so that this category is not as important as it otherwise would be.[43]

(3) A may pay money to B to be applied by B in a certain way. Thus, in *Barclays Bank v Quistclose Investments*,[44] money was lent to a company in financial difficulties on the understanding that it would pay certain dividends previously declared with that money. When the company failed before that purpose had been achieved, the lender claimed the money was held on resulting or constructive trust and succeeded. *Quistclose* singles out one group of creditors (those who have specified that the money they have paid should be used for one purpose only and for no other), and gives them super-priority in an insolvency. This book can only draw attention to the unfortunate proprietary effect of the decision. In particular, it is not quite clear what distinguishes a *Quistclose* purpose from purposes normally pursued with a payment, particularly with the purpose of obtaining a counter-performance.[45]

(4) Money changes hands in the context of a continuing relationship. When that relationship breaks down, the resulting trust may be a useful tool in reversing transfers which were made in the expectation and belief that the relationship would be a continuing one. One category of cases which immediately springs to mind is that involving matrimonial property disputes. These cases are troublesome.[46] The courts will have to take into account a whole plethora of policy considerations, often

---

39 Chambers, 1997.

40 See below, pp 168 ff.

41 For example: *Vandervell v IRC* [1967] 2 AC 291.

42 *In re Denley's Trust Deed, Holman et al v H H Martyn & Co Ltd et al* [1969] 1 Ch 373.

43 There is further the 'anomalous' class of trusts of a public character, as confirmed by the Court of Appeal in *Re Endacott* [1960] Ch 232. Such trusts will only be upheld if they can be effectively administered by the court, and given that they are 'anomalous', the existing scope of these cases should not be extended: see *Re Endacott*, at 246, *per* Lord Evershed, MR. Common examples include trusts for the erection or maintenance of graves or for the maintenance of particular animals.

44 [1970] AC 567.

45 For a more detailed discussion, see Chambers, 1997, Chapter 3: '*Quistclose* Trusts'.

46 Eg *Pettitt v Pettitt* [1970] AC 777; *Gissing v Gissing* [1971] AC 886; *Grant v Edwards* [1986] Ch 638.

informed by family law. For this reason it would not only be difficult to include them in the present discussion, but potentially outright dangerous: policies and arguments successful in family cases should not be extended to the commercial context.[47] Nevertheless, some cases involving continuing relationships cannot and ought not be ignored in the present context. The important case of *Sinclair v Brougham*,[48] can be analysed as a case involving a continuing relationship. A building society had carried on a banking business which was *ultra vires* the society. In consequence the borrowing contracts with the society's depositors were void. When the society went into insolvent liquidation, the unsecured outside creditors were paid off by consent. The question which the liquidator required directions on was whether the *ultra vires* depositors should enjoy priority over the members/shareholders of the society, whether they should rank *pari passu* with the members, or whether the members should be paid in full, leaving nothing for the depositors. The depositors could, of course, not rely on their contracts, as those were *ultra vires* and void. What sort of claim did they have? If they had no right to restitution at all, they would have received nothing, and the members would have been paid in full. If their claim based on an action for money had and received had been successful, they would have had a personal claim, and as unsecured creditors they would have taken priority over the shareholders. Thus the depositors would have been paid in full. The result reached by the House of Lords was pragmatic, but difficult to explain: it was held that depositors and shareholders were to be paid on a *pro rata* basis. In the *Westdeutsche* case[49] the House of Lords finally overruled *Sinclair v Brougham*, although the reasoning employed is open to serious criticism.[50]

9.6 INTEGRATING EQUITY

9.6.1 Resulting trusts

Chambers in his book on resulting trusts[51] sets out to show that resulting trusts are always restitutionary, responding to unjust factors in the 'I didn't mean it' family of claims. The resulting trust, according to Chambers, is 'equity's principal contribution to reversing unjust enrichment'.[52]

Chambers's main thesis is stated in his introduction as follows:

> It will be argued that when property has been transferred to another and the provider of that property did not intend to benefit the recipient, equity responds by imposing a resulting trust. The distinction between express and resulting trusts is that the former are

---

47 The unhappy consequences of doing this can be demonstrated in considering the Canadian law of unjust enrichment, see below, Chapter 13.
48 [1914] AC 398.
49 [1996] AC 669.
50 See Birks, 1996e.
51 Chambers, 1997.
52 *Ibid*, p 1.

created by an intention to create a trust, whereas the latter arise because of a lack of intention to benefit the recipient.[53]

However, the fact that all resulting trusts are restitutionary does not mean, according to Chambers, that equity will always respond to an unjust enrichment of the defendant at the expense of the claimant by imposing a resulting trust. Chambers thus examines the related questions of (i) how the resulting trust responds to unjust enrichment and (ii) what type of unjust enrichment it responds to.[54]

The second question is of relevance in the present context. Chambers points out that unjust enrichments can be analysed in two ways, depending on (i) the type of enrichment or (ii) why the enrichment is unjust. The answers to these questions will determine whether a claimant will have a proprietary claim behind a resulting trust, or whether he will be confined to a personal claim based on an action for money had and received, or for a *quantum meruit/valebat*. As to the first, 'all resulting trusts effect restitution of assets capable of being the subject matter of a trust'.[55] Thus, intangible benefits such as work done or services rendered are excluded from the start,[56] and so are benefits conferred on the recipient by allowing him the use of property or by saving him a necessary expense. This may seem to be similar to the restrictions placed on restitution for failure of consideration at common law, but the similarity is superficial and, it is submitted, accidental. While the restrictive nature of failure of consideration can be explained away as an accident of history stemming from the forms of pleading, the limitation placed on the resulting trust arises because of the logical necessity that a trust must attach to identifiable property. The tracing rules may assist in that exercise, but when it comes to intangible benefits such as work and services, equity has to capitulate. The only claim the claimant can have is then a personal one.

As to the second question, Chambers argues that 'whenever a plaintiff is entitled to restitution of property on the basis of non-voluntary transfer, the resulting trust will apply, provided the defendant does not obtain the unfettered beneficial ownership of that property before the right to restitution arises'.[57] In his chapter on qualified intention, Chambers explains that in order for a resulting trust to arise, the recipient must not have been free to use the assets transferred to him for his own benefit. Thus he identifies three categories of qualified intention which will give rise to a resulting trust: *Quistclose* trusts, situations in which the transferee's ownership is fettered in some other way, and initial failure of purpose. It will be useful to rehearse his arguments in a little detail.

Quistclose *trusts*[58]

The difference between a case of failure of consideration giving rise to a mere personal claim and a *Quistclose* trust is that in the latter case money is paid, in Chambers's words,

---

53   *Ibid*, p 3.
54   *Ibid*, p 105.
55   *Ibid*, p 107.
56   But note the matrimonial property cases, eg, *Pettitt v Pettitt* [1970] AC 777 and *Gissing v Gissing* [1971] AC 886.
57   Chambers, 1997, p 109.
58   *Barclays Bank Ltd v Quistclose Investments Ltd* [1970] AC 567.

'*to be used* for a purpose', as opposed to a payment for a purpose in the former case.[59] Thus, in *Quistclose* itself, the recipient was not allowed to use the money for any purpose other than the payment of the dividends, and Barclays Bank was able to enforce this obligation. For want of a better explanation of the incidence of a resulting trust in this situation, this one will have to do although it is, with great respect to Chambers, not wholly satisfactory: it involves a certain amount of circularity. Why was the money subject to a resulting trust? Because Rolls Razor could not use it freely for its own purposes. Why not? Because it was subject to a resulting trust. Nevertheless, it is suggested that Chambers is making the best of a bad job. He succeeds in identifying a factor which distinguishes *Quistclose*, at least superficially, from other cases of failure of consideration.

Other fetters on ownership

Chambers's main example for this category is Harman J's judgment in *Re Nanwa Goldmines Ltd*.[60] The case concerned share applications requiring applicants to furnish a deposit. The application form stated, however, that deposits were to be held in a separate bank account until the shares were actually issued. When the company was put in receivership, the applicants sought to recover their deposits. Harman J held that the promise on part of the company to keep the money in a separate account was sufficient to raise an equity or a lien on the separate fund in favour of the applicants. Chambers argues that this should have been sufficient to give rise to a resulting trust. Equally, argues Chambers, the trustee of an express trust is never intended and indeed never does enjoy full beneficial ownership of the trust assets. Similarly, the beneficiary's ownership is fettered by the fact that it is subject to the terms of the express trust. If the express trust fails, it is thus clear that a resulting trust in favour of the settlor will arise.

Failure at the outset

This category is problematic, as it is difficult to see what distinguishes a case of failure of purpose at the outset from a case of straightforward mistake. Chambers relies mainly on *Neste Oy v Lloyd's Bank plc*,[61] a case which itself bristles with difficulties. A shipping company employed agents to look after ships entering UK ports. It paid them in advance in respect of expenses to be incurred, such as port costs etc, as well as a fee for each ship. When the agents went into insolvent liquidation, the company applied for a declaration that those moneys not used for the payment of port costs were held in trust for the company. However, Bingham J held as a fact that there was no evidence that the money paid to the agents was to be used for the payment of port costs: there was no requirement of its being held in a separate fund and the agents were free to use it in whatever way they pleased. However, the final payment was received after the agents had ceased trading, and Bingham J held that a constructive trust in respect of that single payment was to be imposed. In respect of this final payment, argues Chambers, there was a failure of consideration at the outset: the agents had decided to stop trading, and did not intend

---

59   *Ibid*, p 148, his emphasis.
60   [1955] 1 WLR 1080.
61   [1983] 2 Lloyd's Rep 658.

to render the required counter-performance. This explanation is certainly much to be preferred to an explanation based on the recipients' lack of good faith.

These are extraordinary cases. Normally, a failure of purpose/consideration will give rise to a personal claim and nothing more. A proprietary claim must be justified by showing that the defendant never acquired an unfettered beneficial interest in the assets, and in the context of failure of purpose that will be rare indeed.

9.6.2 Failure of consideration and resulting trust contrasted

Chambers sees the resulting trust as equity's primary response to unjust enrichment. A resulting trust comes into being where property capable of being the subject matter of a trust is transferred and the transferor did not intend the recipient to receive that property beneficially. Where his intention is qualified rather than vitiated from the start, a resulting trust will only arise where the recipient never obtained unfettered beneficial ownership, that is, where he could not treat the property wholly as his own.

Faced with a failure of purpose, the law (here embracing both common law and equity) has two restitutionary responses at its disposal: first, the personal action for money had and received as on a failure of consideration; secondly, the resulting trust with its proprietary consequences. However, not every failure of purpose triggering a personal claim for money had and received will necessarily give rise to a resulting trust: we have seen that the resulting trust has a number of additional requirements. This is as it should be given that it can have far-reaching consequences for third parties. It is necessary to ask at this point whether every situation giving rise to a resulting trust must necessarily give rise to a personal claim for money had and received as on a failure of consideration. Is it possible to argue that while a resulting trust will require that the recipient must have received property capable of forming the subject matter of a trust and that he must not have enjoyed an unfettered beneficial interest, a claim for failure of consideration requires the existence of a contract and, possibly still, that the failure of consideration must be total? We have seen that the law of resulting trusts does not impose any such requirements.

This question goes to the very heart of Birks's use of resulting trust cases (which often do not involve contracts) as authority for the proposition that an action for money had and received as on a failure of consideration can lie in a non-contractual case. Burrows calls this question 'perhaps the most difficult of all the questions raised by the law of restitution'.[62] The waters have been muddied by Lord Browne-Wilkinson's speech in *Westdeutsche* itself. His Lordship, in direct response to Birks's arguments, strongly opposes the integration of equity into an all-encompassing law of restitution. While the present writer does not agree with his Lordship's approach, it is necessary to point out the considerable difficulties which are still in the way of relying on cases decided in equity as authority for common law propositions.

The jurisdictional chasm running through English law is regrettable, but it is generally acknowledged that it still exists. The majority of the House of Lords again confirmed this when *Westdeutsche* reached them, rejecting the notion that compound interest (normally

---

62 Burrows, 1993a, p 35.

only available to claimants who bring their case in equity) could be awarded in an action for money had and received,[63] although the reluctance of Lord Browne-Wilkinson, Slynn and Lloyd to agree with Lords Goff and Woolf on this point may be explained by the fact that the issue was not fully argued. While the integration of common law and equity should be regarded as long overdue, it is not yet complete. Beatson, in the concluding essay of his *Use and Abuse of Unjust Enrichment*,[64] points out some of the difficulties still to be overcome. Indeed, he stresses that these difficulties are more readily apparent in an area of law which is as yet not fully developed.

The first difficulty he points out stems from the perception of equity as a corrective device, a 'gloss' on the strict rules of the common law. If this view of equity still holds good, deriving principles applicable at law from cases in equity is dangerous if not logically impossible: recourse to the equitable jurisdiction is only required because the common law has failed to provide a remedy. On this view, the case of *Hussey v Palmer*[65] might be regarded as an example of equity doing what it does best: correcting a failure of the common law to do justice, and doing so based on 'equity's conscience'.

The role of equity as a corrective supplement is jealously defended by many writers and judges since, as Beatson points out, the 'integration of the two legal systems is seen ... to imply the inability of judges to continue to develop new correctives and devices to meet new circumstances'.[66] Thus Spry argues that equitable principles 'are of their nature of great width and elasticity and are capable of direct application, as opposed to application merely by analogy, in new circumstances as they arise from time to time'.[67] Against this, Beatson argues that the development of equity has been just as incremental as the common law: there is no radical difference between the two in this respect.[68] However, he recognises that equitable decisions are frequently informed by a number of principles, and thus it may be difficult to 'filter out the restitutionary ones', which 'appear to be inextricably mixed with non-restitutionary ones'.[69]

This can be demonstrated by examining the different analyses that can be placed on *Barclays Bank v Quistclose*.[70] Goff and Jones fail to discuss it as a case of failure of consideration at all. They see the case as demonstrating that a fiduciary relationship can arise even though an action of debt would lie at law, and thus as an example of an unwarranted exception to the general rule that an unsecured creditor ought to be denied a proprietary claim.[71] Burrows mentions the case only once,[72] in outlining the argument that if 'one looks behind the creation of so-called equitable proprietary rights through resulting and constructive trusts one sees that sometimes they appear to rest on the unjust enrichment of the defendant'.[73] On this view, 'a restitutionary analysis could also be

---

63 *Westdeutsche Landesbank v Islington London Borough Council* [1996] AC 669.
64 Beatson, 1991, p 244.
65 [1972] 1 WLR 1286.
66 *Ibid*, p 247.
67 Spry, 1984, p 1.
68 Beatson, 1991, p 247.
69 *Ibid*.
70 [1970] AC 567.
71 Goff and Jones, 1998, pp 91, 705.
72 Burrows, 1993a, p 36, n 18.
73 *Ibid*, p 36.

taken of *Barclays Bank v Quistclose Investments Ltd'*.[74] Burrows does not accept this argument, however: in discussing *Chase Manhattan Bank NA v Israel-British Bank (London) Ltd*,[75] a case involving a mistaken payment which triggered a constructive (but according to Birks really resulting) trust, he expresses the view that this trust must have further-reaching aims than merely giving restitution to the claimant bank, given that it 'became entitled to recover more than $2 m for it had a beneficial entitlement to whatever property represented the $2 m and that property might be worth more than $2 m'.[76] In the end, Burrows is inclined to follow the traditional English view that 'constructive and resulting trusts are not (restitutionary) remedies',[77] because they go further than a pure restitutionary remedy would and must thus be informed by principles over and above the principle of unjust enrichment.

Glover[78] goes further. To him, the 'overlap between equity and the independent restitutionary right is not great'.[79] He argues that '[r]estitution does not explain what is going on, even if the appropriate equitable remedies do sometimes have a restitutionary effect'.[80] He relies on *Quistclose* as evidence for this proposition. In that case, he argues, the 'payer's dispositive intention is perfected by a 'restitutionary' order which restores a payment to the person deprived'.[81] According to Glover, '*Quistclose*'s dispositive reservations were upheld. The House of Lords was not responding to Rolls Razor's enrichment, even if the enrichment was incidentally reversed'.[82] However, his points fail to convince. He himself refers to the resulting trust in *Quistclose* as 'the type of resulting trust which arises upon failure of the consideration, basis or purpose'.[83] Further, what exactly is meant by perfecting the payer's 'dispositive intention'? Is not Glover here describing exactly what Birks means by 'qualification'?

To Birks, the idea of two jurisdictions on occasion reaching opposite results *in the same legal system* is anathema. He writes:

> Again, suppose a jurisdiction generates a vigorous case law under the heading 'resulting trusts', frequently shooting wealth back to a person from whom it has been acquired. The law of unjust enrichment does the same. It shoots back wealth whence it came. The language of resulting trusts and of unjust enrichment is so different that, without a map and a will to use it, the lawyers might never even notice that they ought to check whether they were attacking one and the same problem with two armies. Ignorant armies clash by night: the two forces might indeed wipe each other out before anyone recognised the disaster which soldiers call friendly fire.[84]

---

74   *Ibid.*
75   [1981] Ch 105.
76   Burrows, 1993a, p 37.
77   *Ibid*, p 35.
78   Glover, 1996.
79   *Ibid*, p 101.
80   *Ibid.*
81   *Ibid.*
82   *Ibid*, p 102.
83   *Ibid*, p 101.
84   Birks, 1996b, p 7.

To Birks, a claimant is either entitled to restitution or he is not. It should not matter to his claim whether the pedigree of his cause of action is legal or equitable. To him, 'one large-scale danger to the rationality of our law lies in the exaggeration of the historical mission of equity to do justice, as though it had some special licence to ignore the requirements of legal certainty'.[85] Another great danger to a coherent taxonomy lies in identical or similar cases being decided differently according to the accident whether they fall to be decided at law or in equity.[86] Appeals to conscience are, according to Birks, inherently unreliable as a guide to legal reasoning. He uses a grisly *dictum* by Reinhard Heydrich, a fairly senior Nazi grandee, to illustrate the point: 'For the fulfilment of my task I do fundamentally that for which I can answer to my conscience ... I am completely indifferent whether others gabble about breaking the law.'[87] Thus to Birks the issue is not confined to the law of unjust enrichment, it assumes fundamental constitutional importance. If the law is no longer justifiable, he sees two dangers looming on the horizon: either a complete destruction of our law by the 'Critical Legal Studies' school of thought, or, going the other way, an ossification and restructuring of the law by way of codification.

Beatson, in adopting an intermediate position between Birks, who tends to abhor judicial discretion in any shape or form, and Spry, Glover and others, who seem to abhor firm rules and favour vague principles of justice and equity to inform the broadest possible judicial discretion, argues that unification is desirable and, in the long run, necessary. It is, however, as this short overview demonstrates, far from complete. While this jurisdictional chasm still runs through English law, however, there is nothing to prevent cross-fertilisation between the two jurisdictions. Thus, as Beatson points out, equitable responses to wrongdoing provide powerful arguments to recognise restitution for wrongs at common law, over and above the limited view of the 'waiver of tort' device. Similarly, one powerful argument against the liability mistake bar was that equitable relief for mistake by way of rescission was freely available, whether or not the mistake was as to a supposed liability or not.[88] Cross-fertilisation can also occur the other way, albeit more rarely: far from holding that 'Equity's conscience will rarely be disturbed by the mere retention of an enrichment obtained at the plaintiff's expense unless the defendant is guilty of fraud in its acquisition,'[89] Blackburne J in the recent case of *Omar v Omar* has recognised a strict receipt-based liability in equity.[90]

Beatson concludes his article by reminding us of the necessity to identify the rationales between causes of action both at law and in equity. Once a common rationale is identified, integration is not only possible but required.

---

85 *Ibid*, p 22.
86 *Ibid*, p 49.
87 *Ibid*, p 17, quoting from Campbell, 1946, p 147.
88 Goff J for the first time openly disapplied the bar in *Barclays Bank Ltd v WJ Simms* [1980] QB 677.
89 Glover, 1996 , p 103.
90 *Omar v Omar* (unreported), judgment of 28 November 1996, Chancery Division. I am grateful to Elizabeth Jones QC for bringing this case to my attention.

9.7 LORD MANSFIELD AND THE *CONDICTIO CAUSA DATA CAUSA NON SECUTA*

In *Moses v Macferlan*,[91] Lord Mansfield said as follows:

> This kind of equitable action, to recover back money, which ought not in justice to be kept, is very beneficial, and therefore much encouraged. ... [I]t lies for money paid by mistake; or upon a consideration which happens to fail.[92]

This must have been one of the earliest mentions of 'failure of consideration' in English law. The question must be what Lord Mansfield meant when he uttered those words. A powerful argument, put forward by Birks,[93] is that he was using Roman law concepts and ideas and giving them expression in English law. This would be particularly relevant in this context because, as we have seen, the Roman *condictio causa data causa non secuta*, to which he would have been referring, was indeed designed for non-contractual situations,[94] while the unwinding of contracts was the exception rather than the norm.[95]

Lord Mansfield, unlike many of his contemporaries, never quite lost his fascination with and admiration for classical Roman law. As James Oldham writes: 'A ... source of law that frequently surfaced in Mansfield's opinions was the body of civil law operative on the Continent, and in some measure in Scotland, augmented by the principles of Roman law. Mansfield's learning stretched from Pufendorf to the Pandects, and he did not hesitate to bring these sources into play.'[96]

Birks puts forward the argument that this is indeed what was happening in *Moses v Macferlan*. He argues that the passage quoted from above is 'a species of reception of Roman law. There was English case law to back up what Lord Mansfield said but the particular form in which he streamlined the domestic material is Roman'. The question of when the defendant would receive to the claimant's use was left open by English law, while 'the Roman *condictio* had been settled, albeit with difficulty, into a more informative typology. Lord Mansfield used the Roman typology to answer the question which the English cases untidily left open'.[97]

Birks's evidence for this view is impressive. He takes each of the three parts of Lord Mansfield's statement and points out its Roman roots. First, Lord Mansfield tells us when an action for money had and received will not lie, giving specific examples (payment of time-barred debt, money fairly lost at play etc). These are, argues Birks, expressions of the Roman idea that 'payment which satisfies a "natural" obligation is irrecoverable'.[98] He gives numerous examples from the *Digest* of the identical response of Roman law in similar fact situations.

---

91   (1769) 2 Burr 1005, 97 ER 676.

92   *Ibid*, p 1012.

93   Birks, 1984.

94   See above, pp 140 f.

95   See above, pp 91 f.

96   Oldham, 1992, p 204.

97   Birks, 1984, p 15.

98   *Ibid*, p 17.

Secondly, Lord Mansfield points out situations in which money paid will be recoverable, starting off with mistake and continuing with failure of consideration, imposition, extortion, oppression and an undue advantage taken of the claimant's situation contrary to laws designed to protect persons such as the claimant. Birks matches each of these with their Roman equivalent: he sees mistake 'as a convenient alternative way of indicating the *condictio indebiti* (the term *indebitatus* already being in use in the opposite sense of 'indebted'), failure of consideration as a rough translation of the *condictio causa data causa non secuta* ('consideration', in its original meaning, conveying the same idea as the Roman *'causa'*), and the remaining categories as encompassing what Roman law referred to as the *condictio ob turpem vel iniustam causam'*.[99]

Thirdly, Lord Mansfield describes the action as being founded in natural justice and equity. Birks argues strongly that Lord Mansfield was here not referring to the Chancery jurisdiction, but to Roman ideas of natural law based in reason. His statement is thus to be read in the same light as the Pomponius maxim *'nam hoc natura aequum est neminem cum alterius detrimento fieri locupletiorem'*,[100] which must be seen as the expression of a general principle rather than a positive rule of law.[101] This aspect of *Moses v Macferlan* will be further discussed towards the end of this book.[102]

Birks's argument that Lord Mansfield was bringing an English root (the action of account) 'to Roman flower'[103] is thus formidable, if not incontrovertible. If Lord Mansfield does not directly refer to the *condictiones* of Roman law, he certainly had good reason not to do so, given the frequent allegations made against him that he was corrupting 'the noble simplicity and spirit of our Saxon laws' by allowing himself to be guided by the 'Roman code ... and the opinions of foreign civilians'[104] (into whose legal systems Roman law had of course been received more or less wholesale).

If we thus go back to Lord Mansfield's category of recovery of money paid 'upon a consideration which happens to fail', it will become necessary to read these words through the spectre of Roman law. As Birks has demonstrated, what Lord Mansfield was referring to was the *condictio causa data causa non secuta*, which lay when money was given on a basis which subsequently failed. One obstacle that has to be overcome is Lord Mansfield's use of the word 'consideration' with its (to us) contractual overtones. Birks argues that 'Lord Mansfield was the last person to use "consideration" narrowly',[105] and he cites a number of his cases to support this statement.[106]

This whole discussion must, of course, be taken with a pinch of salt. Lord Mansfield's speech in *Moses v Macferlan* has, it must be remembered, not been universally endorsed by judges who came after him. Its authority is questionable even for the narrow point which it actually decides. Nevertheless, it is hoped that the discussion demonstrates that

---

99   *Ibid*, p 18.
100 Pomp D 12.6.14.
101 Cf below, p 202.
102 See below, pp 250 f.
103 Birks, 1984, p 22.
104 Cf Everett, 1927, p 306; Heward, 1979, p 137.
105 Birks, 1984, p 18.
106 *Pillans v Van Mierop* (1765) 3 Burr 1663, 97 ER 1035; *Atkins v Hill* (1775) 1 Cowp 284, 98 ER 1088; *Rann v Hughes* (1778) 7 TR 350, 2 ER 18; *Hawkes v Saunders* (1782) 1 Cowp 289, 98 ER 1091; *Eastwood v Kenyon* (1840) 11 A & E 438, 113 ER 482.

the original meaning of 'failure of consideration' was closer to the Roman concept of failure of basis in non-contractual cases than to Hobhouse J's understanding of the cause of action as requiring a contractual obligation.

There are, of course, counter-arguments. The most powerful one is this: the English law of contract of today is worlds away from the *numerus clausus* of consensual contracts in Roman law, and very far removed even from the forms of action which dominated English law in Lord Mansfield's day. The two principles which largely inform the modern law are freedom of contract and the maxim '*pacta sunt servanda*'. The gap which existed in Roman law has long since been filled. A party is today able to make enforceable promises in almost any way he wishes, as long as he follows certain minimum requirements laid down by the law of contract and remains within broad bounds set by law and (to a certain extent) morality. The need for the *condictio causa data causa non secuta* has thus disappeared. The only field of application for failure of consideration is thus the law of contracts, and that is where it belongs.

These arguments sound familiar. We have encountered them in the previous chapter when discussing the *condictio causa data causa non secuta* in the guise of § 812 I 2, 2nd alt. They were put forward by those who favour a law of restitution which is based on a general clause of unjust enrichment. One of these is Batsch, who argues vigorously that there is no such thing as the *condictio causa data causa non secuta* in German law, and who, as we will see below, also rejects the elaborate structure which has been constructed to limit the overly broad ambit of the general clause of § 812 I.[107] These arguments are relied on by those who strive for abstraction in German private law, who do not look for concrete reasons for restitution, but are content to base it on the absence of an underlying obligation. Nevertheless, we will see in the next chapter how, even in Germany, where abstraction is almost considered a virtue, these arguments have failed to win the day, and this applies not just to the courts but also to the majority of academic writers.

9.8 CONCLUSION

We arrive at the following tentative conclusions:

(1) Hobhouse J is clearly wrong when he argues that failure of consideration cannot be relied on to recover performances which have been rendered under contracts which were void *ab initio*. This is clear if one considers rescinded contracts, and is further supported by cases such as *Rover v Cannon*.

(2) It is more difficult to find authority to prove that failure of consideration focuses on the qualification of the claimant's will. Wholly non-contractual cases are few and far between. The courts have been reluctant to use the language of consideration in non-contractual cases, and have often chosen the escape route via the law of trusts. This can lead to unwelcome 'proprietary overkill', and shows that on principle the argument is a very strong one.

---

107 See below, pp 225 f.

(3) If Birks is indeed correct that the *condictio causa data causa non secuta* was the action that Lord Mansfield had in mind when he referred to failure of consideration in *Moses v Macferlan* (and all the arguments seem to support him), that would provide a historical argument against Hobhouse J's view of the action for money had and received as on a failure of consideration. However, there are counter-arguments, based upon the fact that the *condictio causa data causa non secuta* is not required in a legal system based on freedom of contract. These arguments mirror similar arguments previously encountered in our discussion of the German law.

We are dealing with two opposing visions of the law of restitution, both in Germany and in England. On the one side, there is what we may call the pragmatic school of thought, seeking to find concrete reasons for restitution. If one subscribes to this school, it is perfectly logical to allow restitution for non-contractual failure of consideration, and it is further not necessary doctrinally to fashion a special category of contractual claims for contractual failures of consideration, as the reasons for restitution are, as we have seen, the same.

This only becomes necessary if one follows the 'abstract' school of thought. To this school, restitution is based on the lack of an underlying obligation. The actual reasons for restitution are not inquired into. A substantive reason for restitution, such as the failure of the 'result contemplated by the legal transaction' in § 812 I 2, 2nd alt, does not fit into their structure, and it is for this reason that it is vigorously opposed. Furthermore, given Stoll's work on *Rücktritt* in Germany and cases such as *Photo Productions v Securicor*[108] in England, contractual cases require separate treatment because it is now established that there is an underlying obligation, in the form of discharged, but nevertheless valid, contract.

---

108 [1980] AC 827, discussed above, pp 128 f.

PART IV
THE CONDICTIO INDEBITI

CHAPTER 10

THE ROLE OF POLICY

It may appear somewhat odd to begin a part entitled 'The *Condictio Indebiti*' with a chapter on policy-motivated restitution. The *condictio indebiti*, it will be remembered, is the claim for an enrichment which was not due. It will become clear in Chapter 11, however, that this is rarely the true reason for restitution. Where a payment is made under a void obligation, the reason for restitution can normally be identified in the reason for the invalidity of the obligation. That reason will not infrequently be policy-motivated. Likewise, in the swaps cases, the true reason for restitution was not, it is suggested, the fact that the contracts were void, but the reason *why* the contracts were void: the *ultra vires* doctrine, a policy in favour of maintaining the integrity of public finances. In this chapter, we will discuss this and other policies which may lead to the invalidity of obligations as well as to restitution of transfers made pursuant to those obligations.

10.1 THE PLACE OF POLICY-MOTIVATED RESTITUTION IN BIRKS'S TAXONOMY

Birks acknowledges that, in a sense, all restitution can be said to be based on policy:

> Thus, even the mistaken payer's right to restitution rests ultimately on a policy or value-judgment to the effect that, even when account is taken of the social interest in the security of receipts, still relief ought to be given for mistakes. In short the right is the product of a decision which balances different goods and bads; and that is nothing if not policy.[1]

The reason why there must be a special unjust factor based on policy is the difficulty of exhaustive classification. There will always be cases which do not precisely fit a proposed typology. It is, therefore, good practice openly to acknowledge this by introducing a catch-all category entitled 'others'. In the case of Birks's typology of the internal structure of the law of unjust enrichment, the category 'others' is best referred to as 'policy-motivated restitution', which excludes all those cases already covered by the more common unjust factors of ignorance, mistake, duress, failure of consideration and, perhaps, unconscientious receipt. Birks himself identifies five examples of policy-motivated restitution,[2] acknowledging that there are many others. This chapter will examine examples of policy-motivated restitution which may tempt us to conclude that restitution is generally based on the invalidity or absence of an underlying obligation. These are: incapacity, illegality and *ultra vires* demands. Again, it is not claimed that this list is complete. Indeed, it is one of the mainstays of the argument presented in this book that it may very well not be complete, with the result that the introduction of a general cause of action in unjust enrichment based on nullity or absence of consideration might have consequences as yet unforeseen and unforeseeable.

---

1   Birks, 1989, p 294.
2   They are: no taxation without Parliament, discouragement of unlawful conduct, encouragement of rescue at sea, protection of creditors and investors and the elimination of anomalies.

10.2 INCAPACITY

One way to categorise incapacity as a reason for restitution is to include it under the heading 'defective intention'. Some natural persons need to be protected from themselves because, as Birks says, they markedly lack 'the social and intellectual advantages of the average citizen'.[3] This categorisation does not work very well, however, when applied to the incapacity of legal persons, such as companies or, indeed, public authorities. There is nothing wrong with the intention of a legal person exceeding its powers – it is just that the law refuses to give effect to it in order to promote policies more important than the right to self-determination of the legal person in question. If one examines the incapacity of natural persons more closely, it becomes apparent that here, too, basing restitution for incapacity on lack of intent recognised by law introduces a certain amount of artificiality. A seventeen year old will normally be more than able to form a proper intention and to express it. If the law does not always recognise the expression of his intention as a valid declaration of will leading to an enforceable contract, this is best explained on the basis of policy.[4]

10.2.1 Minors

The policy to protect minors from themselves finds expression in a number of more or less detailed rules. The application of these rules can in some cases lead to restitution of performances rendered under contracts entered into by minors. The English regime has never been distinguished by its elegance. The general rule is that a minor cannot get out of a fully executed contract, but is not bound to perform his side of the bargain if the contract is still executory. On the other hand, he can enforce the other party's obligations under the contract. There are a number of exceptions to this general rule, which are ostensibly required 'not for the benefit of the tradesman who may trust the infant, but for the benefit of the infant himself'.[5] In reality, the exceptions are in place to protect honest tradesmen who have entered into contracts with minors in good faith.[6] Thus, if the minor has received goods or services which are held to be 'necessaries', he must pay a reasonable sum for them. Further, a minor is required to perform contracts of apprenticeship and such like, but subject to the proviso that the contract as a whole must be for his benefit.[7] There are some contracts which are binding but which can be repudiated during the minor's minority or within a reasonable time after attaining his majority. These include land contracts, marriage settlements, dealings in shares and partnerships. It is clear that the concept of 'necessaries' is very unstable. Likewise, the question whether a contract of service is on the whole for the benefit of the minor is very

---

3 Birks, 1989, p 216.
4 Treitel adopts the same analysis: see Treitel, 1999, p 501. Birks accepts that this is one possible way to categorise incapacity: see Birks, 1993, p 223. On the other hand, the recent draft of the next American *Restatement of the law of Restitution and Unjust Enrichment* lists 'Incapacity of Transferor' under the general topic 'Other Instances of Defective Consent'. See American Law Institute, 2001, pp 255 ff.
5 *Ryder v Wombwell* (1868) LR 4 Ex 32, 38.
6 Cf Treitel, 1999, p 499.
7 Cf *De Francesco v Barnum* (1889) 43 Ch D 165, (1890) 45 Ch D 430.

subjective indeed. English law thus fails to provide clear and universally applicable rules – the issue will in most cases be left to the judge to decide.

The protection afforded to the minor is generally restricted to restitution of his promise, not restitution of his performance. In other words, he cannot be compelled to perform, but once he has performed he cannot recover his performance in unjust enrichment. The unjust factor 'incapacity' is just confined to executory contracts. The policy adopted by English law is that the protection of the minor against his own improvidence is more important than the other party's expectation of a counter-performance, but less important than his interest in the security of his receipt. It is an open question whether, in view of the recognition of change of position, this policy may not have to be reconsidered. It is important, however, that this be done openly and not covertly. A covert way of achieving the same result would be to argue that the minor, in performing the contract which did not bind him, was labouring under a mistake of law: had he known that he was not liable, he would not have performed. This approach would lead to highly arbitrary results: the minor entering into a contract of sale immediately executed (for example, buying wild ducks and champagne in a shop) would not be able to recover: his payment was not caused by his belief in any kind of legal liability: he paid because he fancied ducks and champagne. The minor who ordered the ducks and champagne on credit and later paid believing to be liable, on the other hand, would be able to recover. Distinguishing between these two cases makes very little sense, as the underlying policy should be the same.

German law has developed a sophisticated regime which governs the contracts of minors.[8] The relevant provisions are to be found in §§ 104–13 BGB. German law takes the view that the decision whether a contract is advantageous to the minor or not should not be taken by the court but by the minors' parents or guardian.[9] In a nutshell, minors below the age of seven cannot enter into any legal transactions at all.[10] Older minors can only enter into contracts which exclusively benefit them – that is, most gratuitous contracts, but no contracts which require some counter-performance, however small, however economically advantageous the contract may be. They can only enter into other kinds of contract if they first obtain the permission of their legal representative.[11] Where they enter into a contract without such permission, the contract is subject to a kind of 'qualified invalidity' (schwebende Unwirksamkeit) – the minor's legal representative will have the option to ratify the contract or to refuse to do so; until the contract is ratified or otherwise, the other party is free to cancel the contract: § 109. The legal representative will therefore have to take the decision whether the minor should escape from the contract or whether he should remain subject to it. This decision will depend on the view the legal representative takes of the contract. If he refuses to ratify, the minor will have to make restitution of what he has received under the contract under § 812 I, subject to the

---

8   The regime also applies, *mutatis mutandis*, to mentally ill people. For the sake of simplicity, the discussion will be confined to minors.

9   The word 'legal representative' will be used to encompass both categories from now on.

10 § 104.

11 § 107. This can be said to encompass a 'blanket' permission to deal with a sum of money entrusted to minors by way of pocket money as they please (see the so-called 'pocket money paragraph', § 110), or where the minor has been allowed to carry out a trade, or to enter into a contract of service or apprenticeship to enter into contracts which are usually incidental thereto: see §§ 112, 113.

disenrichment defence in § 818 III, which is even more widely interpreted in the case of minors than it usually is.[12] The availability of restitution is not directly addressed in §§ 104–13. Those provisions merely provide that minors' contracts are in certain circumstances void. The word 'void', although it is not expressly used as relates to contracts entered into by minors above the age of six, triggers the operation of § 812 I. The protective policy of §§ 104–13 is thus carried through to restitution.

It is obvious that the English regime is far less sophisticated. In particular, contracts entered into by minors are not generally void – they are merely not binding on the minor. This was not always the case. By s 1 of the Infants Relief Act 1874, now superseded by the Minors' Contracts Act 1987, all contracts for money lent or goods supplied entered into by minors were absolutely void. Birks has argued, with some hesitation, that the evidence of cases decided under this provision suggests that minors were not entitled to restitution of performances rendered under such void contracts unless they had suffered a total failure of consideration.[13] In *Pearce v Brain*, the claimant minor had exchanged his motorcycle for the defendant's car. The latter turned out to be defective. Although the contract was void, the Divisional Court held that as the claimant had not suffered a total failure of consideration, he was not entitled to restitution. The same result was reached in *Steinberg v Scala (Leeds) Ltd*,[14] in which the claimant, having avoided a contract voidable because it involved share dealings, could not recover the price paid for the shares because she had enjoyed the rights conferred by ownership of the shares for some time and could therefore not be described as having suffered a total failure of consideration. Birks points out, however, that the authority on which these cases were decided, namely *Valentini v Canali*,[15] could have been interpreted as supporting the minor's right to restitution subject to his ability to make counter-restitution.[16] He goes on to point out, however, that this would mean no more and no less than an expression of a policy that the minor should be protected from his own improvident dealings by allowing him a right to restitution of his own performance in certain circumstances. What cannot be derived from that case, therefore, is the automatic triggering of restitution by the word 'void'.

10.2.2 Legal persons with limited capacity

In the case of minors, the policy of English law does not appear to carry through to restitution of performances rendered under contracts which would not otherwise be binding. In German law, we have seen that the position is otherwise. Some contracts entered into by minors are rendered void following precise and well structured rules giving discretion to the minor's legal representative, but not to the court. If the contract is void, restitution is the automatic consequence.

Where legal persons exceed their legal powers by entering into a contract, that contract is void. The fundamental question which underlies this whole book is whether the mere fact that the contract is void will lead to restitution of benefits received under it

---

12 Cf Palandt/Heinrichs, 1997, p 73.
13 Birks, 1993, p 222.
14 [1923] 2 Ch 452.
15 (1889) 24 QBD 166.
16 Birks, 1993, p 223.

(as it does in German law), or whether restitution depends on the question whether the policy underlying the contracts' invalidity will also extend to restitution.

The main importance of the *ultra vires* doctrine has shifted from companies to public bodies. The effect of s 9(1) of the European Communities Act 1972 is that the acts of companies will almost always be *intra vires*, and thus the issue will rarely if ever arise in this context. As for public bodies, the swaps saga has certainly raised the profile of the *ultra vires* doctrine considerably. Again, it is possible to analyse the effect of an *ultra vires* transfer in two ways. On the one hand, the public body can be described as 'a helpless and mindless entity whose affairs have to be managed by natural trustee-like natural persons'.[17] This approach focuses on the voluntariness of the payment: if the natural persons exceeded their powers, they can no longer be said to represent the public authority. As such, the public authority itself did not mean the transfer to take place. It is suggested, again, that it is less artificial to acknowledge that restitution, if it is awarded, is based on a policy to protect the integrity of public finances.[18] This policy could easily explain awarding restitution of moneys paid to banks by local authorities: here, the council tax payers are protected from having their public finances disrupted by their council being exposed to excessive liabilities. It is somewhat more difficult to justify restitution against councils by banks on the basis of the policy underlying the *ultra vires* rule. It is not impossible, however, as a passage by Leggatt LJ in *Westdeutsche* demonstrates. This passage is quoted with approval by Waller LJ in *Guinness Mahon*. He describes it as 'pure policy':

> The parties believed that they were making an interest swaps contract. They were not, because such a contract was *ultra vires* the council. So they made no contract at all. The council say that they should receive a windfall, because the purpose of the doctrine of *ultra vires* is to protect council taxpayers whereas restitution would disrupt the council's finances. They also contend that it would countenance 'unconsidered dealings with local authorities'. If that is the best that can be said for refusing restitution, the sooner it is enforced the better. Protection of council taxpayers from loss is to be distinguished from securing a windfall for them. The disruption of the council's finances is the result of ill-considered financial dispositions by the council and its officers. It is not the policy of the law to require others to deal at their peril with local authorities, nor to require others to undertake their own inquiries about whether a local authority has power to make particular contracts or types of contract. Any system of law, and indeed any system of fair dealing, must be expected to ensure that the council do not profit by the fortuity that when it became known that the contract was ineffective the balance stood in their favour. In other words, in circumstances such as these they should not be unjustly enriched.[19]

This amounts in effect to a principle of fairness which reflects very well the attitude of English law towards public authorities being as much subject to the rule of law as the citizens who are governed by them. The *ultra vires* doctrine demands that where local authorities have been the losers of an interest rate swap transaction, they should be entitled to restitution. Otherwise the very purpose of the ultra vires doctrine would be

---

17   Birks, 1989, p 310, describing the doctrine as it related to companies.

18   Cf *Hazell v Hammersmith and Fulham London Borough Council* [1992] 2 AC 1, 36, *per* Lord Templeman.

19   *Westdeutsche Landesbank v Islington London Borough Council* [1994] 4 All ER 890, 967, *per* Leggatt LJ, cited with approval in *Guinness Mahon & Co Ltd v Kensington London Borough Council* [1999] QB 215, 233, *per* Waller LJ.

undermined. It is the corollary of this, however, that where a local authority has been the winner of an interest rate swap, the bank should likewise be entitled to recover. Otherwise the bank would be 'punished' twice, particularly if it had 'hedged' its exposure under one swap by entering into a mirror image of it with another local authority. As a matter of fact, as was only to be expected, overall the banks were better at betting on interest rate movements and had, overall, been the winners under swap transactions. They were being asked to refund their winnings with interest on a massive scale. It would be difficult to justify, therefore, that the local authorities were allowed to keep their winnings while the banks had to return theirs. It is thus (just) possible to justify restitution on the basis of the policy underlying the *ultra vires* doctrine, but the problem is that the policy has never been fully articulated.[20] In fact, the above quote from Leggatt LJ's judgment in *Westdeutsche* is the most comprehensive discussion there is of the underlying reason for restitution in these cases.

Waller LJ in *Guinness Mahon* recognised that it might be a step too far to award restitution on the basis of absence of consideration alone. He supported restitution because he considered himself bound by the decision of the Court of Appeal in *Westdeutsche*, and because he thought that 'if the matter were considered at a higher level, there may well be further elaboration of the appropriate basis, the result will be the same'.[21] Waller LJ therefore thought that, if the House of Lords had the opportunity to review the closed swaps cases, it might base restitution on a proper articulation of the policy underlying the *ultra vires* doctrine. As we now know, that opportunity never came. The limitation point in *Lincoln* forced the House of Lords to base restitution on mistake of law instead. We have seen above that this does not solve the problem at all. In fact, it can be argued that indeed the *Lincoln* case confirms that there now is a general rule in English law that nullity of an underlying contract leads to restitution without more.[22]

There are not a great number of cases on the consequences of *ultra vires* contracts entered into by local authorities in Germany. A case decided by the *Bundesgerichtshof* in 1956[23] is, however, fairly close to the facts of the swaps litigation: the defendant public body had the function to regulate the fisheries industry. Just before the currency reform after the Second World War, it decided to acquire large fish stocks in order to minimise the risk of the currency reforms. The claimant sold the fish to the defendant, but remained in possession and in fact sold it, as agent of the defendant, generating a profit of just over DM1m. This money was paid over to the defendant. It then came to the claimant's attention that it had been beyond the scope of the defendant's powers to enter into sale transactions for gain. This was because the defendant's function was to regulate the fisheries industry, not to become involved itself in that industry. As the purchase of fish had been outside the purposes of the defendant's powers, it had been '*ultra vires*' the defendant. The claimant argued that for this reason it should be entitled to restitution of the profits of the sale of the fish which it had paid over to the defendant. This argument failed at first and second instance, but was successful in the *Bundesgerichtshof*. The court reasoned that since 'public legal persons are generally only allowed to enter into private

---

20 Cf Birks, 2000b, p 18.
21 *Guinness Mahon & Co Ltd v Kensington London Borough Council* [1999] QB 215, 233–34.
22 See above, p 86–87.
23 BGHZ 20, 119 (28.2.1956).

legal transactions within the framework of the purposes and functions allocated to them ... acts which lie outside this framework are simply devoid of legal effect'.[24] Therefore, concluded the court, the contract by which the defendant purported to buy the fish was wholly void, and both parties had rendered their performances 'without legal ground'. As such, the defendant had to account for the profits of the sale of the fish to the claimant.[25]

It should be pointed out that this kind of case would today be decided by the administrative rather than the civil courts, applying a regime of restitutionary claims which is similar but not identical to §§ 812 ff.[26] Nevertheless, it is striking how the *Bundesgerichtshof* simply concluded that the fact that the contract was void for lack of capacity should lead to restitution. There is no discussion whatsoever of the underlying reasons for restitution. These can only be identified by examining the reasons why the contract was held to be void, and this exercise is useful from an English lawyer's point of view, as it helps us spell out the policy favouring restitution in the swaps cases. It would appear that the answer is prophylaxis: the public authority is required to stay within the law in all its dealings. The best way to remove the temptation to engage in speculative transactions which bear no relation whatsoever to its true functions, is to strip the authority of its winnings if the speculation happens to pay off. Thus, the rationale would appear to be similar to the rationale of restitution in English cases such as *Boardman v Phipps*.[27]

10.3 ILLEGALITY

Whether illegality *per se* can be a ground for restitution is a question of some controversy. We know that it can be a defence to a claim in unjust enrichment. However, at least to the extent that illegality can render a contract void, it must be considered a ground for restitution, each party to the illegal bargain receiving back what he purported to give, namely his own liability to perform. Goff and Jones, Birks and Burrows argue that even where contracts have been executed, illegality can act as a restitutionary unjust factor.[28] In German law, if an illegal contract is void this will trigger restitution unless the defendant can rely on the illegality defence in § 817 *BGB*. Similarly, if English law recognises a doctrine by which nullity as such triggers restitution, it is suggested that the underlying policy must be the invalidating illegality itself.

---

24 See p 124.
25 See p 127.
26 Wolff, 2000, p 222. See further below, pp 192 ff.
27 [1967] 2 AC 46.
28 Goff and Jones, 1998, p 607; Birks, 1989, p 299; Burrows, 1993a, p 333.

10.3.1 German law

In German law, a legal transaction may be void because it violates a legal prohibition (§ 134), because it is extortionate (§ 138 II) or because it is generally 'contra bonos mores' (§ 138 I).[29] This section will concentrate on transactions which are actually illegal. Many of the points made also apply, mutatis mutandis, to extortionate and 'immoral' transactions.

The drafters of the BGB certainly considered 'illegality' to be a ground for restitution. Thus § 134 BGB provides:

Ein Rechtsgeschäft, das gegen ein gesetzliches Verbot verstößt, ist nichtig, wenn sich nicht aus dem Gesetz ein anderes ergibt. [A legal transaction which violates a legal prohibition is void, unless the infringed law indicates otherwise.]

We know that the word 'nichtig' triggers restitution in German law. However, it is interesting to note that § 134 does not declare all illegal transactions void. This recognises the fact that a proper construction of the legal prohibition may reveal that no civil law sanction (such as restitution) is intended in addition to the sanctions (if any) provided for by the relevant legal provision itself.[30] In construing the provision in question, the judge will pay special attention to the purpose of the prohibition – purposive construction is even more important in this context than it generally is in German law.[31] This solution, to make the question whether or not an illegal transaction is absolutely void depend on the proper construction of the prohibiting statute, represents a departure on the part of the BGB from both the precedent of § 79 of the Saxon BGB of 1863, or indeed Art 1133 of the Code Civil.[32]

It should be noted at the outset that § 134 is capable of rendering a transfer void ab initio, with the result that no property will pass between the parties. A case decided by the Bundesgerichtshof in 1953[33] concerned a contract under which the parties purported to trade wood against machinery and furniture. Barter in these goods undermined the rationing regime in force in post-war Germany and was therefore illegal.[34] The court held that, although the goods were exchanged, property never passed. § 134 invalidated the transfer.[35] The result is, effectively, that the claimant is given a proprietary remedy. The concept of tracing being alien to German law, however, this will not apply to money payments and, by the very nature of things, not to the provision of services, so that in the majority of cases the claimant will have to rely on the personal claim in § 812 I.

It should also be pointed out straight away that, as in English law, there is a complex interrelationship between illegality as a ground for restitution (or, as a German lawyer might prefer to call it, as an invalidating factor)[36] and as a defence to a restitutionary

---

29 Cases which would come under the heading 'actual undue influence' would be decided under this provision in Germany.

30 Cf MünchKomm/Mayer-Maly, 1997, p 1087.

31 Ibid.

32 Along with Art 1343 of the Italian Codice Civile, this provides for a 'relative' invalidity, which only has consequences between the immediate parties to the transaction.

33 BGHZ 11, 59 (3.11.1953).

34 Under § 1a 2 of the KWVO.

35 See pp 61–62.

36 § 134 BGB.

claim.[37] § 817 2, which bases a defence to restitution on the illegality of transfer and receipt, is one of the most controversial provisions of the whole law of unjust enrichment. Historically, this defence operated as an adjunct to the *condictio ob rem*, preventing restitution in cases in which the illegal goal which the parties had agreed had not been achieved, and thus providing a disincentive to those willing to pay others to do their dirty work.[38] The second drafting commission of the *BGB*, however, generalised the defence to apply to all cases of enrichment by performance.[39] This has long been criticised as going too far and as leading to inequitable and arbitrary results.[40] In particular, since in practice the illegality of the underlying contract cannot be separated from the illegality of the performance of that contract, this can lead to a direct contradiction between § 134 and § 817 2: where the former declares a contract void as illegal, with the *prima facie* consequence of restitution under § 812 I, § 817 2 may prevent restitution, in effect upholding the state of affairs which § 134 sought to prevent. This leads Zimmermann to observe:

> Cut off from its historical moorings (that is, the *condictio ob rem*), the *in pari turpitidine* rule is lurching through the modern German law of unjustified enrichment without direction and has become one of the most dreaded perils in the sea of legal doctrine.[41]

The modern approach, both in jurisprudence and academic writings, therefore tries to align the two rules on the basis of a purposive interpretation of the prohibiting provision. The question will thus be whether the *status quo* is precisely what the prohibiting statute sought to avoid, in which case the application of § 817 2 will be excluded. For example, where a transfer is in violation of currency regulations, it would make a nonsense of the regulations if it were upheld under § 817 2.[42] This restrictive interpretation of § 817 2 gives a new lease of life to illegality as a ground for restitution in § 134.[43]

This is not the place to give an exhaustive account of what contracts have been found void on the basis of illegality. What I seek to demonstrate is how the German courts base the decision whether or not a contract is declared void on the purpose of the prohibiting provision. The question in each case will be whether or not that purpose would be furthered by restitution. For example, until recently German law regulated shop opening hours very strictly. Even today, it is still an offence for a shop to trade after certain prescribed hours. If this rule is breached, it would make little sense to hold the contract of sale void, requiring the parties to make restitution to each other. The purpose of the statute, namely to prevent the exploitation of shop assistants, would not be furthered by such a rule. On the contrary, the unwinding of the contract would require them to work even longer hours.[44] On the other hand, if a builder and his customer conspire to keep the

---

37 § 817 2 *BGB*.
38 Reuter and Martinek, 1983, p 200.
39 Honsell, 1974, pp 77 ff.
40 Cf Heck, 1925, pp 21 f, 53 ff, who wants to confine the defence to the condictio ob rem; Koppensteiner and Kramer, 1988, pp 61 ff; Honsell, 1974, pp 136 ff, who advocates the abolition of § 817 *in toto*. The courts have long adopted a restrictive interpretation of the defence: cf BGHZ 75, 299 (12.1.1979), p 305.
41 Zimmermann, 1996, p 864.
42 BGH NJW 1956, 338 (4.11.1955); BGHZ 41, 341 (20.5.1964); 63, 365 (8.1.1975).
43 For a more detailed discussion of illegality as a defence in English, see Dannemann, 2000.
44 Cf Medicus, 1997, p 244.

contract for services between them hidden from revenue and social security authorities, they are both committing an offence. The purpose of this rule, namely preventing the evasion of tax and social security levies, is best served by rendering such contracts absolutely void. The worker cannot be sure that he will be paid, and a restitutionary claim will not be available to him.[45] The aim is to dissuade him from entering into such illicit bargains.

It is thus not a foregone conclusion that an illegal contract will be null and void. This will depend on a myriad of policy considerations. The judge retains a great deal of discretion. The word 'nichtig' could only be used as long as the judge retained that flexibility. Otherwise restitution might have to be awarded in circumstances in which it might not be appropriate.

This approach might be criticised as jeopardising legal certainty.[46] However, as Dannemann has pointed out,[47] this discretion must be placed into context. After all, we are dealing here with people who have acted in an illegal or otherwise discreditable manner. Short of allowing or barring restitution in all cases of illegality/immorality, we cannot expect to reconcile justice and certainty in this area, as the unsatisfactory state of English law vividly demonstrates.

10.3.2 English law

In English law, illegality renders a contract absolutely void.[48] Were English law to introduce a rule by which the nullity of a contract triggered restitution of performances under it, this would lead to significant problems.

First, contrary to the position taken by Swadling,[49] it would be necessary to acknowledge that the policy reason for restitution would be the illegality rendering the contract void, and not some other recognised unjust factor which might also be present. This is because the nullity of the contract itself would be based on the illegality, and not the presence of a failure of consideration or mistake. Logic dictates that if the nullity of the contract triggers restitution *ipso facto*, the reason for restitution must be the reason for the nullity, in other words, illegality. If this is correct, we will be faced by the problem that in the current law illegality is not generally a ground for restitution. Thus, in the well known case of *Green v Portsmouth Stadium*,[50] the claimant was a bookmaker who had paid more for entry to a greyhound track than the stadium was permitted to charge him. He failed to recover his overpayment from the stadium because no recognised unjust factor was present and the illegality of the contract itself did not suffice. This must be contrasted with the later case of *Kiriri Cotton v Dewani*,[51] in which the Privy Council ordered restitution on very similar facts. A landlord charged a premium on a lease. To demand

---

45   But see BGHZ 111, 308 (31.5.1990), 312 ff.
46   Cf Virgo, 1999, pp 749–50, arguing that if English law were to adopt a discretionary approach, the law would become too uncertain: 'Justice is dependent on a high degree of certainty and predictability.' *Quaere* whether criminals are entitled to legal certainty in planning their activities.
47   Dannemann, 2000, before n 53.
48   *Mogul Steamship Co v McGregor, Gow & Co* [1892] AC 25, 39, *per* Lord Halsbury.
49   Swadling, 2000, text around n 51.
50   [1953] 2 QB 190.
51   [1960] AC 192.

such a premium constituted a criminal offence. It was held that the law prohibiting the demand of a premium was intended for the protection of tenants, and therefore, if the law was broken, the landlord had to bear responsibility for this. In *Green v Portsmouth Stadium*, on the other hand, the violated statute was not intended to protect bookmakers – in the words of Lord Simonds in *Cutler v Wandsworth Stadium*, it was not a 'charter for bookmakers', but was intended to regulate the conduct of racecourses.[52] The English courts are thus engaging in an exercise similar to that which must be undertaken by German courts applying § 134 and the illegality defence in § 817: would restitution further or hinder the objects of the prohibitory statute? Given that illegality renders all contracts void in English law, nullity as such does not tell us anything about the best restitutionary response.

The next question to face is whether the ground for restitution in *Kiriri Cotton* was indeed the illegality or some kind of inequality between the parties. Following on from this question is the larger question whether in English law illegality can ever be a ground for restitution, as Goff and Jones, Birks and Burrows claim, or whether it only ever operates as a defence. There is very little support for the proposition that in *Kiriri Cotton* itself restitution was based on illegality. Birks puts the case under deficient intent: the tenant is under a transactional disadvantage, the law responds to this by giving him restitution.[53] To say that restitution is based on the illegality is putting this more abstractly, but no less correctly, given that the illegality, as the Privy Council found, is itself a response to the tenant's transactional disadvantage. As Birks admits himself, in one sense all restitution is based on policy. It is important that this policy be spelled out. The policy behind the ordinance in *Kiriri Cotton* was to give tenants an advantage vis à vis landlords. I would suggest, tentatively, that to lump this policy together with cases of vitiated consent obscures the true reason for restitution, just as explaining restitution on the basis of the nullity of the illegal contract would. Absent arbitrary government, there is always a point to illegality. This point can, of course, be that one party is regarded as weaker than the other, and thus worthy of the law's protection. However, there may be other policies underlying illegality which might equally well be furthered by restitution. There is no reason why restitution should not be available in such cases.[54]

Shaw v Shaw[55] concerned an executed contract which violated s 7 of the Exchange Control Act 1947. The claimant had paid the defendant £4,000, for which the defendant had transferred to the claimant a flat in Majorca. The claimant was denied restitution on the basis that his action was based on his own illegal act. Arguably, the result of the case not so much furthers as defeats the purpose of s 7. The contract having been executed without the consent of the Treasury having been obtained, the provision had had no effect whatsoever, the *status quo* was directly contrary to it. The policy underlying s 7 favoured restitution,[56] but that policy alone was not enough. As Lord Denning MR made plain in his short judgment, apart from the illegality defence applying, there was no reason for restitution which the law recognised:

52 *Cutler v Wandsworth Stadium* [1949] AC 398, 404.
53 Birks, 1989, p 167; Birks and Mitchell, 2000, p 557.
54 Cf Birks, 1989, p 300.
55 [1965] 1 WLR 537.
56 Cf the German cases cited above, fn 42, p 187.

No court will lend its aid to a man who founds his cause of 'action upon an immoral or illegal act' ... If the plaintiff is to overcome this bar, he must forward some reason why he should not be defeated by his own illegality. To take a simple illustration: supposing the flat in Majorca had not been conveyed to him and that it had not been handed over to him in return for the £4,000, then I can well see that he could make out a claim. He could say that the money had been paid over on a consideration which had wholly failed, but he does not attempt to do that. On this pleading, it may well be that he has got the flat and yet still wants his money back. He bases himself on nothing but the illegal payment. To my mind, it is clearly bad.[57]

It appears, therefore, that the only cases in which English law allows illegality to operate as a ground for restitution are those cases in which the illegal purpose has not yet been carried out and the claimant repents his involvement, seeking to call a halt to the illegal plan.[58] Although the Law Commission has recently endorsed this view,[59] the matter is not uncontroversial. Swadling,[60] Virgo[61] and Tettenborn[62] all argue that the true reason for restitution in these cases is failure of consideration.

10.4 *ULTRA VIRES* DEMANDS

In the sphere of state imposts, taxes and levies, a number of special interests not encountered elsewhere in the law of unjust enrichment are in play. Some of these favour restitution, others militate against it. This is particularly well demonstrated in the Canadian case of *Air Canada v British Columbia*.[63] The case concerned large sums paid by way of tax by Air Canada to the government of British Columbia under an Act *ultra vires* the state legislature that had passed it. The majority of the Canadian Supreme Court held that these payments were in principle recoverable as paid under a mistake of law, but, Wilson J dissenting vigorously, that in this case the claim could not be allowed to succeed because of the danger of a significant disruption of public finances.

Even though the Supreme Court based the *prima facie* right to restitution on mistake of law, it is suggested that the judgements show that there are two competing considerations in play in this area: on the one hand, there is the concern that government should be subject to the constitution and to the rule of law. On the other hand, there is the acute awareness on the part of judges that what is at stake is *public* money, and that the danger of floodgates is therefore particularly severe.

---

57 *Shaw v Shaw* [1965] 1 WLR 537 at 539.
58 *Robert v Roberts* (1818) Dan 143, 159 ER 862; *Taylor v Bowers* (1876) 1 QBD 291; *Kearley v Thomson* (1890) 24 QBD 742; *Tribe v Tribe* [1996] Ch 107, CA.
59 Law Com CP 157, 1999, paras 2.49–2.56, following Birks, 1989, pp 299–303; see above, fn 28 for further references in support of this view.
60 Swadling, 2000.
61 Virgo, 1999, p 747.
62 Tettenborn, 1996, p 259 .
63 (1989) 59 DLR (4th) 161.

10.4.1 England

In England, the first of these considerations came to a head in *Woolwich Equitable Building Society v Inland Revenue Commissioners (No 2)*.[64] The revenue assessed the Woolwich in respect of taxes levied under the Income Tax (Building Societies) Regulations 1986. The Woolwich's legal advisers considered the Regulations to be invalid and decided to challenge them by way of judicial review. In order to avoid adverse publicity as a recalcitrant taxpayer, however, it nevertheless decided to pay three instalments of tax under the Regulations, although it made these payments without prejudice to its right to recover them should the Regulations have been void. The judicial review proceedings were successful. The revenue repaid the three instalments but refused to pay interest in respect of the period up to judgment. The revenue's argument was essentially that they could not be compelled to repay the money at all – any repayments were effectively made *ex gratia*. As such, s 35A of the Supreme Court Act 1981 could not apply and no interest was due. The Woolwich's main problem was that it was extremely difficult to fit the claim into the traditional system of unjust factors. What, if any, was the ground for restitution? It could not be mistake: the Woolwich had not been mistaken. It had not even been in doubt – it was of the view that the Regulations were *ultra vires* and it expressed that view forcefully. In any event, any mistake would have been a mistake of law, and the case predated the *Lincoln* case by more than half a decade. Duress was not an option, as it requires *illegitimate* pressure. The threat to resort to legal action could hardly be described as illegitimate. Could it be said that there had been a failure of consideration, in the sense of 'failure of basis' advocated above? This was in fact the mainstay of the Woolwich's argument,[65] but on the authorities as they stood at the time a payment to a local authority could only be recovered if made under duress or mistake of fact.[66] In fact, in two influential articles, Cornish[67] and Birks[68] had argued that the true reason for restitution was the principle 'no taxation without Parliament', which could be traced back all the way to the Bill of Rights. Birks in particular argued that any attempt to base the Woolwich's claim on traditional unjust factors would hide rather than reveal the true reasons for restitution:

> [T]he reason for putting aside these private causes of action is to emphasise that our present business is not to inquire into the potential for jiggling facts into some familiar private category. ... On the contrary, it compels us directly to confront the constitutional question whether there is an automatic right to restitution in respect of money demanded officially (*colore officii*) but without lawful authority (*ultra vires*).[69]

The House of Lords, by a bare majority, agreed with Cornish and Birks that the Woolwich should be entitled to restitution as of right. Lord Goff specifically states that this right is

---

64 [1993] AC 70.

65 See Lord Keith's judgment, at 154.

66 Cf Walton J in *William Whiteley v R* (1910) 101 LT 741, 745: '... money paid voluntarily – that is to say, without compulsion or extortion or undue influence, and of course, I may add, without any fraud on the part of the person to whom it is paid, and with knowledge of all the facts, though paid without any consideration, or in discharge of a claim not due, or a claim which might have been successfully resisted, cannot be recovered back.'

67 Cornish, 1987.

68 Birks, 1990b.

69 *Ibid*, p 176.

based on the policy enshrined in Art 4 of the Bill of Rights that taxes should not be levied without Parliamentary authority: '... full effect can only be given to that principle if the return of taxes exacted under an unlawful demand can be enforced as a matter of right.'[70] Lord Browne-Wilkinson, apart from agreeing with Lord Goff in general terms, also based restitution on 'absence of consideration'.[71] This aspect of the case will be further discussed below,[72] but it should be pointed out that, apart from its potential for doing greater harm in the law of unjust enrichment as a whole, it obscures rather than highlights the true reasons for restitution, which is the policy in favour of legality of government.

The next question which had to be faced by the House of Lords was whether the fact that the sums here at stake were public money should have a role to play. Should restitution be limited on this basis? Lord Keith, dissenting, considered that 'the question of possible disruption of public finances must obviously be a very material one',[73] and Lord Jauncey, while expressing some sympathy with Birks's argument that retention of unlawfully levied taxes would violate the principle 'no taxation without Parliament', thought that the danger to public finances posed by the general availability of such a restitutionary claim was just too great.[74]

Lord Goff fully appreciated the problem and was mindful of the floodgates argument, but was not persuaded that these concerns should override the principle of legality which demanded restitution. He acknowledged that the general defences available to restitutionary claims might not be sufficient, and that other limitations might have to be imposed. Ever the comparatist, he referred to German administrative law, with its extremely short limitation periods, as an 'instructive example' of what such limitations might look like.[75]

10.4.2 Germany

If *Woolwich* fell to be decided in Germany today, it would be a case in administrative law. This was not always so. Lord Goff in *Lincoln* refers to a case decided in Germany in 1909, involving the identical issue and decided on the basis of § 812 I by the ordinary courts.[76] Until 1920, the *Reichsgericht* took the view that any claims involving claims to money or property, whether by a citizen against another citizen, by a citizen against the state or *vice versa*, were justiciable in the ordinary courts. In a famous decision in 1920,[77] however, the court changed its mind. The case concerned a dispute over goods which had been requisitioned by the German government in wartime. The *Reichsgericht* declined jurisdiction. Notwithstanding the fact that the dispute involved claims to goods or money, which had previously indicated that the civil courts had jurisdiction even though

---

70 *Woolwich* [1993] AC 70, 172.
71 *Ibid*, at 198.
72 See p 241, below.
73 *Woolwich* [1993] AC 70, 161.
74 *Ibid*, at 196.
75 *Ibid*, at 174.
76 RGZ 72, 152 (29.10.1909); cited by Lord Goff in *Kleinwort Benson v Lincoln CC* [1999] 2 AC 349, 374.
77 RGZ 99, 41 (30.4.1920).

one of the parties was a public body, it involved the question whether the seizure of goods by a governmental body had been lawful or not. As such, it required an examination of the relevant rules of public law. The proper forum to resolve the dispute was therefore the administrative court. This new distinction between private and public law claims had to have consequences for enrichment law. In an influential monograph written in 1921, Gerhard Lassar argued that the application of §§ 812 ff in the public law sphere was wholly inappropriate. While it was tempting to conclude that the reference to a 'legal cause' in that provision could be understood to refer to a public law debt as well as a private law debt, this ignored the fact that the claim in § 812 I was meant to 'eliminate such consequences of abstract transfers which in the view of the legal order are not reconcilable with the demands of justice. These are not exhaustively listed in §§ 812 ff of the BGB, but are found in many other places throughout the BGB'.[78] The underlying argument is therefore that, in contrast to administrative laws which were (and are) largely the responsibility of the individual German states,[79] the BGB is drafted as a coherent, interlocking mechanism. If § 812 bases restitution on the invalidity of underlying obligations, this works well within the context of the code, but need not necessarily work well in the public law sphere. Given that the legal problem 'unjust enrichment' occurs both in the private and in the public sphere, Lassar thus sees the need for a special public law claim, which he refers to simply as 'Erstattungsanspruch' (claim for reimbursement).[80] Nine years later, the Reichsgericht formally recognised this claim.[81] The case concerned a claim by the state against a judge who had resigned from judicial office. The state claimed that he had to repay a proportion of his salary which had been paid to him quarterly in advance. Although the Reichsgericht accepted jurisdiction, it refused to apply the private law rules on unjust enrichment, arguing that the judge as a civil servant was governed exclusively by rules of public law. Private law rules were therefore irrelevant. Applying the relevant rules of public law, the so called 'public law restitutionary claim',[82] the court held that the defendant had to make restitution. The requirements of that claim look identical to § 812 I, in that restitution will follow if there has been a performance 'without legal ground'.[83] There are, however, differences, as we shall see further below.

The underlying reasons for fashioning a separate public law claim were identified above in discussing the *Air Canada* decision of the Supreme Court of Canada: on the one hand, it is 'particularly obnoxious'[84] for the state to enrich itself unlawfully at the expense of its citizens. This suggests that there are circumstances in which the state must be more severely treated than a private citizen would be. On the other hand, there is the threat of a disastrous disruption of public finances. This suggests that, however far reaching the

---

78   Lassar, 1921, p 98.

79   This raises an additional constitutional point: as the BGB is a piece of federal legislation, it cannot without more apply to those areas which are, according to the Basic Law, the sole responsibility of the *Länder*. Cf Weber, 1970, p 18.

80   *Ibid*, p 104. Lassar's argument has been a resounding success. Eckart Weber has more recently remarked that the correctness of his analysis has since not been doubted: Weber, 1970, p 17.

81   RGZ 107, 189 (12.6.1923).

82   '*Öffentlich-rechtlicher Erstattungsanspruch.*'

83   Wolff, 2000, p 238.

84   *Woolwich* [1993] AC 70, 172, *per* Lord Goff.

claim against the state may be, it must be made subject to proper safeguards to keep the floodgates firmly shut.

The right to restitution

The public law restitutionary claim is the creation of judges,[85] although it has found its way into a variety of statutes and statutory instruments since. Most interestingly, overpayments of taxes have long been governed by secondary legislation: § 37 of the *Abgabenordnung* provides for restitution of taxes which were not due under the relevant fiscal legislation.[86] Nevertheless, the principle itself is based on customary law, and is ultimately based on Art 20 III of the German Basic Law.[87] This reads:

> *Die Gesetzgebung ist and die verfassungsmäßige Ordnung, die vollziehende Gewalt und die Rechtsprechung sind an Gesetz und Recht gebunden.* [The legislature is subject to the constitutional order, the executive and judicature are subject to law and justice.]

If a citizen was denied restitution where he paid in response to an unlawful demand by the executive, this would constitute a violation of Art 20 III. The provision therefore demands restitution in those circumstances. However, the application of the general rules on unjust enrichment contained in §§ 812 ff might deny the citizen restitution, which is why the special public law regime is considered necessary. This is demonstrated by a decision of the *Verwaltungsgerichtshof* Mannheim of 1990.[88] A local authority had refused to grant planning permission to a property developer unless he entered into a contract with the authority under which he was to make extra payments in respect of connecting the planned buildings to the utilities. He agreed reluctantly, and later sought to recover his payments under the contract. The court held that the contract was void: the local authority was under a duty to make public utilities available and could not link the granting of planning permission to extra payments being made. The public law restitutionary claim therefore lay. The authority sought to rely on § 814 II *BGB*, which, it argued, should be applicable to the public law claim by way of analogy. It will be remembered that under that provision, a restitutionary claim can be defeated if the defendant can demonstrate that the claimant knew when he made the payment that he was not obliged to do so. This argument is very reminiscent of the *Woolwich* case: on the argument put forward by the authority, the claimant knew all along that he was not obliged to enter into the contract, and that he need not have made any payments under it. The German court, as the House of Lords in *Woolwich*, rejected this argument, however. Although it acknowledged that there could be no objection to applying rules of the private law of unjust enrichment to the public law claim, it argued that in this case § 814 could have nothing to say. Again, the main argument to support this conclusion sounds familiar. The judgment reads:

---

85 Wolff, 1999, p 344.

86 Although the general principle, namely restitution based on the fact that a payment was not due, seems to be the same in public and private law, there are significant differences, the most important of which is a much less generous application of the change of position defence, which, in the public law sphere, is excluded by reckless failure to appreciate the fact that a payment has been made by mistake.

87 Cf Wolff, 2000, p 239

88 VGH Mannheim NVwZ 1991, 583 (18.10.1990)

> Where a public administration uses its dominant position, based on governmental power, to demand that the citizen enter into a contract, the latter will typically be subjected to considerable pressure based on that dominance, to fulfil the contract, as otherwise he has to expect that governmental power is going to be brought to bear against him.[89]

If the authority's view of the facts had been accepted (which it was not), the position would have been exactly similar to the situation the Woolwich found itself in. The general law of restitution would have been no help: the (negative) requirement of a mistake in § 814 would have stood in the way of recovery. However, given the particularly obnoxious nature of the authority's behaviour, the public law claim did not recognise a requirement such as § 814 and thus allowed the claimant to obtain restitution.

The principle of legality in Art 20 III of the Basic Law also means that the state cannot rely on change of position in any circumstances.[90] If § 818 *BGB* were applied to the state, this would mean that a claimant would, in effect, be required to fund public expenditure which he was not legally responsible to fund.

Protecting the public purse

Given that vis à vis the state the public law claim therefore appears rather stricter than the private law claim, this must have consequences for the citizen as well. This takes two forms. First, as Lord Goff has observed, the enforcement of the claim against the state is made subject to strict limitations. Secondly, the state's claim against the citizen is not as weak as a citizen's claim against another citizen would be: the disenrichment defence is severely curtailed.

In German administrative law, an administrative act is generally valid unless it is wholly void *ab initio*, is taken back, vacated, lapses or is avoided on the application of the citizen concerned.[91] § 44 *VwVfG* lays down specific factors which render an administrative act void. These are: (1) the act is based on a particularly gross and obvious error; (2) the authority making the act is not specified in the written notice of the act; (3) lack of writing where writing is required; (4) the act is outside the territorial responsibility of the authority in question; (5) impossibility in fact; (6) it requires the commission of an unlawful act; or (7) it is *contra bonos mores*. There is no general doctrine of *ultra vires*, unless it falls under (1) or (4). The citizen will therefore normally have to seek to avoid the administrative act. Under the relevant secondary legislation, the citizen has one month from the administrative act being communicated to him to object against it.[92] If his objection bears no fruit, he has a further month in which to challenge the act in court.[93] If he is successful, he will be entitled to restitution under the public law principle as of right.[94] If he fails to challenge the act in time, it will be valid and remain valid notwithstanding a successful challenge of the basis of the act by a different party. These limitations are, in Lord Goff's words, 'strong medicine for our taste',[95] but they do protect

---

89 *Ibid*, p 587.
90 Wolff, 2000, p 241.
91 *Verwaltunssverfahrensgesetz (VwVfG)*, § 43.
92 *Verwaltungsgerichtsordnung (VwGO)*, § 70.
93 *VwGO*, § 74.
94 This has now been confirmed by the statute itself: § 49a I *VwVfG*, § 49a I.
95 *Woolwich* [1993] AC 70, 174.

the public purse rather effectively. Again, these rules demonstrate one of the central theses of this book, namely that the German legislator is particularly careful when it comes to using the word *'nichtig'*, given that that word triggers restitution both under § 812 I and under the public law restitutionary claim.

The second way in which German public law compensates for the strictness of the public law claim vis à vis the state is by restricting the availability of the disenrichment defence in claims by the state against the citizen. Thus, where the authority's restitutionary claim is founded on the revocation or avoidance *ab initio* of an administrative act, § 49a II *VwVfG* contains a cross-reference to § 818 III *BGB*, but with the proviso that the defendant's disenrichment will not bar restitution 'where he was aware of the circumstances leading to the revocation or avoidance or should have been aware of them had he not been grossly negligent'.[96] In a case decided in 1985, the highest German administrative court, the *Bundesverwaltungsgericht*, held that the rule amounted to a general principle of administrative law.[97] The case concerned a postal order which had, because of the negligence of the German post office, been paid twice to the defendant beneficiary who was in Italy at the time. The post office, a public body, sought to obtain restitution in the administrative courts, the defendant arguing that she had changed her position in reliance on the payment. On the facts found at first instance, the claimant had received two cheques. The first from her grandmother, the second without any indication as to the sender whatsoever. On these facts, argued the claimant, it was grossly negligent on the part of the defendant to spend the money and she should not be allowed to rely on the disenrichment defence. This argument was successful. The court made a number of interesting observations. There was a clear distinction between the private and the public claim, given that both private parties' claims were subject to the very wide disenrichment defence, while it was settled law that a public defendant could not rely on its own disenrichment in any circumstances. While the citizen's interest in the security of his receipt was to be taken into account where he was being sued by the state, the balance of interests was different to a purely private law case. Thus, the position of the post office was not analogous to the position of a bank, as the latter was not a public body and as such 'not bound by the public good and the principle of legality'.[98] In other words, the limitation of change of position is justified on two grounds: first, to right the balance between the state and the citizen in light of the fact that the state cannot rely on the disenrichment defence at all; second, to take account of the fact that the money at stake is public money misallocated to the defendant.

In conclusion, this excursion into German administrative law has demonstrated that the claim in *Woolwich* is clearly policy based. The German law has drawn consequences from that policy which go further than those currently drawn by English law. Contrary to the conclusion reached by the Supreme Court of Canada in *Air Canada*, however, the German approach does not deny restitution against public bodies altogether. On the contrary, the availability of restitution in circumstances of unlawfully levied taxes is regarded as a legal good of constitutional importance. German law does recognise,

---

96 Similar provisions can be found throughout the German administrative law: eg, *Beamtenrechtsrahmengesetz*, § 53 II; *Bundesbeamtengesetz*, § 87 II; *Bundeshaushaltsordnung*, § 44a II.

97 BVerfGE 71, 86 (12.3.1985).

98 See p 90.

however, that restitutionary rights against the state must be limited if the danger of floodgates is to be avoided.

Even though German administrative law is operating with the concept 'lack of legal ground', it has been demonstrated above that this is nothing but code for the policy identified by Birks: that there should be restitution of taxes and other payments unlawfully demanded by the state.

10.5 POLICY AND NULLITY

Meier, in arguing for a legal ground analysis in English law, makes much of the fact that, although English law does not seem to award restitution based on nullity as such, the thesis that the restitutionary claim requires a total or partial failure of consideration is not supported by the authorities either. She concludes: 'Rather, the availability of restitution depends on the grounds which have rendered the contract defective'.[99] She argues that English law might look at the question from the opposite end: 'It would be possible to derive the basic rule that restitution is based on nullity of a contract [from those cases in which restitution is based on policy grounds], and regard [other] cases [in which void contracts do not trigger restitution] as the exception.'[100]

In the following chapters we will discuss the main challenge to the traditional English taxonomy to the law of unjust enrichment as identified by Birks: should there be restitution based on nothing more than the invalidity or nullity of a transaction?

Meier has suggested that the German approach to enrichment law, based on the concept of the 'legal ground', is superior to the 'casuistic' English approach based on concrete reasons for restitution. We have already encountered this argument in a different context above: Meier argued that restitution for mistake has to be narrowed down in English law, and that the best way to do this would be by adopting 'legal ground' reasoning on the German model. We have rejected this argument for the reasons given above. In the present context, the argument is still more important.

As was pointed out in the introductory chapter, the German approach threatens to encroach on English law in two ways: first, Hobhouse J (now Lord Hobhouse), in *Westdeutsche Landesbank v Islington*, based restitution on 'absence of consideration'. Birks was the first to point out that this amounts to the same thing as *'sine causa'* or the *'ohne rechtlichen Grund'* of § 812 I BGB.[101] The problem with this is that it does not fit the common law taxonomy of unjust enrichment which bases restitution on positive 'unjust factors' rather than a wide negative requirement such as 'absence of legal ground', or, if preferred, 'absence of consideration'. This has wider structural implications which will be discussed below.[102]

The second way in which civilian learning is encroaching on the common law is much more covert. In *Kleinwort Benson v Lincoln*,[103] the House of Lords overthrew the long -

---

99 Meier, 1999a, p 363.
100 *Ibid*, p 365.
101 Birks, 1993, p 232; 2000b, p 20.
102 See pp 243 ff, below.
103 [1999] 2 AC 349.

standing rule that there could be no restitution based on a mistake of law alone. As explained above, the way in which this was done, particularly the way in which mistake was defined, moves English law considerably closer towards the civilian *condictio indebiti*.[104] In effect, restitution will follow the nullity of an underlying transaction (normally a contract) as a matter of course. It is questionable whether English law is ready for this.

In the next chapters we will discuss the issues arising from these two cases from a comparative viewpoint. How was German law able to cope with a wide cause of action in unjust enrichment based on 'absence of legal ground', and would English law not be able to emulate it? It will be argued that Meier is wrong in attempting to force English law into a civilian mould. The second, more specific question, which will also occupy us in the next part of this book, will be how 'restitution for nullity' operates in German law. Here, it will be argued that English law must follow German law in identifying factors militating *against* restitution (which I call 'just factors'), and in developing the nascent change of position defence in the widest possible way.

10.6 CONCLUSION

In this chapter, we have looked at various policies which underlie restitution in cases that cannot easily be explained by any of the traditional unjust factors.

'Incapacity' was the first policy examined. It was argued that it was preferable to treat this category as based on a policy favouring restitution, rather than as belonging to the 'defective intent' based family of unjust factors. Two instances of incapacity were discussed: the incapacity of minors and the incapacity of legal persons. In the case of minors, the law aims to protect the minor on the one hand, and the innocent third parties he deals with on the other. In German law, this is reflected in a complex and sophisticated regime under which contracts entered into by minors are void in certain well defined circumstances. The word 'void' will trigger the law of unjust enrichment, but this is a desired consequence of the German regime. The English law on the subject changed in 1987, when the Minors' Contracts Act was enacted. Now, contracts entered into by minors are simply not binding on the minor. Under the old law, on the other hand, contracts entered into by minors were absolutely void. However, as Birks has argued, there is little evidence that this invalidity had restitution as its inevitable consequence in cases in which the minor had already performed his side of the bargain.

Incapacity of legal persons is dealt with by the *ultra vires* doctrine. This is much more developed in English law than it is in German law. The vital point to grasp is that, if restitution follows where performances have been made pursuant to an *ultra vires* contract, the reason for restitution is not the invalidity of the contract but the policy underlying the *ultra vires* doctrine. As demonstrated by the swaps litigation, there is a danger that the courts will jump to the conclusion that nullity implies restitution without considering or spelling out the policy reasons for this.

---

104 See above, p 82 ff.

Next, illegality was examined as a possible reason for restitution. This area is complicated by the fact that illegality is, in both legal systems, a defence to a restitutionary claim. Only in Germany is it clear that it can also be a reason for restitution, although the courts are given considerable discretion in assessing whether a rule of law which renders a contract unlawful also requires restitution of performances exchanged under it. This assessment will necessitate that the policy reasons for restitution are fully considered and spelled out. In England, it is controversial whether illegality can ever be a ground for restitution. Again, it has been argued here that, where performances have been exchanged pursuant to an illegal contract, it is more transparent to base restitution on the reasons underlying the illegality itself rather than on the accidental presence of some other reason for restitution such as failure of consideration. It would then be necessary to spell out precisely why (or why not) the policy underlying the illegality will be furthered by ordering restitution.

Finally, this chapter looked at payments made following unjustified demands by public authorities. There are two competing policies in play in this area. On the one hand, there is the policy that no taxation should be levied which is not authorised in the way prescribed by the constitution, on the other there is the desire to protect the public finances. In England, these competing policies had to be sorted out in the *Woolwich* case. That case again demonstrated the temptation to conclude that, where a payment is made for no consideration, restitution should automatically follow. The House of Lords, however, resisted that temptation (on that occasion) and instead spelled out the competing policies in a convincing and well reasoned manner. In German law, these policies are also clearly discernable. Indeed, they are considered of such fundamental importance that the whole area is removed from mainstream enrichment law and made subject to a special public law regime, under which legality of government on the one hand is protected by an absolute right to restitution, while the integrity of public finances is safeguarded by extremely short limitation periods.

The discussion of these various policies has aimed to show that nullity as such is not a reason for restitution in either system. The conclusion that nullity must automatically lead to restitution should therefore be resisted. At the very least, it must be regarded as not proven.

CHAPTER 11

ABSENCE OF CONSIDERATION IN GERMAN LAW: A GENERAL CAUSE OF ACTION IN UNJUST ENRICHMENT?

Before we even ask the question whether a general cause of action in unjust enrichment, such as is found in § 812 I 1,[1] could be exported to England and other common law countries, we will ask how the provision is interpreted in Germany itself, and whether it has stood the test of time.

The reader will recall that § 812 I 1 is extremely wide. We noticed in Chapter 2 that this was connected with the abstract nature of the *BGB*.[1] In the civilian tradition, such attempts at a general clause to encompass all cases of unjust enrichment have a long tradition, starting again with Roman law.

11.1 THE ROMAN ROOTS OF § 812 I

It is surprising that many of the battles fought in the modern German law of unjust enrichment are still joined on Roman battlefields, with quotes from the Digest or the Institutes sent into the fray by one side or the other. The question whether enrichment law is based on a number of distinct causes of action, the different *condictiones,* or whether the *condictiones* are merely examples of one underlying cause of action in unjust enrichment has been debated for centuries, and no definite victor has ever emerged. The *condictio,* as we have seen above, was a *stricti iuris* action claiming a *certa pecunia* or a *certa res.* It was characteristically abstract, with the *causa debendi* remaining unspecified – what was important was the fact that the defendant was indebted to the claimant, the *dare oportere.* It was this abstractness which allowed the formula of the *condictio* to be extended from the enforcement of promises made by *stipulatio* to claims founded on the contract of *mutuum* and finally to cover cases we would today describe as cases in unjust enrichment.[2] While it is clear that there was soon a distinct body of case law which could be organised in a number of categories, as long as the formulary procedure endured the condictio was a single claim which could be incidentally used to reverse various forms of unjust enrichment.

It is unlikely classical Roman law ever formulated a general principle.[3] In Justinian's *Digest* the various groups of cases appear as separate causes of action: the *condictio indebiti,*[4] the *condictio ob turpem vel iniustam causam*[5] and the *condictio causa data causa non secuta.*[6] A *condictio* unknown in classical times was added, the *condictio sine causa,*[7] as a general catch-all provision. This latter *condictio,* under the name *condictio sine causa generalis,* competed with all other *condictiones.* Under the name *condictio sine causa specialis*

1 See above, p 28.
2 Liebs, 1986, p 165.
3 Schulz, 1951, pp 610 ff.
4 D 12.6.
5 D 12.5.
6 D 12.4.
7 D 12.7.

it covered those cases which were not caught by any of the other *condictiones*. Increasingly the question was asked what all these categories, all these causes of action based on the old form of action *'condictio'* had in common. The answer might have been provided by a quote which has become the most famous statement of the principle against unjust enrichment, *'nam hoc natura aequum est neminem cum alterius detrimento fieri locupletiorem'*.[8] It is attributed to Sextus Pomponius (2nd century AD). The generality of this proposition, taken out of its original context, is deceptive, however. Classical Roman law made no systematic appeal to a general rule against unjust enrichment. It was probably advanced by Pomponius to support a single decision or argument.

As Roman law was received into European legal systems, the search for a unifying principle continued unabated. The search was given extra urgency by the fact that the Canon law doctrine of restitution was well established in mediaeval theology, but formulated in very general terms.[9] While German writers have claimed that such a general principle was first identified by Savigny, the laurels probably have to go to Hugo Grotius. In the first half of the 17th century, he surveyed the different mechanisms Roman law employed for reversing unjust enrichment. The *condictiones* were clearly most prominent amongst them, but the *actio negotiorum gestorum* was also of great importance.[10] He formulates the general principle in two ways. First, he says that 'obligation from deriving profit (*baet-trecking*) arises when some one without legal title derives or would derive profit from another person's property'.[11] The second mention of the general principle was often said to refer merely to the *condictio sine causa specialis*, but it appears from the context that this view was mistaken: Grotius explicitly relied on natural law, which suggests an extension of the traditional Roman *condictiones*:[12]

> ... repetition of anything which in any other way, without gift, payment, or promise, has come to a man from another man's property apart from any lawful cause.[13]

It is not quite clear whether this was intended as a general principle or as a rule of law of direct applicability. It is indeed questionable whether it is at all possible to draft a clause which is both sufficiently general to encompass all cases of unjust enrichment, and sufficiently precise so as to avoid palm tree justice. In the end we have to know with a high degree of accuracy what enrichments the law considers unjust. § 812 I represents an attempt to encapsulate the condition for every case but, as we have seen, it is pitched at a high level of generality and abstraction. The requirement 'without legal cause' is meant to indicate precisely, albeit abstractly, when an enrichment is unjust.

Building on Grotius' work, Savigny much later, in his monumental *System des heutigen römischen Rechts*, laid down his own general principle against unjust enrichment. It lay in the fact that one person's wealth was increased at the expense of another, while this 'shift of wealth' (*'Vermögensverschiebung'*) was not justified by a valid legal ground, an

---

8   Pomp D 12.6.14.
9   Cf Hallebeek, 1995, p 59.
10   Marginal note in Grotius's own copy of his *Inleidinge*, 3.1.15 – see Feenstra, 1995, p 204.
11   Grotius, H, *Inleidinge* 3.30.1, translation by Feenstra, 1995, p 205.
12   Cf R Feenstra, 1995, p 206.
13   Grotius, H, *Inleidinge* 3.30.18, translation by Feenstra, 1995, p 205.

underlying obligation.[14] This principle was to be elevated to a general clause, § 812 I, in a codification of the law of Germany which Savigny himself had so vehemently opposed.[15]

11.2 THE EARLY DEVELOPMENT OF GERMAN ENRICHMENT LAW

11.2.1 The drafting of the *BGB*

Two commissions and three drafts were needed before the code was finally enacted.[16] As far as enrichment law is concerned the first two drafts are of importance, as no significant changes were made subsequently.

The first commission's draft was, as far as the law of obligations was concerned, based on preparatory work undertaken by Franz von Kübel in 1882. Von Kübel still enumerated different causes of action in unjust enrichment.[17] He argued that a generalised enrichment claim, even as a catch-all provision at the end of the enrichment chapter, should not be resorted to as this would lead back to the highly general and 'incorrect' Pomponius maxim.[18] The first commission followed von Kübel's suggestion in so far as that it retained the enumeration of different causes of action. Thus § 737 of the draft provided:

> *Wer zum Zwecke der Erfüllung einer Verbindlichkeit eine Leistung bewirkt hat, kann, wenn die Verbindlichkeit nicht bestanden hat, von dem Empfänger das Geleistete zurückfordern.* [He who has rendered a performance for the purpose of discharging an obligation can, if the obligation did not exist, demand restitution of the object of the performance from the recipient.]

This was thus an enrichment claim based on the performance or 'Leistung' of the claimant. Other *condictiones* based on performance were provided for, such as the *condictio ob rem* (§ 742), and the *condictio ob causam finitam* (§ 745) in which the liability the claimant seeks to discharge is subsequently destroyed.

However, a general principle, or rather a catch-all provision was added at the very end of the enrichment chapter of the draft, in § 748:

> *Derjenige, aus dessen Vermögen nicht kraft seines Willens oder nicht kraft seines rechtsgültigen Willens ein Anderer bereichert worden ist, kann, wenn hierzu ein rechtlicher Grund gefehlt hat, von dem Anderen die Herausgabe der Bereicherung fordern.* [If another has been enriched from the assets of a person, but not sanctioned by that person's will or legally valid will, that person can, if there was no legal ground for the enrichment, require the other to make restitution of it.]

This comes very close to what German law would today refer to as the '*Eingriffskondiktion*', that is, the enrichment claim which is based upon the infringement of another's rights. As is apparent from the sources accompanying the first draft, the first commission was fully aware of the dangers inherent in this formulation, after all, von

---

14 Savigny, 1841, Vol 5, pp 503 ff.
15 Cf above, pp 14 ff.
16 For the drafting history, see above, pp 16 f.
17 von Kübel, 1884.
18 *Ibid*, p 78.

Kübel's warning had been very clear. The intention of the commission was not to lay down a general principle of unjust enrichment based on equitable considerations, but, following the general pattern of enumerating different enrichment claims, § 748 was to regulate specific groups of cases, such as the consumption or use of property belonging to another.[19]

What all these provisions have in common is that the *reason for restitution* is explicit in all of them to a greater or lesser extent. Thus, § 737 lays down that a performance made with the purpose of discharging an obligation can be demanded back if the obligation did not exist. The ambit of this cause of action is very well defined, the reason for restitution apparent: as the purpose of the performance was the discharge of an obligation, that purpose having failed, restitution should be the natural consequence. The same applies to § 748: the reason for restitution is here that the claimant's property was destroyed or transferred without his consent, and there was no right on the part of the defendant (here referred to as 'legal cause') which justified this infringement of the claimant's rights. This was based on very influential work undertaken by Savigny. As mentioned above, he had re-examined the Roman *condictiones* and had sought to identify a common principle underlying all of them.[20] This he found in the will of the claimant. According to him, enrichments had to be justified by the 'flawless', that is, unvitiated and unqualified, will of the claimant, otherwise a *condictio* would lie.[21] § 748 of the first draft clearly reflects his influence, which is, in many ways, felt to the present day.[22]

However, the first draft was not to survive the scrutiny of the second commission, which was given the brief of fundamentally altering a first draft in the light of its being, as outlined in Chapter 2, in the opinion of some too committed to the pandectists and Roman law.[23] The second commission decided to disregard von Kübel's warnings and rejected the first draft on the basis that it did not place the general principle at the beginning of the chapter, but followed a categorisation based on Roman law, enumerating four different *condictiones* which had their origin in a performance, and only added § 748 for the sake of completeness for all remaining cases. This was perceived to be less elegant than the general delict clause in § 823. The second draft, which was accepted instead, followed the model of Swiss law in that it preceded the chapter on unjust enrichment with a general principle. According to the second commission 'the provisions thereby gained considerably in terms of lucidity and clarity'. Systematically it was perceived to be important 'to place the general principle determining the entire doctrine at the beginning, at least from the point of view of legislative technique'.[24] Whether this was a change of form only or an attempted change of substance is controversial. I would argue that the change away from separate causes of action to a 'general clause' of the kind to be found in § 823 I is an expression of a search for unified causes of action. Obviously, if it was possible to frame a general enrichment action this would be much more in tune with the scheme of the codification, striving for a high level of generalisation and abstraction. It

---

19 Motive II, p 851 ff; cf also Reuter and Martinek, 1983, p 17.

20 See above, p 202.

21 Savigny, 1841, p 523.

22 Cf the examination of Kellmann's work, below, pp 227 ff.

23 Above, p 17.

24 Prot II, p 684.

can thus be concluded that § 812 I, as it subsequently became, was meant as a general clause of unjust enrichment, embracing all the different causes of action provided by the *ius commune* and suggested by the first draft.

11.2.2 Classical German enrichment law

Traditional teaching thus proceeded on the assumption that § 812 I constituted a single cause of action. A direct shift of wealth was regarded as *prima facie* unjustified and requiring justification from the legal relationship between the parties,[25] from the 'legal cause' of the enrichment. The common legal cause for all possible shifts of wealth was seen in its basis in the law of obligations, which Robert Krawielicki[26] typified as follows:

(1) A claim ('*Anspruch*') within the meaning of the definition of § 194, that is, the right to require another to do or refrain from doing a certain thing. Thus, if S sells his car to B, S can claim payment from B, and if B pays S money that claim is a sufficient reason for S to retain the payment.

(2) A so-called 'pure legal cause', that is, a set of facts which, without giving rise to a claim, grants the enriched party the right to retain the benefit. Examples are the gift with immediate delivery (§ 516), the right to retain gambling winnings even though they can never be 'claimed' as a legal debt (§ 762) and can also be found in enrichment law itself, for example, in § 814, which entitles the recipient to retain the benefit if the disenriched party made a '*Leistung*' knowing that there was no obligation to perform or (§ 815) that the purpose of the performance was impossible to realise.[27]

According to Krawielicki, the legal cause was thus 'the acquirer's right to keep the benefit as against the loser. If the acquirer may either (permanently or temporarily) retain the shift of wealth (*sic*), a legal cause exists. If he has to disgorge it (immediately or later), the legal cause is absent'.[28] This rather circular definition becomes less obscure if one starts from the basis that any direct shift of wealth is unjustified to start with, and must be justified by reference to some positive legal right entitling the recipient to retain it.

The requirement of 'directness', tied to the words 'at the expense of', was relied upon to limit the ambit of the enrichment action, and also provided a tool for the identification of its proper parties, particularly in order to avoid a renaissance of the *actio de in rem verso*, a Roman form of action allowing recovery in cases of enrichment through a third party's contract. This, though received into the *ius commune*, had been expressly rejected by the first commission, a view which was upheld by the second commission:[29] it had become a universal remedy for the prevention of 'unjust' enrichment, cut loose from all limitations.[30]

---

25 Krawielicki, 1936, p 4.

26 *Ibid*, pp 6 ff, 47 ff.

27 It should be noted that this analysis is now regarded as outdated. A gift with immediate delivery is now generally regarded as a normal contract. However, though a contract, it does not necessarily give rise to obligations. The parties agree with each other that the bestowal is to be gratuitous, and this is seen as an agreement as to the legal cause ('*Rechtsgrundabrede*'), protecting the donee from the donor's enrichment claim under § 812 I. See Larenz, 1986, p 200.

28 *Ibid*, p 4.

29 Motive II, pp 871 f.

30 Cf Dawson, 1951, pp 89 f.

In three party situations it is often difficult to determine who can sue whom. The simplest example is that of a chain of contractual transfers: A sells a car to B, who sells it to C. If both sales contracts are void for some reason, can A recover the car directly from C? The instinctive answer is that he cannot, for a number of reasons: first, C never entered into any relationship, contractual or otherwise, with A. Why should he suddenly be thrown open to a claim from him? He might have certain defences if sued by B which are not available to him as against A. Secondly, each party should only bear the risk of the insolvency of the party that he himself selected as a contractual partner, which would not be the case if a direct claim A against C were to be permitted. The requirement of directness, defined by insisting that enrichment and disenrichment must flow from the same process, was able to take account of these considerations: the enrichment of C did not spring from a direct transfer of the car from A to C; on the contrary, the car only reached C having first passed through B's assets. The proper actions to bring were B against C and A against B.

11.2.3 Problems with the classical approach

While Krawielicki's work is even today praised as providing an adequate solution, the traditional structure is highly abstract. Nor were the attempts to tie down the ambit of enrichment law by restricting it through the directness requirement universally successful: many writers, used to the clearly defined *condictiones* of the *ius commune*, were puzzled by the very wide formulation of § 812 I. Thus Leo Raape writes in the year 1915,[31] having quoted from the provision: 'These are the ambiguous words of § 812 I 1' Though he stresses that the 'untruth' of the Pomponius maxim had long been realised, given that 'the order of things in society often leads to situations in which one person becomes richer at the expense of the other, or poorer to the other's advantage',[32] he goes on to state, when wondering what is meant by the requirement 'absence of legal cause': 'The shift of wealth is [in some cases] in accordance with legal norms [referring to provisions of property law[33]], and is therefore essentially lawful; it is, however, unjustified in the sense that it appears to work injustice considering the relationship between the parties.'[34] He regrets this conclusion, but, given the wording of § 812 I, he sees himself compelled to make it.

Similarly Carl Crome had written in 1902: 'The question when an acquisition is *unjustified* is not answered by the code in § 812; it is a question of the highest aims of the legal order. It is concerned with the realisation of the substantive principle of justice in the face of legal consequences which the law not infrequently allows for other reasons, such as certainty, speeding up of the legal process and simplification.'[35] In effect, Crome thus asserts that § 812 is to play the role in German law that is played by Equity in the

---

31 Dernburg and Raape, 1915, p 720.

32 *Ibid*, p 721.

33 Raape here refers to provisions such as § 929, which provides for the passing of property in certain circumstances. He fails to see why § 929 should be less of a 'legal cause' than, say, a provision of contract law.

34 *Ibid*, p 723.

35 Crome, 1902, p 979.

common law world. It would, however, of necessity operate without the rigorous discipline which Equity has acquired over many centuries.

It is suggested that it was only due to the admirable constraint of the courts, in particular the *Reichsgericht*, that such a result was avoided. Though the *Reichsgericht* in one case[36] agreed with Raape that an enrichment claim would compensate 'a result brought about by the operation of the code's provisions which the law disapproved of with regard to higher considerations', it insisted that these must be apparent from positive law, and that 'mere considerations of equity can never lead to a situation in which an acquisition sanctioned by the legal order is nevertheless treated as obtained without legal cause'.[37] The court was fully aware that it was applying the provisions of the code, which had to be seen as a coherent whole. It also knew that, given its claim to coherence, the *BGB* often uses language of a very general kind, and that it was the function of the courts to give meaning to such general language.

Nevertheless, it must be wondered how long it would have been able to resist the tempting simplicity of such an unprincipled approach, given that the law itself appeared to be largely devoid of principle and structure.

11.3 THE EMERGENCE OF MODERN GERMAN ENRICHMENT LAW

11.3.1 Walter Wilburg: a revolution in German enrichment law

Wilburg's criticism of the directness requirement

Walter Wilburg,[38] an Austrian scholar writing in the early thirties of the 20th century, was very much concerned about this lack of structure. He deplored the trend to use enrichment law as a kind of legal panacea, a convenient justification for palm-tree justice and was thoroughly unsatisfied with the then dominant approach. He argued that the requirements disenrichment and directness were put in place solely to avoid the concept of unjust enrichment degenerating further into 'a means to compensate for unwelcome harshness of the law and to avoid inequitable results'.[39] This necessary 'positivistic limitation' of enrichment law is, according to Wilburg, based on a 'mere symptomatic phenomenon', the disenrichment of the claimant.[40] Both requirements, argues Wilburg, 'are crutches which enrichment law must not be content with'.[41]

Wilburg's view of the Leistungskondiktion

§ 812 provides that an enrichment is unjust only if it lacks a legal cause. If legal cause is for the moment taken to mean an underlying obligation, this requirement may make

---

36 RGZ 69, 245 (21.9.1908), 246.
37 *Ibid*, pp 246 f.
38 Wilburg, 1934.
39 *Ibid*, p 5.
40 *Ibid*.
41 *Ibid*.

good sense as long as we are concerned with enrichments that are based on a conscious transfer between claimant and defendant. Such a conscious transfer is referred to as 'Leistung' (performance). For Wilburg, the important characteristic of a Leistung is that it depends on the will of the performing party. Restitution of a Leistung is, according to Wilburg, based on a *mistake* as to the legal cause, a mistake as to the underlying obligation. The basis of the transfer can be expressed by reference to that obligation. If the obligation is valid, the performing party may not appeal to the law of unjust enrichment. The contract or other obligation will govern the relationship between the parties. If the obligation is invalid, the performing party was mistaken when the Leistung was rendered, and it is, therefore, proper that restitution should follow. This presupposes that all or most transfers are made in order to discharge an obligation, which is borne out to a certain extent by human experience,[42] particularly if one keeps in mind that German law along with most continental legal systems regards a gift as a contract.[43] Thus enrichment law is able to leave a good many questions of substance to the general law, which prevents duplication of inquiries and also ensures the congruent treatment of similar or identical questions in enrichment law and the general law of obligations.

Classical enrichment law relied heavily on the requirement of a direct link between enrichment and disenrichment in order to identify the proper parties to an enrichment action. According to Wilburg, enrichment law is able to throw away these 'crutches' by looking at the content and the purpose ('Inhalt und Zweck') of the Leistung.[44] In an endeavour to identify the proper parties, ie the party performing and the party receiving the Leistung, 'a debate about directness makes little sense. It is possible to render a Leistung to another both directly and indirectly; the distinction is absolutely meaningless'.[45] Indeed, on any view, if the buyer B decides to pay the seller S by bank transfer, and for this reason requests his bank to pay S and debit the corresponding amount to his account, B is rendering his performance to S, although he is doing so indirectly. If he paid mistakenly believing himself to be liable, should he be denied restitution merely because the 'shift of wealth' was 'indirect'?[46]

Wilburg is here planting the seed of the now dominant understanding of the term 'Leistung', not as a mere bestowal ('Zuwendung'), but as a purposive transfer. This teleological[47] understanding of 'Leistung' has now assumed paramount importance both in the discussion surrounding an adequate definition of 'without legal cause',[48] and in the

---

42 The same observation has been made in England in relation to the now defunct rule that restitution is only available for liability mistakes: In *Morgan v Ashcroft* [1938] 1 KB 49, p 74, Scott LJ said that in 'human affairs the vast majority of payments made without any fresh consideration are made to perform an obligation or discharge a liability'.'

43 See above, pp 60 ff.

44 Wilburg, 1934, p 113.

45 *Ibid.*

46 In cases of Leistung to and through third parties (as in the example of the bank transfer), the then dominant view helped itself with a far from elegant fiction: in such a situation one referred to 'direct shift of wealth by indirect bestowal' ('*unmittelbare Vermögensverschiebung durch mittelbare Zuwendung*'), cf RGRK/Heimann-Trosien, § 812, No 20.

47 The term 'teleological' is used in his book not in the sense it is used in statutory interpretation ('with reference to the aim of the legislator'), but as denoting that the performance is directed at a purpose.

48 See below, p 217.

treatment of three party situations. If an enrichment case involves third parties, the purposes of the various performances can be helpful in identifying the proper parties to an action, which is demonstrated by the above example of a bank transfer, involving the buyer B, the seller S and the bank:

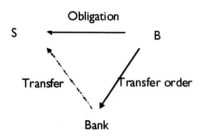

Here the actual transfer takes place between the bank and S, the economic reality of the case is, however, very different. It is B who performs his obligation against S, and the bank that performs its obligation against B. The bank does not pursue a purpose towards S by transferring the money to him, and therefore, if a problem arises between the bank and S, it cannot recover from him, but only from B, provided, of course, that he is solvent. As we have seen, the directness test, if rigorously applied, would in this situation have led to the wrong result, while Wilburg's purposive transfer test reflects the economic reality quite well.

The main reason why German law has such problems with three party situations is the fact that the negative requirement 'without legal cause' does not identify the proper parties to the action, given that it contains no element of intention. Thus, in the above example, there is never a legal cause in the sense of an underlying obligation between the bank and the transferee S, and yet it must somehow be explained that S will not be subjected to an enrichment claim from the bank. It is for this reason that the directness requirement was introduced. Wilburg's model, re-introducing intention by emphasising the concept of mistake, is more elegant, given that it is related to the reason why restitution should or should not be granted. English enrichment law is rather underdeveloped as far as three party situations are concerned, and certainly much work remains to be done in this area.[49] However, it can be argued that the need to analyse these cases has never been as acute as it was (and is) in Germany, given that the English insistence on grounds for restitution often contains within it a reference to the intention of the transferor. It stands to reason that this advantage might well be jeopardised by the introduction of a cause of action in 'no consideration'.[50]

Enrichments not conferred by Leistung — 'Eingriffskondiktion'

Wilburg argues that while the requirement 'absence of legal cause' works satisfactorily in so far as enrichments by *Leistung* are concerned, the great fallacy of the view dominant in

---

49 Again, Birks has made a start: Birks, 2000c.
50 See below, pp 253 f.

Wilburg's day was to transfer the same model to all other enrichments: *'Diese Übertragung verdunkelt das ganze Bereicherungsrecht'*.[51]

What has to be realised first is that there are many enrichments at the expense of another which are not based on a conscious act of transfer on the part of the claimant. The defendant may simply have *taken* something that belonged to the claimant, or he may have exploited the latter's right. Examples range from the defendant who has eaten the claimant's cake without his consent, to the transnational company who has unlawfully used the claimant's patent or trademark. The important quality of enrichments other than enrichments by *Leistung* is that the will or consent of the claimant plays no part in the transfer at all. As such it can, of course, not be flawed, not be vitiated by mistake. That is why Wilburg argues that § 812 contains several causes of action in a single provision: the underlying factor calling for restitution is not identical whether the enrichment is transferred by *Leistung* or in another way.

Not all enrichments at the expense of another are unjust in the eyes of the law. Wilburg observes that we must generally not search for a justification, but for a reason rendering the enrichment 'unjustified'.[52] This is of fundamental importance. It defines Wilburg's entire approach. The question is whether we are to regard enrichments at the expense of another in general as *prima facie* unjust, and allow restitution to follow *unless* they can be justified in some way, possibly by reference to an underlying obligation, or whether we accept that such enrichments are only then to be reversed by the law if we can find a positive factor rendering the enrichment unjust.

Wilburg clearly rejects the former approach. He gives an example: the construction of a railway will cause one plot of land to increase, another to decrease in value; here there is no 'legal cause' of that shift of wealth and yet the enrichment of the one side is not unjust.[53]

He points out that unjust enrichments by *Leistung* and enrichments not based on *Leistung* have in common that they are disapproved of by the law. This is expressed by the negative requirement 'without legal cause' in § 812. Nevertheless, they both have distinct positive features. As explained above, to Wilburg the reason why enrichments by *Leistung* are unjust is that they lack a legal cause in the technical sense, that is, in the sense that the claimant is labouring under a mistake as to the underlying obligation. For other kinds of enrichment, however, the requirement 'absence of legal cause' does not assist to any great extent;[54] they cannot be based on mistake because the claimant does not exercise his will at all.

In searching for a reason for restitution in these cases, Wilburg refers to work by Fritz Schulz which had caused quite a stir in German legal circles some 20 years previously. Schulz had based a single cause of action in unjust enrichment on the unlawful *taking* (rather than the unlawful *possession*) of an enrichment by the defendant.[55] Wilburg, however, sees the root of these restitutionary claims in the purpose of the violated right, which is the *allocation* of certain goods and their use and profits to the owner of the right.

---

51 ('This transference casts a shadow over the whole law of enrichment'), Wilburg, 1934, p 12.
52 *Ibid*, p 14.
53 *Ibid*.
54 Cf *ibid*, p 8.
55 Schulz, 1909, p 1.

It is by looking at the extent to which a right is protected by the legal order that we can decide whether to impose restitutionary liability for its violation.

Property rights are the paradigm case. The *BGB* protects property as such in two ways: § 985 provides that the owner can demand possession of the thing owned from the possessor (*rei vindicatio*). § 1004 provides that the owner can prohibit any interference with his property (*actio negatoria*). Wilburg argues that these two provisions express the purpose of property as allocating a thing exclusively to its owner. Therefore, if the property is lost through the encroachment of somebody else, either by consumption of the thing or by changing its nature in such a way as to acquire property in it, the *value* of the thing will not be lost or transferred, even though the property right may be.[56] An enrichment claim will lie against the person who has acquired or destroyed the property right, and he will be liable to account to the original owner for that value. The positive reason why the enrichment is unjust is the purpose of the property right, which 'lives on in the form of a personal obligation'.[57]

The same restitutionary liability will be imposed on the person who derives profits from somebody else's property. Again we refer to the general (property) law in order to determine whether the purpose of the property right extends to profits. § 993 provides that even a *bona fide* possessor is accountable to the owner of the thing for any profits derived therefrom 'according to the provisions about restitution of unjust enrichments'. What clearer evidence, asks Wilburg, could there be for the function of enrichment law in the protection of property?

These principles, derived from an examination of the protection of property rights, can be applied to other rights: by analogy, the same result is reached for incorporeal hereditaments,[58] intellectual property rights[59] and others. As the law has changed a good deal since the early thirties many of Wilburg's examples, particularly as regards competition and fair trading rules, are now very much out of date.

Summary

Wilburg concludes by stating that 'accordingly, the claim arising from an enrichment in another way has in its origins nothing to do with that arising from an enrichment by *Leistung*'.[60] The former derives from the purpose of an absolute right, the latter from a *Leistung* that has failed.[61] Whether the claimant in the case of an enrichment by *Leistung* actually had a right to confer the benefit, or whether his legal position was in any way protected by the law, is irrelevant: 'That which can be subject of an obligation can be subject of a Leistungskondiktion.'[62] *Leistung* being essentially based on a mistake as to the underlying legal obligation, restitution is justified on that basis alone.

---

56 Wilburg, 1934, p 29.
57 *Ibid.*
58 *Ibid*, p 36.
59 *Ibid*, p 40.
60 *Ibid*, p 49.
61 *Ibid.*
62 *Ibid*, p 50.

By making a distinction between enrichments obtained by *Leistung* and enrichments obtained 'in another way', Wilburg essentially interprets the text of § 812 I in the spirit of § 737 of the first draft, subsequently rejected and replaced in the form of § 812 I by the second drafting commission. By denying the unity of the enrichment claim he contradicts the stated intention of the second drafting commission, in effect the legislator, to frame a general enrichment clause.[63]

11.3.2 Ernst von Caemmerer

Ernst von Caemmerer[64] was writing 20 years or more after Wilburg, and his typology is very much built on the preparatory work done by the Austrian. The recognition of the underlying difference between claims based on *Leistung* and those based on enrichments in another way is clearly Wilburg's achievement. His typology has since, starting with von Caemmerer's influential study, been refined and extended. The great importance of the study was to draw Wilburg's taxonomy to the attention of the legal world in Germany: here was an acknowledged authority in the field of civil law, arguing vehemently against the received wisdom that § 812 represented a general clause, and seeking to give it an altogether different meaning. It was only after von Caemmerer had written his study that the courts started to take notice.

Von Caemmerer points out that even where there is a 'general formula' such as § 812, it will in practice be necessary to develop a typology. The way to go about this is, according to Wilburg and von Caemmerer, to ask why an enrichment is to be considered unjust. As Wilburg has shown, to answer this question by reference to the absence of an underlying obligation is futile, because many enrichments come about without any such obligation, but can nevertheless be retained.

Von Caemmerer takes Wilburg's distinction between '*Leistung*' and '*Eingriff*' as a starting point, and, elaborating the Austrian's typology, adds further categories.

'Leistungskondiktion'

The *Leistungskondiktion* is, according to von Caemmerer, concerned with the reversal of failed transactions and the unwinding of contractual relationships when the contract has proved void or voidable. Thus it is in the same category as contractual rules designed to reverse performances once contracts have been vitiated. Von Caemmerer differs from Wilburg in that he does not seek to justify the *Leistungskondiktion* by reference to a mistake as to the legal cause, but is quite content to state that it is sufficient to show that there was no underlying legal obligation to transfer. This reflects very strongly the view already referred to above,[65] that the discharge of a liability is the only reason for people to transfer value to one another. Von Caemmerer qualifies this later in his study by giving the following definition of *Leistung*: '*Von Leistung kann man nur sprechen, wo*

---

63 See above, p 204.
64 Caemmerer 1954, p 333.
65 See above, p 208.

schuldrechtliche Absprachen durchgeführt oder sonstige Ansprüche erfüllt werden sollen' ('It is only possible to talk of *'Leistung'* where agreements in the law of obligations or other claims are to be fulfilled').[66] This is important, particularly when the *Leistungskondiktion* is to be distinguished from the so-called *'Verwendungskondiktion':*[67] there are some transfers that are not aimed at the discharge of a liability and it would be misconceived to allow restitution in these cases on the basis that the transfer was not owed. It is only where the transfer itself is made with reference to a supposed liability that, argues von Caemmerer, restitution should follow.[68]

It is thus that von Caemmerer can state that 'the actual reasons for restitution lie outside the law of unjust enrichment. The law of restitution would otherwise be overburdened'.[69] Whether a contract is valid, void or voidable is determined by the law of contract, and whether damages for a tort are payable is determined by the law of delict. If those rules decree that there was no liability, it is said to be right to regard any performances given in order to discharge the alleged obligation as conferring an unjust enrichment on the defendant. *The rules of contract and tort are drafted with that consequence in mind.* The legislator's policy which underlies the avoidance of a contract, for instance, is extended to restitution as a consequence of that avoidance. The result is that there is no unnecessary duplication of inquiries. If a contract has been entered into under a mistake of a kind which entitles one party to avoid the contract,[70] and contractual performances have been exchanged, the fact that the claimant was labouring under a mistaken belief in his liability under the contract, or indeed under a mistake as to the facts relevant to the formation of the same is something that the claimant will not have to show in asking for restitution – why should he, as the question has been gone into at length when it stood to be decided whether the contract was voidable or not? Von Caemmerer regards this as desirable, and refers to Anglo-American law to demonstrate the superiority of the German solution: 'Difficulties such as those caused by the co-existence of the different approaches of "condition", "rescission" and restitution for "failure of consideration" are in so far avoided.'[71] 'Issues concerning the doctrine of mistake ... which the continental jurist would assume to find in the Law of Contracts, are dealt with in the Law of Restitution. To control and structure the immense material which American jurisprudence is faced with is almost impossible in this way.'[72]

In the same context, however, von Caemmerer describes the principle of the *condictio* as *'Leistungsrückgewähr bei Zweckverfehlung'* (restitution of the *Leistung* in the case of failure of purpose),[73] and later in his study, when discussing whether the contract with a third party is a sufficient legal ground, he argues that 'according to the German view any intelligible purpose is a sufficient *causa*'.[74] Von Caemmerer here stands in the tradition of Roman law, which had come to regard the *causa* as the purpose of the transaction. The

---

66 Caemmerer, 1954, p 366.
67 See below, p 216.
68 Obviously, there may still be scope for restitution as long as it is not based on the *Leis-tungs-kon-dik-tion*, but on *Eingriff, Rückgriff* etc.
69 Caemmerer, 1954, p 343.
70 See above, pp 64 f.
71 Caemmerer, 1954, p 343.
72 *Ibid*, p 345.
73 *Ibid*, p 343.
74 *Ibid*, p 383.

pandectists had limited the meaning of *causa* to the discharge of underlying obligations, which led to the term being used in an ambiguous and imprecise manner.[75] It should also be remembered that the first draft of the enrichment chapter included the element 'purpose' as a requirement of § 736. While von Caemmerer does not discuss this further, arguing that the only purpose relevant to enrichment law is the discharge of an obligation,[76] the 'purpose' doctrine was later elaborated on, leading to the now dominant opinion that 'failure of purpose' can be described as the positive ground for restitution even in the *Leistungskondiktion*.[77]

Gifts

A common lawyer may wonder how von Caemmerer categorises gifts: is a gift to be seen as a *Leistung*, given that it does not appear to be bestowed 'in order to fulfil an agreement in the law of obligations', nor with the 'purpose' of 'discharging an obligation'? It will be remembered that German law, unfettered by any consideration doctrine, is free to treat gifts as gratuitous contracts.[78] While the case in which a gift is promised in advance (with the requirement of attestation ('*Beurkundung*') by a notary: § 518) fits well into von Caemmerer's analysis, as in this case an obligation is created in advance of the ultimate transfer, gifts do cause problems where delivery and agreement are contemporaneous ('*Handschenkung*'). While the requirement of attestation serves the same function as the requirement in English law that a gratuitous promise be contained in a deed, German law, in very much the same way as English law, makes an unattested gift promise binding if accompanied (or followed) by physical delivery.[79]

It makes little sense to regard this case as a promise preceding delivery by a *scintilla temporis*, and then to treat the transfer as the discharge of a previously agreed obligation.[80] Such an analysis would have little to do with reality. If, then, a gift is not conferred in discharge of an obligation in any meaningful sense, it is difficult to see how von Caemmerer can integrate gifts into his model. While he realises that 'transactions with immediate delivery' ('*Handgeschäfte*') cannot be referred to as obligations', he argues 'that there is no reason to treat the substantive questions differently'.[81] In other words: the reasons for restitution are in the general law. It is not the fact that the defendant never had an enforceable claim which leads to restitution, but the fact some other reason for restitution, such as mistake, duress etc, is present.

The 'condictio ob rem'

Another problem with von Caemmerer's analysis is the '*condictio ob rem*' in § 812 I 2, 2nd alt. It will be recalled that this *condictio* can only be applied to situations where the *Leistung* was to induce the other party to pursue a certain conduct, without binding it to

---

75 Reuter and Martinek, 1983, p 87.

76 Caemmerer, 1954, p 344.

77 See below, pp 218 ff.

78 See above, pp 60 ff.

79 Cf English law: *Irons v Smallpiece* (1819) 2 B & Ald 551, 106 ER 467; *Cochrane v Moore* (1890) 25 QBD 57. German law provides (§ 518 II) that the lack of formality is 'healed' by performance: see p 265, below.

80 That this cannot be right is very much the dominant view: cf Jauernig/Vollkommer, § 516 (1)(b)(aa).

81 Caemmerer, 1954, p 343.

do so (*datio ob rem*), and that it can thus only lie in non-contractual cases.[82] It does not fit into von Caemmerer's model. Its very nature is that it is independent of any underlying obligation. Von Caemmerer has to argue vehemently that the work of the *condictio ob rem* is and should be done adequately by the rules governing frustration. These arguments have been discussed above.[83] Von Caemmerer regards the *condictio ob rem* as a 'historical relic', left over from Roman law with its *numerus clausus* of contractual forms. Yet if that is so, why does the *BGB* contain the *condictio ob rem* at all? Should the provision just be ignored? The *condictio ob rem* threatens von Caemmerer's model of the *Leistungskondiktion* (the *condictio ob rem* being a sub-category of the same), based on the absence of an underlying liability, and thus he has to ignore it.

'Eingriffskondiktion'

This is the most important sub-category of 'enrichment in another way', arising in cases in which 'a stranger's assets are utilised, consumed or made into something else' (*'fremdes Gut gebraucht oder genutzt, verbraucht oder verwertet wird'*).[84] The *'Eingriffskondiktion'*, a claim for restitution of an 'enrichment in another way', fulfils quite a different function from the *Leistungskondiktion*. While the latter, as we have seen,[85] is very much akin to contract and has an important role to play in the rules governing consensual transfers of benefits, the function of the former is the continued protection of property and other rights which have been interfered with by the defendant. It is in the same category as the *actio negatoria*, the *vindicatio* and the action based on tortious interference with property rights.[86]

The reference back to the general law, so important to von Caemmerer's view of the *Leistungskondiktion*, is not quite so simple here. As Wilburg observed, it is difficult to argue that the reason why the enrichment is unjust is because it lacks a foundation in the law of obligations. With Wilburg, von Caemmerer therefore argues that the substantive reason why the enrichment is unjust is that it is *contrary to the allocation of the benefit* (*'Zu-wei-sungs-ge-halt'*). Thus a property right over an asset allocates the *'uti, fruti, abuti'*[87] of the asset to its owner.[88] If the property right is lost by a third party's interference, conferring a benefit on that third party, he has obtained something that by rights should belong to the owner of the lost property right. Whether an enrichment by interference is unjust is thus again decided by reference to the general law.[89] Absolute rights, like property itself, clearly allocate the benefit to the owner of the thing, and are thus equally unproblematic.[90] For other rights the inquiry must be directed at the extent to which the

---

82 See the detailed discussion above, Chapter 8.
83 See above, pp 153 f.
84 Caemmerer, 1954, p 352.
85 See above, p 212.
86 Caemmerer, 1954, p 353.
87 *Ibid*.
88 Cf § 903: '*Der Eigentümer einer Sache kann, soweit nicht das Gesetz oder Rechte Dritter entgegenstehen, mit der Sache nach Belieben verfahren und andere von jeder Einwirkung ausschließen.*'
89 Typically this will be the law of property, or the law governing absolute rights.
90 Caemmerer, 1954, p 354.

law protects the right against outside interference, and whether a restitutionary claim is justifiable on that basis.

Additional condictiones

Von Caemmerer goes on to identify cases of 'enrichments in another way' which are not based on *Eingriff*. Thus if a third party discharges another's debt, German law allows him to recover in restitution. Von Caemmerer calls this claim *'Rückgriffskondiktion'*, and asserts that this is 'the third important group of enrichment claims'.[91] He sees the ground for restitution not in any form of compulsion or lack of consent on the part of the third party, but simply in the fact that the enrichment of the primary debtor is 'contrary to the final allocation of burdens intended by law'.[92]

Likewise, where a person spends money in order to improve property not in his possession (property in his possession being subject to the special regime in §§ 994 ff), or where §§ 994 ff are displaced by contrary contractual relationships between the parties (for example, the tenant who improves his flat without the knowledge of the owner), enrichment law provides a remedy, the so-called *'Verwendungskondiktion'*. The special feature of these cases is that, unlike the other groups of situations of 'enrichment in another way', they involve a conscious act on the part of the claimant. Yet as von Caemmerer defines *Leistung* as a transfer with a view to discharging a liability, the rules governing the *Leistungskondiktion* cannot be adequately applied. Von Caemmerer argues that *prima facie* a restitutionary claim should lie in these situations, but recognises that problems may arise where defendants are seeking to subjectively devalue the benefit conferred on them (*'aufgedrängte Bereicherung'*). As long as the claimant's property can be removed without damaging the defendant's structure or chattel, specific restitution will be ordered (§§ 951 II 2, 997, 258). This is in keeping with the general preference of German law for specific remedies.[93] Von Caemmerer admits, however, that much work remains to be done in this field of German law,[94] particularly as regards benefits conferred in the form of labour and services, where specific restitution is obviously not possible.

Von Caemmerer stresses that his list of categories of claims based on unjust enrichment is not meant to be exhaustive, and that it is inherent in the nature of a general provision such as § 812 that it 'remains open for new fact situations which arise in this life, while new categories will, of course, as has been the case in the development of the law of tort, have to be legitimised with reference to the recognised causes of action in unjust enrichment, their inherent value judgments and limitations'.[95]

---

91 *Ibid*, p 360.

92 *Ibid*.

93 Thus specific performance is the primary remedy of German law: § 249. Likewise in enrichment law the primary claim is for recovery of the actual thing which has been transferred to or taken away by the defendant; it is only in those cases where specific restitution is 'impossible because of the nature of the thing' (§ 818 II) that restitution will be in money instead.

94 Caemmerer, 1954, p 367.

95 *Ibid*, p 376.

11.3.3 Summary

Looking back at the work of Wilburg and von Caemmerer, it becomes clear that German law has not been able to dispense with reasons for restitution. As regards the *Leistungskondiktion*, Wilburg argues that recovery of enrichments by Leistung could be justified on the basis that the *Leistungskondiktion* is 'based on a mistake as to the legal cause'.[96] Von Caemmerer does not seek to justify recovery by reference to an underlying mistake. He argues that there are substantive reasons for restitution which can be determined by reference to the general law.[97] Given that von Caemmerer regards a Leistung as a transfer made with a view to discharging a liability, Wilburg's analysis still holds good: the claimant sought to discharge a liability, yet, unbeknown to him, that liability had never existed or had ceased to exist – he was mistaken as to the existence of the liability. However, not even Wilburg makes it a requirement of recovery that the claimant be mistaken in making the transfer; his reference to mistake is merely an explanation of the defendant's restitutionary liability. The 'unjust factor' ultimately relied upon by both authors is essentially the policy underlying the avoidance of the transaction the transfer was based on. On this view, the *Leistungskondiktion* dispenses with the need for a positive unjust factor by reference back to the general law, it represents the largest group of cases that do not require a positive unjust factor.

It is much clearer that German law cannot dispense with a substantive ground for restitution in the other categories of restitutionary claims, that is, those not based on enrichments by *Leistung*. It is here the interference with an asset which the law allocates to the claimant that calls for restitution. That is as much an unjust factor as mistake or ignorance, and indeed, an argument can be made that 'interference with property rights' can be regarded as an unjust factor in English law.[98]

What both Wilburg and von Caemmerer clearly reject is a generalised unjust enrichment claim. Their main thesis is that enrichments by conscious transfer with a view to discharging an obligation (von Caemmerer's definition of *Leistung*) are rendered unjust by different factors than enrichments which have accrued to the defendant in another way. *The very reason for the differentiation is thus the identification of a substantive reason for restitution.*

---

96 See above, p 208.

97 See above, p 212.

98 Cf Goff and Jones, 1993, p 108, rejecting 'ignorance' as an unjust factor: '... even where the plaintiff is ignorant of what is happening, recovery of the asset or its value must depend upon some specific ground of recovery, relating the plaintiff to the asset and rendering it unjust for the defendant to retain it.' Also cf the interference with ownership analysis in *Calland v Loyd* (1840) 6 M & W 26, 151 ER 307.

11.4 DEVELOPMENT AND ACCEPTANCE OF THE NEW TYPOLOGY

11.4.1 The *Leistungsbegriff*

The new typology had to be refined and developed by later writers. In particular, the precise definition and requirements of a *Leistung* as well as the requirements of the *Eingriffskondiktion* still needed to be worked out. In the present context the former is of particular relevance. What, precisely, is a *Leistung*?

Writing in the same year as von Caemmerer, and building on Wilburg's work, Hans-Wilhelm Kötter answered this question in a most influential article.[99] He identified three central requirements of a *Leistung*: first, he pointed out that *Leistung* must be a way in which another person is in some way enriched. Another's assets must therefore be increased as a result of the *Leistung*. This is referred to as '*Vermögensvermehrung*'.[100] Secondly, the transferor must be conscious of the fact that he is increasing another's assets.[101] Thirdly and finally, the transferor must be pursuing a purpose towards the enriched party. Kötter's main concern was with three-party situations, but his article was instrumental in shaping the modern definition of *Leistung*, the so-called '*Leistungsbegriff*' subsequently adopted by the *Bundesgerichtshof*, defining *Leistung* as a '*bewußte und zweckgerichtete Vermehrung fremden Vermögens*' (conscious and purpose-related increasing of another's assets).[102] To Kötter, it was the purpose of the transfer which turned it from a mere *Zuwendung* (bestowal) into a fully-fledged *Leistung*.

11.4.2 The purpose of the transfer

As has been mentioned before,[103] the view that the substantive reason for restitution of a Leistung is that the transferor did not achieve his purpose in making the Leistung has now achieved dominance. As Reuter and Martinek write: '*Rechtsgrundlosigkeit ist ... Zweckverfehlung*' – 'lack of legal cause is failure of purpose.'[104] This goes back to Hugo Kreß, writing in 1929 (even before Wilburg), who emphasises the importance of the concept of 'purpose' for the entire law of obligations and even calls it '*die Seele des Schuldverhältnisses*' ('the soul of the obligatory relationship').[105] Kreß argues that people 'do not transfer goods in order to transfer them, do not create legal obligations in order to create them',[106] but are driven by economic aims, are pursuing economic purposes. If the law were to disregard these, argues Kreß, it would soon become too abstract, too far removed from reality.[107]

---

99   Kötter, 1954, p 193.
100 *Ibid*, p 195.
101 *Ibid*.
102 BGH NJW 74, 1132 (14.3.1974), II 2 (a), (aa).
103 See above, p 213.
104 Reuter and Martinek, 1983, p 110.
105 Kreß, 1929, p 59.
106 *Ibid*, p 35.
107 Kreß, 1934, p VI.

The teleological definition of Leistung discussed above was, as we have seen, mainly developed for the adequate identification of the proper parties to an enrichment action in three party situations, the purpose of the Leistung enabling us to determine who was performing towards whom.[108] It reflects Kreß's conception of the law of obligations as a whole in that it takes into account that the increase of another's assets is in most cases tied to the realisation of a plan, a purpose.

We have seen that the function of the *Leistungskondiktion* is to reverse failed performances.[109] Of its three requirements, that is, enrichment (benefit or '*erlangtes Etwas*'), *Leistung* and lack of legal cause, it is the lack of legal cause that tells us when a *Leistung* has failed: a *Leistung* has failed if it was conferred without a legal cause (whatever that may mean). If we start with the premise that a *Leistung* is a transfer with a purpose, we are also able to assert that a *Leistung* has failed if its purpose has not been achieved. It is thus an almost mathematical conclusion that the formula: 'lack of legal cause = failure of purpose' must be correct. Thus, the search for an adequate solution to the problem of three party enrichment situations has thrown up unexpected fruits: the identification of a positive unjust factor in the context of enrichments by *Leistung*.

Thus if the buyer of a car pays the purchase price, he can be said to make that payment in order to fulfil his obligations under the contract of sale. If, now, that contract is rendered void (for example, by dissent) or is avoided (for example, for mistake), that purpose has failed because there never was an obligation to fulfil in the first place. The concept of 'purpose' thus provides a convenient link between the claimant's (subjective) state of mind and the (objective) situation in the law of obligations. While the general law still determines the ultimate question of whether restitution is to follow (the policy of contract law deciding), the claimant's purpose directed at the discharge of a purported obligation explains why the failure of an obligation should have restitutionary consequences.

The subjective conception of legal cause or '*Rechtsgrund*' also has the advantage that it can help solve some of the conceptual problems with the Wilburg/von Caemmerer analysis referred to above: it enables us to dispense with fictions when assessing the position of gifts in enrichment law, while making it possible to categorise the *condictio ob rem* alongside the other forms of '*Leistungskondiktion*', it being no longer necessary to treat it as an anomalous exception nor to dispute its continued existence.

We have seen that gifts are contracts in German law. One of the purposes that a donor pursues in making a gift is thus to give rise to a legal relationship between the parties, providing that the transfer is to be gratuitous, and that the donee is to be enriched by the gift.[110] The contract arises in that situation by the very act of making the transfer. If that purpose fails for some reason (the agreement might be vitiated by legally relevant mistake or duress), the donor can demand restitution. The purpose of the transfer has failed, thus the transfer lacks a legal cause and must be reversed. The result may be no different from the one von Caemmerer would have reached, however, the reference to the purpose of the *Leistung* has the advantage that we can dispense with the fiction relied on by von Caemmerer that the gift is to be treated as though it is made in response to a pre-existing obligation.

---

108 See above, p 217.
109 See above, p 212.
110 Cf Reuter and Martinek, 1983, p 91.

Turning to the *condictio ob rem*: it in fact provides the main support for the subjective view in that it expressly refers to the 'result' or 'success' ('*Erfolg*') of the *Leistung*, a concept very much akin to 'purpose'. We have seen that the *condictio ob rem* is independent of any underlying liability, and that the reason for restitution is that a condition on which the *Leistung* was made has failed. The person performing is seeking to induce the recipient of the *Leistung* to pursue a certain conduct which is not legally enforceable. If that purpose fails, he will be able to reclaim the benefit conferred in unjust enrichment. Thus the *condictio ob rem* is the paradigm case of failure of purpose, and cannot be explained in any other way. The great advantage of the subjective theory is thus that it enables us to keep the *condictio ob rem* within the fold of the general *Leistungskondiktionen*. It can even be argued that the proponents of the subjective view cannot make do without the *condictio ob rem*. Consider a case in which A makes a payment to B in anticipation of a contract to be concluded between them, as the claimant did in *Chillingworth v Esche*.[111] Similarly, A might have started work on a building project before, but in the certain expectation of, being awarded a formal contract. If negotiations break down, it is difficult to argue that B ought to make restitution because A performed for the purpose of discharging a supposed obligation. A more realistic construction to be placed on the facts is to say that A performed in order to induce B to enter into a contract with him, and that restitution should therefore follow under the *condictio ob rem*. On the other hand, if a contract is in fact entered into subsequently to one party commencing his performance, most would agree that the proper cause of action should that contract turn out to be void for some reason would be the *condictio indebiti*.

This is the most important *Leistungskondiktion*. The *Leistung* is made in order to discharge an underlying liability. It may, and has,[112] been argued that in these cases the intermediate inquiry whether or not the purpose of the *Leistung* has been achieved is unnecessary, given that the law is framed in such a way as to make a policy avoiding a liability carry through to the consequence of restitution. Indeed, the results reached by either method will always be the same. The question that has to be asked is whether or not the underlying liability exists and can thus either be relied on as the legal cause itself (objective view), or enable the person performing to achieve his purpose of discharging the liability (subjective view). It has been suggested that for this reason the dispute between subjectivists and objectivists is largely irrelevant.[113] However, I would argue that the great advantage of the subjective approach is that it provides an acceptable *explanation* for why restitution should be granted, without affecting the actual result. To say that the enrichment was unjust because the purpose pursued by the performing party has not been achieved is intuitively more satisfactory than the alternative explanation that it is

---

111 [1924] 1 Ch 97, discussed above, pp 163 ff.
112 MünchKomm/Lieb, § 812, No 138.
113 Kupisch, 1985, p 2370.

unjust because the performance was made in response to a supposed liability which either did not exist or was rendered void by the operation of the general law of obligations. If a *Leistung* was made with the purpose of discharging a liability that purpose will necessarily have failed if the liability did not in fact exist. As Hermann Weitnauer put it while debating about the correctness of the purpose doctrine during a seminar dedicated to the memory of the late Detlev König:

> While I do not consider the objective view to be necessarily incorrect, I do consider it to be an incomplete expression of a correct thought.

To Weitnauer, the danger inherent in that view is that if the purpose of the *Leistung* is confined to the purpose of discharging an obligation alone, one will often be forced to imply promises and obligations and 'discharge' them fictitiously.[114]

Relevant purposes

There is some debate as to whether purposes lying behind the immediate purpose of discharging a contractual obligation should be of restitutionary relevance (based on the *condictio ob rem*). In other words, is it possible to base restitution of a contractual performance on the failure of a purpose which is not given expression in the contract itself? As we have seen above,[115] the dominant academic opinion has now come down firmly in favour of the view that it is not.[116]

This dominant view can be supported by an analogy to the English law relating to mistakes. In an action for restitution based on the claimant's mistake, different rules apply in a situation where recovery would upset a contractual arrangement from a situation where no such contractual element is involved. In the former case the mistake must be 'fundamental' or 'basic',[117] in the latter it need merely be causative.[118] Thus, if the validity of a contract is put in issue, a mistake which would otherwise found a good restitutionary claim ceases to be of restitutionary relevance if it is not of a kind as would enable the claimant to avoid the contract. Similarly in German law, it is first of all the contract which governs the relationship between the parties. If the failure of purpose relied on for the restitutionary claim is not due to a circumstance which vitiates the contract rendering it void or voidable, it is thus of no restitutionary relevance and cannot

---

114 König, 1984, p 107. An English translation of the proposal can be found appended to Zimmermann, 1995, p 425.

115 See above, pp 149 ff.

116 See MünchKomm/Lieb, § 812, No 165; Reuter and Martinek, 1983, pp 155 f; Larenz and Canaris, 1994, p 153; *contra* still Palandt and Thomas, § 812, Nos 67 f, Liebs, 1978.

117 *Bell v Lever Brothers Ltd* [1932] AC 161.

118 *Barclays Bank Ltd v WJ Simms & Son Ltd* [1980] QB 677.

lead to restitution. Thus it is always just the outer, as opposed to the inner purpose of a Leistung whose failure has restitutionary consequences.[119] It is only in situations where no outer purpose (such as the discharge of a liability or creation of an underlying contract) exists, that such purposes as referred to above come to the fore, that is, in the cases of the *datio ob rem*. We thus end up with three categories of relevant purposes:

(1) *Datio solvendi causa*. The claimant pursues the purpose of discharging his liability to the defendant. That purpose might, for example, fail due to the fact that there never was a contract giving rise to the liability. Equally, it is possible that the *Leistung* was not of a kind such as to be suitable to discharge the liability: C owed D a car, but delivered a bicycle (delivery of an *'aliud'*).

(2) *Datio donandi/obligandi causa*. The claimant conferred the Leistung in order to give rise to a contract by the very act of performing. That contract may be a gift, or a loan agreement (of the 'will you lend me a fiver' kind). In both these cases the contract arises only at the point of performance. If it fails to arise for some reason, an enrichment claim lies.

(3) *Datio ob rem*. In the absence of a contract governing the relationship between the parties, the claimant seeks to induce the defendant to engage in a certain conduct. That purpose or goal fails, and the claimant can recover his outlay.

This typology of relevant purposes was first suggested by Esser,[120] and is accepted by Reuter and Martinek.[121] One of these purposes will always be present.[122] If it is, it is relevant to the exclusion of all others, that is, if it was one purpose of the *Leistung* to discharge an underlying liability, and that liability is in fact discharged, the payment cannot be recovered back notwithstanding the fact that some other purpose pursued by the payment was not in fact realised.

One major dispute in the academic literature, and indeed between academic writers and the courts, is how (or indeed whether) it must be brought to the attention of the other party which of these relevant purposes the *Leistung* pursues. While the courts still take the view that the recipient must objectively be able to determine what purpose is being pursued by the *Leistung* and, indeed, who is conferring the *Leistung* (the doctrine of the 'horizon of the recipient' or *'Lehre vom Empfängerhorizont'*), the dominant academic view holds that the purpose must at least be implied by the performing party. While this dispute is of considerable importance and one of the major current battlegrounds in unjust enrichment law, for present purposes it suffices to be aware of its existence.

---

119 It should, however, be noted that under § 781 *BGB*, it is possible for one party to recognise that he owes a certain performance, usually the payment of a debt, to another party. This is the so-called abstract recognition of a debt, or *'abstraktes Schuldanerkenntnis'*, itself a contract in German law. Its effect is similar to that of a promissory note or even a cheque under English law: the 'creditor' can sue on the abstract contract and does not have to point to reasons why it came into existence. It could be argued that such a contract only has an outer purpose, the creation of the debt, and that the inner purpose is irrelevant. However, under § 812 II the abstract contract itself is considered a performance, so that the inner *causa* (ie, the purpose of discharging some other obligation) will acquire restitutionary relevance. The effect of the abstract contract is thus merely a shifting of the burden of proof (again this is similar to the English law on promissory notes or cheques). See Markesinis, 1997, p 727.

120 Esser, 1971, p 340.

121 Reuter and Martinek, 1983, p 90.

122 *Ibid*, p 91.

Purpose and mistake

From an English point of view, the problem with the purpose doctrine is that the suggestion that people render performances in order to discharge contractual obligations, to the exclusion of their underlying purposes, has a touch of unreality. In a different context, namely the distinctions between mistakes in expression and mistakes in motive, Titze has expressed the same objection rather well:

> ... the power to give rise to legal obligations which the individual enjoys is never an end in itself; on the contrary, the private autonomy which he is endowed with is meant to enable him to take an active part in economic life in general and to satisfy his own needs in particular in a planned and orderly manner. Nobody has ever entered into contracts simply out of interest in legal phenomena and in order to enjoy the aesthetic pleasure of experiencing the workings of the legal order.[123]

The same idea can be transferred from the creation of contracts to their performance. It is unrealistic to say that a party who pays money for a car does so in order to discharge his obligations under the contract of sale. The much more pressing reason is that he wants the car and can only get it by paying the price. The obligation is a means to an end, not an end in itself. It is therefore odd if restitution is made dependent on the invalidity of the legal transaction, rather than on the realisation of the (primary) purpose of the payment, namely, that the buyer obtains and may keep the car.

The typology of relevant purposes outlined above represents a compromise which satisfies a need for a positive reason for restitution on the one hand without jeopardising the elegant automation identified by von Caemmerer on the other. The substantive, primary reasons for restitution, as we have seen throughout this book, are already built into the general law.

In order to determine whether the purpose of the *Leistung* has failed (in most cases: whether the purpose of discharging a liability has succeeded), one will have to refer back to the general law and ask whether the liability existed or not. Thus, failure of purpose is still more abstract than Birks's system of 'unjust factors', but that abstraction is a price willingly paid for having many substantive questions answered in that area of the law where they most belong; in most cases the general law of contract.

11.4.3 The response of the courts

While the highest German appellate courts, that is, the *Reichsgericht* and later the *Bundesgerichtshof*, applied the criteria of classical enrichment law for a long time, the *Bundesgerichtshof* gave in to the force of Wilburg's and von Caemmerer's arguments in 1963 – the so-called '*Elektrogerätefall*' (electrical appliances case).[124] The facts of the case were relatively simple. The defendant developer had contracted with a firm of electricians to provide a number of houses that were being developed with electrical installations,

---

123 Titze, 1940, pp 92–93.
124 BGHZ 40, 272 (31.10.1963).

including the delivery and connection of electrical appliances. The company ordered 22 electric stoves and 22 hot-water boilers from the claimant supplier, upon which the claimant sent the defendant a so-called 'confirmation of order'. The defendant replied straight away, pointing out that it had not given any such order and that if such an order had been received from the company, the claimant should contact it rather than the defendant. The appliances were delivered anyway, accepted by a worker of the company and duly installed. The company having presumably gone into liquidation, the claimant brought an action against the defendant, claiming the return of or payment for the appliances, the property in which it had now lost as they had become fixtures in the defendant's houses. It was held that no claim in unjust enrichment would lie against the defendant. The court did not, however, base this decision on the fact that there had been no direct shift of wealth between claimant and defendant (the goods having been delivered to the company), but on the basis that there had been no *Leistung* as between claimant and defendant. The court defines the term as 'a conscious and purposive increasing of a stranger's assets',[125] basing that definition on 'more recent literature', but denies the existence of a *Leistung* in this case on the ground that the purpose of discharging an obligation towards the defendant had not been declared by the claimant, and indeed the defendant had no way of knowing that it was not the company that was performing. The only party that might rely on the *Leistungskondiktion* was, according to the court, the company, but only if the contract between it and the defendant was invalid.

Having thus denied a *Leistungskondiktion*, the court goes on to examine the possibility of what it expressly calls an '*Eingriffskondiktion*', and agrees with Esser[126] that an *Eingriffskondiktion* can only lie when there has been no *Leistung* at all (subsidiarity of the *Eingriffskondiktion*). Thus the *Bundesgerichtshof*, referring expressly to von Caemmerer's study,[127] accepted the distinction between *Leistungs-* and *Eingriffskondiktion*.

In applying the new typology, the *Bundesgerichtshof* has sometimes encountered difficulties. One famous case,[128] and the subject of intense debate amongst scholars, concerned a minor who took a Lufthansa flight from Munich to Hamburg. Once arrived there, he joined the transit passengers and managed to get back onto the plane to fly to New York. There he was refused entry, as he did not have a visa. Having asked him to sign a form certifying that he owed them some $250, the airline took him back to Munich on the same day. As he was a minor, any legal transactions he had entered into had to be ratified by his parents, who refused to do so. The airline's claim for some DM 2,200 was therefore based on unjust enrichment. The *Bundesgerichtshof* saw the main problem of the case in the fact that clearly no enrichment survived in the defendant's assets – it was difficult to say that his position had been improved in any way by the flight. However, the *Bundesgerichtshof* throughout assumed that Lufthansa had rendered a performance. This is, of course, fraught with difficulty. The airline pursued no purpose of its own in

---

125 *Ibid*, p 277.
126 Esser, Schmidt and Köndgen, 1971, p 127.
127 *Ibid*, p 276.
128 '*Flugreisefall*', BGHZ 55, 128 (7.1.1971).

allowing the minor onto the plane, there was no supposed or actual liability it intended to discharge, and thus most commentators are agreed that this was a case of *Eingriffs-* rather than *Leistungskondiktion*.

Similarly, in another case,[129] the *Bundesgerichtshof* simply assumed a performance in the following circumstances: an aunt had let a building and an adjacent plot of land to her nephew. She also allowed him to build an extension to the house onto the adjacent land. She made a will under which he would have inherited both the house and the land, and he paid the legal costs of having the will attested by a notary. He built the house and started to run a public house there. Some years later, the aunt cut him out of her will, leaving everything to the defendant, and died seven days later. He claimed restitution of the value of the extension from the defendant and succeeded. The question whether there had been any performance at all was not raised at all. However, the nephew had not intended to increase the aunt's assets at all by building the extension. This was therefore not a conscious and purposive increasing of another's assets (*'bewußte und zweckgerichtete Mehrung fremden Vermögens'*) and did thus not fulfil the modern requirements of a *Leistung*. Thus, it might have been better to regard this claim as a so-called *Verwendungskondiktion*. As we have seen, this lies where a party mistakenly improves somebody else's property.[130] The issue was never discussed by the *Bundesgerichtshof*, however, and in the end it is doubtful whether a different result would have been reached if it had.

Nevertheless, the new typology, including the so-called *Leistungsbegriff*, is frequently applied by the courts, particularly in difficult cases involving three parties. Although increasingly subjected to adverse criticism in this context,[131] it is here that the *Leistungsbegriff* comes into its own. A 1984 decision of the *Bundesgerichtshof*[132] bears striking resemblance to the English leading case of *Barclays Bank v Simms*.[133] It will be remembered that that case involved a stopped cheque, and that the bank was able to recover its mistaken payment. The facts underlying the German decision differ from that case only in that they concerned a countermanded standing order:[134] a brewery ordered its bank to stop payments of rent to the brewery's landlords. It felt to be entitled to do so because of alleged defects in the demised premises. The bank continued to pay, the defendant landlords to receive the monthly payment of rent. To the landlords, it appeared that the brewery had not put its threats to stop paying rent into action. They thought the payments were coming out of the brewery's account. The bank's action against the defendants therefore failed. The performance relationship, as perceived by the defendants, was between the brewery and the defendants – the bank's involvement was merely instrumental in getting the brewery's money to the defendants. It was only the application of the Wilburg/von Caemmerer taxonomy which led to this result, although the court stressed that slavish adherence to any typology should be avoided.[135]

---

129 BGHZ 44, 321 (29.1.1965).
130 See above, p 216.
131 Most influentially: Canaris, 1973, p 799.
132 BGHZ 89, 376 (19.1.1984).
133 [1980] QB 677.
134 An earlier case was almost identical to *Barclays v Simms*: BGHZ 61, 289 (18.10.1973). In that case, too, the bank was unsuccessful in recovering its mistaken payment.
135 Other examples of the application of the new typology: for many BGHZ 58, 184 (24.2.1972), 188; BGH NJW 1974, 1132 (14.3.1974); BGHZ 72, 246 (26.10.1978), 248.

This acceptance of the Wilburg/von Caemmerer taxonomy by the highest German appellate court confirms authoritatively that the attempt of a general enrichment clause, undertaken by the second drafting commission against the warnings of von Kübel, has finally failed. The court accepts that § 812 is best interpreted as containing different and distinct causes of action, and thus reverts back to the conception underlying the first draft of the *BGB*.

11.5 CRITICS OF THE MODERN TYPOLOGY

The old, traditional view that § 812 I should be seen as a general cause of action in unjust enrichment can today be said to be largely defeated. It made its last stand in the late sixties and early seventies, and the remainder of this chapter will examine some attempts then made to revive the, by then largely discredited, traditional view of German enrichment law.

11.5.1 Karl Ludwig Batsch (1968)[136]

At the time Karl Ludwig Batsch was writing, the Wilburg/von Caemmerer dichotomy had been largely accepted by academic writers, while the courts were only just beginning to react to the new academic theories. Batsch makes one final, almost desperate attempt to stop the inevitable acceptance of the Wilburg/von Caemmerer typology by the courts. His arguments are largely founded on the drafting history of the *BGB*. We have accepted above that the second commission did indeed intend to draft an all-embracing enrichment clause in § 812 I, and so these arguments put forward by Batsch need not detain us.

Batsch takes the view that there is no reason why a general cause of action should not work in practice. § 812 I is only too wide if the requirement of a direct shift of wealth (*'unmittelbare Vermögensverschiebung'*) is not complied with. One of the problems with that requirement, says Batsch, was that it appeared to deny restitution where the claimant's property had been used by the defendant in such a way that the use gave the defendant a 'plus' but without a clearly definable 'minus' on the part of the claimant. It was mainly this problem, according to Batsch, which made the development of the new typology necessary.

According to Batsch, however, the perceived problem disappears if one considers the following: an absolute right can be defined as the power that the owner has to dispose of the use of his property, to make decisions as to how his property is to be used.[137] One such use is the transfer of the right to use the property on another in return for valuable consideration. If the defendant without permission uses another's property, he thus

---

136 Batsch, 1968.
137 *Ibid*, p 109.

deprives the owner of that decision making power which is one of the owner's assets. Therefore, even though it may not be immediately apparent, there has been a direct shift of an asset.[138]

While some of these insights are of interest to English enrichment lawyers, in particular in tackling the question whether the phrase 'at the expense of' should denote a loss on part of the claimant, Batsch fails to answer the majority of arguments put forward by Wilburg and von Caemmerer. The most important of these is that the 'direct shift' requirement must always be an artificial barrier to a claim, a barrier which has little or nothing to do with the underlying reasons for restitution.

Batsch is desperate to maintain the general cause of action in unjust enrichment. To him, the scheme of the *BGB* envisages that an enrichment must be justified if it is to be retained. It is this which characterises the approach of most if not all of the critics of the new typology. On this basis we can explain Batsch's reluctance to accept the continued role of the *condictio ob rem*.[139] The *condictio ob rem* is the one enrichment claim which specifies its own reason for restitution: the failure of the purpose of the transfer. Such a claim has no place in Batsch's typology. If § 812 I is to be an all-embracing, general clause of 'unjustified' enrichment liability, it will simply leave no room for an enrichment claim requiring positive reasons for restitution. However, while Batsch is content to base his view of the general cause of action on the legislative and drafting history of the *BGB*, he disputes the validity of such arguments when it comes to attacking the *condictio ob rem*. He cannot have it both ways.

11.5.2 Christof Kellmann (1969)[140]

Christof Kellmann's examination of German enrichment law starts with a comparison to the German law of delict. § 823 I reads:

> *Wer vorsätzlich oder fahrlässig das Leben, den Körper, die Gesundheit, die Freiheit, das Eigentum oder ein sonstiges Recht eines anderen widerrechtlich verletzt, ist dem anderen zum Ersatze des daraus entstehenden Schadens verpflichtet.* [He who intentionally or negligently injures or violates life, body, health, liberty, property or other right of another unlawfully, is liable to the other to compensate him for the resulting damage.]

The words 'or other right' do in this provision not give rise to a separate cause of action. On the contrary, their meaning is, according to the dominant view, to be derived from the rights enumerated in the section. Thus 'other rights' comprise on the one hand absolute rights similar to property (and reflected by the express mention of property) and such rights to privacy and self-determination as reflected by the express reference to life and liberty.

---

138 *Ibid*, p 110.
139 See above, pp 156 ff.
140 Kellmann, 1969.

Kellmann compares these words to the phrase 'or in another way' in § 812. The formulations are, according to him, so similar that one has to conclude that 'in another way' comprises *all* modes in which enrichments come about, and that the *Leistungskondiktion* is merely a sub-category of such importance that it merits to be specifically mentioned, just like life and property are such important rights that they deserve special emphasis in § 823 I.[141]

Kellmann agrees with Wilburg, however, in that he accepts that the lack of a basis in the law of obligations cannot be a sufficient requirement as far as the *Eingriffskondiktion* is concerned, given that, as Wilburg has pointed out,[142] an enrichment can be justified without being based on such a relationship with the disenriched party. However, having come to this conclusion, Wilburg, according to Kellmann, went further than he should have done by denying that *Leistungskondiktion* and *Eingriffskondiktion* have anything in common. Wilburg here, says Kellmann, overlooks the obvious *'tertium comparationis'*,[143] the obvious common basis of the two claims: an enrichment by the one at the expense of the other *without his will or consent* is unjust.

To Kellmann, the 'legal cause' is thus for both *Leistungskondiktion* and *Eingriffskondiktion* not necessarily a contractual agreement (*causa*), but the 'flawless consent of the owner of the right to the use or transfer of his assets'.[144] Kellmann suggests that the relevance of factors vitiating the claimant's will is to be determined according to the general principles of the law of obligations. He declines, however, to discuss this further,[145] although he admits that the real problems lie in the differentiation between legally relevant and legally irrelevant mistakes and other factors vitiating consent.[146] It is doubtful that §§ 116 f, which deal with these questions, are suitable for this purpose, as Kellmann suggests. While the German law of mistake (§ 119) is probably wider than the English equivalent in contract law (§ 119 II allows for the avoidance of contracts on the basis of a mistake 'as to a feature of the person or the object that is regarded as relevant in the marketplace' (cf above, pp 57 f)), it is not as wide as the English law of mistake in the law of unjust enrichment. The interests that stand to be protected are quite different in the two areas: in contract, the law is protecting expectations, mostly based on bargain and exchange, while in the law of unjust enrichment the only interest at stake is the recipient's interest in the security of his receipt. English law is thus justified in treating the former less generously than the latter. Kellmann proposes to treat them both equally (in accordance with the *BGB*'s underlying philosophy to legislate for recurring problems in a 'General Part'). However, Kellmann does not even attempt to argue that the authors of the *BGB* ever intended to define 'without legal cause' as 'without the plaintiff's unvitiated consent', and thus the provisions in the general part do not necessarily fit enrichment law. Indeed, a good argument could be made that they would be too narrow.

Kellmann would clearly be in agreement with this book's thesis that the 'no consideration' approach adopted in the *Westdeutsche* decision should be rejected. First, he

---

141 *Ibid*, p 98.
142 Cf above, p 211.
143 Kellmann, 1969, p 99.
144 *Ibid*, p 102.
145 *Ibid*.
146 *Ibid*, p 103.

attempts to bring German law down onto a lower level of abstraction. Second, he argues for *substantive reasons for restitution*, in effect unjust factors of the kind we know in England, to be adopted in German law. Given that he does not start from the proposition that all enrichments are *prima facie* unjustified, he then needs criteria by which to decide which enrichments the law should regard as unjust, and opts for the lowest possible level of abstraction.

Kellmann's attempts to disprove the dominant view of restitution in Germany, though ultimately unsuccessful and, as a matter of German law, highly questionable, show that some German lawyers try to reduce the level of abstraction necessary in unjust enrichment law and replace the currently dominant classification with a more 'down to earth', positive set of 'unjust factors', telling us in each particular case why an enrichment should be regarded as unjust.

11.5.3 Christian-Michael Kaehler (1972)[147] and Jürgen Costede (1977)[148]

These two authors are discussed together because they are very much in agreement, in fact Costede expressly bases himself on Kaehler's work in adding some more general points of his own.[149]

Kaehler's study compares English and German law. It is interesting in that it appears to be the only German monograph which analyses restitutionary principles taken as a whole, that is to say that it does not confine itself to enrichment law proper (§§ 812–22) but includes principles of vindication (§§ 985–1007) and the law of *Rücktritt* (§§ 346–61). This is a rare phenomenon in German law. It would appear that German lawyers find it difficult to transcend the categories prescribed by the *BGB*. It is striking that those who succeed in doing so, such as Kaehler or von Caemmerer in his seminal essay[150] or Zweigert and Kötz, adopt a comparative approach.

Kaehler attempts to point out a common function of all these 'restitutionary' provisions, and argues that they should follow the same principles. Differences between these different remedies must be based on substantive differences in the relevant fact situations that they are designed to deal with, according to the principle that equal fact situations ought to be treated equally.[151]

At the beginning of his discussion of enrichment law proper, Kaehler makes an assertion which he claims holds true for enrichment law in all the systems he discusses: 'He who has acquired a beneficium at the expense of another, has to return it, unless his acquisition is justified.' His authority for this proposition is § 1 of the American Restatement of Restitution, the first edition of Goff and Jones and § 812 I. He accords the individual a general freedom to enrich himself ('*allgemeine Bereicherungsfreiheit*'), but argues that this comes to an end as soon as the legally protected interests of another legal subject are involved. He derives from this proposition that the enrichment of the one at

---

147 Kaehler, 1972.
148 Costede, 1977.
149 *Ibid*, p 41.
150 Caemmerer, 1954.
151 *Ibid*, p 35.

the expense of the other is generally prohibited and calls, if it occurs, for restitution.[152] In certain situations the legal order allows, however, that the legally protected interests of another are infringed, and in these the acquisition is justified, however, only exceptionally. Thus the relationship between 'enrichment at the expense of another' and 'justification of this enrichment' is seen as a logical 'rule-exception relationship'. § 812 follows the rule that an enrichment at the expense of another is to be returned, and only as an exception allows for the situation in which the enrichment is justified and in which it can therefore be retained. It is inherent in such a relationship, argues Kaehler, that it is impossible to give a conclusive definition for that which remains once the exceptions have been subtracted from the general rule. Thus he argues that it is impossible positively to define those cases in which an enrichment is unjustified.[153] This is, according to Kaehler, the explanation of the phenomenon that neither English nor German lawyers have come up with a positive definition of 'unjustified enrichment'.[154]

The search for a definition in both countries was, according to Kaehler, based on the fact that statistically the rule-exception relationship is turned on its head, ie that statistically the rule is that enrichments are generally justified while the exceptions are formed by those situations in which they are not. In Germany, Kaehler argues, the search was not so much directed towards a single definition, but enrichment claims were categorised according to the way in which they could be justified. Costede remarks that this is tantamount to typifying delictual claims in accordance with their defences.[155]

Kaehler, starting with the 'rule' that all enrichments are *prima facie* unjustified, then presents a typology of 'exceptions'. According to him, an analysis of both English and German law shows that an enrichment is justified if (1) retention is in accordance with the legally binding will of the claimant, (2) the claimant infringed good morals or a law in conferring the enrichment, (3) the defendant was *bona fide*, (4) *restitutio in integrum* is impossible or, in Germany, the so-called '*Saldotheorie*', (5) the defendant has changed his position, or (6) is able to subjectively devalue, (7) the recipient is subject to a legal incapacity or (8) there is a public interest that the defendant retain the benefit, to name but a selection. Instead of relying on a requirement of a 'direct shift of assets', Kaehler thus enumerates situations in which he regards the retention of an enrichment at the expense of another as justified.

Kaehler, whilst criticising the failure of English and German law to construct a positive definition of unjustified enrichments, himself fails to provide a closed definition of 'justified' ones. His entire logical exercise in constructing 'rule -exception relationships' is thus self-serving. The logic of seeing enrichments as unjustified as a rule, and regarding situations in which a conferred benefit can be kept as the exception is flawed in itself: Kaehler bases his entire argumentative structure on the proposition that the 'general freedom of the individual to enrich himself' ends where the legally protected interests of another are involved. These are themselves left undefined. In a concrete fact situation it would accordingly be necessary to point out the 'legally protected interests' whose existence makes restitution necessary. Kaehler's thesis thus presupposes that which he is setting out to establish.

---

152 Kaehler, 1972, p 154.
153 *Ibid*, p 155.
154 *Ibid*.
155 Costede, 1977, p 51.

All things being equal it makes no difference whether one regards an enrichment at the expense of another as generally unjust and calling for a legally recognised justification, or whether on the contrary one sees such an enrichment as *prima facie* just and requires the claimant calling for restitution to show that it was, for some legally relevant reason, unjust. In both cases we are left with a difficult definition, namely, what counts as a justification in the first and what as an 'unjust factor' in the second case. That is, all things being equal. However, Kaehler himself admits that statistically the rule-exception relationship is the reverse of his model. The question is whether the law should not reflect this experience. As a matter of evidence law, it is always the rule that 'he who asserts must prove'. It is more often than not the claimant, that is, the disenriched party, who asserts that an enrichment ought to be returned, and it is he who accordingly bears the burden of proof. If we follow Kaehler, it would be more 'logical' to require the defendant, whose enrichment is, after all, *prima facie* 'unjustified', to point to the relevant 'just factor', that is, to one of the grounds listed by Kaehler on which an enrichment can be retained. It is thus inherent in the rule 'he who asserts must prove', that a claimant be required to show why an enrichment is unjust, rather than to require the defendant to put forward reasons why it should be retained.

In making the wide assertion that 'he who has acquired a *beneficium* at the expense of another has to return it, unless his acquisition is justified', Kaehler bases himself on the Restatement, Goff and Jones and § 812 I. It is, however, highly questionable that at least the first two of these are of any assistance to him. The Restatement does not use the word 'unjustified' at all, but calls for restitution if an enrichment is 'unjust'. Goff and Jones follow a similar pattern, pointing out reasons why an enrichment might be seen as unjust by the law. It is only § 812 I, with its heading 'Unjustified Enrichment' which gives any support to Kaehler's assertion. It is thus not some general 'logical' rule, but a rule which is derived from the formulation of the *BGB* itself. A formulation which was made in an attempt of founding a general cause of action in unjustified enrichment by providing a negative definition, an attempt which, it was argued in this chapter, ultimately failed.

11.5.4 Jan Wilhelm (1973)[156]

Wilhelm argues for a single generalised enrichment action, independent from the way in which the enrichment was acquired. He bases his discussion on Savigny's teachings, who, according to Wilhelm, based the enrichment claim on the continuation of a lost right, the *condictio* replacing the lost *rei vindicatio*.[157] He replaces the criterion of unlawful acquisition, which Schulz had made the basis of his system, with the criterion of unlawful having.[158]

---

156 Wilhelm, 1973.
157 *Ibid*, p 22.
158 *Ibid*, p 98.

Wilhelm advocates that the *Leistungskondiktion* be reintegrated into a system based on the enrichment of the defendant from the assets of the claimant.[159] The *Leistung* is to be seen as the enrichment of the defendant which was effected by the claimant in accordance with his legally relevant will. The criterion 'failure of purpose' is replaced by an inquiry into the justification of a shift of assets, whether that justification follows from the law or from a legally valid transaction. Thus, Wilhelm concentrates on the requirement 'at the expense of' which he amplifies as 'from the assets of'. On this basis, both kinds of *condictio* are one and the same. To Wilhelm the mere having of a benefit which according to the rights or legal positions of the claimant pertain to him is an indication that the having is unlawful and requires justification.[160] In both *Eingriffs-* and *Leistungskondiktion* both transactional and generally legal justifications of the enrichment from somebody else's assets are possible. Thus a *Leistung* can be justified by an obligation imposed by law, such as, for instance, a delict claim.[161]

It is striking that Wilhelm cannot sustain his system without reference to the '*Zuweisungstheorie*' which is very much part of the dominant view of the *Eingriffskondiktion*. Whether a benefit pertains to the claimant 'according to his rights or legal positions' can only be determined by asking whom the benefit is allocated to. On the other hand, Wilhelm criticises the '*Zuweisungstheorie*' as an 'empty formula'.[162] The two are difficult to reconcile.

Wilhelm, while putting forward a view reconcilable with the *BGB*, suggests a general enrichment claim which is very broad, and necessarily very abstract. Like all those who advocate a unified enrichment action, he has to start from the position that all enrichments at the expense of another are *prima facie* unjustified and thus require justification, even though he puts it rather differently. He criticises the dominant view with its distinction of *Leistungs-* and *Eingriffskondiktion*, but does not put anything in the place of the restrictions and categorisations that distinction brings. His system gives no definite answer to the question why an enrichment is unjust. While traditional enrichment law attempted to limit the ambit of the enrichment claim by the requirement of a direct shift of wealth, Wilhelm tries to make do without any such limiting criterion, and throws himself open to the same objections that can be levelled against restitution for 'no consideration'.

11.5.5 Ernst Wolf (1978)[163]

Wolf's textbook on the law of obligations is the only major textbook that does not follow the dominant view of enrichment law. He rejects the distinction between the different *condictiones* and instead bases himself on the text of § 812 I itself when formulating his general principle:

> If a person (enriched party) has obtained an advantage (enrichment) and if another has foregone an advantage which belonged or legally pertained to him (disenrichment), the enrichment and the disenrichment being caused by the same circumstance (shift of an

159 *Ibid*, p 99.
160 *Ibid*, p 173.
161 *Ibid*.
162 *Ibid*, p 89.
163 Wolf, 1978, pp 412 ff.

advantage or '*Vorteilsverschiebung*'), and this shift of an advantage having occurred directly between the parties while no reason existed which would exclude a restitutionary liability, the enriched party is obliged to make restitution to the disenriched party.[164]

The basis of his system is that 'the shift of an asset is necessarily abstract, that is, requires a ground of acquisition if it is to be lawful'.[165] Like all other proponents of a 'general clause', Wolf must deny that enrichments need to be shown to be unjust if they are to be returned, and state the opposite. His support for this proposition is that in German law the transfer of property is abstract from the underlying transaction (principle of abstraction or '*Abstraktionsprinzip*'). Thus, if I contract with you to sell you my car, that contract does not affect the property of the car at all. It is only when I deliver the car to you, giving you possession of the car, and enter into a separate or 'abstract' contract with you that property in the car is now to pass, that the car becomes yours (see above, p 18). Wolf quotes a nineteenth century writer who expresses his opinion that the 'reasonableness of this system is so much beyond doubt, and for reasons equally relevant to all nations, that every legal system will reach the same decision sooner or later'.[166] Wolf transfers the pattern reflected by the principle of abstraction onto enrichment law: property has been lost, according to the rules of the law of property (otherwise the vindication, not the enrichment action, would lie). However, since the rules of property law are abstract, if there was no underlying obligation to transfer the property, if there was no legal ground, the property must be returned. Thus, whenever there is a shift of an advantage, an underlying obligation is required.

Wolf's insistence on a 'shift of an advantage' as the basis of an enrichment claim is in accordance with traditional enrichment doctrine. He also retains the old requirement that the shift be 'direct' between the parties, though he defines this requirement slightly differently in order to avoid some of the problems it caused to traditional enrichment law. Thus limiting the enrichment action, he can make the broad assertion that 'an advantage, which legally belongs or pertains to a person, can lawfully only then be acquired by another person if this is covered by the terms of a legally causal relationship ('*Rechtsgrundverhältnis*') between the two persons. If this does not exist, the acquisition of the advantage is unlawful vis à vis the person it pertains or belongs to'.

Wolf 'borrows' the structure of his enrichment action from the principle of abstraction, which underlies the *BGB*. However, does it necessarily follow that just because a transaction in the law of obligations is abstract from the passing of property that every passing of property requires a transaction in the law of obligations? Admittedly, the structure has a certain attraction as it results in an internal consistency of the *BGB*. However, there are many transactions in which the conferring of the benefit is not in fact abstract: contracts for services, for instance, do not fit the model, and yet surely such services are benefits which can be the subject of a restitutionary claim.

Wolf's aim is to find a general, unified cause of action in unjustified enrichment. That aim is identical to the aim of the drafters of the *BGB*. Whether a system based on the negative requirement of 'lack of legal cause' alongside a positive requirement of a direct

---

164 *Ibid*, p 412.
165 *Ibid*.
166 *Ibid*, p 413, quoting Zitelmann, 1888, p 210.

shift of wealth, or, as Wolf puts it, a direct shift of an advantage, can function in today's society is a different question.

11.5.6 General assessment of the critics

If one takes the strict wording of § 812 I as a starting point, the critics of the dominant view have a point: it seems almost incontrovertible that the provision seeks to lay down a general clause of unjust enrichment, a generalised enrichment claim with the negative requirement of the absence of a legal cause. Kellmann's parallel to the law of delict seems to have substance. Besides, a look at the drafting history of the *BGB* makes it clear beyond doubt that a generalised enrichment action was sought for, and that different groups of enrichment claims based on the mode of acquisition, as first proposed, were expressly and intentionally rejected.[167]

It also has to be admitted that in some cases the distinction between *Leistungskondiktion* and *Eingriffskondiktion* is exceptionally difficult to draw, and that it is, as far as the restitutionary consequences are concerned, often irrelevant. This can be illustrated by reference to the 'Stowaway case' ('*Flugreisefall*'),[168] in which a minor had smuggled himself onto a plane to New York. The question for the *Bundesgerichtshof* was whether he was liable to make restitution of the value of the flight to the airline, and if so, on what basis. It could either be argued that the airline had allocated the minor a seat for the purpose of discharging its liability from a supposed contract. That would be an argument for a *Leistungskondiktion*. However, it can also be argued that the airline was not, in fact, aware of the fact that the minor did not possess a ticket and that, far from being *allocated* a place he simply took one himself, interfering with the airline's right to decide for itself whom to carry on its plane. Both arguments are perfectly viable, and while the *Bundesgerichtshof* came down in favour of a 'general intention to perform' ('*allgemeiner Leistungswille*') on part of the airline, and thus granted restitution on the basis of a *Leistungskondiktion*, many academic commentators disagree with the highest civil court. Medicus merely states that the distinction is almost impossible to draw, and in the final analysis irrelevant (given that the remedy, restitution, is the same whatever *condictio* we are concerned with).[169] He admits, however, that the difficulty of drawing the distinction is one strong argument against the prevalent view.

However, the traditionalists' last stand was so unsuccessful. It is suggested that this was so for a number of reasons:

First, the suggested principle does not tell us when an enrichment is unjust. It tells us when it is not unjust (that is, when it has a legal cause). This necessitates a reversal of the relationship between 'just' and 'unjust' enrichment situations. While statistically and as a matter of political philosophy all enrichments are *prima facie* 'just', any negative definition of 'unjustified' cannot but declare that the rule is the 'unjustifiedness' of enrichments, with 'just' enrichments being the exception.

---

167 See above, pp 203 ff, esp p 204.
168 BGHZ 55, 128 (7.1.1971).
169 Medicus, 1993, p 408.

Secondly, it follows from this that the minority view finds it difficult to cope with examples such as the bridge built by a philanthropist which benefits the entire region, or the tradesman who 'steals' his competitors' customers. Some of these examples can admittedly be solved by reference to the 'directness' requirement. This, however, is not explicit in the text of § 812 I, which deprives the minority view of its greatest support: its faithfulness to the wording of the *BGB*.

Thirdly, the starting point of the minority opinion (enrichment without legal cause) is simply too broad. It therefore becomes necessary to limit the principle, if one is to avoid an enrichment law which is not based on principle but on vague notions of justice and equity. This limitation is achieved with the help of the requirement of a direct shift of wealth. As that requirement has nothing to do with the ultimate reason for restitution its importance as a limiting device is liable to be underestimated, the requirement may ultimately be watered down (as indeed arguably happened in the first half of this century, making the work of Wilburg and von Caemmerer necessary).

Possibly the most persuasive argument has been put forward by Medicus: he calls for continuity and consistency in the area of enrichment law, remarking that even now students get entangled in a myriad of theories when attempting the solution of even simple enrichment cases. He also draws attention to the danger that if the academic literature were to perform another U-turn it might in future be completely ignored by the courts.[170]

As yet the courts pay at least some attention to academic opinion. In a 1978 decision[171] the *Bundesgerichtshof* rejected the arguments put forward by the critics of the dominant view and stated that 'according to now well established case law a Leistung within the meaning of § 812 I is a conscious and purposive increasing of a stranger's assets'. The *Bundesgerichtshof* has thus shown itself unwilling to revert to a general clause of unjust enrichment and is satisfied that the dominant view is functionally adequate and leads to correct and equitable results.

The attempts to reverse the effects of Wilburg's and von Caemmerer's work have thus been wholly unsuccessful. The less abstract and more sensible view that the claimant must point to reasons why an enrichment at his expense should be considered unjust has prevailed.

The attempt of the second drafting commission to frame a 'general clause of unjustified enrichment' must likewise be considered a failure. Admittedly neither Wilburg nor von Caemmerer would openly agree that the second commission did in fact make such an attempt. They repeatedly argue that German law clearly distinguishes between the different types of enrichment claim, pointing to the various provisions of the *BGB* that refer exclusively to the *Leistungskondiktion*. Von Caemmerer concedes that the *BGB* has chosen to include the different claims in a general norm 'in an unfortunate manner'.[172] However, reference to the drafting minutes, and an objective reading of the text of the provision make it clear, and here I agree with the critics of the dominant view,

---

170 *Ibid*, p 409.
171 BGHZ 72, 246 (26.10.1978).
172 Caemmerer, 1954, p 342.

that § 812 was supposed to lay down a 'general principle',[173] in effect a general clause of unjustified enrichment. 'The multifariousness of legal fact situations and particularly the increasing involvement with transactions of third parties'[174] made its operation cumbersome and difficult. Enrichment law threatened to degenerate into a mechanism for palm tree justice. While the courts were still resisting that temptation, the structure of the law was changed by interpretation, reverting to several causes of action, each well defined and with its own particular requirements, each telling us why an enrichment is considered unjust by the law, but still troubled by the very wide wording of the code, on which it is ostensibly based.

On a reference from the German ministry of justice, König was asked to draw up a proposal for the reform of German unjust enrichment law.[175] It is striking that he proposes *different* sections for *Eingriffs-* and *Leistungskondiktion*. This can be taken to mean simply that he regards the wording of § 812 I, along with von Caemmerer, as 'unfortunate', but it is also evidence for the proposition that § 812 I as it stands does in fact not naturally bear the meaning that the dominant view seeks to ascribe to it. The proposal, now, following König's untimely death, unlikely to be adopted, can thus be seen as a final admission of the failure of the second commission's attempt to frame a 'general clause of unjustified enrichment'.

11.6 CONCLUSION

In this long chapter we have looked at the development of the general enrichment action in German law, § 812 I, starting with its roots in Roman law and its enactment late in the 19th century. We have seen how the abstract and open-ended nature of the provision led to problems in the early days of the *BGB*, and followed the laborious process of developing a typology to contain it. After unsuccessful attempts by Krawielicki and Schulz, the typology suggested by Wilburg, as developed by von Caemmerer, was finally accepted. It now represents both the view of the courts and the dominant view in the academic literature.

The modern German typology, in contrast to the traditional English typology of unjust enrichment law, is not based on the reasons for restitution but on the way in which an enrichment has come about. This enables the German law to maintain the elegant automation intended by the drafters of the *BGB* at least where enrichments come about by conscious transfer (performance). The so-called *Leistungskondiktion* is more abstract than the other *condictiones* in that the true reasons for restitution, as demonstrated in Chapter 10, are to be found in the policies which render the supposed obligation void. In contrast, the other *condictiones*, such as the *Eingriffs-* and *Rückgriffskondiktion*, cannot dispense with positive unjust factors.

---

173 Cf above, pp 203 ff.
174 RGRK/Heimann-Trosien, § 812, No 20.
175 König, 1984.

Even where the *Leistungskondiktion* is concerned, many academic writers were dissatisfied with a restitutionary claim based on a negative requirement (absence of legal ground). As a consequence, the so-called 'purpose doctrine' was developed. This bases restitution on the fact that the purpose of a performance, normally the discharge of an underlying obligation, has not been achieved. While it has been argued here that this approach is a little artificial, given that the legal obligation will normally be just a means to an end, this does demonstrate that even a system as sophisticated as the German one finds it difficult to dispense wholly with positive reasons for restitution.

Finally, this chapter has outlined a number of views critical of the modern typology. In the end, however, the critics fail to convince. An open ended general unjust enrichment clause is simply too wide and uncertain. It must be contained by a principled typology. This, then, is the lesson for English law: if a general rule that nullity will trigger restitution is introduced into our law, we will have to learn how to deal with this. Until that process is complete, mistakes are inevitable.

CHAPTER 12

ABSENCE OF CONSIDERATION IN ENGLISH LAW

If it is correct that *Kleinwort Benson v Lincoln* makes restitution generally available where a performance is based on a supposed void or non-existent obligation, the line of authority based upon Hobhouse J's judgment in the *Westdeutsche* case will no longer be relied upon in such cases. The *Lincoln* model of restitution for mistake of law represents a much more secure basis for claims of this kind. As was argued in Chapter 5, however, the results will be no different. The focus is not on the performing party's state of mind but on the validity and existence of the underlying obligation.[1] In essence, this version of 'absence of consideration' amounts to an importation of the German *Leistungskondiktion* into English law. In this chapter, we will discuss the question whether 'restitution for nullity' can be defended on the basis of authority and principle. We will then consider the remaining scope of the *Westdeutsche* line of authority. The language of 'absence of consideration' is out there now. It is possible that it will not be possible to restrict it to cases to which German law would apply the *Leistungskondiktion*. There is a danger that the contagion will spread further. The result would be a general and as yet unprincipled general cause of action in unjustified enrichment. This danger will be addressed in the second part of this chapter.

12.1 ABSENCE OF CONSIDERATION: A LOOK AT AUTHORITY

12.1.1. The annuity cases

Under the Grants of Life Annuities Act 1777, any annuity or rent-charge was to be registered in Chancery; if it was not, it was to 'be null and void to all intents and purposes'. Cases decided under that Act in the early 19th century provide the main authority for Hobhouse J in *Westdeutsche*.[2] According to him, they show that, in English law, nullity automatically triggers restitution. If this is indeed correct, it is difficult to fault either the 'absence of consideration' doctrine or indeed the wide approach to mistake of law adopted by the House of Lords in *Lincoln*.

The annuity cases concerned claims to recover money paid by one or both parties under instruments that had not been so registered. The fact that in most of these cases restitution was allowed leads Hobhouse J to conclude that they 'establish that the right of restitution existed in respect of payments made under void contracts even though there were payments both ways and therefore on a contractual analysis there was no 'total failure of consideration'.[3] Indeed, there is a strong similarity between the situation in the annuity cases and the swaps saga: the purchaser of an annuity, very much like a party

---

1   This is the result of the argument put forward in Chapter 5 above.
2   The cases had been unearthed by Nicholas Lavender, Junior Counsel for Kleinwort Benson. They had previously escaped the notice of unjust enrichment scholars.
3   *Westdeutsche Landesbank Girozentrale v Islington London Borough Council* [1994] 4 All ER 890, 923.

entering into a swap, makes a bet as to the future. Payments are made both ways. When the underlying transaction is void, the restitutionary consequences have to be faced up to. If it is right that the annuity cases unequivocally said that the voidness of a contract will lead to the recovery of benefits transferred thereunder, that would provide strong support for the 'absence of consideration' doctrine.

Birks has argued, however, that 'the annuity cases cannot bear the load',[4] and that Hobhouse J can only rely on the annuity cases because he takes an 'unduly restrictive view of failure of consideration'.[5] Birks rightly points out that restitution for non-contractual failure of consideration would in all cases have led to the same result; however, the suggestive power of a contract's absolute invalidity must not be underestimated. While some cases refer to failure of consideration as the ground for restitution,[6] most of the annuity cases appear to assume that the contract's invalidity alone is sufficient for restitutionary liability. This becomes particularly clear in *Davis v Bryan*,[7] the very case on which Birks places great reliance. The annuitant had died, and his executrix, finding that the annuity had yielded less than her husband had paid, relied on the 1777 Act and sought restitution. It was obvious to Bayley J that she should not be allowed to succeed: 'Here a bargain was made, and the testator paid a consideration of £300, and the defendant agreed for that to pay a certain annuity. The testator received the whole of that which he bargained for'.[8] It was obvious that if restitution was allowed, the original bargain would be undermined. However, Bayley J did not make this the basis of his decision. Indeed, he seemed to proceed on the assumption that the voidness ab initio of the instrument in question would indeed lead to a *prima facie* right to restitution. He is thus obliged to construe the Act so as to read 'voidable' for 'void', and to argue that the claimant could not take advantage of his own negligence (his failure to register the instrument) in claiming restitution: 'The Act of Parliament says, that unless a memorial be duly enrolled, the deed of which no memorial is enrolled shall be void; but in many cases such words have been held to make the instrument voidable only at the will of the party, and I think we are at liberty to put that construction upon them in the present case.'[9] This represents a considerable departure from the wording of the Act. It is not at all clear from the Act which party is obliged to register the annuity. A strong case could have been made that the grantor should be the one to bear that obligation, as it is normally in the business of granting annuities and is thus in a better position to comply than the grantee. To say that for 'null and void to all intents and purposes' read 'voidable at the option of the grantor' is stretching statutory construction rather far.

Thus, while it must be admitted that the annuity cases seem to have been decided on the assumption that invalidity *per se* will lead to restitution, *Davis v Bryan* is a good example of a case in which such a rule would lead to unacceptable results. It is possible to

4   Birks, 1993, p 214.

5   *Ibid*, p 216.

6   In *Scurfield v Gowland* (1805) 6 East 241, p 244, 102 ER 1279, Lord Ellenborough CJ said, finding for the claimant, that 'the consideration for the money has failed'. Birks further relies on Lord Tindal CJ's speech in *Cowper v Godmond* (1833) 9 Bing 748, 131 ER 795. Lord Tindal CJ, however, appears to speak of 'an action for money had and received for the recovery of the consideration money' (at 753), and no mention is made of failure of consideration.

7   (1827) 6 B & C 651, 108 ER 591.

8   *Ibid*, at 655.

9   *Ibid*, at 655 f.

explain the annuity cases on the basis of failure of consideration, and they have been so explained by the editors of 9 *Halsbury's Laws* (4th edn), para 669, as Hobhouse J himself points out.[10] They have not been subsequently relied upon. There is no unequivocal statement that the invalidity of the contract itself is to be the ground for restitution. If the annuity cases teach us one thing, it is to resist the instinctive response to allow restitution as a consequence of the mere invalidity of a contract.

12.1.2 *Woolwich*

In expressing his preference for 'absence of consideration' over 'failure of consideration' in non-contractual cases, Hobhouse J relies on *dicta* in *Woolwich Building Society v Inland Revenue Commissioners (No 2)*.[11] That well known case concerned an *ultra vires* demand of taxes. The claimants had paid under protest, intending to challenge the assessment of the commissioners, but anxious not to incur the consequences of being seen to be a recalcitrant taxpayer. The *dicta* referred to by Hobhouse J can be found in the speeches of Lords Goff and Browne-Wilkinson. In his judgment, Lord Goff refers to Birks's essay, *Restitution from the Executive: A Tercentenary Footnote to the Bill of Rights*,[12] in which, says Lord Goff, Birks argues that 'money paid to a public authority pursuant to an *ultra vires* demand should be repayable, without the necessity of establishing compulsion, on the simple ground that there was no consideration for the payment'.[13] It has subsequently been pointed out that Birks is here being misquoted: he was arguing for a special rule flowing from the constitutional principle 'no taxation without Parliament' enshrined in the Bill of Rights 1689, and the words 'no consideration' appear nowhere in his article.[14]

Lord Goff refers to *Campbell v Hall*,[15] which concerned restitution of taxes levied in the colonies. His Lordship points out that the ground of restitution itself was not discussed in that case, as the important issue related to the power of the Crown to levy taxes, the Crown accepting that the relevant taxes had to be repaid if they had not been duly levied. Nevertheless, says Lord Goff, 'the simple fact remains that recovery was stated to be founded on absence of consideration for the payment'.[16] However, it is important to note that Lord Goff does not base his decision on 'absence of consideration'. This becomes especially clear when he points out the possible objections to the Woolwich's claim. The first of these he sees 'in the structure of our law of restitution'. The passage is so important for present purposes that it deserves to be quoted in its entirety:

> That law might have developed so as to recognise a *condictio indebiti* – an action for the recovery of money on the ground that it was not due. But it did not do so. Instead, as we have seen, there developed common law actions for the recovery of money paid under a mistake of fact, and under certain forms of compulsion. What is now being sought is, in a

---

10 *Westdeutsche Landesbank Girozentrale v Islington London Borough Council* [1994] 4 All ER 890, 921.
11 See above, pp 191 f; [1993] AC 70.
12 Finn, 1990, p 164.
13 *Woolwich* [1993] AC 70, 166.
14 Swadling, 1994, p 75.
15 (1774) 1 Cowp 204, 98 ER 1045.
16 *Woolwich* [1993] AC 70, 166.

sense, a reversal of that development, in a particular type of case; and it is said that it is too late to take that step.[17]

Lord Goff provides two answers to this objection. The first is based on the fact that it is 'particularly obnoxious' for the state to exact taxes without the authority of Parliament; indeed, such is contrary to the Bill of Rights of 1688. This is in fact the argument put forward by Birks in the article his Lordship had previously referred to. The second answer given by Lord Goff is based on the coercive power of the state backing a demand for tax. In effect, Lord Goff here formulates an exception to the rule that pressure of law cannot be duress. Whether or not that is right, it is clear that his Lordship refuses to endorse the view that the money should be returned 'on the simple ground that there was no consideration for the payment'. He is not about to introduce the *conditio indebiti* into English law. On the contrary, he is extending the categories of substantive, positive reasons for restitution.

Lord Browne-Wilkinson refers to 'two streams of authority relating to moneys wrongly extracted by way of impost. One stream is founded on the concept that money paid under an *ultra vires* demand for a tax or other impost has been paid without consideration'.[18] He refers to *Campbell v Hall* and other cases in which the principle was subsequently applied:[19]

> Although this stream seems subsequently to have run into the sand, I find the approach attractive: money paid on the footing that there is a legal demand is paid for a reason that does not exist if that demand is a nullity. There is in my view a close analogy to the right to recover money paid under a contract the consideration for which has wholly failed.[20]

The second stream of authority Lord Browne-Wilkinson bases his decision on is based on compulsion, and on the fact that 'the payer and the payee were not on an equal footing and it was this inequality which gave rise to recovery'.[21] According to Lord Browne-Wilkinson, in *Woolwich*:

> ... both the concept of want of consideration and payment under implied compulsion are in play. The money was demanded and paid for tax, yet no tax was due: there was a payment for no consideration. The money was demanded by the state from the citizen and the inequalities of the parties' respective positions is manifest (sic) even in the case of a major financial institution like the Woolwich Building Society.[22]

Lord Browne-Wilkinson's approach, as opposed to Lord Goff's, represents a whole-hearted endorsement of the 'absence of consideration' doctrine. In view of this, it is regrettable that his judgment is so short. However, given that *Woolwich* was decided by a 3:2 majority of their Lordships, with only Lord Browne-Wilkinson basing his decision on want of consideration, and even then only taken in conjunction with elements of illegitimate pressure of some kind, the authority of this endorsement is to be doubted.

---

17 *Ibid*, at 172.
18 *Ibid*, at 197.
19 *Dew v Parsons* (1819) 2 B & Ald 562, 106 ER 471; *Steele v Williams* (1853) 8 Exch 625; *Queens of the River Steamship Co Ltd v River Thames Conservators* (1899) 15 TLR 474.
20 *Woolwich* [1993] AC 70, 197.
21 *Ibid*, at 198.
22 *Ibid*.

Nevertheless, Lord Browne-Wilkinson's speech does represent the most authoritative support for Hobhouse J's decision based on absence of consideration.

12.2 ABSENCE OF CONSIDERATION IN THE LIGHT OF THE GERMAN EXPERIENCE

As Waller LJ points out in *Guinness Mahon*, the English law of unjust enrichment is at a cross-roads (*Guinness Mahon v Kensington and Chelsea* [1999] QB 215, 233). There are essentially two ways in which it may develop:

(1) The abrogation of the mistake of law bar in *Kleinwort Benson v Lincoln* amounts to an importation of the German *'Leistungskondiktion'*. Payments made in order to discharge a supposed legal liability can generally be recovered if the liability turns out not to exist. This is also a possible interpretation of the 'absence of consideration' doctrine. *Woolwich Building Society v IRC (No 2)*, in which the phrase was first referred to,[23] did not involve a contract at all, but concerned tax overpaid in response to *ultra vires* demands by the Inland Revenue. Lord Browne-Wilkinson, in allowing restitution, said that '[m]oney paid on the footing that there is a legal demand is paid for a reason that does not exist if that demand is a nullity. There is in my view a close analogy to the right to recover money paid under a contract, the consideration for which has wholly failed'.[24] Dillon LJ, in the Court of Appeal in *Westdeutsche*, based his decision in part on this *dictum* and similar such *dicta* in *Woolwich*. The whole approach (particularly the reference to the 'reason' for payment) is very reminiscent of the subjective approach to the *Leistungskondiktion* in Germany. It is possible that 'absence of consideration' will be restricted in this way, which would render the concept largely superfluous in the light of the *Lincoln* decision. If this is correct, it will still be necessary for English law to develop an infrastructure within which the equation 'invalidity = restitution' is correct in all cases.

(2) Birks fears that it will be difficult to limit the cause of action in 'absence of consideration' to contractual payments. He argues that '[t]here will be a foreseeable temptation to use it often, to escape every difficulty in pinning down more specifically the precise unjust factor which calls for restitution'.[25] In effect, Birks is warning that 'absence of consideration' may bring about a generalised right to restitution. Any enrichment of a defendant at the expense of a claimant, as long as the defendant did not have a contractual right to it, will have accrued for 'no consideration'.

Birks writes: 'If the common law is drawn into an enrichment law in which an enrichment is unjust when it is obtained or retained "without consideration (in the eye of the law)" or, in Latin, *sine causa*, it will have at the same time to learn what civilian systems mean by insufficient legal cause. ... It is neither to its credit nor discredit that it will not do so, certainly not at the necessary speed.'[26]

---

23 *Woolwich* [1993] AC 70.
24 *Ibid*, at 197.
25 Birks, 1993, p 232.
26 *Ibid*.

An argument can be made, however, that as long as it is authoritatively laid down that the ambit of 'no consideration' is to be confined to failed performances, the common law will be able to guard against the dangers of a generalised right to restitution. We have seen that German law in the early years of this century attempted to give substance to the requirement that an enrichment must be 'unjust' by laying down a single negative criterion ('*ohne rechtlichen Grund*'), irrespective of the way in which the enrichment accrued to the defendant. German enrichment law then ran into the danger of degenerating into a system based on vague notions of justice and equity, and that danger was only averted by recognising that such a general negative definition was rather too ambitious. Instead, it was realised that the only group of cases where a negative definition was feasible was that of 'enrichments by performance'; the performance bears within it a plan, a concept of why the transfer is made, and it is thus possible to say that the failure of that plan can justify restitutionary consequences. The great advantage of this negative definition, in the context of enrichments by performance, is that the substantive question whether or not an enrichment is unjust in the eyes of the law is answered by the area of law governing the underlying obligation. Credit in no small measure is due to the drafters of the *BGB* for laying down such a system, and to von Caemmerer for drawing attention to it.

It is possible that the common law might also benefit from those advantages if 'absence of consideration' is confined to 'restitution for nullity'. This is the argument put forward by Meier and Zimmermann.

12.2.1 The *Leistungskondiktion* in the common law

An introduction of restitution for nullity would represent a rejection of the traditional unjust factor approach as far as cases of enrichments by performance are concerned. The true reason for restitution would then be found in the rule of law rendering the underlying obligation void or non-existent. However, it would leave 'enrichments in another way' unscathed. These would continue to be governed by traditional unjust factors, namely 'ignorance' and helplessness. Restitution for wrongs would, of course, likewise remain unaffected.

Over the past five to eight years, Zimmermann and Meier have led a concerted civilian attack on the system of unjust factors in English law. Zimmermann first articulated his misgivings about the English system in an article which appeared in the *Oxford Journal of Legal Studies* in 1995. In this article, he argues that in England 'we have a rather complex and fragmented system of specific grounds for redressing unjustified enrichment. These grounds have developed, over the centuries, in a rather haphazard way.'[27] Pointing to Birks's typology of 'unjust factors', he writes: 'It may well be that the compilation of this kind of list is a particularly convenient way of organizing the casuistry of the English common law. In comparison with the modern civilian approach, and viewed against the background of the principle of unjust enrichment, it does not, however, appear to be a scheme distinguished by its elegance.' Zimmermann levels five main charges at the common law:

---

27   Zimmermann, 1995, p 415.

'Untidiness'

Zimmermann deplores the fact that most unjust factors involve performance, while ignorance does not.[28] This criticism is clearly made from a German perspective. As long as we do not start with a general negative definition of what constitutes an 'unjust' enrichment, there is little utility in distinguishing between enrichments by performance and enrichments in another way.

'English law is not comprehensive'

Zimmermann further remarks that 'new unjust factors may be recognized',[29] and that the law accordingly remains uncertain. This is a general feature of the common law. New grounds of liability may be recognised. Lord Atkin did in *Donoghue v Stevenson*,[30] and, less spectacularly, judges have always had the task of 'fine tuning' the legal system, allowing it to respond to social change and changes in political philosophy. To that extent Zimmermann is right: 'The law remains uncertain.' However, new unjust factors will, or should, fit neatly into the typology of unjust factors as identified by Birks. As was pointed out above, there are a number of 'families' of grounds for restitution, the most prominent amongst them being that the claimant did not mean to give. That broad family is then subdivided into the individual unjust factors, such as mistake, duress, undue influence, or, indeed, failure of consideration (a case of qualified rather than vitiated intent).

Moreover, the Wilburg/von Caemmerer typology is likewise not immune to change. We saw that von Caemmerer himself admits that his enumeration of *condictiones* will never be complete, and that it is inherent in the nature of a general provision such as § 812 that it 'remains open for new fact situations which arise in this life, while new categories will, of course, as has been the case in the development of the law of tort, have to be legitimised with reference to the recognised causes of action in unjust enrichment, their inherent value judgments and limitations'.[31]

'Judges and academics are required to analyse ten or more specific grounds of restitution'

The argument here is that there are often substantial problems of delimitation between unjust factors. We can willingly concede the point. However, it is recognised in England that it is quite open to the claimant to claim both in contract, tort and unjust enrichment, all at the same time. Likewise, it makes no practical difference if the claimant recovers, once he brings an action in unjust enrichment, in failure of consideration or for mistake. He can frame his action in such a way as to allow for both causes of action, the additional ground for restitution giving him an additional string to his bow.

It can be argued that Zimmermann is again rather injudicious in throwing stones: after all, one of the major problems in German enrichment law is the exercise of delimitation between *Leistungskondiktion* and *Eingriffskondiktion*. Medicus, as we have seen, regards this as the most powerful argument put forward by the critics of the

---

28 *Ibid*, p 416.
29 *Ibid*.
30 [1932] AC 562.
31 von Caemmerer, 1954, p 376; see above, p 216.

modern accepted view. While not necessarily giving rise to differences in outcome, this difficulty of delimitation is, if anything, more serious in a civilian system than it is in the common law.

'Unnecessary fragmentation' and 'lack of internal economy of the legal system'

Zimmermann argues that 'placing the focus on the single issue of "transfer without legal ground" does not lead to runaway liability. The civil law systems provide the proof'.[32] He sees the fragmentation of English law as potentially harmful and argues that in any event specific unjust factors do not contribute to the internal economy of the legal system. He points to the fact that this will lead to a duplication of inquiries:

> Mistake, in certain circumstances, invalidates the contract. Mistake also provides the basis for a claim for restitution. What is the relationship between these two inquiries? Why deal with one and the same issue in two different contexts? ... It is difficult to see why the law of unjustified enrichment should be saddled with the task of sorting out the fate of the contractual relationship between recipient and transferor.[33]

This argument is easily Zimmermann's most powerful, and must be dealt with in detail. To start with the second limb of the argument: Zimmermann deplores the fact that English law seems to inquire twice into the same issue. He uses mistake in contract and unjust enrichment as an example. It is true, if a contract is rendered void by mistake it is possible to argue that, in order to obtain restitution, the mistaken party will have to start the argument all over again and show to the satisfaction of the court that he was mistaken in making his performance. However, in practice this is never going to present much of an obstacle, given that a mistake sufficiently serious to render a contract void will always be a sufficient unjust factor to found a restitutionary claim. In addition, it has been demonstrated in Chapter 5 that it is well nigh impossible to render contracts void on the basis of mistake in English law, and so the situation is going to arise extremely rarely in practice.

Some mistakes vitiating contracts will not lead to the contract being void, but render it merely voidable,[34] giving the mistaken party a power to strip away the contract. This is so both in Germany and in England.

In Germany, § 119 allows one party to avoid the contract for certain defined types of mistake, but does not provide a remedial framework for the subsequent unwinding of the mutual contractual performances. That task is left to the law of unjust enrichment. The code operates as a coherent system, one part taking over where another leaves off: § 119 provides that the contract is rendered void, § 812 I that, now there no longer being a contract, each party has a claim for restitution against the other. It is this smooth working in tandem of the laws of contract and unjust enrichment which is probably the most attractive feature of the German law in this context,[35] and one of the main advantages of the German way of doing things.[36]

---

32 Zimmermann, 1995, p 416.
33 *Ibid.*
34 *Solle v Butcher* [1950] 1 KB 671; mistakes may render contracts void at common law, but only voidable in Equity. See above, p 69.
35 Cf von Caemmerer's enthusiasm for it, above, p 213.
36 Cf Chapter 4 for a discussion of the German law on mistake.

In English law the mistaken party is, if his mistake was sufficiently fundamental, entitled to rescind. Rescission is a remedy responding to a limited range of vitiating factors. On the analysis adopted in this book, rescission is itself a response to unjust enrichment, whether the contract is fully executed, partially executed or executory. The rescinding party gets back what he handed over to the other contracting party, be this an actual performance or merely his obligation to perform.

It is for this reason that, where a contract is rescinded, restitution of tangible benefits conferred follows as a matter of course. If this is correct (and the cases certainly give that impression[37]), restitution could be said to follow merely because a contract has been rendered void. It is this perception which has led English writers on contract to conclude that it must hence be logical that restitution should follow if a contract is not avoided, but void from the start.[38] Indeed, the latter case does appear to be *a fortiori* the former.

The question is whether that is the correct conclusion to draw. Rescission, after all, is the law's response to a limited number of situations in which it is perceived to be unjust to bind a person to his bargain and to deny restitution of benefits which have passed to the other party before the situation became clear. Vitiating factors triggering rescission include mistake, undue influence, fraud and misrepresentation. Within these, again, the remedy of rescission may vary in its scope and operation from one vitiating factor to another. *Thus the law, in allowing rescission, is fully aware of the restitutionary consequences.* Restitution is, so to speak, part of the plan. The law is able to do this because it knows that any vitiating factor leading to the rescission of a contract will also be a sufficient ground for restitution in unjust enrichment.

Birks hesitates in denouncing the *ratio* in *Westdeutsche* on the ground that 'there is no doubt that in almost every detail German law would have reached the same conclusions'.[39] As was pointed out in Chapter 10,[40] the swaps litigation would have taken place in an administrative court, if at all. If swap transactions were indeed *ultra vires* local authorities in German law, the legislature would be at pains to make clear whether restitution should follow or not. This might be done in one of two ways:. The relevant rule might provide that, though the transaction is unenforceable, any performances thereunder cannot be recovered. This mechanism is used, for instance, to provide that wagering contracts are unenforceable while not triggering restitution, § 762 I making sure that the loser will not be able to recover his stake under § 812. Another mechanism is that of 'qualified invalidity', giving an interested party (for example, the parents in the case of a minor's contract – § 108) the option to render the contract void or to let it stand.[41] It is only *nullity* as such that triggers restitution, and German law knows this to be the case. The inquiry into the consequences of vitiating a transaction can thus be undertaken in that area of law governing the underlying obligation. Since to date nullity has, in English law, not had automatic restitutionary consequences, the inquiry is here best undertaken in unjust enrichment. Thus I would go further than Birks in stating that, in a common law system, *Westdeutsche* is indeed 'absolutely wrong'.[42]

---

37   Cf Bowen LJ in *Newbigging v Adam* (1886) 34 Ch D 582, 595.
38   Chitty, 1999, p 22.
39   Birks, 1993, p 205.
40   See above, pp 192 f.
41   See above, p 181.
42   Birks, 1993, p 205.

My fundamental argument is that English law, given that unlike German law it is not codified, does not contemplate the consequence of restitution when avoiding a contract. While where the law allows contracts to be rescinded restitution is clearly 'part of the plan', the same is not true of contracts that are void from the beginning. The reasons which underlie the voidness of the contract may not be reasons for restitution. They are directed at avoiding obligations, not at the return of benefits.

This conclusion is not changed if English law were to subscribe to the subjective view of the *Leistungskondiktion* now prevalent in German law, basing a claim in unjust enrichment on the fact that the purpose of a performance has failed. As was pointed out in Chapter 11, the purpose doctrine only serves as an explanation of restitutionary liability, the ultimate result will in most cases still depend on the existence or non-existence of an underlying legal obligation, the decision as to which being determined by the law of obligations. The substantive reason for restitution will still have to be located in the general law.

Zimmermann is thus basing himself on a wrong premise when he argues that German law provides the proof that 'the focus on the single issue of 'transfer without legal ground' does not lead to runaway liability'. The only assertion he would be justified in making is that the focus on 'transfer without legal ground' does not lead to runaway liability in German law. That, in itself, is not proof for the proposition that a similar technique would not lead to runaway liability in the common law. It proved dangerous to introduce rabbits into Australia, where they had no natural enemies. It led to an explosion of the rabbit population. Likewise, it is dangerous to introduce a civil law concept into the common law, which lacks the interdependence of a civilian code. It might indeed, contrary to Zimmermann's argument, lead to runaway liability. The only way to minimise that danger would be by a complete overhaul of the law, identifying situations in which contracts are rendered void and deciding, for each situation, whether or not restitution should be the consequence of invalidity. It is to be doubted if the common law will be able to effect these adjustments at the necessary speed, although we will attempt a tentative start in the next chapter.

Sonja Meier's legal ground analysis of the common law

We have already encountered the arguments put forward by Meier in her book *Irrtum und Zweckverfehlung*. It will be remembered that they are mainly based on her view that, without a legal ground analysis, the unjust factor 'mistake' is overinclusive.[43] It was argued in Chapter 5 that it is far from clear that this is in fact the case. In any event, Meier regards Hobhouse J's judgment in *Westdeutsche* as a step in the right direction, towards an adoption of legal ground thinking in English law. In a recent contribution to the debate in English, Meier presents a survey of the English authorities on void contracts. She concludes that the restitutionary consequences of invalidity are unclear in some cases (*ultra vires* contracts being one of them), while there is no restitution in cases relating to the contracts of minors, in cases of minor illegality and lack of formality. She then identifies a large group of cases (contracts void for misrepresentation, compulsion,

---

43 See above, pp 77 ff.

exploitation and the annuity cases) in which, she argues, restitution is always possible.[44] On this basis, she presents the following argument, which needs to be set out in full:

> That there should be restitution after full execution in many cases of defective contracts, like cases of misrepresentation, compulsion, minority or even ultra vires, is not objected to by Birks. However, the reason for restitution, he argues, is then not the void contract, but a special unjust factor, such as mistake, compulsion, inequality, incapacity, illegality, *ultra vires* or another special policy. But it is remarkable that these unjust factors do nothing else than to mirror the reasons why the contract is invalid. The question whether a contract which was influenced by a mistake or some form of compulsion or which was concluded by a minor or prohibited by the law should be void is answered differently in different countries and is ultimately a question of policy. If there is a policy requiring the invalidity of the contract, and if the same policy in most cases requires mutual restitution, why should not one say that a policy invalidating a contract regularly requires restitution and that, therefore, an invalid contract principally triggers restitution?[45]

The problem with this argument is that it assumes that a legal ground analysis based on the invalidity of a contract as a reason for restitution is necessarily superior to the common law approach. However, as will be argued below, notwithstanding the suggestive power of a void contract, there is much to be said for sticking to the traditional common law model, based on pragmatic reasons for restitution. Moreover, while the policies of English law in deciding in what circumstances contracts are invalidated are reasonably clear, the same cannot be said of the restitutionary consequences of those policies. As was demonstrated in Chapter 10, German law possesses a sophisticated infrastructure which ensures that a defective contract will only lead to restitution where this is desired. English law does not possess a comparable infrastructure, even though statistically it may be correct that most cases in which a contract is void restitution will follow.

Meier has a strong preference to the 'no consideration' approach over the alternative solution based on mistake of law, as she makes clear in a postscript to her recent article.[46] She argues, first, that the mistake of law approach as adopted by the House of Lords in the *Lincoln* case will make it necessary to exclude certain claimants from restitution. This problem will be addressed in Chapter 14. She further argues that basing restitution on mistake of law circumvents the necessity for a legal ground analysis. In other words, there will be too much restitution because restitution for all causal mistakes, be they of fact or law, is simply too wide. She also points out that mistake of law 'merely adds one further unjust factor to the long and probably as yet still not exhaustive, complex list of possible unjust factors for recovery after void contracts', while 'no consideration' might lead to 'a simple unified regime for all cases of invalid contracts'.[47] In part, this argument has already been dealt with above:[48] given that the German law of unjust enrichment is far from 'simple', a suggestion that an adoption of civilian doctrine will simplify English law must be treated with some scepticism. The great danger of 'absence of consideration' which Meier wholly ignores, however, is that it may give rise to a wide and unprincipled

---

44 Meier, 2000, p 207.
45 *Ibid*, p 211.
46 *Ibid*, pp 212 f.
47 *Ibid*, p 213.
48 See above, p 245.

general cause of action in unjust enrichment. We would then have to wait for an English Wilburg to bring order into the ensuing chaos. While it is one merit of the approach based on mistake of law that this danger is somewhat reduced, we will now turn to consider this 'worst case scenario'.

12.2.2 'No consideration' as a generalised right to restitution

So far we have been optimistic. We have assumed that the common law will be able to learn the fundamental lesson that the 'no consideration' doctrine must be confined to what German law would regard as a performance or *Leistung*. The transfer in *Woolwich* would already have been a borderline case, given that the building society confidently asserted that the tax was *ultra vires* and only paid in response to other pressures, such as the loss of business reputation if censured as a recalcitrant tax-payer. Yet while *Woolwich* can just about be fitted within the mould of the German *Leistungskondiktion*,[49] it must clearly be a case of 'this far and no further'. As soon as the new cause of action is extended to enrichments not obtained by performance, the common law will be in serious trouble.

Birks seems to have some trepidation that 'no consideration' reasoning might lead to the adoption of a generalised right to restitution in England, 'however much Hobhouse J may have meant to confine these phrases within the context of void contracts'.[50] It is undeniable that the new doctrine does have the potential to be interpreted in that way, and that, to quote Birks, might be the most persuasive argument against leaving it 'casually lying around'. This would not be the first attempt in the long history of English law to lay down a generalised right to restitution. In the past, however, the common law has been successful in fending off such attempts.

Pomponius and Lord Mansfield

In *Moses v Macferlan*,[51] Lord Mansfield made the following remarks on the action for money had and received:

> The gist of this kind of action is, that the defendant, upon the circumstances of the case, is obliged by the ties of natural justice and equity to refund the money.

The similarity with the Pomponius maxim is obvious and not surprising considering Lord Mansfield's background in Roman law. It is, however, arguable that his Lordship was merely identifying the general principle behind the categories of claim recognised by the law. He also said that the action 'lies for money paid by mistake; or upon a consideration which happens to fail; or for money got through imposition ... or extortion ...; or an undue advantage taken of the plaintiff's situation'.[52] Thus he was listing *unjust factors*, he was pointing out *when* the law would hold that 'by the ties of natural justice

---

49 Indeed, many German lawyers would not have any problems with this. However, if Hobhouse J's principle is to be limited to contractual payments, that limitation is already breaking down in a *Woolwich* scenario.

50 Birks, 1993, p 232.

51 (1760) 2 Burr 1005, p 1012, 97 ER 676.

52 *Ibid*, p 1013.

and equity' the defendant would be obliged to refund the money. Thus subsequent rejections of *Moses v Macferlan* would appear to have misunderstood what his Lordship really meant.[53]

Like the Pomponius maxim, Lord Mansfield's doctrine, the principle against unjust enrichment, should be just that, a *principle*, underlying the law, ensuring, in Birks's words 'a stable pattern of reasoning', and guarding against fragmentation.[54] As Lord Wright said of the doctrine in *Fibrosa*:[55]

> Like all large generalisations, it has needed and received qualifications in practice ... The standard of what is against conscience in this context has become more or less canalised or defined.

Westdeutsche is a threat to that development. Its reasoning destroys the dams and canals built up by centuries of case law, the wild waters of unjust enrichment are no longer confined by principle and precedent but are allowed to flow freely into a sea of judicial discretion. The fact that 'no consideration' was given or received for an enrichment is, as has been pointed out repeatedly, not a sufficient criterion to determine when an enrichment is 'unjust' in the eyes of the law. That decision, in the absence of further guidelines, must then be up to the discretion of the judge.

'The authoritative text-book'

In the third edition of Goff and Jones we find the following argument:

> In our view the case law is now sufficiently mature for the courts to recognise a generalised right to restitution. Indeed there are decisions, including those of the House of Lords, which can be best explained on the simple ground that the court considered that the plaintiff should succeed because the defendant had been unjustly enriched.[56]

The recognition of such a general right cannot but represent a break with the common law approach to unjust enrichment, defining 'unjust' by reference to decided cases and established categories. However much one may claim that 'the recognition of this general right is not a recognition of palm tree justice',[57] it is difficult to see in what way the discretion of the courts is to be limited. Goff and Jones in their third edition do not tell us, and it appears that in their fourth edition they have realised the error of their ways. For now the relevant passage reads as follows:

> English law is now sufficiently mature to follow the example of other common law jurisdictions and to recognise that the principle of unjust enrichment unites all restitutionary claims.[58]

---

53 Cf *Holt v Markham* [1923] 1 KB 504, 513, where Scrutton LJ called Lord Mansfield's doctrine 'discarded', and described the history of the action for money had and received as a 'history of well-meaning sloppiness of thought'. Sir William Greene MR in *Morgan v Ashcroft* [1938] 1 KB 49, 62 said: 'Lord Mansfield's view upon those matters, attractive though they be, cannot now be accepted as laying the true foundations of the claim.'

54 Birks, 1989, pp 19 f.

55 [1943] AC 32, at 62 f.

56 Goff and Jones, 1986, pp 15 f.

57 *Ibid*, p 16.

58 Goff and Jones, 1993, p 15.

We find no more mention of a generalised right to restitution, and in a later passage, in which the third edition was propounding the view that the recognised categories of restitutionary claims (unjust factors) should be seen as 'illustrations of a generalised right to restitution',[59] we now read that 'nowadays it is possible to identify substantive categories which form the basis of the restitutionary claim that the defendant has received a benefit which is *unjust* for him to retain'.[60]

The current edition of Goff and Jones continues along the same lines:

'Unjust enrichment' is, simply, the name which is commonly given to the principle of justice which the law recognises and gives effect to in a wide variety of claims of this kind.[61]

This change can only be described as a U-turn. There is a world of difference between recognising that certain categories of claim are united by a common underlying principle, and claiming that those categories are merely 'illustrations' of a generalised right, instances of enrichments which the judges have found to be 'unjust', but in no way limiting the exercise of their discretion.

Different reasoning techniques

The contrast is between deductive and inductive reasoning. While the one starts with a general principle, and applies it to fact situations, the other 'looks down to the cases' and seeks to identify the general principle behind existing categories. Whatever line of reasoning is adopted, it is necessary to find a structure which effectively hedges in judicial discretion.

The common law has always preferred the inductive technique. As Lord Asquith said in *Chapman v Chapman*: 'Nor ... does English jurisprudence start from a broad principle and decide cases in accordance with its logical implications. ... General rules are arrived at inductively, from the collation and comparison of these decisions; they do not pre-exist them.'[62] Inductive reasoning is safer, as it gives very little scope for judicial discretion right from the start, while deductive reasoning puts little or no limits on discretion until a structure has been developed by jurists and judges.

We can thus offer some explanation for the very different histories of unjust enrichment in England and Germany. While in England the law started off without any separate category entitled 'unjust enrichment', and had to develop it laboriously on a case by case basis, with judges tentatively extending existing categories, often with the assistance of legal fictions such as the implied contract theory, the opposite was the case in Germany (if one takes the enactment of the *BGB* as a beginning). There we had a broad general clause of unjust enrichment, which was then laboriously limited by academics and judges, so as to avoid enrichment law becoming a general discretionary panacea. The outcome, as we have seen, is surprisingly similar in both countries, and while enrichment

---

59 Goff and Jones, 1993, p 29.
60 *Ibid*, p 39.
61 Goff and Jones, 1998, p 12.
62 *Chapman v Chapman* [1954] AC 429, 470.

law in England still lags behind in some respects (given its more recent recognition), it will surely soon catch up with its German counterpart.

'No consideration' threatens to undo the laborious process of inductive reasoning in England. If we agree that it cannot be a sufficient criterion to establish that an enrichment is 'unjust', additional criteria will have to be developed, the very wide formula will have to be limited. The process will have to start afresh. On a case by case basis judges will have to identify reasons why enrichments are *not* to be considered unjust even though they are not supported by consideration. English law would be where German law was in the early decades of this century.

Three party situations

Even those advocating a generalised right to restitution might not be comfortable with the negative definition ('no consideration') suggested by Hobhouse J. We have seen above that in Germany, in the early decades of this century, the formulation in § 812 I caused two problems: the first was the potential increase in judicial discretion brought about by a generalised right to restitution; the second, and one that is to the present day very much in the forefront of the German jurist's mind, is the problem of three party situations and the difficulty in identifying the proper parties to an enrichment action.[63] In this book this important area has been somewhat marginalised.[64] However, its importance must not be underestimated.

We have seen that the negative definition of an 'unjustified' enrichment in the *BGB* makes it difficult to identify the proper parties to an action by reference to their respective intentions. The element of intention is only brought in by the roundabout route of defining the term '*Leistung*' with reference to its purpose. It is thus the purpose at which a *Leistung* is directed that tells us who the proper parties to an enrichment action are.[65] Take the case of X who pays £50 to D, although he intended to pay C, to whom he is indebted to that amount.[66] Can C recover from D? According to German law as formulated in the *BGB*, there is *prima facie* no reason why he should not: if D had not received the £50, C would have received it. D's enrichment is therefore 'at C's expense' in that sense. D had no claim to the money as against C, and thus there is no 'legal cause' for the enrichment. This result can only be avoided (and that it should be avoided is almost unanimously agreed on in Germany, starting with the first drafting commission of the *BGB*) either by reading a directness requirement into the words: 'at the expense of', or by relying on the Wilburg/von Caemmerer model by denying C's claim on the basis that he never performed and never pursued a purpose which could have failed, replacing the negative requirement of 'lack of legal cause' with the positive requirement of a *Leistung* as a purposive transfer.

English law is not concerned about three party situations to the same extent as German law,[67] and it has been suggested above that this is in some measure due to the fact that the element of intention is built into most unjust factors. In the above example, C

---

63   See above, p 209.

64   For a detailed discussion, see Birks, 2000c.

65   Cf above, pp 217 ff.

66   The example is taken from Burrows, 1993a, p 46.

67   Burrows devotes some nine pages in his chapter on fundamental ideas to 'Benefits Conferred by Third Parties' (Burrows, 1993a, pp 45–54), while Canaris, in a textbook on the law of obligations, needs no less than 57 (Larenz and Canaris, 1994, pp 197–253).

cannot claim from D because he was not mistaken, X was. The only claim that C has is against X (on the original debt), while X may have a claim against D on the ground that he was mistaken in making the payment.[68] 'No consideration', understood as a general restitutionary cause of action, would not have that advantage. The problems faced by English law would then be no less serious than those which German law has now been grappling with for over a century. English law would have to rely on privity[69] or directness,[70] but both are more or less artificial, and 'may represent more of a legal conclusion than an explanation'.[71]

12.3 CONCLUSION

In this chapter, we have examined the proposition that restitution will follow nullity in English law both on authority and principle. As far as the 'absence of consideration' approach is concerned, it was argued that it cannot be supported either on the basis of the annuity cases or on the basis of the House of Lords decision in *Woolwich*.[72]

In considering the question on principle, the argument presented here amounted to this: while the German approach is undoubtedly elegant and works well in German law, there is no evidence to suggest that it would work equally well in English law. Moreover, there is no reason to change the traditional English approach, given that it cannot be shown to lead to unjust or unsatisfactory results.

It must be admitted that the choices available to English law are limited by the decision of the House of Lords in *Lincoln*. Unless the original Law Commission recommendations are enacted, which must now be regarded as extremely unlikely, the focus will no longer be on a claimant's state of mind but on the validity of the obligation which his performance was meant to discharge. English law will now have to deal with the consequences as best it can.

It is to be hoped that the decision in *Lincoln* represents the demise of the language of 'no consideration'. However, as was pointed out above, that language is still out there, and it has been repeatedly endorsed by the Court of Appeal. The danger is thus present that it will be used by claimants unable to identify any other plausible reason for restitution, not even mistake of law. It is easy to argue that a defendant has been enriched 'without legal ground' or 'without consideration' in a legal system which does not know what is meant by those phrases.

---

68 Cf Burrows, 1993a, p 47.
69 *Ibid*, p 46.
70 *Ibid*, p 47.
71 *Ibid*.
72 [1993] AC 70.

This can be demonstrated by reference to common law Canada, where an approach to unjust enrichment based on the absence of a 'juristic reason' is already firmly established, under the strong influence of civil law Quebec. A book of this kind cannot forego the opportunity of a quick excursion to the other side of the Atlantic.

CHAPTER 13

THE CANADIAN EXPERIENCE[1]

If 'restitution for nullity' or 'absence of consideration' indeed establish themselves in English common law, our law will not be the first to be mixing elements of civilian and common law enrichment law. Some 20 years ago, common law Canada embarked on a similar experiment, introducing the concept of the 'juristic reason' into its enrichment law. In this chapter we will briefly examine the experiences made in common law Canada. Has civilian doctrine been successfully introduced?

13.1 THE MATRIMONIAL CASE LAW[2]

The phrase 'juristic reason' first appeared in *Rathwell v Rathwell*.[3] The case concerned a standard matrimonial property dispute. Of the nine judges of the Supreme Court, two held that the wife was entitled to a half share because a resulting trust could be found, three would have imposed a constructive trust, and four would have found in the husband's favour, on the basis that there was no common intention to the effect that the wife was to have a beneficial interest. The crucial passage in Dickson CJC's minority judgment reads as follows:

> As a matter of principle, the Court will not allow any man unjustly to appropriate to himself the value earned by the labours of another. That principle is not defeated by the existence of a matrimonial relationship between the parties; but, for the principle to succeed, the facts must display an enrichment, a corresponding deprivation, and the absence of any juristic reason – such as a contract or disposition of law – for the enrichment.[4]

The formulation 'juristic reason' is highly reminiscent of civilian doctrine, in particular the Roman *condictio sine causa* and § 812 I in German law. However, as Lionel Smith has pointed out, it would be simplistic to assume that here the civil law influence of Quebec has simply 'contaminated' Canadian common law. As Smith explains, in Quebec law the claim for *réception de l'indu*, or receipt of a benefit that was not due, occupies most of the field. This claim, however, is oriented towards specific reasons for restitution, as it requires a claimant to show that he paid under mistake or duress,[5] while the general enrichment claim, a judicial development of the Roman *actio de in rem verso*[6] later codified

---

1 I am exceedingly grateful to Dr Lionel Smith for his very helpful comments on an earlier draft of this chapter, and for drawing some recent case law and literature to my attention. As always, the remaining errors are my own.

2 In fairness to Canadian lawyers, it should be pointed out that matrimonial cases involve their very own considerations. It is for this reason that they have been largely excluded from our discussion of the English case law. However, in Canada the principles developed in matrimonial cases have now, as will be seen in the following sections, assumed fundamental importance for the whole law of unjust enrichment.

3 (1978) 83 DLR (3d) 289.

4 *Ibid*, at 306.

5 Smith, 2000, p 217.

6 *Cie Immobilière Viger Ltée v Lauréat Giguère Inc* [1977] 2 SCR 67.

in the Civil Code of Quebec,[7] which does work on a *'sans cause'* basis, is merely of subsidiary application.[8]

In *Pettkus v Becker*,[9] the formulation was accepted by a majority of the Supreme Court of Canada itself. Again, the case concerned a standard matrimonial dispute, even though the parties were not formally married but living together as if they were husband and wife. The claimant common law wife paid the rent and all expenses for the first five years, enabling the defendant to save his entire income. They purchased a farm with money taken from the defendant's bank account and started a bee-keeping business. More farms were bought. When the claimant left, alleging maltreatment, the defendant gave her a small sum of money. The claimant commenced an action for a declaration that she was entitled to a one-half interest in the assets acquired by the joint efforts of the parties. Her action was dismissed at trial, but her appeal to the Ontario Court of Appeal was allowed. Dickson J, on appeal to the Supreme Court, applied the principles he had first outlined in *Rathwell*. He first states that the 'principle of unjust enrichment lies at the heart of the constructive trust', and relies on Lord Mansfield's words in *Moses v Macferlan* to the effect that 'the gist of this kind of action is that the defendant, upon the circumstances of the case, is obliged by the ties of natural justice and equity to refund the money'. Dickson J does not attempt to define the circumstances in which an unjust enrichment will arise, indeed, he states that such an attempt 'would be undesirable, and indeed impossible'. He goes on:

> The great advantage of ancient principles of equity is their flexibility: the judiciary is thus able to shape these malleable principles so as to accommodate the changing needs and mores of society, in order to achieve justice. The constructive trust has proven to be a useful tool in the judicial armoury ... How then does one approach the question of unjust enrichment in matrimonial causes? In *Rathwell* I ventured to suggest there are three requirements to be satisfied before an unjust enrichment can be said to exist: an enrichment, a corresponding deprivation and absence of any juristic reason for the enrichment. This approach, it seems to me, is supported by general principles of equity that have been fashioned by the Courts for centuries, though, admittedly, not in the context of matrimonial property controversies.[10]

The majority agrees with him. Martland J, leading the minority, warned of the dangers of the new approach:

> In my opinion, the adoption of this concept involves an extension of the law as so far determined in this Court. Such an extension is, in my view, undesirable. It would clothe Judges with a very wide power to apply what has been described as 'palm tree justice' without the benefit of any guide-lines. By what test is a judge to determine what constitutes unjust enrichment? The only test would be his individual perception of what he considered to be unjust.[11]

---

7   Articles 1493–96.
8   Smith, 2000, p 216.
9   (1980) 117 DLR (3d) 257.
10 *Ibid*, at 273 f.
11 *Ibid*, at 262.

13.2 *PETTKUS V BECKER* – THE RIGHT WAY FORWARD?

13.2.1 The principle

From an English perspective, it is difficult not to share Martland J's concerns about the imposition of constructive trusts in response to what is perceived to be an unjust enrichment. Let us take the facts in *Pettkus v Becker* itself, and ask how Dickson J arrives at the conclusion that the defendant had been unjustly enriched at the expense of the claimant. Is he dispensing 'palm tree justice', or is he applying established principles?

First, he reiterates the formula he had first laid down in *Rathwell*. The claimant has to show three things:

(1) an enrichment;

(2) a corresponding deprivation; and

(3) absence of any juristic reason for the enrichment.

As we have seen in our discussion of § 812 I in German law, while this looks like a well - structured list of requirements, it does not tell us very much. In fact, it does nothing more than translate the phrase 'unjust enrichment' into 'enrichment without juristic reason'. It is thus the third requirement that is crucial. As Dickson J acknowledges, the 'common law has never been willing to compensate a plaintiff on the sole basis that his actions have benefited another'. Thus, he says, it 'is not enough for the Court simply to determine that one spouse has benefited at the hands of another and then to require restitution. It must, in addition, be evident that the retention of the benefit would be "unjust" in the circumstances of the case'.[12]

Dickson J thus admits that his formula is, as such, not very helpful. The absence of a juristic reason for the enrichment will not suffice. It is in fact code for the word 'unjust', which still needs to be filled. At first brush, it appears that Dickson J seeks to fill that word by relying on the unjust factor 'free acceptance', or, as it is now more frequently called, 'unconscientious receipt':

> Miss Becker supported Mr Pettkus for five years. She then worked on the farm for about 14 years. The compelling inference from the facts is that she believed she had some interest in the farm and that that expectation was reasonable in the circumstances. Mr Pettkus would seem to have recognized in Miss Becker some property interest, through the payment to her of compensation, however modest. There is no evidence to indicate that he ever informed her that all her work performed over the 19 years was being performed on a gratuitous basis. He *freely accepted*[13] the benefit conferred upon him through her financial support and her labour.
>
> On these facts, the first two requirements laid down in *Rathwell* have clearly been satisfied: Mr Pettkus has had the benefit of 19 years of unpaid labour, while Miss Becker has received little or nothing in return. As for the third requirement, I hold that where one person in a relationship tantamount to spousal prejudices herself in the reasonable expectation of

---

12 *Ibid*, at 274.
13 Emphasis added.

receiving an interest in property and the other person in the relationship freely accepts benefits conferred by the first person in circumstances where he knows or ought to have known of that reasonable expectation, it would be unjust to allow the recipient of the benefit to retain it.[14]

Dickson J clearly states, in the second of the above two paragraphs, that 'without juristic reason' means nothing more than 'unjust'. He seeks to apply the unjust factor 'free acceptance'. However, that unjust factor does not really seem to fit the facts. Birks argues that '[a] free acceptance occurs where a recipient knows that a benefit is being offered to him non-gratuitously and where he, having the opportunity to reject, elects to accept'.[15] It appears that the test applied by Birks is objective, that is, would the reasonable person have realised the non-gratuitous intent of the transferor? It is suggested that Dickson J's purported application of the principle goes a good deal too far. In the loving relationship between two people, living as husband and wife, it is difficult to see why one party should regard the general contributions to living expenses etc as non-gratuitous. If anything, this is the paradigm case of *gratuitous* benefit. Dickson J criticises resulting trust reasoning, and the search for an elusive (and in most cases illusory) common intention, but it is suggested that it is just as difficult to discern a reasonable expectation to acquire title on the part of the wife.

The truth of the matter is that Dickson J is not applying unjust factors at all. Having determined that there is an enrichment, a disenrichment, and 'no juristic reason' for the enrichment, the court under the palm tree is in session. Dickson J can now dispense justice, or what he perceives to be justice. The above passage represents an attempt to justify the result he reaches, but not on the basis of principle, but for reasons of 'fairness' and 'equity'.

13.2.2 The *Pettkus v Becker* formula in commercial disputes

Dickson J's formula risks to be applied not just to matrimonial cases, but to *all* cases involving unjust enrichment, even commercial ones. We have seen how it took German law 30 years or more to work out a workable structure to contain a similar formula. The same process is only just beginning in Canada, even though the Canadian courts have the civilian Quebec jurisprudence to fall back on.

While Canadian text-books on the law of restitution introduce the subject by reference to *Pettkus v Becker*,[16] they still refer to traditional unjust factors such as mistake[17] and duress.[18] Is not all lost, then? Is it the case that, while paying lip-service to the principle of unjust enrichment in *Pettkus*, Canadian judges are still applying unjust factors in order to determine when an enrichment has been obtained 'without juristic reason', and thus, unjustly? To a certain extent this is indeed the case, as Smith has convincingly demonstrated.[19]

---

14 (1978) 83 DLR (3d) 289, 274.
15 Birks, 1989, p 265.
16 Fridman and McLeod, 1982, pp 16 ff; Klippert, 1983, p 27.
17 Fridman, 1992, Chapters 3 and 4; Klippert, 1983, Chapter 6, C, 1.
18 *Ibid*, Chapter 5; Chapter 6, C, 2.
19 Smith, 2000, pp 229 ff.

Problems arise, however, when none of the traditional unjust factors seem to fit the facts, while the court is still sympathetic to the claimant.

In *Hunter Engineering Co v Syncrude Canada Ltd*,[20] the British Columbia Court of Appeal had applied the *Pettkus* principle to a commercial dispute. The majority of the Supreme Court, however, held that the doctrine did not apply. Dickson CJ (as he had then become) in particular was adamant that the British Columbia court had carried the doctrine 'beyond the breaking point'.[21] However, Wilson J thought that the doctrine was applicable: 'Although both *Pettkus v Becker* and *Sorochan v Sorochan* were 'family' cases, unjust enrichment giving rise to a constructive trust is by no means confined to such cases.'[22] Fridman suggests that the 'differing attitudes expressed in this case suggest that there remains some uncertainty about the true nature of the role to be played by the doctrine of unjust enrichment and the constructive trust in purely commercial cases not involving any familial or similar content.'[23]

The subsequent case of *Atlas Cabinets & Furniture Ltd v National Trust Co*[24] confirms Fridman's view. The case revealed similar divisions in the British Columbia Court of Appeal. It concerned the construction of a condominium development on Vancouver Island. The defendants were to advance 75% of the cost of the land and the construction on the security of a first mortgage to the developers. A percentage of the payments made to the developers was withheld on a so-called 'Mechanic's Lien Holdback', pending the completion of the project. During construction, the property market declined and the developers got into financial difficulties. Some of their contractors remained unpaid, and threatened to stop work. They were assured by a representative of the defendant mortgage company not only that there was a sufficient fund being held back to satisfy their claims, but also that they would be paid if they finished their jobs. When the developer got into arrears, the defendant foreclosed and acquired full title to the development. The contractors remained unpaid, and brought proceedings against the defendant. A number of arguments were put forward why they should be entitled to the holdback fund. One of them was based on unjust enrichment. Lambert JA, speaking for the majority, accepted this argument. He applied the *Pettkus v Becker* doctrine to the case, arguing that it was applicable generally, though easier to apply in family cases.[25] The test in commercial disputes, he argued, was 'the injustice of the enrichment as being against sound commercial conscience'.[26] Lambert JA was thus able to hold that to retain the moneys was 'unfair in the circumstances', given the assurances made to the contractors by the defendant. A remedial constructive trust could therefore be imposed. No 'unjust factor' as we understand it was specified.

In *Atlas* there is a strong dissent by Southin JA. She would not invoke the *Pettkus* doctrine, doubting its role in commercial disputes: 'I, of course, cannot say where the breaking point is of *Pettkus v Becker*. That is for the Supreme Court of Canada to say but I

---

20 (1989) 57 DLR (4th) 321.
21 *Ibid*, at 353.
22 *Ibid*, at 383.
23 Fridman, 1992, p 443.
24 (1990) 68 DLR (4th) 161.
25 *Ibid*, at 171.
26 *Ibid*, at 172.

do know that *Pettkus v Becker* has not yet been applied by it in a commercial setting.'[27]
She further argued that in commercial relationships:

> ... a man, if he wants the same legal rights as if he had a promise, should ask for it in clear terms. It is one thing to apply the remedy of constructive trust or analogous remedies to relationships such as husband and wife where, in common human experience, the parties rely at the outset on affection as a guarantee of reward and quite another to apply such remedies to relationships which, in the reasonable expectations of the participants, are governed by bargains clearly made with the intention of creating legal obligations on both sides.[28]

She found no reason to give the holdback fund to the contractors and would have allowed the defendant's appeal.

13.2.3 Two voices speaking

Smith has convincingly argued that common law Canada suffers from a 'contradiction of the fundamental orientation of the common law of unjust enrichment',[29] with judges sometimes looking for positive reasons for restitution, sometimes for reasons for retention. He argues that the law has to choose one approach or the other, and that a combination of the two simply will not do. The reason is that the *sine causa* language supposes an underlying infrastructure. Birks agrees with this analysis. According to him, Canadian judges have not yet appreciated that a system of enrichment law based on the absence of a juristic reason requires that underlying structure. He continues:

> Meanwhile, till it is in place Canada might be said to have the worst of both worlds, more abstraction, unintelligible to the lay litigant, without the elegant automation that is supposed to be bought at that price.[30]

---

27   *Ibid*, at 194.
28   *Ibid*, at 196.
29   Smith, 2000, p 243.
30   Birks, 2000a, p 232.

PART V
LIMITING THE INCIDENCE OF RESTITUTION

CHAPTER 14

'JUST FACTORS'

In Chapter 10 we saw that sometimes restitution is desired although none of the usual unjust factors are available. Restitution is based on policy in those cases, and it was argued that it is desirable to identify and spell out that policy as clearly as possible. Most of the cases looked at in that chapter also involved void contracts. This was explained on the basis that the policy leading to the nullity or voidability of the contract is in some, but not all, cases carried through to restitution. In those cases the policy is best served by unwinding an executed transaction. Merely rendering an executory transaction unenforceable is not enough. Sometimes, however, there is no underlying transaction or obligation at all, or it is wholly void, but nevertheless restitution is not a desirable consequence. A system which makes restitution available on the basis of nullity as such, or which bases restitution on mistake of law widely interpreted, must take care to keep restitution within acceptable bounds. One way to do this, of course, is by putting in place wide and robust defences, particularly a strong change of position defence. It will be suggested in the next chapter that this may well be the only option for English law following *Westdeutsche* and *Lincoln*, at least in the short to medium term.

Apart from its wide disenrichment defence, the primary mechanism by which German law imposes limits on restitution for nullity, as we have seen repeatedly throughout this book, is by using the word '*nichtig*' sparingly and carefully, always bearing the restitutionary consequences of its use in mind. It will be necessary for English lawyers to examine afresh all those instances in which transactions are declared void, asking whether in those cases restitution of executed transactions is really a desirable result, and it is hoped to make a modest start in this chapter. Careful use of invalidating language may not be enough, however. Again, German law demonstrates this, particularly in its use of the concept of the natural obligation, and its treatment of time-barred claims, both of which will be examined below.

It is, of course, true that even a system wholly based on unjust factors requires 'just' factors, or, as they are more elegantly referred to, 'factors justifying retention'. Tettenborn devotes a major heading of his introductory chapter to this concept.[1] To him, the main 'factors justifying retention' are subjective devaluation, *bona fide* purchase, receipt from a third party, incidental benefit and receipt under a contract with the claimant. From this list, we can eliminate subjective devaluation and receipt from a third party, as they raise the issues of 'enrichment' and 'at the expense of the claimant', with which this book is not primarily concerned. '*Bona fide* purchase' and 'receipt under a contract with the claimant' both look suspiciously like 'legal grounds', and indeed this is how Meier accounts for receipts under contracts.[2] In this chapter, we are concerned with enrichments which, by definition, lack a legal ground, so that it will not be necessary to discuss these issues again. The one remaining 'factor justifying retention' identified by Tettenborn is therefore 'incidental benefit'. What does Tettenborn mean by this? He uses the old American case of

---

1   Tettenborn, 1996, pp 19–30.
2   Meier, 1999a, p 99.

Ulmer v Farnsworth[3] as an example. In that case the owners of two neighbouring quarries had a dispute when one of them pumped out his quarry, thereby lowering the water level in the neighbouring quarry and saving the other owner considerable expense. On these facts, there was simply no unjust factor, and therefore no reason, at common law, to work with 'just factors'. Tettenborn therefore 'invents' an unjust factor and argues that nevertheless there should be no restitution because the benefit in question is merely an 'incidental benefit'. On his hypothetical version of the facts, a public authority has ordered the claimant to pump out his quarry following pressure from the defendant. The unjust factor Tettenborn identifies is 'compulsion, or lack of voluntariness'.[4] I would argue that, even on Tettenborn's hypothetical, there is no unjust factor which requires a countervailing 'just factor': assuming that the public authority is acting lawfully, the pressure exercised is not 'illegitimate', and therefore the unjust factor 'duress' has nothing to say. In reality, the true facts in *Ulmer v Farnsworth* raise much more difficult questions against the background of a law of unjust enrichment which bases restitution on 'absence of consideration'. We have seen how the modern German law uses a framework based on the way in which an enrichment has come about to deal with this problem. Thus a modern German court would decide the case on the basis that there had been no *Leistung*, that is, no purposive transfer, by the claimant to the defendant, nor had the defendant interfered with the claimant's rights in any way. Thus, the basic requirements of a claim under § 812 I are simply not present. English law has no comparable typology. However, it may not, after all, be necessary to develop one. As was pointed out above, it is likely that 'absence of consideration' will now run into the sand, given that mistake of law will almost invariably be available. If that is the case, the fact that a mistake, even on the House of Lords' wide interpretation of what constitutes a mistake, is required, will in any event exclude restitution on the facts of *Ulmer v Farnsworth*.

The remainder of this chapter will examine cases of void contracts in which restitution may nevertheless not be a desired consequence.

14.1 FORMALITIES

Formality requirements may be imposed by the law in the interest of the parties themselves or in the public interest. The parties themselves may benefit because they are prevented from taking ill thought-out, hasty steps which might have serious consequences, and because a formal transaction is easier to prove subsequently. The frequent requirement of notary attestation also ensures the provision of appropriate legal advice, so that the parties are prevented from entering blindly into a transaction the consequences of which they do not fully understand. Formalities also benefit the state: transactions are recorded in order to keep public registers up to date and to levy taxes and fees. The question for the law of unjust enrichment is how to respond to cases in which the relevant formality requirements have been disregarded by the parties.

---

3   16 Atl 65 (1888).
4   Tettenborn, 1996, p 28.

14.1.1 German law

§ 125 1 *BGB* provides that, where legal formality requirements are not complied with, the transaction is absolutely void.[5] This general rule, however, does not apply across the board. In particular, in certain cases the provision imposing the formality requirement makes sure that § 125 1 will have no restitutionary consequences.

§ 313 requires that land contracts must be attested by a notary. If they are not, they should be void according to § 125 1. The second sentence of § 313, however, provides that where the land contract has been fully performed and the new owner registered at the land registry (*Grundbuchamt*), the lack of form is 'cured' and the contract becomes binding. Full performance is therefore seen as a factor militating against restitution. Registration itself is a formal act, and the purpose of § 313 is thus largely achieved by registering the new owner's title.[6] Unwinding the transaction at this stage would mean compromising the integrity of the register, which is a further reason to bar restitution.

Similarly, § 518 I provides that gift promises require attestation by a notary. If they are not attested, they are thus void according to § 125. However, § 518 II provides that again lack of form is cured by full performance, which must be a relief to all children on their birthdays. Again, once the gift promise has been fully performed, the gift handed over, there are obvious strong reasons militating against restitution which make § 518 II necessary.

A final example is provided by § 766. This lays down the requirement that a guarantee or surety agreement must be in writing. Otherwise § 125 will apply. The purpose of this requirement is that, since the surety does not have to pay any money at the time of agreeing to guarantee the main debt, he should be warned against the potential adverse consequences of that step.[7] The second sentence of § 766 again provides that once the surety pays up and satisfies the creditor, the lack of formality is cured. There is no longer any need to warn the surety at that stage. Indeed, even if the surety mistakenly believes to be bound by the guarantee, this will not help him.[8] The payment is, in other words, a ground of retention which trumps the *prima facie* voidness of the guarantee. The fact that the obligation was void at or just before the time of payment does not trigger restitution.

14.1.2 English law

Under s 2 of the Law of Property (Miscellaneous Provisions) Act 1989, a contract for the sale or other disposition of an interest in land can only be made in writing, all the terms must be contained in one document, or, where contracts are exchanged, in each, and the relevant documents must be signed by or on behalf of each party to the contract. It must follow that where these formalities are not complied with, the agreement in question

---

5   This can lead to hard cases, which have indeed led to bad law: the courts have tried to temper the inflexibility of the rule in cases in which its application would lead to results 'not in accordance with the requirement of good faith': BGHZ 16, 334 (18.2.1955), 336 f; 29, 6 (3.12.1958), 10 f; 48, 396 (27.10.1967), 397 f.

6   Cf Larenz, 1987, p 73.

7   BGH NJW 1993, 1126 (28.1.1993).

8   Cf Larenz and Canaris, 1994, p 5.

must be void and of no effect. Where one party refuses to perform such an agreement, the courts will not assist the other by ordering specific performance or by awarding him damages. The question in the present context is, however, whether such an agreement, once performed, will subsequently have to be reversed, or will be reversible at the instance of one party or the other. If restitution must necessarily follow where performances have been exchanged pursuant to a void contract, that should clearly be the result.

Tootal Clothing Ltd v Guinea Properties Ltd[9] concerned a lease under which the tenant was to carry out certain shop fitting works to the demised premises. The landlord, Guinea Properties, was to contribute to the costs of these works. Its obligation to do so, however, was contained in a separate document. Having taken possession of the property, and having completed the works, the tenant sued for recovery of the landlord's contribution. The landlord argued that the agreement was void and unenforceable because under s 2 of the 1989 Act all the relevant terms should have been in one document. This argument succeeded at first instance before Douglas Brown J, dealing with the question as a preliminary issue. He held 'without any enthusiasm at all' that s 2 applied to the contract and that therefore all the terms of the contract had to be incorporated in one document. In the Court of Appeal, Scott LJ, with whom Boreham J and Parker LJ agreed, held that Guinea's defence missed the point of s 2 of the 1989 Act. If the argument was sound, the result would be that executed agreements would have to be unravelled. It was therefore necessary to ask what policy was pursued by s 2. This question had been addressed previously by Hoffmann J (as he then was) in *Spiro v Glencrown Properties Ltd*.[10] He had held that s 2 'was intended to prevent disputes over whether the parties had entered into a binding agreement or over what terms they had agreed'. As such, argued Scott LJ, s 2 was of relevance only to executory contracts. He continued:

> If parties choose to complete an oral land contract or a land contract that does not in some respect or other comply with section 2, they are at liberty to do so. Once they have done so, it becomes irrelevant that the contract they have completed may not have been in accordance with section 2.[11]

While *Tootal Clothing* did not concern a restitutionary claim, the conclusion that s 2 had no relevance to executed contracts was necessary to avoid the conclusion which Douglas Brown J had felt compelled to draw at first instance.

For present purposes, *Tootal Clothing* can be interpreted in two ways: on the one hand it can be argued that the case clearly demonstrates that nullity as such will not lead to restitution where both parties have obtained what they bargained for, in other words, where there has been no failure of consideration or other substantive reason for restitution; and on the other hand, it is arguable that lack of formality renders a contract unenforceable rather than void, or that the lack of formality is 'cured' by subsequent performance. This would mirror the position in German law.

---

9   (1992) 64 P & CR 452.
10   [1991] Ch 537, at 541.
11   64 P & CR 452, at 455.

14.2 NATURAL OBLIGATIONS

The concept of the natural obligation has been known since the times of classical Roman law. In Roman times, the majority of the population lacked legal capacity, namely slaves, children and women in power. What if these entered into contracts? Were such contracts legally irrelevant? The answer given by Roman law was that this depended on whether the contract was executory or had been executed. If the contract was wholly executory, it could not be enforced. Any transfer effected under such an unenforceable contract, however, was allowed to stand, because it did not lack a legal ground, even though the claim would have been unenforceable.[12] In other words, even though the law will not lend itself to enforce an obligation, it will do nothing to reverse a transfer effected under it.

14.2.1 GERMAN LAW

As Zimmermann points out, even though the concept has been abolished in name, German law still recognises it, even though the transactions falling into this category are fundamentally different.[13] The main examples now are gambling and marriage brokerage contracts. Thus § 762 I provides that a bet does not give rise to an obligation. This is commonly justified not by moral objections but by the inherent dangers of gambling contracts.[14] The provision goes on, however, to say that any performances under a bet cannot be recovered on the basis that no obligation existed. The second sentence of § 762 I thus effectively disapplies § 812 I.

§ 656, which applies to marriage brokerage, is in almost identical terms. Again, it provides that a promise to pay in consideration of marriage brokerage services does not give rise to an obligation, and again it goes on to say that if such a promise is nevertheless honoured the fact that no obligation existed cannot be relied on to demand restitution of any payments made.

These natural obligations[15] are good examples of cases in which German law considers that even the strongest form of invalidity, the total absence of an obligation, should not lead to restitution if performances are made. Even though the policies underlying these rules may appear somewhat outdated and paternalistic,[16] the legislator was quite clearly aware that both forms of 'natural obligations' would be caught by the very wide § 812 I unless it was made clear that the latter provision should not apply. Although they are not obligations properly so-called, 'natural' obligations thus form legal grounds; in other words, they entitle the recipient to retain the benefit conferred – they are reasons for retention.

§ 814 alt 2 is not strictly a natural obligation, but it is sufficiently similar to be included under this heading. The whole provision reads:

---

12 Zimmermann, 1996, p 7.
13 *Ibid*, p 8.
14 Jauernig/Vollkommer, § 762, No 1.
15 For criticism of the term see Larenz, 1987, p 21.
16 Zimmermann, 1996, p 8.

Das zum Zwecke der Erfüllung einer Verbindlichkeit Geleistete kann nicht zurückgefordert werden, wenn der Leistende gewußt hat, daß er zur Leistung nicht verpflichtet war, oder wenn die Leistung einer sittlichen Pflicht oder einer auf den Anstand zu nehmenden Rücksicht entsprach. [That which as been performed for the purpose of discharging a liability cannot be demanded back if the performing party knew that he was under no liability to perform, or *if his performance was pursuant to a moral duty.*]

The second part of this provision is meant to apply to cases in which the claimant was labouring under a mistake: he thought, the law enforced moral obligations rather more strictly than turned out to be the case. When he finds out that he need not have paid after all, he is denied restitution. In fairness, it should be pointed out that there is a dearth of modern case law on this, and this has been taken to indicate that the provision has lost its importance.[17] Nevertheless, two cases decided by the *Reichsgericht* are, I think, instructive. In the first, decided in 1906, a married couple petitioned for divorce. Under the family law of the time, the alimony payable by the husband depended heavily on the relative blameworthiness of the parties. Initially, the husband admitted to have been the guilty party. On that basis, he had to make payments to his wife enabling her to live according to the style to which she had become accustomed while married to him. The divorce court found that both parties had been equally to blame for the breakdown of the marriage. On this basis, she was only entitled to just enough to keep her out of the poorhouse. The husband sought to recover restitution of payments at the higher rate made in the run-up to and during the divorce proceedings and failed. To make the higher payments to the woman who was, after all, still his wife accorded with his moral obligations, and therefore he was unable to recover.[18] In contrast, in a decision of the *Reichsgericht* of 1910,[19] the claimant paid maintenance to a woman whom he thought to be the mother of his child. When it later became clear that he was not the father after all, he demanded his money back and was successful. The court argued that a mistaken intention to discharge a moral obligation did not bring the case under § 814, 2nd alt. The mistake had not just been a mistake as to the claimant's supposed liability in law, as in the previous case, but as to the underlying facts giving rise not just to the supposed legal, but also to the supposed moral obligation. This demonstrates that if § 814, 2nd alt ever applies at all, it is likely to apply to cases of mistake of law rather than mistake of fact.

14.2.2 English law

One obvious difference between English law and German law is that English law still insists on the presence of some consideration before a promise will be enforced as a contract. In the well known case of *Eastwood v Kenyon*[20] a guardian decided to improve his young ward's matrimonial prospects by renovating a house which belonged to her. He raised the necessary funds on a promissory note. The scheme bore fruit, and soon the ward was engaged to be married. The bridegroom, feeling morally obliged to do so, promised to pay the promissory note. Once the couple were married, however, he

---

17 von Staudinger/Lorenz, 1999, p 207.
18 RGZ 63, 38, (8.3.1906), 42.
19 RG JW 1910, 752, No 12 (6.6.1910).
20 (1840) 11 A & E 438.

changed his mind. When sued upon his promise it was held that, contrary to Lord Mansfield's view,[21] a moral obligation was not sufficient consideration to support a promise. Any consideration furnished by the guardian was past consideration, and as such no consideration at all. In order to make my point, I have to change the facts slightly: what if the defendant had already honoured his promise, in the mistaken belief that he was bound to do so? English law has never had to address this question, because the mistake of law bar has prevented it from arising. Now, following *Westdeutsche* and *Lincoln*, the husband, in a restitutionary claim against the guardian, would be able to rely on two compelling arguments in favour of recovery. First, he could say that, in paying, he had made a mistake of law. Unknown to him, his promise did not bind him. He should therefore recover. Secondly, he could argue, the contract which he thought compelled him to pay never came into being because the three requirements of contractual liability, offer, acceptance and consideration, were never present. There should thus be restitution based on 'absence of consideration'.

Restitution in such a case, however, is not desirable. The general policy of the law should be that people should honour their promises, the doctrine of consideration being merely a means to make sure that promises will not be enforced which were not given seriously, with intention to give rise to legal relations. English law will thus have to deal with this case in some way, following the recent developments in the law of unjust enrichment. Meier suggests that the only way to deal with this situation is a wholesale adoption of the *condictio indebiti*. She argues that the underlying promise, though not binding as a contract, would still be sufficient to give rise to a legal ground. In other words, payment in accordance with an unenforceable promise will have to be considered a 'just factor', a reason for retention. As Meier rightly recognises, this would constitute the final acceptance by English law that the German solution is superior.

The modified *Eastwood v Kenyon* raises another question, addressed in German law by § 814: the defendant was under a moral obligation to reimburse the claimant. The latter, although he had spent his money 'voluntarily', had spent it on improving his ward's property. English law would probably deny him a restitutionary claim against the ward based on some kind of 'moral compulsion' or necessity: *Nicholson v Chapman*,[22] *Falcke v Scottish Imperial Insurance*.[23] It is nevertheless easy to see why the ward's later husband would feel obliged to his wife's former guardian and reimburse him for his expenditure. Should he be able to reclaim that reimbursement on the basis that he paid for 'no consideration' or because he had believed[24] himself legally obliged to pay? Again, English law might have to make an exception to the general rule, might have to recognise yet another 'just factor'.

---

21 Expressed in *Lee v Muggeridge* (1813) 5 Taunt 36, 46, when he was still Sir James Mansfield CJ.

22 (1793) 2 H Bl 254.

23 (1886) 34 Ch D 234.

24 In German law, that belief might well have been right, because German law recognises claims based on *negotiorum gestio*: cf §§ 677 ff.

14.3 CONCLUSION

This chapter has outlined some of the areas in which an restitution based on nullity without more will lead to problems in English law. It was pointed out that German law is set up in such a way as to avoid those problems. If English law follows German law in its approach to the question when restitution will generally be available, it will also have to follow it in restricting the availability of restitution, given that wide principles have the drawback that one tends to get more than one bargained for.

We have highlighted two areas which will lead to particular problems. One concerns performances under contracts which are void for lack of form. A look to Germany demonstrates that restitution may not be desirable in such cases, and an examination of English law confirms that our own attitude to such contracts is the same. English law will therefore have to come up with a mechanism designed to deal with this problem.

The same applies to obligations which are referred to in civil law countries as 'natural obligations'. Performances under stale claims can also be conveniently dealt with under this heading. The problem is compounded in English law because our law still adheres to the doctrine of consideration. Can it really be said that performances under a contract void for lack of consideration can be recovered back? Again, English law will have to devise some mechanism to deal with these cases.

The chapter does not claim to be complete. Indeed, it is part of my argument that there may still be much beneath the surface of which we are as yet unaware, many problems which may suddenly spring up as a result of restitution suddenly being triggered by the mere nullity of a transaction. This is the reason why the next chapter is so important. If the English law of unjust enrichment is likely to become increasingly unstable as a result of the decisions in *Westdeutsche* and *Lincoln*, robust defences are needed now more than ever.

CHAPTER 15

THE DEFENCE OF CHANGE OF POSITION

15.1 THE ENGLISH DEFENCE OF CHANGE OF POSITION

15.1.1 The late recognition of change of position

It is generally acknowledged that the development of the English law of unjust enrichment was held back because of its refusal to recognise a defence of change of position. In the absence of any such defence, it was necessary to restrict the availability of restitution at the liability stage. Thus, as we have seen, English law until recently refused to allow restitution based solely upon the claimant's mistake of law. The liability mistake rule can be explained in the same way as can the requirement that a failure of consideration had to be total if it was to trigger restitution.

Where mistake of law is concerned, the link between the unavailability of the defence and the mistake of law bar is particularly clear. In *Brisbane v Dacres*[1] a naval captain paid part of freight he had earned on the carriage of bullion over to the Admiral in command. He thought that legally freight earned by naval ships had to be treated as prize money, but in this he took a mistaken view of the law. When he discovered this, he sought to recover the payment from the Admiral's widow and failed. Mansfield CJ, not to be confused with the great Lord Mansfield, argued:

> It would be most contrary to *aequum et bonum* if he were obliged to repay. For see how it is! If the sum be large, it probably alters the habits of his life, he increases his expenses, he has spent it over and over again; perhaps he cannot repay it at all, or not without great distress. Is he then, five years and eleven months after to be called on to repay it?[2]

Although restitution was denied because the captain's mistake had been a mistake of law rather than fact, Gibbs J, along with Mansfield CJ, rationalised the bar by reference to the likelihood that the money would have been spent.[3]

In the light of the various more or less arbitrary restrictions which were placed in the way of a successful restitutionary claim, it is understandable that English law refused to acknowledge that those instances in which restitution was actually available were based on a common principle, namely the principle against unjust enrichment, and this, in turn, explains the late discovery of our subject as a subject in its own right. It is thus not surprising that the case which recognised that the principle against unjust enrichment formed part of English law, *Lipkin Gorman v Karpnale*,[4] was also the first case in which the defence of change of position was consciously applied for the first time. The facts of the case are well known. Cass, a partner of a solicitor's' firm, a gambling addict, and a thief,

---

1 (1813) 5 Taunt 143, 128 ER 641.
2 *Brisbane v Dacres* (1813) 5 Taunt 143, 128 ER 641, 162.
3 '... he has spent it in the confidence that it was his and perhaps has no means of repayment.' *Ibid*, at 153.
4 [1991] 2 AC 548.

'borrowed' £323,222.14 from his firm's client account and used this money to finance his gambling at the defendant's club, the 'Playboy' club. He may have intended to return the money, but in the end he was only able to replace £100,313.16. The balance of £222,908.48 could not be recovered from Cass. In total, he staked £561,014.06 at the club, and won £378,294.06. The overall losses suffered by Cass over the period of his activities were calculated to be £174,745, £20,050 of which, it was agreed, represented his own funds. Assuming the club was liable to the solicitors in unjust enrichment, the question was whether they should be liable for £200,000 or £150,000. It was held that they were liable for the latter sum, and this conclusion was based on the defence of change of position.

The two Law Lords delivering detailed reasoned judgments, Lords Templeman and Goff, arrived at this result by different routes, which will be interesting when we come to compare the different approaches with the German position. Lord Templeman took the view that, to the extent that the club changed its position in reliance on the receipt from Cass, it ceased to be unjustly enriched. He said:

> If Cass had given £20,000 of the solicitors' money to a friend as a gift, the friend would have been enriched and unjustly enriched because a donee of stolen money cannot in good conscience rely on the bounty of the thief to deny restitution to the victim of the theft. Complications arise if the donee innocently expends the stolen money in reliance on the validity of the gift before the donee receives notice of the victim's claim for restitution. Thus if the donee spent £20,000 in the purchase of a motor car which he would not have purchased but for the gift, it seems to me that the donee has altered his position on the faith of the gift and has only been unjustly enriched to the extent of the second hand value of the motor car at the date when the victim of the theft seeks restitution. If the donee spends the £20,000 in a trip round the world, which he would not have undertaken without the gift, it seems to me that the donee has altered his position on the faith of the gift and that he is not unjustly enriched when the victim of the theft seeks restitution. In the present case Cass stole and the club received £229,908.48 of the solicitors' money. If the club was in the same position as a donee, the club nevertheless in good faith allowed Cass to gamble with the solicitors' money and paid his winnings from time to time so that when the solicitors' sought restitution, the club only retained £154,695 derived from the solicitors. The question is whether the club which was enriched by £154,695 at the date when the solicitors sought restitution was unjustly enriched.[5]

Thus Lord Templeman not so much recognises a change of position defence, but he changes the nature of the action for money had and received. The claim is no longer for the enrichment received, but for the enrichment surviving. The unjust enrichment action is thus directed at the enrichment which is still held by the defendant at the time the claim is made, always providing that the defendant acted in good faith.

Lord Goff's approach is more defence oriented, and it is his speech which, with great respect to Lord Templeman, has been the more influential of the two. The vital passage reads as follows:

> At present I do not wish to state the principle any less broadly than this: that the defence is available to a person whose position has so changed that it would be inequitable in all the circumstances to require him to make restitution, or alternatively to make restitution in full.[6]

---

5   *Lipkin Gorman v Karpnale* [1991] 2 AC 548, p 560.
6   *Ibid*, at 580.

As is typical of the common law, but, as we shall see, not just of the common law, Lord Goff was anxious that 'nothing should be said at this stage to inhibit the development of the defence on a case by case basis, in the usual way'.[7] The common law prefers to be pragmatic in these matters. For the time being, however, this leaves us with a number of important and difficult questions. Many of these questions are questions of detail, and their resolution will depend on the answer we give to the 'big question', namely how readily available the common law should make the defence of change of position.

Although Lord Goff in *Lipkin Gorman* said that the development of the defence would be left to future cases, he did give us some hints as to what he understood the defence to mean. Apart from those hints, the way in which their Lordships applied the defence to the facts of *Lipkin Gorman* itself does give us some clues as to how it should be interpreted.

Lord Goff made it clear that the principle which underlies the defence is that it should be available where it would, in the light of the change of position, be inequitable to require the defendant to make restitution. This, of course, does not get us very far. The inherent danger of wide principles, and the dislike the common law has of such principles, was the main reason why the defence was denied in previous cases.[8] Lord Goff was careful to point out that, just as the principle against unjust enrichment did not give the court *carte blanche* to order restitution whenever it is felt that the claimant has suffered an injustice, so the defence of change of position had to be founded on legal principle.[9] It is implicit in his judgment that the minimum requirement for the defence to be made out is that the relevant change of position must have been caused by the receipt of the benefit. Thus, the defence should not be available where the defendant would have incurred the expenditure he now relies on as a change of position in the ordinary course of things. His Lordship gave some further indications of the limitations of the defence:

> It is, of course, plain that the defence is not open to one who has changed his position in bad faith, as where the defendant has paid away the money with knowledge of the facts entitling the claimant to restitution; and it is commonly accepted that the defence should not be open to a wrongdoer. These are matters which can, in due course, be considered in depth in cases where they arise for consideration. They do not arise in the present case.[10]

One can only speculate as to what Lord Goff meant by this. Are all 'wrongdoers' to be disqualified from relying on the defence, even though they were wholly innocent? Some wrongs, such as conversion and trespass, do not require any fault on the part of the defendant. Did his Lordship have the innocent converter or trespasser in mind? If some fault is required to make the defendant a wrongdoer who cannot rely on the defence, what kind of fault? Is negligence sufficient? This question gives rise to a larger and more important question: what of the defendant who has parted with the enrichment in circumstances in which he should have been aware of 'the facts entitling the claimant to restitution'? In other words, what kind of knowledge is required: actual or constructive?

---

7   *Lipkin Gorman v Karpnale* [1991] 2 AC 548, 580.

8   Cf *Baylis v Bishop of London* [1913] 1 Ch 127, 140, *per* Hamilton LJ: '... we are not now free in the 20th century to administer that vague jurisprudence which is sometimes attractively styled "justice between man and man".'

9   *Lipkin Gorman v Karpnale* [1991] 2 AC 548, 578.

10 *Ibid*, at 580.

We can go even further: what of the defendant who *knew* 'the facts entitling the claimant to restitution', but who simply did not realise their significance, from stupidity, ignorance of the law or simply carelessness?

Lord Goff did not attempt to answer any of these questions, given that there was no need to decide them in *Lipkin Gorman* itself. He did go on, however, to refer to change of position as a defence 'which in fact is likely to be available only on comparatively rare occasions'.[11] On the other hand, it was plain to Lord Goff that the new defence, however rarely available, would 'enable a more generous approach to be taken to the recognition of the right to restitution, in the knowledge that the defence is, in appropriate cases, available'.[12]

A law of unjust enrichment which is put upon a proper footing of principle, and which has developed well-defined rules which determine the question what enrichments are to be considered 'unjust', can afford to leave the defendant's interest in the security of his receipt to a relatively narrowly defined change of position defence. When *Lipkin Gorman* was decided, the English law of unjust enrichment appeared to have reached a level of sophistication which allowed this step to be taken. Where a restitutionary claim is available 'as of right', and not merely on the basis of the exercise of judicial discretion, in the light of what is 'just and equitable', it is more difficult to justify a wide change of position defence. After all, the claimant has a valid claim against the defendant, and thus the question why the defendant's ill-considered or even foolish change of position should defeat that claim becomes increasingly difficult to answer.

15.1.2 Cases after *Lipkin Gorman*

There have been three important first instance decisions since Lipkin Gorman which may give us some indication of the likely development of the new defence. The first is *South Tyneside Metropolitan Borough Council v Svenska International plc*,[13] in which Clarke J held that the defence had no role to play where the defendant changed his position before he actually received the enrichment. In such cases, reasoned his Lordship, the defendant was not relying on the security of his receipt when he changed his position. Allowing change of position would, in such circumstances, amount to enforcing the (void) contract pursuant to which the payment was made.[14] The question whether change of position should be allowed as a defence in cases of 'anticipatory reliance' is one on which reasonable people can disagree. We will see below that German law, at least in cases in which the defendant changed his position for purposes connected to the underlying (now invalidated) transaction, has no problem with anticipatory reliance.[15] It is merely important at this stage to note that of two possible versions of the defence, Clarke J

---

11 *Lipkin Gorman v Karpnale* [1991] 2 AC 548, 580.

12 *Ibid*, at 581.

13 [1995] 1 All ER 545.

14 *South Tyneside Metropolitan Borough Council v Svenska International plc* [1995] 1 All ER 545, 568, *per* Clarke J.

15 See below, p 282. See also the detailed comparative analysis by Jewell, 2000, p 1, where he examines the position in German administrative law, with the same result.

favoured the *narrower*. The *Svenska* case thus gave an indication that the new defence would indeed, in Lord Goff's words, 'be available only on comparatively rare occasions'.[16]

In two more recent cases, the defence was actually applied.[17] The main importance of these cases, which is not of immediate concern to this paper, is that both defendants sought to rely on the defence of estoppel: they had been assured by the claimant that the money they had received was indeed theirs to spend as they pleased. Prior to the recognition of change of position, estoppel was a complete defence to a restitutionary claim, and the question was whether this state of affairs could continue in the light of the much more sensitive change of position defence now being available. In both cases, it was held that estoppel could no longer be relied upon. This may explain to some extent why in both cases the change of position defence was interpreted comparatively widely. In *Scottish Equitable v Derby* the defendant had received significant overpayments under an individual pension policy, amounting to just over £200,000. When the payments were made, he made inquiries whether he was indeed entitled to the money, and was categorically assured by the claimant pension company that he was. When the claimant realised the mistake, he argued that he had changed his position in the following ways: £150,600 had been reinvested into a new individual pension policy provided by a different pension company, £41,700 had gone towards reducing his mortgage, while the approximate balance of £9,600 had been used to improve his lifestyle in a moderate way. He further contended that he now found himself in a most difficult financial position because of an impending divorce from his wife. The court correctly held that his liability would only be reduced by £9,600, rejecting an invitation by the defendant's counsel to engage in a balancing exercise in order to consider 'what would be fair and equitable as between the parties, bearing in mind the consequences for both sides'.[18] In upholding the defence in respect of the £9,600, the court did not require the claimant to prove that he had indeed spent that money in reliance on the validity of the overpayment, since in any event the claimant was no longer pursuing the claim in respect of that sum.

In *Philip Collins v Davis*, on the other hand, the court did have to resolve evidential difficulties of this kind. The defendants had been part of a group of musicians accompanying the 'well known popular musician'[19] Phil Collins on a world tour in 1990. They were entitled to royalties in respect of sales of an album containing recordings of live performances made during the tour. These royalties were miscalculated because of a mistaken construction of the contract between the parties. This had resulted in overpayments over several years, which the claimant now sought to set off against future royalty entitlements. The defendants argued that they had spent the overpayments on general living expenses. The problem facing them was that, due to their 'unconventional' lifestyles, they were unable to establish that they would not have spent an equivalent amount of money in any event. Jonathan Parker J held that the defendants had merely an

---

16 *Lipkin Gorman v Karpnale* [1991] 2 AC 548, 580.
17 *Scottish Equitable plc v Derby* [2000] 3 All ER 793; *Philip Collins Ltd v Davis* [2000] 3 All ER 808.
18 *Ibid*, at 802.
19 *Philip Collins Ltd v Davis* [2000] 3 All ER 808, 810, *per* Jonathan Parker J.

evidential burden to make good the defence. In applying the defence itself, the court should then 'beware of applying too strict a standard'. His Lordship continued:

> Depending on the circumstances, it may well be unrealistic to expect a defendant to produce conclusive evidence of change of position, given that when he changed his position he can have had no expectation that he might thereafter have to prove that he did so, and the reason why he did so, in a court of law.[20]

Given that, the judge was satisfied that 'had the defendants been paid the correct sums by way of royalties their levels of expenditure would have been lower',[21] but unable to assess with any precision how much lower, he concluded, rather pragmatically, that the claim should be reduced by one-half. While the defendants might not have appreciated this, this ruling can only be described as generous towards the defendants, who were not required to come up to strict proof in establishing their change of position.

The current state of play can therefore be summed up as follows: the *dicta* in *Lipkin Gorman* are very wide indeed. So far, they have only been applied in first instance decisions, and we are consequently able to make out only faint of contours of the new defence. On the basis of *Svenska* it would appear that the defence is going to be interpreted more narrowly than it might be, and that it is probably not going to extend to anticipatory reliance. *Scottish Equitable v Derby* has once and for all made it clear that the defence cannot be relied on merely on the basis of the defendant's general hardship – there has to be a causal link between the original enrichment and the change of position, and this is certainly a very welcome clarification. The *Philip Collins* case suggests that the courts are unlikely to give defendants a particularly hard time to prove reliance where the evidential problems seem insurmountable. This case, therefore, suggests an interpretation of the defence which may be more generous towards defendants. Many questions of fundamental importance remain open, however, and there is accordingly everything left to play for: does the defence protect honest but foolish defendants, in other words, defendants who should have realised, but did not, that they were not entitled to the benefit received? Should knowledge of the claimant's entitlement to restitution be fatal to the defendant's chances of relying on the defence in all cases? What about defendants who use the benefit in a way which can only be described as extremely unreasonable? Take the example of a 'modern art sceptic' who is given a Picasso painting by mistake and decides to burn it. Should he be able to rely on the defence? It is difficult to predict the common law's reaction to such extreme scenarios.

As the courts have so far told us relatively little, academics naturally play a more important role than that to which they are normally accustomed in the common law world.

---

20 *Philip Collins Ltd v Davis* [2000] 3 All ER 808, p 827.
21 *Ibid*, at 830.

15.1.3 Academic views

The academic debate is best summed up by saying that most commentators favour a wide but principled defence. There is a general realisation that the recent liberalisation of the law of unjust enrichment makes it imperative that the defence should be fairly wide.

Birks originally favoured a comparatively narrow version of the defence – he was fearful of a 'woolly' defence doing more harm than good to the nascent law of unjust enrichment. He had particular problems with the situation in which the enrichment is lost in circumstances not amounting to reliance by the defendant on the security of his receipt.[22] There is indeed an unreported first instance decision, prior to *Lipkin Gorman*, which confirms this view.[23] It is interesting to note that, in German law, this is the central case of 'Wegfall der Bereicherung' under § 818 III.[24]

As the subject gained more and more acceptance he later revised this view, and is now in favour of a wide defence, protecting defendants who changed their position in the anticipation of an enrichment which was subsequently received as well as defendants who should have known that they were not entitled to the benefit received, but negligently or foolishly failed to realise this.[25] Birks is, however, unable to find a satisfying rationale for the defence.[26] To him, the defence is therefore merely 'the price which must be paid for a sensitive reconciliation of the demand for restitution and the interest in security of receipts'.[27] It might be going too far to say that he therefore regards the defence as a necessary evil, but he is certainly keenly aware of the fact that in a system which regards the enrichment creditor as *entitled* to restitution on the grounds of unjust enrichment, the defence is difficult to justify.

Goff and Jones likewise favour a wide version of the defence, criticising the *Svenska* decision as leading to 'arbitrary distinctions',[28] and arguing that 'the honest, if foolish defendant who, knowing all the facts, ought to have surmised that he should make restitution of the value of the benefit conferred, should be allowed, in an appropriate case, to invoke the defence of change of position. He has not acted with a want of probity'.[29]

Burrows is a little more ambivalent about these issues. First, he argues, well before *Svenska* was decided, that anticipatory reliance should not make the defence available, although he arrives at this conclusion 'tentatively'.[30] He further suggests that a defendant may well be denied the defence where he is clearly more at fault than the claimant in not realising that he was not entitled to the benefit.[31] He argues that this approach finds some

---

22 Birks, 1992b, pp 142 f.
23 *Streiner v Bank Leumi* (1985) unreported, 31 October, cited by Tettenborn, 1996, p 251.
24 See below, pp 281 f; the German law played a major role in changing Birks's mind on this point: see Birks, 1996a, p 61.
25 Birks, 1996a, p 49.
26 *Ibid*, p 54.
27 *Ibid*, p 51.
28 Goff and Jones, 1998, p 823.
29 *Ibid*, p 826.
30 Burrows, 1993a, p 424.
31 *Ibid*, p 430.

support in s 142(2) of the American *Restatement of Restitution*. Furthermore, he thinks that the manner in which the defendant changes his position may be relevant in extreme cases – criminal expenditure, for example, or intentional destruction of the benefit.[32] To some extent, Burrows's ambivalent attitude to the defence may be traced to the difficulties which are encountered in justifying the defence.

Tettenborn favours a still narrower defence. He argues that the defendant must establish three things before he can rely on the defence:

(1) that having got the benefit in question, he assumed he would be allowed to retain it;

(2) that he had no reason to know of the possibility of his being liable to restitutionary action; and

(3) action taken by him as a result is such that it would be unjust to make him refund.[33]

He thus clearly regards negligence on the part of the defendant where he had reason to doubt the security of his receipt as barring the defendant from the defence. Tettenborn also raises the possibility that a defendant 'who has himself caused the events leading to the restitution claim against him' will find it more difficult to rely on the defence.[34] He points to *dicta* in two first instance decisions, *Saronic v Liberia Huron*[35] and *R v Secretary of State for the Environment, ex p London Borough of Camden*,[36] to the effect that a misrepresentor cannot resist a restitutionary claim based on the very mistake which he himself induced on the basis of his change of position, given that the 'equities are very weak' in his favour.[37]

It is interesting, but not surprising, that academic writing about the new defence often has a comparatist flavour, and that German law takes pride of place. Thus, the standard work on the law of restitution, Goff and Jones,[38] devotes a whole page to the German position in a passage owing much to Zweigert and Kötz in the translation by Tony Weir. They point out how widely the change of position defence has been interpreted in Germany, and although they do refer to criticisms of the dominant view put forward by 'German jurists as distinguished as Rabel and Flume',[39] they come to the conclusion that a similarly wide interpretation of change of position should be adopted in England.[40] Birks, in a recent article on the defence, refers extensively to German law, concluding that 'at least in outline English law is in effect the same as German law as set out in § 818(3) of the *BGB*'.[41]

Virgo, in the latest textbook on restitution to be published, argues that on one test, which he calls the 'loss of benefit test of causation', 'the defence of change of position is open to the defendant if he or she no longer retains the actual benefit which had been received from the claimant', remarking in a footnote that '[t]his interpretation of the

---

32 *Ibid*, p 431.
33 Tettenborn, 1996, p 250.
34 *Ibid*, p 254.
35 [1979] 1 Lloyd's Rep 341, at 365.
36 (1995) unreported, 17 February.
37 Tettenborn, 1996, p 254.
38 Goff and Jones, 1998, pp 824 f.
39 *Ibid*, p 825.
40 *Ibid*.
41 Birks, 1996a, p 73.

defence is also recognised in German law'.[42] In a recent edition of our own journal – the *Restitution Law Review* – we find a whole article devoted to a comparative analysis of change of position in England and Germany by Michael Jewell.[43] He concentrates on two issues: pre-enrichment change of position and the role of fault. It is particularly interesting that he focuses on German administrative law rather than just private law. He reaches two conclusions: first, that English law should follow the example of German administrative law relating to overpaid salaries of civil servants and allow the defence where the expenditure in question is made before the enrichment is actually received; and, secondly, that matters of fault are not matters for the English law of unjust enrichment, even though German administrative law takes the defendant's fault into account and does not allow the grossly negligent defendant to rely on the defence.

15.2 THE GERMAN DISENRICHMENT DEFENCE IN § 818 III

In turning to the German law, I will concentrate in particular on the relationship between the unjust enrichment claim in § 812 I and the disenrichment defence. To this end, it will first be helpful briefly to examine the drafting history of these two provisions. It will then be necessary to look in some greater detail at the scope of the defence itself as it is currently understood. Having thus prepared the ground, I will then examine a number of critical approaches to the defence, but always bearing in mind the relationship between the defence and the restitutionary claim itself.

15.2.1 Drafting history

When it comes to looking at the drafting history of the German law of unjust enrichment, it is important to realise that the draftsmen had at best a very hazy idea of how the subject was to be structured internally. Although the modern typology of German enrichment law is on its face based on § 812 I *BGB*, it is quite unlikely that at the drafting stage anyone would have had that, or a similar typology, in mind (see above, pp 203 f).

Therefore, when they said that restitution was to follow whenever an enrichment lacked a 'legal ground', the drafters of the *BGB* knew quite well that a cause of action which is so widely drafted at the liability stage requires a strong and wide-ranging defence to keep the floodgates firmly shut. Thus the first drafting commission proposed that a *bona fide* defendant who is no longer enriched at the time he becomes aware of the claim against him should not be liable to the extent that he has been disenriched. It is interesting that the first commission did not go into great detail in defining the ambit of the defence: a hundred years before *Lipkin Gorman* they preferred to leave the working out of the details to 'legal scholarship and practice'.[44] On the other hand, the commission made it clear that it expected the provision to be interpreted widely: the recipient should be able to rely on any change of position caused by the receipt, as long as the causal link between receipt and change of position was 'adequate', that is, not too remote.[45]

---

42 Virgo, 1999, p 712.
43 Jewell, 2000.
44 Motive II, p 837.
45 *Ibid.*

When this draft came before the second drafting commission, a proposed amendment which would have severely curtailed the defence failed to find a majority. The reasoning behind the rejection of the amendment is interesting: the majority argued that the claimant was *prima facie* entitled to restitution because of equitable considerations. Given that the claim arose merely *ex aequo et bono*, the defendant should under no circumstances be prejudiced by the claim over and above the amount of his surviving enrichment.[46] Thus, the uncertain basis of the claim was understood to bear a direct relationship to its comparative weakness.

15.2.2 The scope of the disenrichment defence

As pointed out above, while the drafting commissions envisaged a wide defence, counterbalancing the wide general unjust enrichment clause in § 812 I, they were content to leave the concrete scope of the defence to be worked out by academics and practitioners. It is doubtful, however, whether it was subsequently appreciated that § 818 III was capable of a more restrictive interpretation, which might have seemed to be indicated when the enrichment claim itself was stabilised by Wilburg and von Caemmerer. The consequences were that, to the present day, the defence has been interpreted extremely widely.

From the outset, the *Reichsgericht* relied on § 818 III to define the very ambit of the enrichment claim in § 812 I. The court argued that the 'something' which has to be given back in § 812 I was not just any value which had found its way from the claimant to the defendant, but 'the benefit received taking into account what has been given up in return and all encumbrances resting upon it'.[47] This idea, that § 818 III does not just contain a defence, but lays down the measure of restitution, has been very influential in Germany, and it will be remembered that Lord Templeman's thoughts in *Lipkin Gorman* were very much along the same lines.[48] The *Reichsgericht* repeatedly confirmed that § 818 III contains the 'paramount principle of enrichment law', namely that the defendant must never be worse off as a result of making restitution than he was before he received the enrichment.[49]

The *Bundesgerichtshof* immediately adopted the *Reichsgericht*'s interpretation of the defence.[50] As long as there was a causal link between the enrichment and the disenrichment, the court generally held that the defence was available.[51] In giving examples of cases in which the defence has been successfully relied on, it is useful to distinguish between a number of categories:

---

46   Prot II, pp 706 f.
47   RGZ 54, 137, 141 (14.3.1903); 75, 361 (6.3.1911), 362.
48   See above, p 272.
49   RGZ 118, 185 (11.10.1927), 187.
50   BGHZ 1, 75 (19.1.1951), 81.
51   BGH NJW 1981, 277 (23.10.1980), 278.

Loss of the benefit itself

Where the received benefit itself is lost or destroyed, it follows from the wording of § 818 III that the recipient will have a defence. It does not matter whether the loss or destruction occurred accidentally, or was caused by the recipient's negligence. Thus, where the sum of money received is embezzled by the recipient's employee[52] or where it is seized by a foreign power in times of war as enemy property,[53] the defendant can rely on the defence. From an English perspective, it is particularly interesting that this category involves no reliance on the security of receipt on the part of the defendant. It nevertheless constitutes the least controversial, not to say the paradigm example of a relevant disenrichment. Most critics of the wide scope of the defence leave this category unscathed. In fact, it is argued that, since § 812 I itself is directed at the benefit received ('*das Erlangte*'), it is beyond doubt that the loss of that very benefit, without substitute, is to be regarded as a relevant disenrichment. On this interpretation of § 812 I, the application of the defence becomes more problematic when it comes to all those changes of position which do not involve the loss of the benefit received, but which occur in relation to the defendant's other assets.

This special treatment of the loss of the benefit itself goes so far as to allow the defence in the event of the recipient's insolvency.[54] Given that the defendant has lost all his assets, it is regarded as obvious that he will also have lost the very benefit he received. This has been criticised because the enrichment could well have meant a reduction of the estate's overall liabilities.[55] The insolvent's creditors gain a windfall at the expense of the claimant which is not easily justified. This again shows the very wide approach of the courts in interpreting § 818 III.

Uneconomic use of the benefit

Where the defendant uses money received for unsuccessful speculations in the market, or where he has gambled the money away, he will be able to shift his losses to the claimant.[56] Where he sells the received object at an undervalue, the loss will fall on the claimant, not on him.[57] Where he has sold it to an insolvent third party, he will likewise be able to rely on the defence: although the benefit has been replaced by a claim against the third party, that claim is worthless and he is therefore disenriched.[58] Where he has used money received to pay off his own existing debts, however, he is clearly still enriched to the extent that his liabilities have been reduced.[59] It is not quite clear how this can be reconciled with the case in which the defendant has become insolvent, which has been held to constitute a disenrichment 'by exhaustion' as discussed in the previous paragraph.

---

52 RGZ 68, 269 (13.4.1908).
53 RGZ 120, 297 (10.3.1928), 299.
54 BGH 1957, 598 (28.6.1956), 599; BGH NJW 1958, 1725 (19.3.1958).
55 von Staudinger/Lorenz, § 818, No 34.
56 OLG Hamm NJW-RR 1991, 155 (6.11.1989).
57 RGZ 75, 361 (6.3.1911); RG JW 1931 (3.11.1930).
58 BGHZ 72, 9 (29.5.1978), 13.
59 BGH NJW 1985, 2700 (18.4.1985).

Expenditure incurred in connection with the benefit

The most obvious case under this head is where the recipient spends money on the received object. In this case, whether or not the expenditure is objectively useful in raising the value of the object, he can insist on being reimbursed before he has to return the object itself. Thus, in a case decided by the *Bundesgerichtshof* in 1980, the claimant had rescinded the gift of a plot of land. The defendant had already started building works on the land and relied on § 818 III when the claimant sued him for re-transfer of the land. The court held that the defendant was only obliged to re-transfer the land in return for any expenditure he had incurred in building on it.[60]

Cases in which the expenditure is incurred in the acquisition of the benefit also fall into this category. Examples include money spent on freight, duties, estate agent's fees[61] and notary attestation of the underlying contract.[62] These cases typically involve expenses which are incurred before receipt of the enrichment. The point that the law is here protecting not the recipient's security of receipt but his expectation of that receipt is generally not taken. The only commentator who refers to it is Heimann-Trosien,[63] who notes that the wording of § 818 III seems to be restricted to disenrichments occurring after the enrichment. He argues, however, that this is irrelevant, and that the provision must be interpreted widely. It is interesting that Heimann-Trosien is a retired judge of the *Bundesgerichtshof*, writing in a commentary of the *BGB* which is compiled by former and present members of that court. His extremely wide approach to § 818 III sets him apart from most academic writers, but may be some indication of the judicial attitude towards the provision.

Other expenditure causally connected to the enrichment

This, as the previous head, relates not to the received object itself, but to dispositions of the recipient's other assets made in reliance on the enrichment received from the claimant. There is a great variety of cases which fall into this category. They include the paradigm case of the defendant who, when he is given a valuable painting, takes a luxury holiday even before he has managed to sell the painting, or the defendant who inherits a large amount of money and decides to make a substantial donation to charity of money in a different bank account.

As mentioned above, the courts seek to distinguish between relevant and irrelevant dispositions according to a broad causation test: would the disposition have been made but for the enrichment? The more modern academic literature regards this as too broad. It is argued that the defendant must show not just a causal link between enrichment and disenrichment, but also an element of reliance on his security of receipt. A well worn example is usually relied upon to illustrate the point: a dog is transferred 'without legal ground'.[64] The defendant feeds it and looks after it. The ungrateful animal, however,

---

60 BGH NJW 1980, 1789 (11.1.1980).
61 BGH NJW 1970, 2059 (30.9.1970); 1993, 648 (15.10.1992), 652.
62 RGZ 72, 1 (11.6.1909).
63 RGRK/Heimann-Trosien, § 812, No 57; § 818, Nos 22, 24.
64 Characteristically, the writers who use this example (and they almost all do) never explain the circumstances more fully, simply referring to the *'indebite geleisteter Hund'*. We are therefore left in the dark as to why the dog has to be returned to its original owner.

repays him by tearing up his valuable Persian rug. To what extent can the defendant rely on § 818 III? The test commonly applied by the courts, asking for a causal link between the enrichment and the loss, would yield the result that the defendant can refuse to return the dog unless he is paid the cost of dog food and, more importantly, the cost of the damaged rug.[65] Most commentators, however, would argue that the damage to the rug was not incurred in reliance on the belief that the defendant could keep the animal, and for that reason should not be relevant where the disenrichment defence in § 818 III is concerned. If the defendant decides to keep a dog, he has to accept the consequences.[66] Heimann-Trosien argues that to insist on reliance in the application of the defence is not warranted by the wording of § 818 III and misses the point of the provision. He argues that if damage caused by the dog is not to be deducted, the defendant 'would suffer a reduction of his assets as a result of the enrichment which would put him in a position worse than the position he was in before; but this is precisely what the idea expressed in § 818 III is designed to prevent'.[67] It should be remembered that the *Reichs-ge-richts-rä-te-kom-men-tar*, in which Heimann-Trosien is writing, is compiled by current and former members of the *Bundesgerichtshof* and can therefore be taken to reflect judicial *practice* more accurately than the other standard commentaries of the *BGB*.

As mentioned above,[68] Heimann-Trosien is the only commentator who argues that the wording of § 818 III is in fact too *narrow*, in that it seems to exclude disenrichments which are incurred before the relevant enrichment is actually received. The cases in which prior disenrichments were held to be deductible all concerned expenditure incurred to facilitate the acquisition of the enrichment, such as estate agent's fees, freight etc. The only cases in which defendants who spent their own money in reliance on the expectation of an enrichment were able to rely on the defence, are cases involving civil servants who had been overpaid over a period of time.[69] Originally, the *Reichsgericht* applied § 818 III to such cases, but later held that such cases were covered by administrative law. Where administrative law does not recognise a defence equivalent to § 818 III, however, the Reichsgericht held that the defence constituted a general principle of law which was applicable both in a private and a public law context.[70] As Jewell has pointed out,[71] the German administrative courts have had no problems in making the defence available to civil servants who changed their position in anticipation of an overpayment from their employers.[72]

---

65 This result is still supported by Heimann-Trosien (RGRK/Heimann-Trosien, § 818, No 26.)
66 von Staudinger/Lorenz, § 818 No 40; Larenz and Canaris, 1994, p 300.
67 RGRK/Heimann and Trosien, § 818, No 26.
68 See above, p 282.
69 See Jewell, 2000, p 1.
70 RGZ 107, 189 (12.6.1923).
71 Jewell, 2000, pp 12 ff.
72 *Oberverwaltungsgericht* Hamburg NVwZ 1988, 73 (17.3.1987), cited by Jewell, 2000, p 12, n 67. It should be pointed out, however, that in the public law field the defence is lost where the recipient has been negligent in failing to spot the fact that he has been overpaid. The wide interpretation of the defence adopted by administrative courts should therefore be treated with caution.

The generosity of the courts towards overpaid employees is not limited to anticipatory reliance. Generally, it is made very easy for defendants to establish the defence. For example, the courts simply assume that where an employee receives an increased salary he will raise his standard of living accordingly, rather than use the money to save or pay off existing debts.[73] In a case decided in 1959,[74] the *Bun-des-ge-richts-hof* allowed the defence where the defendant had used the money to buy new furniture which could only be realised for a fraction of its cost. The maxim that the defendant must not suffer any patrimonial harm as a result of the enrichment claim is thus generally taken very seriously.

This overview of circumstances in which the defence has been held to be available was not intended to be exhaustive. It should simply give an impression of the very wide approach to the defence which has been adopted by courts and commentators alike. Two more issues need to be addressed before we can turn to the critics of this wide approach: the problem of transfers both ways, and the question in what circumstances the defence will be lost.

Transfers both ways and § 818 III – the 'Saldotheorie'

In Chapter 6, we already referred to the so-called '*Saldotheorie*'.[75] It will be remembered that this seeks to take account of the fact that mutual payments under a bilateral contract are linked to each other by restricting the restitutionary claim to the balance between them. While the underlying concern of the *Saldotheorie* cannot be dismissed, this approach has two main problems, one peculiar to German law, the other of more general relevance. The first problem lies in the contrary solution having been adopted in § 350 *BGB*, which applies where contracts have been terminated pursuant to §§ 325, 326 or indeed § 467 (*Wandelung*, the equivalent of rejection of goods of unsatisfactory quality). Where a buyer terminates the contract of sale because the goods are of unsatisfactory quality, § 350 provides that the risk of accidental loss or destruction of the goods will be borne by the seller. Under the *Saldotheorie*, on the other hand, the risk will remain with the buyer, who would not be able to demand restitution of the price if he himself were unable to return the goods. The problem is a peculiarly German one because it is doubtful whether the policy pursued by § 350 itself can be supported.

The problem of more general relevance is that the *Saldotheorie* only applies where performances have actually been exchanged. Thus, where the buyer has not yet paid the price, the risk of loss or destruction of the goods, whether by negligence or otherwise, will be borne by the seller. Different results according to whether the buyer has already paid or not are difficult to justify.

A number of attempts have been made to solve the above problems, but this is not the place to discuss them. Suffice it to say that, where exchanged performances are

---

73 It will be remembered that Jonathan Parker J in the *Philip Collins* case adopted a similar approach, but limited the extent to which the defendants could rely on the defence to one-half of their disenrichment: see above, p 274.

74 BGH MDR 1959, 109 (20.10.1958).

75 See above, pp 101 ff.

concerned, there is general agreement that the change of position defence needs to be modified or disregarded completely.

Circumstances in which the defence is lost

§ 818 IV provides that where process has been served on the defendant, his liability is determined by the 'general rules'. He will either be treated as any other debtor,[76] or, if the enrichment consists of an object rather than money, as involuntary bailee of that object.[77] In other words, the protection of § 818 III will be lost completely.

§ 819 provides that the defendant is to be regarded as having had process served upon him in two sets of circumstances: first, if he knew that the benefit was conferred upon him 'without legal ground', or if he later finds out that this was the case; and second, if he acted illegally or in a manner *contra bonos mores* in accepting the benefit. The first of these has been interpreted narrowly so as to allow a defendant to rely on the defence even in circumstances in which any reasonable person would have realised that he was not entitled to keep the enrichment. In other words, if he is to lose the defence, the recipient must actually be aware not only of the relevant facts, but also of their legal consequences. Mere negligence or even recklessness does not suffice.[78]

Conclusion

In general, the disenrichment defence in § 818 III has been interpreted in accordance with the intentions of the drafters of the *BGB*, who envisaged a wide defence to counterbalance the equally wide general unjust enrichment clause in § 812 I. The defence has generally been held to be available where a loss suffered by the defendant can be said to be causally connected to his enrichment. The 'first principle of enrichment law', namely that the recipient must under no circumstances end up worse off than before the enrichment, permeates both the jurisprudence of the courts and academic writings. The principle is further given full effect by interpreting § 819 I narrowly, so as to make the defence available even to a defendant who has been grossly negligent in failing to appreciate the fact that he was not entitled to keep the enrichment.

It is unsurprising that a disenrichment defence as wide as this has not enjoyed universal support. Particularly after § 812 I was re-interpreted by Wilburg and von Caemmerer it was no longer obvious that such an extremely wide defence was needed. Thus it would be misleading to take the German approach as it presents itself in the jurisprudence of the *Bundesgerichtshof* and the majority of academic writings as a model for the English defence of change of position without putting it in its context and without being aware of critical voices which have recently become more and more frequent in the German debate.

---

76 Where the enrichment consists of a distinct sum of money, he will be treated as an involuntary bailee of the money, which means he will only be liable for loss of the money if he is 'at fault': BGHZ 83, 293 (25.3.1982). This would seem to cover Birks's 'busy businesswoman'.

77 von Staudinger and Lorenz, § 818, No 50.

78 Cf RG WarnR 1927, No 91 (27.4.1927): 'Mere knowledge of the facts leading to invalidity' of a contract of sale was held not to be enough. See also RGZ 93, 227 (2.7.1918), 230.

15.2.3 Academic criticism

Andreas von Tuhr

The emphasis on protecting the recipient at all costs provoked academic criticism very soon after the *BGB* had become law. As early as 1907, Andreas von Tuhr thought that a wide and undifferentiated disenrichment defence was inappropriate.[79] He argued that such a wide defence might be suitable for cases of mistaken transfers, but not necessarily for other cases. He pointed out that there was an important parallel between the solutions adopted by the *BGB* in respect of mistake in contract law (§ 119 ff *BGB*) and the measure of recovery in the law of unjust enrichment. When a person avoids a contract for mistake, § 122 *BGB* provides that he must make good the other contracting party's reliance loss. Von Tuhr argues § 818 III leads to the same result where a person mistakenly confers a benefit on another, and is now seeking restitution of that benefit: any losses which the other party has incurred in reliance on the receipt are to be borne by the party demanding restitution. If this result is correct in the context of mistake in contract law, it must likewise be correct where a transfer is made in the mistaken belief in the existence of an obligation. Von Tuhr argues that it was cases of this kind which the drafters of the *BGB* mainly had in mind in drafting § 818 III. He points out, however, that mistaken transfers are not the only way in which an unjust enrichment can arise. He mainly relies on § 816 as an example. This provides that where the possessor of property belonging to another passes title to that property to a third party, he is liable to make restitution of what he obtained in return to the original owner. This is a special case of an 'enrichment in another way' mentioned in § 812 I. Take the following example: the buyer of a house finds that the seller has left a number of items of furniture behind. He mistakenly believes that these have become his property along with the house. He sells them at a car boot sale. According to the German rules on *bona fide* purchase, he passes good title to the buyers. To celebrate this windfall, he takes his family out for a meal on the proceeds. Von Tuhr asks: is it really appropriate to allow him to resist the original owner's claim under § 816 with the argument that he is no longer enriched, given that he would not have taken his family out for a meal had he not been so successful in selling the furniture? Von Tuhr argues that the loss which the defendant has suffered is a loss which can be suffered by anyone who overestimates his means,[80] and that there is no reason whatsoever to allow him to rely on § 818 III.

Von Tuhr's work is remarkable because he argues for different measures of restitution according to the way in which the enrichment came about. Von Tuhr's approach was endorsed by Ernst Rabel (possibly the greatest comparative lawyer ever),[81] but was otherwise almost completely ignored.

Walter Wilburg

It was almost 30 years before his argument was taken up and refined by Walter Wilburg,[82] an Austrian writing in 1934. Wilburg was dissatisfied with the way in which

---

79   von Tuhr, 1907.
80   *Ibid*, p 317.
81   Rabel, ZSchwR NF 27 (1908) 291 ff, 320.
82   Wilburg, 1934.

§ 812 I had been interpreted, namely as a general cause of action in unjust enrichment. He argued that restitution could not be based simply on the absence of an underlying obligation in all cases, but that it was necessary to differentiate between cases in which a benefit had been conferred under a supposed obligation, and cases in which the benefit had been obtained 'in another way'. Without drawing this distinction, the wording of § 812 I was simply far too wide. It was thus wrong to regard it as a general cause of action in unjust enrichment, in fact it contained a number of separate causes of action with wholly separate requirements. His typology was thus based on the ways in which enrichments can come about.

Wilburg's arguments led to a reappraisal of liability in unjust enrichment in German law, and his typology, with some refinements added by Ernst von Caemmerer in 1954,[83] is now generally accepted both by academic writers and the courts. In the light of the importance of Wilburg's work on the liability stage, it is somewhat surprising that his work on the disenrichment defence, contained in the same monograph, was all but ignored. Wilburg argues that if the liability stage is refined in accordance with his suggested typology, this cannot be without consequences for the defence stage. If the different enrichment claims have different requirements and different functions, it would be odd if they shared one wholly undifferentiated defence.

To Wilburg, the wide and all embracing disenrichment defence in § 818 III reflects a mechanistic view of enrichment law ignoring the 'reason for and purpose of the claim'.[84] He argues that the argument that a wide interpretation of the disenrichment defence should be adopted in order to do equity between the parties was inconclusive and dangerous. The different enrichment claims are not simply founded on considerations of equity, whatever the second drafting commission might have thought. Just like any other claim, an enrichment claim is based on the rules of positive law.

Just because an enrichment claim does not require fault on the part of the recipient is not to say that the parties' conduct should be irrelevant when it comes to deciding the extent of their liability. The erasure of the enrichment should, argues Wilburg, be regarded as a loss which has to be allocated to one or the other of the parties. It would not be in accordance with the function and purpose of the different enrichment claims if that loss were to be borne by the enrichment creditor in each and every case.

To Wilburg, the conduct of the parties must be used as the main criterion of loss allocation. A party will, according to Wilburg, have to bear the loss if he is responsible for the facts leading to the enrichment. In most cases of the *Eingriffskondiktion* this will be the defendant, while in most cases of the *Leistungskondiktion* it will be the claimant. To this extent, Wilburg agrees with von Tuhr. However, according to Wilburg it would not be correct to generalise. To him, it is important to determine which party has 'induced' the enrichment. He argues that it is not possible to lay down rules of general applicability according to which it can be determined in advance who is to bear the loss in any given case. It is clear that where a party brings about the enrichment in circumstances amounting to actual fault, he will have to accept any resulting loss whether by allowing

---

83   von Caemmerer, 1954, p 333.
84   Wilburg, 1934, p 143.

the other party the disenrichment defence or by being denied to rely on it himself. Yet Wilburg even argues that *'verkehrswidriges Verhalten'*, which one might attempt to translate as 'unconventional conduct', not itself amounting to fault, should suffice to deprive a defendant on the defence. Thus, where the defendant induced the claimant's mistake which caused the latter to make the transfer, for example by approaching him with an unfounded claim, Wilburg would not allow the defendant to rely on his subsequent disenrichment as reducing his liability.[85] Similarly, where the claimant allows his sheep to stray so that some of them get mixed up with the defendant's herd, any disenrichment on the part of the defendant should continue to be relevant, for example if the defendant sold his entire herd at a fixed price which takes no account of the precise number of animals in the herd. Even though the claimant's claim is based on the *Eingriffskondiktion*, he must allow the defendant to reduce his liability on the basis of § 818 III.

Nevertheless, von Tuhr and Wilburg agree in one fundamental respect: the disenrichment defence as it is generally interpreted is simply too wide. Wilburg prepares the ground for a more restrictive interpretation of the defence by proposing a coherent taxonomy which will enable the law to decide in what circumstances an enrichment is to be considered unjust. By eliminating the uncertainty which characterised the enrichment claim in the first few decades of the *BGB*, Wilburg has no more need for a sweeping disenrichment defence which was meant to counteract it.

On the other hand, Wilburg's approach of typifying enrichment claims according to the manner in which the enrichment came about is not itself suitable to be carried through to the defence stage, as Wilburg himself points out. This is because the way in which the enrichment came about does not in itself tell us anything about the reasons for restitution. These are to be found in the general law, and are just as much obscured by the Wilburg typology as they are by the abstract formula in § 812 I.

Werner Flume

Flume, writing in 1953, agrees with Wilburg that § 818 III is a questionable provision, and that German law is generally too generous towards disenriched defendants.[86] In particular, he agrees that it is inappropriate to apply the same disenrichment defence to all cases of unjust enrichment, even though the different causes of action in unjust enrichment are themselves totally different. Flume does not, however, regard Wilburg's approach to limiting § 818 III as feasible, both because it simply contradicts the provision as laid down in the code, and for more fundamental reasons of principle. While he accepts that fault might have a role to play in deciding whether or not the defendant should be able to shift his disenrichment onto the claimant, he argues that short of fault, the parties' *'verkehrswidriges Verhalten'* should not determine the availability of the disenrichment defence.

Flume argues that, since the application of the 'but for' test would make the defence available whenever a disenrichment would not have happened but for the enrichment received from the claimant, a narrower approach to causation is required. Many

---

85   Wilburg, 1934, p 149.
86   Flume, 1953, pp 103, p 148.

disenrichments are based on economic decisions[87] taken by the defendant. According to Flume, the disenrichment defence should be not be available where the disenrichment is based on an economic decision which is made irrespective of the legal ground of the enrichment, in other words, an economic decision which is not made in reliance on the recipient's security of receipt. In the popular example of the dog which chews up the defendant's rug, for instance, Flume bases the result that the defendant has to return the dog notwithstanding the damage to his rug on the fact that the decision to keep a dog was an 'economic decision' on the part of the defendant which was wholly unrelated to the question whether or not the contract of sale in respect of this particular animal was valid. 'If he wishes to protect himself against losses of this kind, he should not keep dogs.'[88] Where, on the other hand, the defendant incurs expenditure which he would not have incurred had he known that he would have to make restitution, such expenditure constitutes a relevant disenrichment.[89]

The advantages of Flume's analysis become clear where the recipient has, albeit pursuant to a contract which subsequently turns out to be void, paid for the benefit. It is in this area of exchanged performances that there is almost unanimity in Germany that § 818 III needs to be limited, and we have seen how the *Reichsgericht* sought to deal with this problem by developing the so-called *Saldotheorie*.[90] One of the major problems of that approach, as we have seen, is that it only leads to satisfactory results where both parties have actually performed. It breaks down in circumstances in which only one party has performed when it becomes clear that the underlying transaction is void. If the recipient has changed his position in such circumstances, the *Saldotheorie* does not assist the other party: as he has lost his entitlement to receive his expected counter-performance, he will bear the loss occasioned by the recipient's disenrichment. Flume's approach based on the recipient's economic decision helps in these cases. Flume argues that where a benefit is obtained in return for a counter-performance, or indeed in the expectation of having to render a counter-performance, any disenrichments suffered by the recipient must be borne by him up to the value of that counter-performance. After all, it was the value of that counter-performance which he staked in receiving and dealing with the relevant benefit.

Thus, while Flume's approach does not produce dramatically different results where a benefit has been obtained gratuitously, it does offer an elegant and convincing alternative to the *Saldotheorie* as applied by the German courts.

Axel Flessner

Flessner, writing in 1970,[91] starts from the premiss that the defendant's disenrichment constitutes a loss which needs to be allocated to one or the other of the parties. He argues, however, that it is impossible to lay down *ex ante* rules which determine which of the parties is to bear this loss in any particular case.[92] He nevertheless lays down a number of

---

87 A rather inaccurate translation of Flume's term *'vermögensmäßige Entscheidung'*, meaning a 'decision in relation to one's assets'.
88 Flume, 1953, p 155.
89 *Ibid*, p 156.
90 Cf above, pp 101 ff, 282.
91 Flessner, 1970.
92 *Ibid*, p 114.

criteria, drawn from the law of contractual and delictual damages. Thus, the loss may be allocated according to who caused and was responsible (a) for the enrichment accruing to the defendant, (b) for the lack of legal cause and (c) for the disenriching event. The judge is to compare the parties' relative causative contributions and their *relative* blameworthiness, and this, according to Flessner, is only possible with hindsight.

The loss may also be allocated according to whose 'sphere' it occurred in. Flessner is critical of cases in which § 818 III was available to defendants whose own employees had embezzled the funds which were now subject to an enrichment claim[93] – he would prefer to hold the recipient liable for the loss in such circumstances, given that he should bear the risk of his employees' dishonesty. Likewise, where the recipient deliberately or negligently damages or loses the received benefit, a loss allocation according to 'spheres' of risk would suggest that he should bear this loss himself.

Particularly interesting from the point of view of the present argument is Flessner's suggestion to link the availability of the disenrichment defence to the purpose of the rule of law which has given rise to the enrichment claim in the first place. This, as Flessner stresses, is not to be found in § 812 I. The decision whether or not to reverse an enrichment is taken elsewhere, in the general law.[94] Flessner gives a number of examples: if a contract turns out to be void because one of the parties is a minor, it is well settled that the minor will be able to rely on § 818 III if he has changed his position, while he will be able to demand his own performance back. To that extent, the *Saldotheorie* is disapplied. The policy declaring contracts entered into by minors void also demands that minors should not be exposed to losses when an executed contract is unwound. Flessner argues that the same argument should prevent the party of full capacity to rely on § 818 III so as to deny the minor restitution.[95] Similarly, where an expectant heir sells his inheritance without observing the relevant formality requirements,[96] this is to protect him against rushed and ill-considered decisions. If the buyer, having taken possession of the estate and lost part of it, were to be able to rely on § 818 III in resisting the original heir's restitutionary claim, the policy of the formality requirement would be defeated, as the seller would, to the extent that parts of the estate have been lost, be bound by the sale.[97]

Flessner's work is characterised by his dissatisfaction with the present approach to § 818 III, and by his agonised search for a more appropriate solution. In the end, he fails to come up with a workable, systematic approach, but nevertheless many of his ideas are of great interest, particularly his argument that more regard should be had to the actual reason for restitution when making the decision whether a defendant can rely on his disenrichment.

---

93   RGZ 65, 292 (14.3.1907); 79, 285 (26.4.1912); Flessner, 1970, p 123.
94   Flessner, 1970, p 136, referring to von Caemmerer, 1954, p 343.
95   *Ibid*.
96   § 2371 *BGB*.
97   Flessner, 1970, p 137.

Bernhard Rengier

Rengier, writing in 1977,[98] agrees with Flessner that § 818 III needs to be narrowed down. He argues, however, that Flessner's proposals would lead to unacceptable legal uncertainty, given that he fails to develop any workable system according to which the availability of the disenrichment defence can be determined in advance.[99] He proposes to confine the applicability of § 818 III to cases in which the actual benefit received by the defendant is lost, damaged or destroyed, excluding all those cases in which the defendant, in reliance on his enrichment, disposes of assets not directly related to that benefit. Reliance losses of this kind can only be set off or recovered, says Rengier, where the general law provides a remedy. Given the radical nature of this particular proposal, it is unsurprising that its impact has been minimal. For purposes of the present argument it is relevant in that it shows that the basic tenet of German enrichment law, that the defendant must not suffer more than the loss of the actual enrichment, is far from generally accepted, and that some are prepared to turn it right on its head. Rengier's main justification for his radical re-interpretation of § 818 III is once again the changed perception of German enrichment law: if the restitutionary remedy is not based on judicial discretion, but rather on 'hard nosed' rules of law, it is not obvious why those rules of law should not lead to the disenrichment of the defendant who has, after all, received a benefit which should not have accrued to him at all.

15.2.4 The current state of play

The boundaries of the defence

As stated above, the *Reichsgericht* regarded it as 'the highest principle of enrichment law that the defendant's liability to make restitution must not lead to a diminution of his estate which is greater than his true enrichment', and that only such disenrichments are to be taken into account which are causally connected to the receipt. Directly after the war, the *Bundesgerichtshof* made it clear that it was not going to depart from the jurisprudence of the *Reichsgericht* where the disenrichment defence was concerned.[100] Thereafter, the court took every opportunity to reaffirm this view.[101]

However, on occasions the courts have more or less openly refused to apply the disenrichment defence. One obvious example is the *Saldotheorie*, which disapplies the disenrichment defence in cases in which performances have been exchanged by the parties.[102]

Where the courts refuse a defendant the protection of § 818 III, this can sometimes be interpreted as a response to the kind of criticism just discussed. Thus, in 1942 the *Reichsgericht* had to decide the following case:[103] two brothers jointly owned the family farm. They both had existing debts, amounting to RM 15,000 for brother A, and RM

---

98 Rengier, 1977, p 418.
99 *Ibid*, p 428.
100 BGHZ 1, 75, 81 (19.1.1951).
101 See, eg, BGHZ 14, 7 (3.6.1954), 9 f; 26, 185 (16.12.1957); BGHZ 1957, 598 (28.6.1956).
102 See above, pp 101 ff.
103 RGZ 170, 65 (30.10.1942).

184,000 for brother B. To avoid breaking up the farm, they agreed that both these debts should be secured on the land and that they were to be jointly liable for their combined debts so secured. In consideration of this, brother B agreed to enter into an inheritance contract with brother A, under which he was to leave his share of the estate to brother A.[104] Everything went well for three years. Repayments of the now joint debt were made from the profits earned by the farm. In 1936, however, brother B decided to get married, which had a profound effect on the subsisting arrangement between the brothers, as by German family law a widow is entitled to inherit a certain proportion of her deceased husband's estate. This rendered the inheritance contract between the parties voidable under §§ 2079 and 2081 *BGB*, and brother B duly avoided it. Brother A went to law, arguing *inter alia* that the rescission of the inheritance contract also rendered the main agreement between A and B void, and that therefore, for some three years, he had been discharging part of the liabilities of B 'without legal ground'. He asked for restitution of RM 23,454,39. This claim was successful at first instance. Appealing against that decision, B did not dispute that A was entitled to be repaid, but argued that the total sum should be reduced by at least RM 8,000. Given that half his debts had been discharged from A's half of the earnings of the farm, his own earnings had been greater than they otherwise would have been, and in consequence he had incurred a greater tax liability than he otherwise would have done. There was no way in which that tax could now be reclaimed, and therefore B argued that he was no longer enriched to the extent of the overpaid tax. The *Reichsgericht* did not accept the argument, although it was in no doubt that the increased tax liability could constitute a relevant disenrichment:

> In calculating the enrichment which has to be given up, it is necessary to compare the defendant's wealth after receipt of the benefit with the hypothetical wealth which the defendant would have had if the benefit had never been received; every diminution of his wealth which is causally connected to the receipt of the benefit must be taken into account. ... An increased tax liability, caused by the receipt of the enrichment, cannot as such be disregarded, provided the enriched party is unable to obtain restitution of overpaid tax from the revenue.[105]

The court pointed out, however, 'rescission of the inheritance contract was a step which was motivated solely by the defendant's self-interest and the interests of his newly-founded family'.[106] For this reason, it would be unjust, said the court, if A, who had to accept B's rescission of the contract, were to suffer a loss as a result. The court based this conclusion on three arguments, the first indifferent, the second exceedingly interesting, the third disgraceful:

(1) The principle of good faith in § 242 required that B should not be able to cause loss to his brother by his self-motivated, unilateral act. Anything can be justified by reference to § 242, and on its own this argument would not be particularly convincing.

---

104 In German law, such a contract is binding if it complies with the formality requirements laid down in §§ 2274 ff.

105 RGZ 170, at 67.

106 *Ibid*, at 68.

(2) The analogy with § 122 (reliance losses arising from rescission for mistake) suggested that where a contract was avoided for reasons which were wholly one-sided, the avoiding party had to compensate the other up to his reliance interest. It will be remembered that von Tuhr had first drawn attention to this analogy.[107] Where a party is entitled to rely on a contract and does so rely, he should not suffer a loss when the contract becomes invalidated for a reason which the other party is solely responsible for.[108] This rule, which can be derived from § 122, is not confined to rescission for mistake but of general validity.

(3) Hitler had decreed that where the *lex scripta* led to results which did not accord with Nazi ideology, it could simply be set aside. The court, and this undermines the authority of the decision considerably, based the non-availability of § 818 III on this decree.

If confined to the second line of reasoning, this decision makes quite a lot of sense, and is obviously heavily relied upon by critics of the wide interpretation of § 818 III such as Flume[109] and Flessner.[110] It may well be due to the disgraceful third basis of the decision that it was largely ignored by the *Bundesgerichtshof*. Thus Heimann-Trosien, as a former member of that court, argues that the decision cannot be relied upon 'because it is based on irrational considerations stemming from then prevailing political conditions'.[111]

If the above case is an example of the court taking into account the circumstances under which the restitutionary claim arose, there are circumstances in which the courts refuse the defendant the protection of § 818 III in order to uphold the policy underlying the restitutionary claim. In a case decided by the *Bundesgerichtshof* in 1953,[112] the claimant's employee embezzled a large number of vouchers which were to be exchanged for coal (under the rationing regime in force in post-war Germany). He sold these to X, who sold them on to the defendants, who used them to obtain coal worth some DM 13,000. When the claimant claimed this sum from the defendants, they sought to set off the purchase price which they had paid to X. The court held that they were unable to do so. The reasoning is less than convincing: the court held that, in return for the purchase price, the defendants had obtained contractual rights against X. Given that these amounted to more than the purchase price itself, they could not claim that they were disenriched. This argument, however, is inconsistent with earlier judgments of the *Reichsgericht*.[113] In those cases, the defendant had sold the received benefit to a third party who turned out not to be good for the purchase price. The court in those cases did not allow the claimant to argue that the defendant was still enriched because it had received claims for the purchase price in return for the loss of the benefit – it preferred the more realistic view that those claims were in fact worthless. In effect, the benefit had been used in an uneconomic way by the recipient, and this qualified him for the disenrichment

---

107 See above, p 286.
108 See p 69.
109 Flume, 1953, p 151 (Flume draws attention to the objectionable 'phraseology', but agrees with von Tuhr and Wilburg that the analogy with § 122 is valuable in applying § 818 III).
110 Flessner, 1970, p 117.
111 RGRK/Heimann-Trosien, § 818, No 30.
112 BGHZ 9, 333 (7.5.1953).
113 RGZ 98, 64 (20.1.1920); 86, 340 (20.3.1915), 349.

defence.[114] The same arguments must apply in circumstances in which the purchase price was paid to a non-owner, where the claim against the non-owner based on the contract of sale is unlikely to be realisable.[115] A more convincing reason for not allowing the deduction of the purchase price paid to a non-owner would appear to be that the restitutionary claim, here in the form of the *Eingriffskondiktion*, is intended to extend the protection of the *rei vindicatio* in § 985 in circumstances in which the property right itself is lost because of the defendant's act. A *bona fide* possessor of goods belonging to another, however, is unable to resist the owner's vindication claim on the basis that he has paid money to a third party in order to obtain title to the goods. This, it is generally thought, cannot change merely because the defendant is no longer in possession – thus the application of § 818 III would lead to results inconsistent with §§ 985 ff. The purpose of the restitutionary claim – in this case to extend the *rei vindicatio* – thus militates against an application of the disenrichment defence.

A case decided in 1971[116] is further evidence of this phenomenon. The claimant (C) sold building materials to a builder (B). The contract contained a retention of title clause extending to the proceeds of any sale or use of the materials. Subsequently, the defendant bank took a global assignment of B's book debts. When B became insolvent, it enforced its security and called in the book debts, including those debts which, under the title retention clause, belonged to C. C therefore sued the bank, who argued that, although it faced an enrichment claim under § 816 I, it was no longer enriched because it had extended additional credit facilities to B, believing to have sufficient security to do so. Had D known that the debts in fact belonged to C, it would not have done so. In a previous case, the *Bundesgerichtshof*, on essentially the same facts, had decided that the bank could in such circumstances rely on its disenrichment.[117] In this case, however, the *Bundesgerichtshof* pointed out one crucial difference: the global assignment to the bank had been held to be void because it had been found to be *contra bonos mores* under § 138 *BGB*. If D had been allowed to rely on the disenrichment defence, the risk that the global assignment might be void on that ground would have been allocated to C, who had nothing at all to do with the transaction.

Whether this justification of the result is correct is open to serious doubt.[118] It is, however, plain that the court was trying to do two things: first, to take account of the fact that it was the bank, not the claimant, who had 'induced' the enrichment, with the consequence that it should now not be able to shift the consequential loss to the claimant, who had been unlawfully deprived of its rights; and secondly, the court sought to give effect to the policy underlying the finding that the global assignment had been *contra bonos mores* under § 138. That policy would have been frustrated if the bank had been allowed to pass the loss on to the claimant.

These are just a few examples of cases in which the courts have decided to ignore § 818 III in circumstances where it would defeat the policy which underlies the

---

114 Cf above, p 280.
115 Cf RGRK/Heimann-Trosien, § 818, No 30; but see BGHZ 55, 176 (11.1.1971) which adopts the reasoning of BGHZ 9, 333 (7.5.1953).
116 BGHZ 56, 173 (12.5.1971).
117 BGHZ 26, 185 (16.12.1957).
118 Cf RGRK/Heimann-Trosien, § 812, No 59; Olschewski, 1971, p 2307.

restitutionary claim. The courts are finding it difficult, however, to spell this out. It is suggested that the reason for this lies in the fact that the German law of unjust enrichment is so abstract that it is sometimes difficult to keep sight of the true objects of the restitutionary claim.

Suggested reform

In the late seventies and early eighties, the Federal Justice Ministry was considering a far reaching reform of the German law of obligations. König, an eminent comparative lawyer, was entrusted with the difficult task of drawing up suggestions for reform of the law of unjust enrichment. These were published in 1981, and although the law of unjust enrichment was not included in the current programme of reform of the law of obligations, König's proposals are important as they constitute the first serious attempt to put the results of academic and judicial work in this area of the law into legislative form.

König builds on the Wilburg/von Caemmerer typology of enrichment law, in that he distinguishes between three kinds of enrichment claim (*Leistungskondiktion*, *Eingriffskondiktion* and *Aufwendungskondiktion*, that is, enrichment by performance, interference and through payment of another's debt or improvement of another's property). For present purposes, it is of particular interest that König abandons the attempt to formulate one comprehensive disenrichment defence for all of these different claims. Instead, the proposal includes separate defences specifically tailored for each enrichment claim. It will be useful to look at each formulation of the disenrichment defence in turn.

The most complex version of the defence is intended to govern situations in which the defendant has received the enrichment by way of the claimant's performance. § 1.4 draws a sharp line between the loss of the received object itself and dispositions made by the recipient of other property in reliance on the security of his receipt. In the former case, the current solution in § 818 III is not departed from and the defence will generally be available. In the latter case, however, the availability of the defence is significantly curtailed. First, the proposal puts it beyond doubt that more than a mere causal link is required: the disposition must have been made in reliance on the security of the receipt. Even then, however, the defence will not be available where that reliance was not induced by the claimant, or where the claimant cannot be held responsible for having induced it. This solution is aimed at those cases in which the defendant's unjustified demand caused the claimant to make a payment or transfer property. König gives the example of the beneficiary under a will who receives an invoice from one of the testator's creditors and pays, little knowing that the testator had long discharged the debt. Here, argues König, it is the defendant's own mistake which induces the payment, and thus the defendant should not be allowed to rely on dispositions of his other property which he made in reliance on his receipt.

Where performances have been exchanged pursuant to a void contract, König goes even further than Flume in proposing that the defence should generally not be available.[119] He only makes an exception to this general rule where the inapplicability of

---

119 § 1.5(1).

the defence would frustrate the policy which underlies the invalidating rule of law. Thus, argues König, where a minor rents a car and suffers an accident resulting in the total destruction of the car, he should be able to rely on the defence given that his contract with the rental company is void precisely in order to protect him against this kind of risk.[120]

In the context of the *Eingriffskondiktion*, the disenrichment defence is not available if the defendant was grossly negligent in thinking that he was entitled to take the benefit in question. König thus proposes, contrary to § 818 III, to disallow the defence in circumstances in which the defendant was at fault. The second sentence of the provision puts it beyond doubt that the defendant cannot claim to have been disenriched by paying the purchase price to a non-owner.

Where the *Aufwendungskondiktion* is concerned, ie, cases in which the defendant is enriched because the claimant has paid and discharged his debt, and cases in which the claimant has 'improved' the defendant's property, the proposal expresses the disenrichment idea not by way of a defence but as part of the liability stage, asking whether the defendant is subjectively enriched by the claimant's act at the time the claim is made.

This very quick overview of the relevant provisions of the proposed draft hardly does them justice. For present purposes, however, it is possible to make a number of points which conveniently demonstrate the trend of the German debate over the past few decades:

Firstly, the proposal envisages far less protection for the enrichment defendant than the corresponding provisions of the *BGB*. Such extensive protection of the defendant is felt to be unnecessary in view of more precisely defined requirements of liability in unjust enrichment. The most striking practical consequence is that the parties' respective fault is taken into account in deciding whether or not the disenrichment defence should apply.

The second point is related to the first, in that the now accepted typology of enrichment law is relied upon in framing different versions of the disenrichment defence according to the different ways in which enrichments can come about.

Thirdly, even if different versions of the defence apply to different kinds of enrichment claim, the Wilburg/von Caemmerer typology alone is not without more sufficient to reach the correct result in every case. Particularly where the *Leis-tungs-kon-dik-tion* is concerned, it is necessary to modify the defence in accordance with the underlying reasons for the enrichment claim. These, as König realises, are to be found in the general law. Thus, the proposal modifies the defence in § 1.4 (3) depending on who has 'induced' the enrichment. Similarly, § 1.5 (1), which is concerned with the problem of exchanged performances (currently addressed by the *Saldotheorie*), takes into account the policy of the invalidating rule of law. It is suggested that the proposal therefore accepts that the high level of abstraction which runs through the entire German law of unjust enrichment can no longer be maintained when it comes to deciding whether or not the disenrichment defence should be available. In making that decision, the law will sometimes have to look behind the abstraction and identify the concrete reasons for restitution.

---

120 König, 1984, p 1547.

15.3 THE FUTURE DEVELOPMENT OF THE ENGLISH DEFENCE

The overview of the German debate demonstrates that it would be misleading for an English comparative lawyer to point out that § 818 III is extremely wide without drawing attention to the fact that German commentators have been attempting to restrict the ambit of that defence for as long as the BGB has been in force. The development of the German defence shows the clear link between restitutionary liability and defences: a wide liability stage will favour a wide defence, while a narrow liability stage will allow the defence to be applied more restrictively and sensitively. Particularly where the basis of restitutionary liability is not clearly identified, a wide disenrichment or change of position defence will be a necessity. Lack of precision in defining the basis of the claim will necessarily lead to an increase in judicial discretion. Only a wide and generally applicable defence will ensure that defendants can arrange their affairs without fear of that discretion being exercised to their disadvantage. This was appreciated by the drafters of the BGB, who still conceived of enrichment law as an equitable corrective of the more 'hard nosed' rules of the general law, and who therefore resisted attempts to introduce a more limited disenrichment defence into the BGB. Calls for a limitation of the very wide defence which was accordingly introduced naturally became more frequent and persuasive when a coherent structure of the German law of unjust enrichment had been developed. What lessons can be derived from this for English law?

It has been argued throughout this book that the English law of unjust enrichment has recently become destabilised by the intrusion of civilian structures into a legal system ill-fitted to accommodating them. This was not foreseeable in 1991, when *Lipkin Gorman* was decided. If Lord Goff thus foresees a limited role for the defence, this must now be heavily qualified in the light of subsequent developments.

15.3.1 The system of unjust factors and change of position

Mindy Chen-Wishart has recently pointed out that, in English law, unjust factors have a role to play in deciding whether the change of position defence should be available.[121] Having pointed out that both English and German law bar the bad faith defendant from the defence, she argues that:

> Whether the defendant should be regarded as in bad faith must be influenced by the operative unjust factor. The clearest cases are the defendants tainted by unconscientious procurement. Where fraud, duress or actual undue influence involving pressure is found, the defendant should normally have to account for any depletion of the enrichment received. The same applies to defendants tainted by unconscientious receipt.[122]

In other words, the unjust factor itself can be used to determine whether change of position will be available as a defence: if the unjust factor suggests that the defendant behaved badly, he should be barred from the defence. This is straightforward for the unjust factors mentioned in the above passage, namely fraud, duress, actual undue influence involving pressure and unconscientious receipt. In these cases, the defendant must, by definition, be in bad faith. Chen-Wishart stresses that the position is virtually identical in German law: 'Where duress or fraud under paragraph 123 of the BGB are

---

121 Chen-Wishart, 2000.
122 *Ibid*, after n 39.

triggered, defendants are in practice disqualified from the value surviving measure.' The only difference between the two legal systems lies in the fact that in German law there is a duplication of inquiries (!): the defendant's *mala fides* come under scrutiny both in establishing the fact of fraud or duress, and in showing under § 819 I that the defendant knew from the time of his receipt that he was not entitled to keep the enrichment, disqualifying him from the disenrichment defence.

Chen-Wishart explains how the unjust factor can have the opposite effect, namely in the case of bad faith minors.[123] The reason for restitution, in English law, is the minor's incapacity itself, the policy pursued is one of protecting the minor from himself. This policy would be frustrated if the minor were denied restitution under the change of position defence, even in circumstances where he can be said to be in bad faith. Chen-Wishart makes much of the fact that in German law the result would be no different. Her quote from Zweigert and Kötz is particularly apposite: '... in all legal systems liability depends on considerations appropriate to the particular type of case' and that 'these considerations ... oust or temper the abstract rules of liability preformulated in general terms.'[124] The advantage of English law is, of course, that the rules of liability are not abstract – the unjust factor itself, incapacity, tells us that change of position should be available whether or not the recipient minor acted in bad faith.

The same phenomenon, namely that the availability of the defence, bad faith aside, can be influenced by the reason for restitution, can be observed in cases in which restitution is made available in order to protect other defendants from improvidence.[125] The unjust factor is called 'presumed undue influence' in English law. It is to be distinguished from actual undue influence in that the defendant may well be wholly innocent. The cases commonly involve a surety who places his family home at risk to stave off their spouses' or family members' bankruptcy. If the law takes the view that such a person should be protected from their own good-natured gullibility, it would then 'hardly make sense to negate that intended protection by invariably allowing lenders to shift the loss, entailed in making the loans, to the sureties via change of position'.[126] Again, the policy pursued by the unjust factor would be subverted.

The big question which must be faced, however, is how long the link between the unjust factor and the availability of change of position can be maintained. There are cases, as Chen-Wishart herself points out, which involve a more covert 'balancing of the equities'. Thus, in the case of *Allcard v Skinner*,[127] which Chen-Wishart cites,[128] a novice nun made over her worldly goods to the Mother Superior of the convent she had joined. When she changed her mind, she was held to be *prima facie* entitled to restitution on the grounds of presumed undue influence. Chen-Wishart points out that Cotton LJ was nevertheless reluctant to make the morally blameless Mother Superior liable for money spent for charitable purposes, given that the money was handed over precisely for such

---

123 *Ibid*, before n 42.
124 Zweigert and Kötz, 1998, p 594.
125 Chen-Wishart, 2000, before n 45.
126 *Ibid*, after n 45.
127 (1887) 36 Ch D 145.
128 Chen-Wishart, 2000, at n 51; her other example for the same phenomenon is the case of *Cheese v Thomas* [1994] 1 WLR 129.

purposes. According to Chen-Wishart, '[l]imiting change of position to this type of loss minimises the risk of subverting the protective policy underlying undue influence'.[129]

The problem with this approach is that it is now necessary to look beyond the unjust factor itself. This suggests that the link between the unjust factor and change of position becomes unstable where the unjust factor does not itself establish the defendant's bad faith.

While Chen-Wishart's work does demonstrate that a system which bases restitution on unjust factors does have certain advantages over the more abstract civilian approach when it comes to developing a more refined change of position defence, it cannot be suggested that unjust factors solve all the problems.

Let us take 'failure of consideration' as an unjust factor first. The claimant is entitled to restitution because he conferred a benefit on the defendant, typically expecting the defendant to render some kind of counter-performance.[130] It is tempting to argue that in these cases the defendant should never be able to avail himself of the defence of change of position – after all, he knew that the transfer was made on a certain condition, and that that condition had not yet been fulfilled. In many cases this will certainly be the case, but there are a number of cases where it will not. In the famous *Fibrosa*[131] case, for example, a contract to supply machinery was frustrated when the buyer had already paid the price. It was able to recover the money it had paid in full. Would the seller have been able to rely on change of position where it had already used part of the money on purchasing the machines? On such facts, it would simply not do to dismiss the availability of the defence merely because the ground of restitution happens to be failure of consideration. Thus, while the unjust factor is helpful when it comes to applying the defence, the example confirms yet again that the link between unjust factor and change of position must not be taken too far.

This becomes more obvious in relation to mistake as an unjust factor. It will be remembered that von Tuhr, back in 1907, had relied on the analogy between mistake in contract (§ 119 *BGB*) and the disenrichment defence.[132] This would suggest that, bad faith aside, change of position should always be available where the unjust factor is mistake. This would ignore, however, cases of 'induced mistake', in which the party who is primarily to blame for the mistake is not the claimant but the defendant. As Wilburg points out for the German law, it is not obvious that, in such a case, the defendant should be allowed to rely on change of position.[133]

As has been pointed out above,[134] there are *dicta* in recent cases suggesting that a defendant who spends money received as a result of his own misrepresentation cannot defend an action for money had and received by relying on his change of position. In *R v*

---

129 *Ibid*, before n 48.
130 Cf Chapters 7 and 9, above.
131 [1943] AC 32.
132 See above, p 286.
133 See above, p 287.
134 See above, p 278.

Secretary of State for the Environment, ex p London Borough of Camden,[135] Camden had received payments out of central funds amounting to about £7 m. For two distinct reasons these payments had been *ultra vires* and void, and the Secretary of State sought to recover them under the so-called *Auckland* principle,[136] according to which taxpayer's money can only be removed from central funds in a manner authorised by Parliament – money which is removed without such authority can be recovered. The question arose whether Camden could rely on change of position. Although the question was not finally decided, Schiemann J said, *obiter*, after discussing whether change of position could ever be an answer to claims based on the *Auckland* principle:

> It is worth noting that even if a defence of change of position is an answer to some claims based on the *Auckland* principle, there is, to put it no higher, an argument for saying that where the *ultra vires* payment has been made following representations of entitlement by the recipient, the defence should be inapplicable.

In *Larner v London County Council,*[137] Lord Denning expressed a similar view, albeit in the context of the estoppel defence, which back then was the best chance the defendant had to avoid making restitution. He said:

> Speaking generally, the fact that the recipient has spent the money beyond recall is no defence unless there was some fault, as, for instance, breach of duty – on the part of the paymaster and none on the part of the recipient. ... But if the recipient was himself at fault and the paymaster was not – as, for instance, if the mistake was due to an innocent misrepresentation or a breach of duty by the recipient – he clearly cannot escape liability by saying that he has spent the money. That is the position here.[138]

This demonstrates quite clearly that the link between the unjust factor and the applicability of the defence must break down when it comes to induced mistakes.

It can thus be concluded that while under the system of unjust factors a more restrictive and sensitive system of different change of position defences would be more easily developed than under the Wilburg/von Caemmerer typology in German law, English law would nevertheless encounter significant problems. Although the English system is less abstract in identifying the reasons for restitution, which makes it easier to maintain a link between the reason for restitution and the availability of the change of position defence, there would still be considerable problems. Ultimately, where the unjust factor, (for instance, mistake,) is neutral as to the *bona fides* of the recipient, we end up on a slippery slope towards an open 'balancing of the equities', surrendering the decision whether or not to allow the defence ultimately to the discretion of the judge. This is well demonstrated by the law of New Zealand, to which we now turn.

15.3.2 The New Zealand experience

It is interesting that New Zealand introduced the defence by statute as early as 1958, but limited it mistaken payments. The relevant provision reads:

---

135 (1995) unreported, 17 February; cited by Tettenborn, 1996.
136 *Auckland Harbour Board v R* [1924] AC 318.
137 [1949] 2 KB 683.
138 *Ibid*, at 688 f.

Relief, whether under ninety-four A of this Act or in equity or otherwise, in respect of any payment made under mistake, whether of law or of fact, shall be denied wholly or in part if the person from whom relief is sought received the payment in good faith and has so altered his position in reliance on the validity of the payment that in the opinion of the Court, having regard to all possible implications in respect of other persons, it is inequitable to grant relief, or to grant relief in full, as the case may be.[139]

The first reported case to apply the defence was *Thomas v Houston Corbett*.[140] The defendant, a junior doctor, asked one of his friends, a law clerk employed by the claimant firm of solicitors, to invest £400 for him. Some weeks later, when the defendant wanted to purchase a new car, he asked his friend to return the money. He was told that a large sum of money was to be paid into his account, and that he should write him a cheque for £840 in respect of the excess. The defendant, unversed in business matters, and trusting his friend, did so. When he checked his account a few days later, he found that he had indeed received £1,380 from the claimant firm. He assumed that the investment which his friend had arranged had made him a profit of £140. In fact, the friend had stolen the £1,380 from the claimants' client account. When the claimants discovered this, they sought to recover that money from the defendant as money paid by mistake induced by their clerk's fraudulent misrepresentation. The question was to what extent the defendant could rely on the defence of change of position in order to reduce the claim against him. In other words, could the defendant argue that he had changed his position by paying over £840 to his rogue friend, thus reducing the claimants' claim to £540? Speight J at first instance had held that the defendant could not avail himself of s 94B, for two reasons. First, he held as a fact that the defendant handed over the cheque a few hours before the £1,381 was paid into his account – therefore it could not be said that he changed his position *in reliance* on the enrichment. Even if he was wrong on this point, the learned judge thought that the defendant should have realised that his friend was a rogue and was defrauding both him and his employers, saying:

> [The defendant] had been ... too trusting and possibly a trifle foolish in risking his money in this way, in particular, with an unqualified person who sounds as if he was leading a rather fancy life.[141]

The New Zealand Court of Appeal disagreed with Speight J on both points. First, their Honours held that it could not make a difference whether the defendant changed his position before or after he actually received the money from the claimants.[142] Secondly, the judges thought that Speight J's balancing of the equities was wholly inadequate. On this point the Court of Appeal was agreed, although there was some difference of opinion as to how the equities should be balanced properly. Turner J thought that this was a case in which 'two reputable and responsible professional men put their trust in a scoundrel, in circumstances in which neither of them was in the circumstances under a legal duty to the other'.[143] He felt that he could not 'distinguish between them so as to visit one with the consequences of this disaster more heavily than the other'.[144] In these circumstances,

---

139 Judicature Act 1908, Section 94B, as inserted by Judicature Amendment Act 1958, s 2.
140 [1969] NZLR 151.
141 Cited from the transcript by Turner J, at 170.
142 At 164, *per* North J; at 169 f, *per* Turner J; at 176, *per* McGregor J.
143 At 171, *per* Turner J.
144 At 170, *per* Turner J.

equality was equity, and he would have divided the loss equally between the parties. The other two members of the court disagreed, holding that, as the rogue was, to outward appearances, a trusted servant of the claimant firm of solicitors, the latter had to accept the greater responsibility for it 'was in a far better position to judge the character of Cook than was the [defendant]'.[145] As such, the claimant had to bear two thirds, the defendant one third, of the loss.

In the recent case of *National Bank of New Zealand v Waitaki*[146] the New Zealand Court of Appeal applied similar reasoning to the general common law change of position defence as recognised by *Lipkin Gorman*.[147] The facts of the case were curious. The defendant meat processing company had become involved in foreign currency trading, which had brought it into a business relationship with the claimant bank. For reasons best known to itself, the bank took the view that it owed the defendant US$500,000 and informed the defendant of this. The defendant pointed out that it had no record of such a sum being owed to it. After some debate, the defendant nevertheless accepted the payment, in the words of Henry J, 'under protest'.[148] It first invested the money in government stocks, but after a month this safe investment was replaced by a mortgage over a development property held by a nominee company. By the time the claimant discovered that it had indeed been mistaken in making the payment, the nominee company had collapsed, the security had proved worthless and the money had been lost.[149] The question for the court was which party was to bear that loss. Gallen J at first instance had concluded that 'justice would be done' if the bank recovered 10% of the amount at issue, that is, US$50,000. This was upheld by the New Zealand Court of Appeal, which confirmed that the relative fault of the parties was relevant in applying the general *Lipkin Gorman* change of position defence. The Court of Appeal's approach has much in common with the one suggested by Flessner for German law.[150] The judges were fully aware of the fact that they were allocating losses, and they were carrying out this exercise by reference to factors normally relevant only in the area of civil wrongs. The relevant factors included: that the claimant bank had put pressure on the defendant to accept the payment, failed to follow its own procedures in determining whether the money was in fact due and that there was a long delay between the payment and the bank's discovery of the true state of affairs. On the other hand, the court accepted the bank's argument that it was unacceptable for the defendant to invest the money in the property market, particularly if the investment was placed through a nominee company. The Court of Appeal thought that the judge had probably come down too strongly in favour of the defendant, but was not prepared to interfere with his judgment given that his general approach had been correct.

---

145 At 165, *per* North J.

146 [1999] 2 NZLR 211.

147 [1991] 2 AC 548; see above, pp 219 ff.

148 *National Bank of New Zealand Ltd v Waitaki International Processing (NI) Ltd* [1999] 2 NZLR 211, 222.

149 Why the mortgage proved worthless did not become entirely clear at the hearing: see Henry J, at 215.

150 See above, pp 289 f.

The members of the Court of Appeal relied on one of Birks's articles in support of this approach.[151] Birks there argues that knowledge as such should not disqualify a defendant in every case. He gives the example of a businesswoman who notices that she has been overpaid. Being intensely busy, she simply does not get round to doing anything about this for three days, although she firmly intends to repay the money. Her bank collapses. According to Birks, she should still be able to avail herself of the change of position defence. The underlying question is whether a recipient in her position, assuming she cannot rely on the defence, will be subject to an absolute liability to return the enrichment. We have seen that German law solves this problem by making the defendant liable 'according to the general rules'. The equivalent in English law would be to model the enrichment defendant's liability on the liability of an involuntary bailee, which would probably result in the busy businesswoman not being liable even if the defence of change of position is not available to her. Someone in her position would then only be liable for her own fault, not for inevitable losses of the enrichment.

> In light of these considerations, the result in *Waitaki* appears to be insupportable. The defendant was not *forced* to accept the payment, and it knew that the money probably did not belong to it. It should therefore not have taken any risks whatsoever with the money – taking it out of government stock and putting it into a shady property investment was not justifiable. To take the fault of the claimant in making the mistake into account simply confuses the issue.

The curious thing about *Waitaki* is that the loss allocation exercise, undertaken on the basis of the parties' relative faults, leads to the defence being available where, on a more orthodox interpretation, it would not be. This does not mean, however, that the case widens the defence. On the contrary, the emphasis on the fault of the parties gives rise to a great increase of judicial discretion, which can, by definition, cut both ways. The New Zealand Court of Appeal is fully aware of this. Thomas J points out that his interpretation of the defence is not shared by the majority of academics and judges in other common law jurisdictions, and that it should rest on the net enrichment rather than 'the notion of justice in the sense of the relative fault of the parties', referring to the work of Birks, Burrows, Mason and Carter and others. Thomas J goes on to observe:

> At least in part this criticism is based on a cerebral fear that the remedy will place undue discretion in the hands of the Judges. A better ordering of the elements of unjust enrichment is sought so that judicial discretion is reduced to a bare minimum. Of course, the academics chase a will o' the wisp. Unjust enrichment involves more than merely stripping defendants of their enrichments. Factors such as risk allocation and fault will inevitably intrude. ... To preclude a balancing of the equities in appropriate cases is the antithesis of equity's attempt to do justice in the individual case.[152]

An English court would, I think, refuse to go down this road, given the greater emphasis on certainty in English courts generally and the greater importance of London as a centre of international trade in which legal certainty is at a premium in particular. The New Zealand experience is nevertheless interesting. It demonstrates that there is a certain

---

151 Birks, 1996a.
152 *National Bank of New Zealand Ltd v Waitaki International Processing (NI) Ltd* [1999] 2 NZLR 211, 229.

dissatisfaction with a wide and indiscriminate defence in parts of the common law world, and a desire to make the defence more 'sophisticated', in the sense of being more responsive to the facts of the individual case. The approach in *Waitaki* itself may pass as a first attempt to develop such a defence, as a model for other jurisdictions it certainly leaves much to be desired. We should not be prepared to give up the search for a defence of change of position which is at once just *and* certain – to confer wide discretion on judges is, to my mind, not the way forward.[153] However, as pointed out above, an undesirable increase in judicial discretion may well be the price to pay for a more 'sensitive' defence. It is, to my mind, not a price worth paying, even in a system which boasts a stable taxonomy of the law of unjust enrichment, in other words, a system which has largely eliminated discretion from the liability stage. It would be still more dangerous to introduce a 'sophisticated' change of position defence when the liability stage is anything but stable.

15.3.3 The recent liberalisation of unjust enrichment and change of position

Whatever the ultimate future of the defence, it is argued in this book that now is not the time for attempts to make the defence more sophisticated and restricted. We have seen that, in the development of the German defence, great care was taken to counter-balance a wide and badly defined cause of action in unjust enrichment with an extremely widely drafted change of position defence. It was only as the cause of action settled down and became more stable that serious attempts to limit the defence were made, and to this day, rightly or wrongly, such attempts have been largely unsuccessful.

Following *Lipkin Gorman*, it might have been possible to develop a more sophisticated and restrictive version of the defence, incrementally, on a case by case basis, as envisaged by Lord Goff. Such a defence could well have been operated against the background of the system of unjust factors. At the time of *Lipkin Gorman*, it appeared that this system provided the necessary stability for the law of unjust enrichment as a whole. All that has changed now, as this book has demonstrated. The irony is that the unprecedented liberalisation of the law of unjust enrichment was only possible because the change of position defence was in place. It would therefore be wholly misguided to restrict it in any of the ways suggested for German law. Indeed, Birks has argued that 'change of position' has to be interpreted even more widely than the German disenrichment defence. According to him, the name 'change of position' suggests a wider concept than just 'disenrichment'.[154] This wider defence he then relies to solve the problem of spent mistakes. It will be remembered that the void contracts in *Kleinwort Benson v Lincoln* had been fully performed. The banks nevertheless sought restitution based on mistake of law. Birks always felt unhappy about that result, even if it could be argued that the banks had indeed made a mistake. In his seminal article on 'absence of consideration', he therefore introduced the doctrine of spent mistake in a footnote.[155] The argument runs that where a

---

153 This is demonstrated by the fact that the judges of the Court of Appeal would have 'weighed the equities' rather differently than did the Gallen J at first instance – which gives some idea of the unpredictability of the current version of the defence in New Zealand.

154 Birks, 2000a, pp 220 ff.

155 Birks, 1993, p 230, n 137.

mistaken party has received all he has bargained for, the mistake has spent its force. Originally, Birks did not formulate this in terms of change of position, which may account for the fact that the argument was given short shrift in *Lincoln*. Birks now formulates the same idea as follows:

> … the facts which happened after the mistake was made had the effect of depriving the mistake of all adverse effect, in that the disappointment inherent in the mistake never materialised and could never do so. Supervening circumstances thus arguably rendered it inequitable to rely on the mistake at all, despite the enrichment of the defendant.[156]

This suggested extension of the change of position defence to deal with problems caused by the extensive interpretation of what constitutes a mistake provides a further indication that our law has become unstable. I would suggest that the problem would best be addressed at the liability stage: has a mistake been made which justifies restitution?[157] The danger of allowing the change of position defence to 'mop up' all those cases in which restitution is not desired notwithstanding the presence of a *prima facie* restitutionary claim is that the whole law of unjust enrichment could become more and more discretionary. Given that our law now refuses to carry out this inquiry at the liability stage, it appears that this is inevitable at present.

15.4 CONCLUSION

While it was always clear that the English law of unjust enrichment could not be liberalised until a change of position defence was in place, it was argued in this chapter that the mere presence of the defence does not justify a liberalisation of the law on the scale that we have witnessed in recent years. This is particularly true because the defence is as yet largely untested: as was pointed out above, there is no knowing how the defence will be interpreted and how it will be applied by the courts.

In this chapter, it was argued that the defence should be widely rather than narrowly interpreted. It would be a mistake, however, to base this argument on the German example without more. This is because German writers, as was demonstrated above, are increasingly unhappy with the sheer width of the German disenrichment defence. This book has been very critical of unreflected and superficial comparative law, and it would be fatal to fall into that very trap in the last substantive chapter. The argument has therefore been rather more refined: when the disenrichment defence was drafted, the liability stage of German enrichment law was still very much open-ended and largely unprincipled. At that stage in its development, German law desperately needed a wide disenrichment defence. As § 812 I was subsequently 'tamed' and narrowed down by a laborious process of interpretation, it is arguable that the defence is now rather too wide. The lesson for English law is that a narrow change of position defence might well be desirable once English law has settled down and developed a principled approach to restitutionary liability, but not before then. It has been argued in this book that civilian

---

156 Birks, 2000a, pp 220 ff.
157 See above, pp 34 f.

doctrine is threatening to encroach on English law, and while English law deals with that challenge, and possibly develops the structures necessary to integrate and absorb the foreign approaches, mistakes will be inevitable. A strong change of position defence is therefore a necessity, at least for now.

CHAPTER 16

CONCLUSION

As Waller LJ said in *Guinness Mahon*,[1] the English law of unjust enrichment is at a crossroads: the choice is between two different models of enrichment liability. This book has presented an argument in favour of the traditional common law approach to unjust enrichment, basing restitution on positive, identifiable and articulated unjust factors rather than wide principles based on the absence of a legal ground for an enrichment. It is probable that this argument comes too late, particularly in light of *Kleinwort Benson v Lincoln*. If that is the case, the book has pursued a subsidiary aim, namely to provide an introduction to the infrastructure which makes an approach based on absence on legal ground possible in Germany.

16.1 COMMON LAW AND CIVILIAN MODELS OF UNJUST ENRICHMENT

Both the 'common law model' and the 'civilian model' of enrichment liability are informed by the structure of the legal systems they operate in: while the common law model is based on *inductive* reasoning, proceeding cautiously from case to case, and discovering wider principles behind the cases, the civilian model is based on *deductive* reasoning, starting off with a general principle which then needs to be refined, confined and controlled. The oft-quoted Pomponius maxim in Justinian's Digest must be regarded as expressing such a general principle: '*nam hoc natura aequum est neminem cum alterius detrimento fieri locupletiorem*'. This is in exactly the same category as '*alterum non laedas*' and '*pacta sunt servanda*' – useful general principles, but not rules which can be used to determine the incidence of liability in individual cases.

Opposed to this is the common law model, based on inductive reasoning. Here, we are only just beginning to identify the common principles behind restitutionary claims. It has taken many years for the courts to acknowledge, in *Lipkin Gorman v Karpnale*,[2] that there is such a thing as the principle against unjust enrichment. However, such principles, in English law, are never tantamount to statutory provisions. English law cannot dispense with concrete *unjust factors*. These unjust factors tell us in a non-theoretical and pragmatic manner when restitution is available. It is only when precedent runs out that the courts may resort to higher level principle in order cautiously to extend the categories of recognised unjust factors, as happened recently in the *Woolwich* decision.[3] The list not being closed, English law will always be able to formulate unjust factors which support a restitutionary award in appropriate cases.

---

1   *Guinness Mahon v Kensington and Chelsea* [1999] QB 215, 233.
2   [1991] 2 AC 548.
3   *Woolwich Building Society v Inland Revenue Commissioners (No 2)* [1993] AC 70.

16.2 THE UNJUST FACTOR 'MISTAKE'

In the chapters on mistake, it was argued that a mistake which causes a transferor to make a transfer which he would not have made but for the mistake triggers a presumption in favour of restitution. This presumption is rebuttable by showing either that restitution would undermine contractual risk allocations or that it would lead to the transferee ending up in a worse position than he was in before the transfer was made.

The system based on 'unjust factors' has been criticised by Meier as allowing restitution in inappropriate cases. Meier has particular problems with the unjust factor 'mistake'. The only way in which the availability of restitution can be appropriately narrowed down, she argues, is by introducing a 'legal ground' analysis into English law – in effect an importation of the structure which underlies the German law of restitution. The decision of Hobhouse J in *Westdeutsche Landesbank v Islington* suggests that this is indeed happening.

Against these arguments, it has been argued in Chapters 3–5 that to base restitution on any causal mistake does not lead to unacceptable results. There is nothing wrong with the unjust factor 'mistake'. Even if the fear of manufactured mistakes should cause the law to narrow down the categories of mistake which trigger restitution, there is absolutely no reason why this should be done by reference to a legal ground analysis. It will then, however, be necessary to answer the question how serious a mistake has to be so that the transferor is allowed to reverse his transfer. Neither legal system discussed here has so far come up with a satisfactory answer to this question, which provides further support for the argument that the current causal mistake approach adopted by the common law represents the best solution. If this is correct, the argument put forward by Meier loses much of its force.

16.3 THE UNJUST FACTOR 'FAILURE OF CONSIDERATION'

Failure of consideration is the second important unjust factor in English law. The underlying reason for restitution is that a transfer is made on a basis which then fails. Again, the presumption in favour of restitution is raised in that the transfer is no longer sanctioned by the transferor's consent. This is so whether the 'failure of consideration' occurs in a contractual or a non-contractual context, and whether it was 'total' or merely partial. If this is correct, then Hobhouse J's main reason for basing restitution on 'absence of consideration' simply falls away.

It was also seen in Chapters 6–9 that the modern view that a contract is not destroyed *ab initio* by frustration or discharge for breach, but that it continues to subsist in modified form, represents a challenge to any system based on a legal ground model. If the contract survives, how is it that it no longer forms a 'legal ground' of any enrichments transferred under it? This in part explains why in German law there is in place a separate restitutionary regime applying to contracts discharged by breach or frustration.

A system exclusively based on legal ground analysis also has great difficulty accounting for restitution for failure of consideration outside contractual cases. This is demonstrated by the German debate relating to the *condictio ob rem*. However, if the presumption in favour of restitution is indeed triggered in such cases, the unjust factor 'failure of consideration' is clearly required here.

16.4 THE USE OF COMPARATIVE LAW: TRANSPLANTING DOCTRINES AND STRUCTURES

The civilian dissatisfaction with the common law unjust factor approach has led to suggestions that the legal ground approach be introduced in England. If it is correct that this dissatisfaction cannot be based on the over-inclusiveness of the unjust factor 'mistake' or the inadequacy of the unjust factor 'failure of consideration', it must be based on the fact that the civilian model appears more elegant than the common law model, with the different inquiries taking part in the parts of the law best suited to carry them out. However, it was seen in Chapter 11 that this elegant automation must be bought at the price of greater abstraction. German law has no problem with this. In fact, as was made clear in Chapter 2, German law regards abstraction more as a virtue than a vice.

Part IV of this book should be taken as a warning against certain abuses of comparative law. The comparatist should not simply be counting heads. Just because a solution works in one system does not necessarily mean that it will work in another. We have seen that the formula 'restitution if an enrichment lacks a legal ground' is not without more particularly informative. It was made the basis of an elaborate typology of enrichment law in Germany, and only along with that typology or a similar one can it function correctly. To introduce that formula in England, under the guise of 'restitution for absence of consideration' would be dangerous.

The decision of the House of Lords in *Kleinwort Benson v Lincoln* suggests a different alternative. If restitution is based not on 'absence of consideration' but on the fact that an underlying obligation has turned out to be void or non-existent, then English law is already close to an adoption of an equivalent of the German *Leistungskondiktion*. This is not as dangerous as a wholesale adoption of the 'without legal ground' formula, given that it is considerably narrower. Could English law therefore emulate the civilian 'elegant automation' in this way? The answer given in this book has been: probably not. This is because even the *Leistungskondiktion*, however it is interpreted, depends on being part of a system of private law which knows that the word 'void' implies automatic restitutionary consequences. The policies which lead to nullity of contracts in English law have not been tested in this way, however, as was argued in Chapters 10 and 14. If the effect of the *Lincoln* case is therefore indeed an introduction of the German *Leistungskondiktion*, it will be necessary to develop an infrastructure within which it can operate.

The reader was forewarned in the introductory chapter that this book would refuse to present an argument in favour of either model of unjust enrichment liability. The danger is not so much the adoption of the German model by English law, but a combination of the two approaches. If English law chooses to adopt the civilian 'legal ground' model, it should do so consciously and openly. Only then will it be able to reap the benefits.[4]

16.5 THE AVAILABILITY OF RESTITUTION

In this book, it has been suggested that this infrastructure must contain reasons for retention and a wide change of position/disenrichment defence. Reasons for retention will exclude certain claimants from restitution where restitution is not desired even though the underlying obligation in question has turned out to be void. The wide change of position defence is necessary because it is inevitable that mistakes will be made while the system of reasons for retention is put in place.

16.6 THE PROPER ROLE OF COMPARATIVE LAW

Comparative law is an invaluable tool for any lawyer. But it is also easily abused. The single most important message which this book hopes to convey to the reader is that just because an approach functions well in one system it will not necessarily function well in others. In the law of unjust enrichment it is particularly tempting to adopt a civilian model which is based on a much longer development, and which appears to be working well in Germany. It should never be forgotten that English law and German law are not just different in their methods – they belong to two different families of legal systems.

Comparative law can highlight similarities, show how problems are dealt with by others, and help us better understand our own law. Our enthusiasm should not carry us away, however. The context is important. This is true for unjust enrichment as indeed it is for all areas of the law.

---

4   The recent draft of the American *Restatement* seems to go down the road of combining the two approaches. § 6(2) of the draft, under the general heading 'Benefits Conferred by Mistake', provides for restitution based on 'a mistake by the payer as to the existence or extent of the payor's obligation to an intended recipient'. The provision is headed: 'Payment of Money Not Due'. See American Law Institute, 2001, p 20. In the end, it does not become clear why it is necessary to single out liability mistakes in this way, given the seemingly generous treatment of mistaken gifts (cf above, pp 80 f).

TRANSLATION OF SOME BGB PROVISIONS

This appendix attempts a rough translation of those provisions of the BGB which are of particular relevance to this book. It is meant as an aid for the English reader of this book, and should not be taken as an authoritative translation. A more authoritative translation can be found in Markesinis, Lorenz and Dannemann, *The German Law of Obligations*, Vol I, p 816. There is also a complete translation of the BGB by Simon Goren (2nd edn by Forrester, Goren und Ilgen), 1994, Rothmans.

Erstes Buch. Allgemeiner Teil	**First Book. General Part**
...	...

Erster Titel – Geschäftsfähigkeit

First title – Capacity

§ 104 [Geschäftsunfähigkeit].

§ 104 [Incapacity]

Geschäftsunfähig ist:

A person who

(1) wer nicht das siebente Lebensjahr vollendet hat;

(1) is less than seven years of age;

(2) wer sich in einem die freie Willensbestimmung ausschließenden Zustande krankhafter Störung der Geistestätigkeit befindet, sofern nicht der Zustand seiner Natur nach ein vorübergehender ist.

(2) is in a state of mental illness which makes a free exercise of the will impossible, as long as that state is not merely temporary;

(3) (Aufgehoben)

(3) (Repealed)

is not of legal capacity.

§ 105 [Nichtigkeitsgründe bei Willenserklärungen]

§ 105 [Avoiding factors for declarations of will]

(1) Die Willenserklärung eines Geschäftsunfähigen ist nichtig.

(1) The declaration of will of a person not of legal capacity is void.

(2) Nichtig ist auch eine Willenserklärung, die im Zustande der Bewußtlosigkeit oder vorübergehender Störung der Geistestätigkeit abgegeben wird.

(2) A declaration of will which is made in a state of unconsciousness or during an episode of temporary insanity is likewise void.

§ 106 [Beschränkte Geschäftsfähigkeit Minderjähriger]

§ 106 [Restricted capacity of minors]

Ein Minder-jähriger, der das siebente Lebensjahr vollendet hat, ist nach Maßgabe der §§ 107 bis 113 in der Geschäftsfähigkeit beschränkt.

The capacity of a minor above the age of seven is restricted in accordance with §§ 107 to 113.

§ 107 [Einwilligung bei Minderjährigen

§ 107 [Permission]

Der Minderjährige bedarf zu einer Willenserklärung, durch die er nicht lediglich einen rechtlichen Vorteil erlangt, der Einwilligung seines gesetzlichen Vertreters.

The minor requires the permission of his legal representative for a declaration of will which is not exclusively legally advantageous.

§ 108 *[Wirksamkeit von Verträgen ohne Einwilligung]*

(1) *Schließt der Minderjährige einen Vertrag ohne die erforderliche Einwilligung des gesetzlichen Vertreters, so hängt die Wirksamkeit des Vertrags von der Genehmigung des Vertreters ab*

(2) *Fordert der andere Teil den Vertreter zur Erklärung über die Genehmigung auf, so kann die Erklärung nur ihm gegenüber erfolgen; eine vor der Aufforderung dem Minderjährigen gegenüber erklärte Genehmigung oder Verweigerung der Genehmigung wird unwirksam. Die Genehmigung kann nur bis zum Ablaufe von zwei Wochen nach dem Empfange der Aufforderung erklärt werden; wird sie nicht erklärt, so gilt sie als verweigert*

(3) *Ist der Minderjährige unbeschränkt geschäftsfähig geworden, so tritt seine Genehmigung an die Stelle der Genehmigung des Vertreters.*

§ 108 [Validity of contracts made without permission]

(1) If the minor enters into a contract without the required permission of the legal representative, the validity of the contract will depend on the latter's ratification.

(2) If the other party requests the representative to clarify whether or not he is going to ratify, ratification will only be effected if communicated to the other party; a ratification or refusal to ratify previously declared to the minor becomes ineffective. The contract can be ratified for a period of two weeks following the other party's request; if it is not ratified, ratification shall be deemed to be refused.

(3) If the minor has become of full legal capacity, his ratification replaces the ratification of his representative.

§ 109 *[Widerrufsrecht des Vertragspartners]*

(1) *Bis zur Genehmigung des Vertrags ist der andere Teil zum Widerrufe berechtigt. Der Widerruf kann auch dem Minderjährigen gegenüber erklärt werden.*

(2) *Hat der andere Teil die Minderjährigkeit gekannt, so kann er nur widerrufen, wenn der Minderjährige der Wahrheit zuwider die Einwilligung des Vertreters behauptet hat; er kann auch in diesem Falle nicht widerrufen, wenn ihm das Fehlen der Einwilligung bei dem Abschlusse des Vertrags bekannt war.*

§109 [The other party's right to revoke]

(1) Prior to ratification the other party is entitled to revoke. Revocation can be communicated to the minor.

(2) If the other party was aware of the minority, he can only revoke if the minor untruthfully stated that the representative had permitted the contract. He cannot revoke even in this case if he knew about the lack of permission.

§ 110 *[Vertragsschluß durch Bewirken der vertragsmäßigen Leistung, 'Taschengeldparagraph']*

Ein von dem Minderjährigen ohne Zustimmung des gesetzlichen Vertreters geschlossener Vertrag gilt als von Anfang an wirksam, wenn der Minderjährige die vertragsmäßige Leistung mit Mitteln bewirkt, die ihm zu diesem Zwecke oder zu freier Verfügung von dem Vertreter oder mit dessen Zustimmung von einem Dritten überlassen worden sind.

§ 110 [Executed contract, 'pocket money paragraph']

A contract entered into by a minor without permission of his legal representative is valid from the start if the minor renders the contractual performance with means given to the minor by the representative or a third party with the representative's consent for this purpose or at the minor's free disposal.

...

Zweiter Titel. Willenserklärung

...

§ 119 *[Erklärungs- und Inhaltsirrtum]*

(1) *Wer bei der Abgabe einer Willenserklärung über deren Inhalt im Irrtume war oder eine Erklärung dieses Inhalts überhaupt nicht abgeben wollte, kann die Erklärung anfechten, wenn anzunehmen ist, daß er sie bei Kenntnis der Sachlage und bei verständiger Würdigung des Falles nicht abgegeben haben würde.*

(2) *Als Irrtum über den Inhalt der Erklärung gilt auch der Irrtum über solche Eigenschaften der Person oder der Sache, die im Verkehr als wesentlich angesehen werden.*

...

§ 123 *[Anfechtungsgrund Täuschung oder Drohung]*

(1) *Wer zur Abgabe einer Willenserklärung durch arglistige Täuschung oder widerrechtlich durch Drohung bestimmt worden ist, kann die Erklärung anfechten.*

...

§ 125 *[Nichtigkeit bei Verstoß gegen Formerfordernis]*

Ein Rechtsgeschäft, welches der durch Gesetz vorgeschriebenen Form ermangelt, ist nichtig ...

§ 134 *[Nichtigkeit bei Gesetzesverstoß]*

Ein Rechtsgeschäft, das gegen ein gesetzliches Verbot verstößt, ist nichtig, wenn sich nicht aus dem Gesetz ein anderes ergibt.

...

§ 138 *[Nichtigkeit infolge von Sittenwidrigkeit]*

(1) *Ein Rechtsgeschäft, das gegen die guten Sitten verstößt, ist nichtig.*

(2) *Nichtig ist insbesondere ein Rechtsgeschäft, durch das jemand unter Ausbeutung der Zwangslage, der Unerfahrenheit, des Mangels an Urteilsvermögen oder der erheblichen Willensschwäche eines anderen sich oder einem Dritten für eine Leistung Vermögensvorteile versprechen oder gewähren läßt, die in einem auffälligen Mißverhältnis zu der Leistung stehen.*

...

Second title. Declaration of will

...

§ 119 [Mistake]

(1) He who, when making a declaration of will, is mistaken about the content of that declaration or did not mean to make such a declaration at all, can avoid the declaration if it can be assumed that he would not have made it had he had full knowledge of the facts and an opportunity reasonably to appreciate the situation.

(2) A mistake about such qualities of a person or a thing which are generally considered relevant is to be treated as a mistake about the content of a declaration.

...

§ 123 [Rescission due to deliberate misrepresentation or duress]

(1) He who has been induced to make a representation by fraudulent misrepresentation or unlawfully by threats can avoid the declaration.

...

§ 125 [Voidness due to lack of form]

A legal transaction which lacks the form prescribed by law is void ...

§ 134 [Voidness for illegality]

A legal transaction which violates a legal prohibition is void, unless the infringed law indicates otherwise.

...

§ 138 [Voidness for immorality]

(1) An immoral [*contra bonos mores*] legal transaction is void.

(2) In particular, a legal transaction will be void if it allows one party to be promised or to obtain pecuniary advantages out of all proportion to his own performance, if it was procured by exploiting another's predicament, inexperience, lack of judgment or considerable weakness of will.

...

§ 142 [*Anfechtungswirkung*]

(1) *Wird ein anfechtbares Rechtsgeschäft angefochten, so ist es als von Anfang an nichtig anzusehen.*

(2) *Wer die Anfechtbarkeit kannte oder kennen mußte, wird, wenn die Anfechtung erfolgt, so behandelt, wie wenn er die Nichtigkeit des Rechtsgeschäfts gekannt hätte oder hätte kennen müssen.*

...

Zweites Buch. Recht der Schuldverhältnisse

Erster Abschnitt – Inhalt der Schuldverhältnisse

Erster Titel – Verpflichtung zur Leistung

§ 241 [*Leistungsverpflichtung aus dem Schuldverhältnis*]

Kraft des Schuldverhältnisses ist der Gläubiger berechtigt, von dem Schuldner eine Leistung zu fordern. Die Leistung kann auch in einem Unterlassen bestehen.

§ 242 [*Treu und Glauben*]

Der Schuldner ist verpflichtet, die Leistung so zu bewirken, wie Treu und Glauben mit Rücksicht auf die Verkehrssitte es erfordern.

...

§ 249 [*Schadensersatz durch Naturalrestitution*]

Wer zum Schadensersatze verpflichtet ist, hat den Zustand herzustellen, der bestehen würde, wenn der zum Ersatze verpflichtende Umstand nicht eingetreten wäre. Ist wegen Verletzung einer Person oder wegen Beschädigung einer Sache Schadensersatz zu leisten, so kann der Gläubiger statt der Herstellung den dazu erforderlichen Geldbetrag verlangen.

§ 251 [*Geldentschädigung statt Wiederherstellung*]

(1) *Soweit die Herstellung nicht möglich oder zur Entschädigung des Gläubigers nicht genügend ist, hat der Ersatzpflichtige den Gläubiger in Geld zu entschädigen.*

(2) *Der Ersatzpflichtige kann den Gläubiger in Geld entschädigen, wenn die Herstellung nur mit unverhältnismäßigen Aufwendungen möglich ist ...*

...

§ 142 [Effect of Rescission]

(1) If a voidable legal transaction is avoided, it is to be considered void from the beginning.

(2) He who knew or ought to have known that a legal transaction was voidable will, if it is avoided, be treated as if he had known or ought to have known of the voidness of the legal transaction.

...

Second Book. The law of obligations

First Section. Content of obligations

First title. Obligation to perform

§ 241 [Duty to perform based on the obligation]

By virtue of the obligation the creditor is entitled to demand that the debtor render a performance. The performance can also consist of an omission.

§ 242 [The principle of good faith]

The debtor is obliged to render the performance in such a way as good faith requires, having regard to general practice.

...

§ 249 [Restitutio in integrum]

A party who is obliged to make compensation has to restore the injured party to the position the latter would have been in had the circumstance calling for compensation not occurred. If the duty to make compensation arises because of the injury of a person or damage to a thing, the creditor can insist that the debtor make compensation in money rather than in kind.

§ 251 [Damages instead of restoration]

(1) In so far as restoration is not possible or not sufficient to compensate the creditor, the party obliged to make compensation has to pay damages to the creditor.

(2) The party obliged to make compensation can pay damages, if restoration in kind would necessitate disproportionate efforts or expenditure on his part ...

314

...

...

§ 275 [Nicht zu vertretendes Unmöglichwerden]

(1) Der Schuldner wird von der Verpflichtung zur Leistung frei, soweit die Leistung infolge eines nach der Entstehung des Schuldverhältnisses eintretenden Umstandes, den er nicht zu vertreten hat, unmöglich wird.

(2) Einer nach der Entstehung des Schuldverhältnisses eintretenden Unmöglichkeit steht das nachträglich eintretende Unvermögen des Schuldners zur Leistung gleich.

§ 276 [Umfang der Verschuldenshaftung]

(1) Der Schuldner hat, sofern nicht ein anderes bestimmt ist, Vorsatz und Fahrlässigkeit zu vertreten. Fahrlässig handelt, wer die im Verkehr erforderliche Sorgfalt außer acht läßt ...

(2) Die Haftung wegen Vorsatzes kann dem Schuldner nicht im voraus erlassen werden.

...

§ 275 [Impossibility for which the debtor is not responsible]

(1) The debtor is released from his obligation to perform, if after the obligation is created his performance becomes impossible due to a circumstance for which he is not responsible.

(2) The debtor's subsequent inability to perform is to be treated in the same way as impossibility to perform arising after the obligation is created.

§ 276 [Extent of fault-based liability]

(1) Subject to contrary provisions, the debtor is responsible for intentional and negligent acts and omissions. A person is negligent if he fails to observe the care necessary in the circumstances ...

(2) Liability for intentional acts or omissions cannot be excluded in advance.

...

Zweiter Abschnitt – Schuldverhältnisse aus Verträgen

Zweiter Titel – Gegenseitiger Vertrag

...

§ 323 [Von keinem zu vertretendes Unmöglichwerden]

(1) Wird die aus einem gegenseitigen Vertrage dem einen Teile obliegende Leistung infolge eines Umstandes unmöglich, den weder er noch der andere Teil zu vertreten hat, so verliert er den Anspruch auf die Gegenleistung; bei teilweiser Unmöglichkeit mindert sich die Gegenleistung nach Maßgabe der §§ 472, 473.

(2) Verlangt der andere Teil nach § 281 Herausgabe des für den geschuldeten Gegenstand erlangten Ersatzes oder Abtretung des Ersatzanspruchs, so bleibt er zur Gegenleistung verpflichtet; diese mindert sich jedoch nach Maßgabe der §§ 472, 473 insoweit, als der Wert des Ersatzes oder des Ersatzanspruchs hinter dem Werte der geschuldeten Leistung zurückbleibt.

(3) Soweit die nach diesen Vorschriften nicht geschuldete Gegenleistung bewirkt ist, kann das Geleistete nach den Vorschriften über die Herausgabe einer ungerechtfertigten Bereicherung zurückgefordert werden.

Second Section. Contractual obligations

Second title. Bilateral contract

...

§ 323 [Performance becomes impossibility with neither side responsible]

(1) If in a bilateral contract the performance due from one party becomes impossible due to a circumstance which neither he nor the other party is responsible for, he loses his claim to counter-performance; in the case of partial impossibility his obligation to counter-perform is reduced according to §§ 472, 473.

(2) If one party requests the giving up of the replacement obtained in place of the thing originally owed or the assignment of a claim to compensation, he remains obliged to counter-perform; his counter-performance is however reduced under § 472, 473 in so far as the value of the replacement or claim to compensation is smaller than the performance originally owed.

(3) If a counter-performance, no longer required under these provisions, has already been rendered, the benefit conferred can be demanded back according to the rules of unjust enrichment.

§ 324 *[Unmöglichwerden bei Vertretenmüssen des Gläubigers]*

(1) *Wird die aus einem gegenseitigen Vertrage dem einen Teile obliegende Leistung infolge eines Umstandes, den der andere Teil zu vertreten hat, unmöglich, so behält er den Anspruch auf die Gegenleistung. Er muß sich jedoch dasjenige anrechnen lassen, was er infolge der Befreiung von der Leistung erspart oder durch anderweitige Verwendung seiner Arbeitskraft erwirbt oder zu erwerben böswillig unterläßt.*

(2) *Das gleiche gilt, wenn die dem einen Teile obliegende Leistung infolge eines von ihm nicht zu vertretenden Umstandes zu einer Zeit unmöglich wird, zu welcher der andere Teil im Verzuge der Annahme ist.*

§ 325 *[Unmöglichwerden bei Vertretenmüssen des Schuldners]*

(1) *Wird die aus einem gegenseitigen Vertrage dem einen Teile obliegende Leistung infolge eines Umstandes, den er zu vertreten hat, unmöglich, so kann der andere Teil Schadensersatz wegen Nichterfüllung verlangen oder von dem Vertrage zurücktreten. Bei teilweiser Unmöglichkeit ist er, wenn die teilweise Erfüllung des Vertrags für ihn kein Interesse hat, berechtigt, Schadensersatz wegen Nichterfüllung der ganzen Verbindlichkeit nach Maßgabe des § 280 Abs. 2 zu verlangen oder von dem ganzen Vertrage zurücktreten. Statt des Anspruchs auf Schadensersatz und des Rücktrittsrechts kann er auch die für den Fall des § 323 bestimmten Rechte geltend machen.*

(2) ...

§ 327 *[Rücktritt bei Unmöglichkeit]*

Auf das in den §§ 325, 326 bestimmte Rücktrittsrecht finden die für das vertragsmäßige Rücktrittsrecht geltenden Vorschriften der §§ 346 bis 356 entsprechende Anwendung. Erfolgt der Rücktritt wegen eines Umstandes, den der andere Teil nicht zu vertreten hat, so haftet dieser nur nach den Vorschriften über die Herausgabe einer ungerechtfertigten Bereicherung.

...

§ 324 [Creditor responsible for performance becoming impossible]

(1) If in a bilateral contract the performance due from one party becomes impossible because of a circumstance the other party is responsible for, he keeps his right to counter-performance. He must, however, give credit for what he has saved by being freed of his counter-performance or what he obtains by employing his labour elsewhere, or that which he intentionally fails to obtain.

(2) The same applies, where the performance of one party becomes impossible due to a circumstance he is not responsible for arising when the other side is late in accepting.

§ 325 [Debtor responsible for performance becoming impossible]

(1) in a bilateral contract the performance due from one party becomes impossible due to a circumstance he is responsible for, the other party can ask for damages for non-performance or terminate the contract. If the impossibility is only partial he can, if the partial performance of the contract has no interest for him, claim damages for non-performance of the entire obligation according to the rules in § 280 II or terminate the entire contract. Instead of claiming damages or terminating the contract he can rely on the same claims as specified by § 323.

(2) ...

§ 327 [Termination in cases of impossibility]

The right to terminate provided for in §§ 325, 326 is governed by the same rules as the contractual right to terminate in §§ 346 to 356. If the contract is terminated for a reason which the other party is not responsible for, he will only be liable according to the rules applying to the restitution of unjust enrichment.

...

Fünfter Titel. Rücktritt

§ 346 [Rücktrittsfolgen]

Hat sich in einem Vertrag ein Teil den Rücktritt vorbehalten, so sind die Parteien, wenn der Rücktritt erfolgt, verpflichtet, einander die empfangenen Leistungen zurückzugewähren. Für geleistete Dienste sowie für die Überlassung der Benutzung einer Sache ist der Wert zu vergüten oder, falls in dem Vertrag eine Gegenleistung in Geld bestimmt ist, diese zu entrichten.

§ 347 [Haftung im Falle der Rückgewähr]

Der Anspruch auf Schadensersatz wegen Verschlechterung, Unterganges oder einer aus einem anderen Grunde eintretenden Unmöglichkeit der Herausgabe bestimmt sich im Falle des Rücktritts von dem Empfange der Leistung an nach den Vorschriften, welche für das Verhältnis zwischen dem Eigentümer und dem Besitzer von dem Eintritte der Rechtshängigkeit des Eigentumsanspruchs an gelten. Das gleiche gilt von dem Anspruch auf Herausgabe oder Vergütung von Nutzungen und von dem Anspruch auf Ersatz von Verwendungen. Eine Geldsumme ist von der Zeit des Empfanges an zu verzinsen.

§ 348 [Verpflichtungserfüllung Zug um Zug]

Die sich aus dem Rücktritt ergebenden Verpflichtungen der Parteien sind Zug um Zug zu erfüllen. Die Vorschriften der §§ 320, 322 finden entsprechende Anwendung.

§ 349 [Erklärung des Rücktritts]

Der Rücktritt erfolgt durch Erklärung gegenüber dem anderen Teile.

§ 350 [Zufälliger Untergang]

Der Rücktritt wird nicht dadurch ausgeschlossen, daß der Gegenstand, welchen der Berechtigte empfangen hat, durch Zufall untergegangen ist.

§ 351 [Verschuldeter Untergang]

Der Rücktritt ist ausgeschlossen, wenn der Berechtigte eine wesentliche Verschlechterung, den Untergang oder die anderweitige Unmöglichkeit der Herausgabe des empfangenen Gegenstandes verschuldet hat. Der Untergang eines erheblichen

Fifth title. Termination of contracts

§ 346 [Consequences of termination]

If one party to a contract has negotiated a right to terminate the contract, the parties are, once he exercises this right, obliged to make restitution of the performances received. For services rendered as well as for the use of a thing the objective value has to be paid, or, if the contract makes provision for a counter-performance in money, this is to be paid.

§ 347 [Liability in case of restitution]

The claim to compensation because of deterioration, destruction or impossibility of restitution for some other reason is determined in the case of termination from the time of receipt of the performance according to the rules which apply to the relationship between owner and possessor from the time the owner's vindication claim becomes pending. The same applies to the claim for delivery up, payment for emoluments or repayment of disbursements. A sum of money bears interest from the time of receipt.

§ 348 [Contemporaneus discharge of obligations]

The obligations of the parties flowing from the termination of a contract are to be discharged contemporaneously. The rules laid down in §§ 320, 322 are applied *mutatis mutandis*.

§ 349 [Declaration of termination]

A contract is terminated by declaration to that effect to the other party.

§ 350 [Accidental destruction]

Termination is not excluded by the fact that the benefit received by the person entitled to declare it has been accidentally destroyed.

§ 351 [Destruction through fault]

Termination is excluded, if the person entitled to declare it has by his fault caused the significant deterioration, the destruction or other impossibility of delivery up of the object received. The destruction of a significant part is

Teiles steht einer wesentlichen Verschlechterung des Gegenstandes, das von dem Berechtigten nach § 278 zu vertretende Verschulden eines anderen steht dem eigenen Verschulden des Berechtigten gleich.

equal to the significant deterioration of the object, any fault of a third party whom the person entitled to declare termination is responsible for under § 278 is equal to that person's own fault.

§ 352 [Rücktrittsausschluß durch Verarbeitung und Umbildung]

§ 352 [Exclusion of termination by processing or changing]

Der Rücktritt ist ausgeschlossen, wenn der Berechtigte die empfangene Sache durch Verarbeitung oder Umbildung in eine Sache anderer Art umgestaltet hat.

Termination is excluded where the entitled person has changed the object received by processing or remodelling it into a different object.

§ 353 [Ausschluß bei Veräußerung und Belastung des Gegenstandes]

§ 353 [Exclusion of termination in cases of alienation]

(1) Hat der Berechtigte den empfangenen Gegenstand oder einen erheblichen Teil des Gegenstandes veräußert oder mit dem Rechte eines Dritten belastet, so ist der Rücktritt ausgeschlossen, wenn bei demjenigen, welcher den Gegenstand infolge der Verfügung erlangt hat, die Voraussetzungen des § 351 oder des § 352 eingetreten sind.

(1) If the entitled person has legally disposed of the object or a significant portion thereof, or charged the same to a third party, termination is excluded if the conditions of § 351 or § 352 are satisfied in respect of the person who has received the object in consequence of such alienation.

(2) Einer Verfügung des Berechtigten steht eine Verfügung gleich, die im Wege der Zwangsvollstreckung oder der Arrestvollziehung oder durch den Konkursverwalter erfolgt.

(2) A disposition effected by enforcement by way of execution or distraint or by the liquidator or trustee in bankruptcy is equivalent to a disposition effected by the entitled person.

Vierundzwanzigster Titel. Ungerechtfertigte Bereicherung

Twenty-fourth title. Unjust enrichment

§ 812 [Herausgabeanspruch]

§ 812 [Claim for delivery up]

(1) Wer durch die Leistung eines anderen oder in sonstiger Weise auf dessen Kosten etwas ohne rechtlichen Grund erlangt, ist ihm zur Herausgabe verpflichtet. Diese Verpflichtung besteht auch dann, wenn der rechtliche Grund später wegfällt oder der mit einer Leistung nach dem Inhalte des Rechtsgeschäfts bezweckte Erfolg nicht eintritt.

(1) He who obtains something through somebody else's performance or in another way at his expense without a legal cause, is obliged to make restitution to the other. This obligation arises also where the legal cause later disappears or where the result contemplated by the legal transaction is not attained.

(2) Als Leistung gilt auch die durch Vertrag erfolgte Anerkennung des Bestehens oder des Nichtbestehens eines Schuldverhältnisses.

(2) The contractually acknowledged existence or non-existence of an obligation is equivalent to performance.

§ 813 [Rückforderung der Erfüllung trotz Einrede]

§ 813 [Restitution of performance made despite defence]

(1) *Das zum Zwecke der Erfüllung einer Verbindlichkeit Geleistete kann auch dann zurückgefordert werden, wenn dem Anspruch eine Einrede entgegenstand, durch welche die Geltendmachung des Anspruchs dauernd ausgeschlossen wurde. Die Vorschrift des § 222 Abs. 2 bleibt unberührt.*

(2) *Wird eine betagte Verbindlichkeit vorzeitig erfüllt, so ist die Rückforderung ausgeschlossen; die Erstattung von Zwischenzinsen kann nicht verlangt werden.*

§ 814 *[Bewußte Leistung ohne Leistungsverpflichtung; Sitten- oder Anstandspflicht]*

Das zum Zwecke der Erfüllung einer Verbindlichkeit Geleistete kann nicht zurückgefordert werden, wenn der Leistende gewußt hat, daß er zur Leistung nicht verpflichtet war, oder wenn die Leistung einer sittlichen Pflicht oder einer auf den Anstand zu nehmenden Rücksicht entsprach.

§ 815 *[Ausschluß der Rückforderung bei Erfolgsverfehlung]*

Die Rückforderung wegen Nichteintritts des mit einer Leistung bezweckten Erfolges ist ausgeschlossen, wenn der Eintritt des Erfolges von Anfang an unmöglich war und der Leistende dies gewußt hat oder wenn der Leistende den Eintritt des Erfolges wider Treu und Glauben verhindert hat.

§ 816 *[Verfügung durch einen Nichtberechtigten]*

(1) *Trifft ein Nichtberechtigter über einen Gegenstand eine Verfügung, die dem Berechtigten gegenüber wirksam ist, so ist er dem Berechtigten zur Herausgabe des durch die Verfügung Erlangten verpflichtet. Erfolgt die Verfügung unentgeltlich, so trifft die gleiche Verpflichtung denjenigen, welcher auf Grund der Verfügung unmittelbar einen rechtlichen Vorteil erlangt.*

(2) *Wird an einen Nichtberechtigten eine Leistung bewirkt, die dem Berechtigten gegenüber wirksam ist, so ist der Nichtberechtigte dem Berechtigten zur Herausgabe des Geleisteten verpflichtet.*

(1) That which has been performed in order to discharge an obligation can be demanded back where the claim was permanently barred by a defence. The rule in § 222~ II is not affected.

(2) If an obligation is discharged before it becomes due, restitution is excluded; no interest can be claimed for the time until performance would have been due.

§ 814 [Performance in knowledge of absence of duty to perform; moral duties to perform]

That which as been performed for the purpose of discharging a liability cannot be demanded back if the performing party knew that he was under no liability to perform, or if his performance was pursuant to a moral duty.

§ 815 [Exclusion of restitution where contemplated result is not attained]

Restitution for non-attainment of the intended result of a performance is excluded where the attainment of the result was impossible from the start and where the party performing was aware of this, or where the party performing has prevented the attainment of the intended result contrary to the principle of good faith.

§ 816 [Disposition by a non-owner]

(1) If an non-owner disposes of an object in such a way that the disposition is valid against the owner, he is obliged to make restitution to the owner of what he obtained by the disposition. If the disposition is made gratuitously, the same obligation applies to the person who obtains an immediate advantage by the disposition.

(2) If a performance effective against an authorised person is rendered to an unauthorised person, the latter has to give up to the former what has been performed.

§ 817 [Leistungszweck gegen gesetzliches Verbot oder gute Sitten]

§ 817 [Purpose of performance against legal prohibition or good morals]

War der Zweck einer Leistung in der Art bestimmt, daß der Empfänger durch die Annahme gegen ein gesetzliches Verbot oder gegen die guten Sitten verstoßen hat, so ist der Empfänger zur Herausgabe verpflichtet. Die Rückforderung ist ausgeschlossen, wenn dem Leistenden gleichfalls ein solcher Verstoß zur Last fällt, es sei denn, daß die Leistung in der Eingehung einer Verbindlichkeit bestand; das zur Erfüllung einer solchen Verbindlichkeit Geleistete kann nicht zurückgefordert werden.

If the purpose of a performance is such that the recipient violates a legal prohibition or good morals by accepting, he is obliged to make restitution. The claim to restitution is excluded when the performing party is to blame in the same way, save for cases in which the performance consisted of the entering into an obligation, performances made in order to discharge such an obligation cannot be claimed back.

§ 818 [Umfang des Herausgabeanspruchs]

§ 818 Measure of Restitution

(1) Die Verpflichtung zur Herausgabe erstreckt sich auf die gezogenen Nutzungen sowie auf dasjenige, was der Empfänger auf Grund eines erlangten Rechtes oder als Ersatz für die Zerstörung, Beschädigung oder Entziehung des erlangten Gegenstandes erwirbt.

(1) The obligation to make restitution extents to profits made from any benefit received as well as of what the recipient obtains because of a right he has obtained or as compensation for destruction, damage to or deprivation of any object received.

(2) Ist die Herausgabe wegen der Beschaffenheit des Erlangten nicht möglich oder ist der Empfänger aus einem anderen Grunde zur Herausgabe außerstande, so hat er den Wert zu ersetzen.

(2) If restitution is impossible because of the nature of what was received or if the recipient is unable to deliver it up for some other reason, he has to make restitution in money.

(3) Die Verpflichtung zur Herausgabe oder zum Ersatze des Wertes ist ausgeschlossen, soweit der Empfänger nicht mehr bereichert ist.

(3) The obligation to make restitution of the value is excluded in so far as the recipient is no longer enriched.

(4) Von dem Eintritte der Rechtshängigkeit an haftet der Empfänger nach den allgemeinen Vorschriften.

(4) From the time an action becomes pending the recipient is liable according to the general rules.

§ 819 [Haftungsverschärfung bei Bösgläubigkeit]

§ 819 [Increased liability of mala fide recipient]

(1) Kennt der Empfänger den Mangel des rechtlichen Grundes bei dem Empfang oder erfährt er ihn später, so ist er von dem Empfang oder der Erlangung der Kenntnis an zur Herausgabe verpflichtet, wie wenn der Anspruch auf Herausgabe zu dieser Zeit rechtshängig geworden wäre.

(1) If the recipient knows of the lack of legal cause at the time of receipt or gets to know of it later, he is, from the time of receipt or knowledge, obliged to make restitution as if the claim to restitution had become pending at that time.

(2) Verstößt der Empfänger durch die Annahme der Leistung gegen ein gesetzliches Verbot oder gegen die guten Sitten, so ist er von dem Empfange der Leistung an in der gleichen Weise verpflichtet

(2) If the recipient violates a legal prohibition or public policy by accepting the performance, he is obliged in the same way from the time of receipt.

§ 820 [*Haftungsverschärfung bei unsicherem Erfolgseintritt*]

(1) *War mit der Leistung ein Erfolg bezweckt, dessen Eintritt nach dem Inhalte des Rechtsgeschäfts als ungewiß angesehen wurde, so ist der Empfänger, falls der Erfolg nicht eintritt, zur Herausgabe so verpflichtet, wie wenn der Anspruch auf Herausgabe zur Zeit des Empfanges rechtshängig geworden wäre. Das gleiche gilt, wenn die Leistung aus einem Rechtsgrunde, dessen Wegfall nach dem Inhalte des Rechtsgeschäfts als möglich angesehen wurde, erfolgt ist und der Rechtsgrund wegfällt.*

(2) *Zinsen hat der Empfänger erst von dem Zeitpunkt an zu entrichten, in welchem er erfährt, daß der Erfolg nicht eingetreten oder daß der Rechtsgrund weggefallen ist; zur Herausgabe von Nutzungen ist er insoweit nicht verpflichtet, als er zu dieser Zeit nicht mehr bereichert ist.*

§ 820 [Increased liability if attainment of desired result uncertain]

(1) If the performance pursued a result whose realisation was regarded as uncertain within the terms of the legal transaction, and the result is then not attained, the recipient is liable to make restitution as if the claim had become pending at the time of receipt. The same applies if the performance is made for a legal cause which the legal transaction contemplated might subsequently disappear, if the legal cause subsequently disappears.

(2) The recipient only has to pay interest from the time at which he learns that the result of the performance has not been attained or that the legal cause has disappeared; he will no longer be obliged to make restitution of profits made in so far as he is no longer enriched at that time.

§ 821 [*Bereicherungsanspruch als Einrede*]

Wer ohne rechtlichen Grund eine Verbindlichkeit eingeht, kann die Erfüllung auch dann verweigern, wenn der Anspruch auf Befreiung von der Verbindlichkeit verjährt ist.

§ 821 [Enrichment claim as defence]

He who enters into an obligation without legal cause, can refuse performing it even if the claim to be freed from the obligation has become time-barred.

§ 822 [*Herausgabepflicht bei unentgeltlicher Zuwendung*]

Wendet der Empfänger das Erlangte unentgeltlich einem Dritten zu, so ist, soweit infolgedessen die Verpflichtung des Empfängers zur Herausgabe der Bereicherung ausgeschlossen ist, der Dritte zur Herausgabe verpflichtet, wie wenn er die Zuwendung von dem Gläubiger ohne rechtlichen Grund erhalten hätte.

§ 822 [Duty to make restitution in cases of gratuitous bestowal]

If the recipient bestows the received benefit onto a third party, the latter is obliged to make restitution as if he had received the bestowal from the creditor without legal cause, if the recipient's duty to make restitution is excluded by the bestowal.

BIBLIOGRAPHY

A

Adams, J and Brownsword, R, *Understanding Contract Law*, 1987, London: Fontana

American Law Institute, *Restatement of the Law Third – Restitution and Unjust Enrichment, Tentative Draft No 1 (6 April 2001)*, 2001, Philadelphia: American Law Institute

Arens, H, '*Die "abgekaufte" Strafanzeige*' (1971) JuS 355

Arrowsmith, S, 'Mistake and the role of the "submission to an honest claim"', in Burrows, A (ed), *Essays on the Law of Restitution*, 1991, Oxford: Clarendon, p 17

Atiyah, PS, *An Introduction to the Law of Contract*, 3rd edn, 1981, Oxford: Clarendon

B

Barnett, RE, 'A consent theory of contract', in Frey, RG and Morris, CW (eds), *Liability and Responsibility*, 1991, Cambridge: CUP

Barker, K, 'Restitution of passenger fare' (1993) LMCLQ 291

Batsch, KL, *Vermögensverschiebung und Bereicherungsherausgabe in den Fällen unbefugten Gebrauchens bzw Nutzens von Gegenständen*, 1968, Marburg: Elwert

Batsch, KL, 'Zum Bereicherungsanspruch bei Zweckverfehlung' (1973) NJW 1639

Beatson, J, *The Use and Abuse of Unjust Enrichment*, 1991, Oxford: Clarendon

Beatson, J, *Anson's Law of Contract*, 1998, Oxford, New York: OUP

Birks, PBH, 'English and Roman learning in *Moses v Macferlan*' (1984) CLP 1

Birks, PBH, *An Introduction to the Law of Restitution*, revised edn, 1989, previous edn, 1985, Oxford: Clarendon

Birks, PBH, 'Restitution after ineffective contracts: issues for the 1990s' (1990) 2 JCL 227 [1990a]

Birks, PBH, 'Restitution from the executive: a tercentenary footnote to the Bill of Rights', in Finn, PD (ed), *Essays on Restitution*, 1990, North Ryde, NSW: LBC, p 161 [1990b]

Birks, PBH, 'Restitution without counter-restitution (*Guinness v Saunders*)' [1990] LMCLQ 330 [1990c]

Birks, PBH, 'In defence of free acceptance', in Burrows, A (ed), *Essays on the Law of Restitution*, 1991, Oxford: Clarendon, p 109 [1991a]

Birks, PBH, 'The English recognition of unjust enrichment (*Lipkin Gorman v Karpnale; Woolwich v IRC*)' [1991] LMCLQ 473 [1991b]

Birks, PBH, 'Review of Maddaugh and McCamus, *The Law of Restitution*' (1991) 70 CBR 814 [1991c]

Birks, PBH, 'Restitution and resulting trusts', in Goldstein, SR (ed), *Equity and Contemporary Legal Developments*, 1992, Jerusalem: H & M Sacher Institute [1992a]

Birks, PBH, *Restitution – The Future*, 1992, Sydney: Federation [1992b]

Birks, PBH, 'No consideration: restitution after void contracts' (1993) 23 UWALR 195

Birks, PBH, 'The remedial constructive trusts: proprietary rights as remedies', in Birks, P (ed), *The Frontiers of Liability*, 1994, Oxford: OUP, Vol 2, p 214

Birks, PBH (ed), *Laundering and Tracing*, 1995, Oxford: Clarendon [1995a]

Birks, PBH, 'Overview: tracing, claiming and defences', in Birks, P (ed), *Laundering and Tracing*, 1995, Oxford: Clarendon, p 289 [1995b]

Birks, PBH, 'Change of position: the nature of the defence and its relationship to other restitutionary defences', in McInnes, M (ed), *Restitution: Developments in Unjust Enrichment*, 1996, North Ryde, NSW: LBC Information Services [s 1], Deakin Law School: Legal Resources Project [1996a]

Birks, PBH, 'Equity in the modern law: an exercise in taxonomy' (1996) 26 UWALR 1 [1996b]

Birks, PBH, 'Failure of consideration', in Rose, FD (ed), *Consensus ad Idem: Essays in Honour of Günter Treitel*, 1996, London: Sweet & Maxwell, p 179 [1996c]

Birks, PBH, 'Inconsistency between compensation and restitution' [1996] 112 LQR 375 [1996d]

Birks, PBH, 'Trusts raised to reverse unjust enrichment: the *Westdeutsche* case' (1996) RLR 3 [1996e]

Birks, PBH, 'Mistakes of law' (2000) 53 CLP 205 [2000a]

Birks, PBH, 'Private law', in Birks, PBH and Rose, FD, *Lessons of the Swaps Litigation*, 2000, London: Mansfield, p 1 [2000b]

Birks, PBH, 'At the expense of the claimant: direct and indirect enrichment in English law' (2000) Oxford University Comparative Law Forum 2 at http://oudf.iuscomp.org [2000c]

Birks, PBH and Chambers, R, *The Restitution Research Resource*, 1997, 2nd edn, 1997, Oxford: Mansfield

Birks, PBH and McLeod, G, *Justinian's Institutes*, 1987, London: Duckworth

Birks, PBH and Mitchell, C, 'Unjust enrichment', in Birks, P (ed), *English Private Law*, 2000, Oxford: OUP, Vol 2

Birks, PBH and Rose, FD, *Lessons of the Swaps Litigation*, 2000, London: Mansfield

Bridge, M, *The Sale of Goods*, 1997, Oxford: Clarendon

Brox, H, *Allgemeines Schuldrecht*, 21st edn, 1993, München: Beck [1993a]

Brox, H, *Besonderes Schuldrecht*, 19th edn, 1993, München: Beck [1993b]

Burrows, A, 'Free acceptance and the law of restitution' (1988) 104 LQR 576

Burrows, A (ed), *Essays on the Law of Restitution*, 1991, Oxford: Clarendon

Burrows, A, *The Law of Restitution*, 1993, London: Butterworths [1993a]

Burrows, A, 'Restitution of payments made under swaps transactions' [1993] 143 NLJ 480 [1993b]

Burrows, A, 'Swaps and the friction between common law and equity' [1995] RLR 15

C

von Caemmerer, E, 'Bereicherung und unerlaubte Handlung', in Festschrift für Rabel, 1954, Tübingen: Mohr, Vol 1, p 333

von Caemmerer, E, 'Mortuus redhibetur', in Festschrift für Karl Larenz zum 70 Geburtstag, 1973, München: Beck, p 621

Campbell, AH, 'Fascism and legality' (1946) 62 LQR 141

Canaris, C-W, 'Ansprüche wegen „positiver Vertragsverletzung" und „Schutzwirkung für Dritte" bei nichtigen Verträgen' (1965) JZ 475

Canaris, C-W, 'Der Bereicherungsausgleich im Dreipersonenverhältnis', Festschrift für Larenz, 1973, München: Beck, p 799

Canaris, C-W, 'Der Bereicherungsausgleich im bargeldlosen Zahlungsverkehr' (1980) WM 354

Carter, JW, 'Discharged contracts: claims for restitution' (1997) 11 JCL 130

Carter, JW and Tolhurst, G, 'Restitution for failure of consideration' (1997) 11 JCL 162

Cartwright, J, 'Solle v Butcher and the doctrine of mistake in contract' (1987) 103 LQR 584

Cartwright, J, Unequal Bargaining, 1991, Oxford: Clarendon

Chambers, R, Resulting Trusts, 1997, Oxford: Clarendon

Chen-Wishart, M, 'In defence of unjust factors: a study of rescission for duress, fraud and exploitation' (2000) Oxford University Comparative Law Forum 2 at http://ouclf.iuscomp.org

Chitty, J, Law of Contracts, Guest, AG (ed), 28th edn, 1999, London: Sweet & Maxwell

Collatz, W, Ungerechtfertigte Vermögensverschiebung: Ein Beitrag zum Recht des bürgerlichen Gesetzbuches, 1899, Berlin: Struppe & Winckler

Conring, H, De origine iuris Germanici commentarius historicus, 1643, Helmstedt: Müller

Corbin, AL, Corbin on Contracts, 1993, St Paul, Minn: West, Vol 1

Cornish, WR, '"Colour of office": restitutionary redress against public authority' (1987) 14 Journal of Malaysian and Comparative Law 41

Cornish, WR, Nolan, R, O'Sullivan, J and Virgo, G (eds), Restitution: Past, Present and Future, Essays in Honour of Gareth Jones, 1998, Oxford: Hart

Costede, J, Dogmatische und methodologische Überlegungen zum Verständnis des Bereicherungsrechts, 1977, Bern: Stämpfli

Crome, C, System des deutschen Bürgerlichen Rechts II: Recht der Schuldverhältnisse, 1902, Tübingen: Mohr

D

Dagan, H, 'Mistakes', 2000, Social Science Research Network Electronic Library: (http://papers.ssrn.com/sol3/papers.cfm?abstract_id=255344)

Dannemann, G, *An Introduction to German Civil and Commercial Law*, 1993, London: British Institute of International and Comparative Law

Dannemann, G, 'Restitution for termination of contract in German law', in Rose, FD (ed), *Failure of Contracts*, 1997, Oxford: Hart, p 129

Dannemann, G, 'Illegality as a defence against unjust enrichment claims' (2000) Oxford University Comparative Law Forum (http://oud.iuscomp.org)

Dawson, JP, *Unjust Enrichment: A Comparative Analysis*, 1951, Boston: Little, Brown

Dernburg, H and Raape, L, *Die Schuldverhältnisse nach dem Recht des Deutschen Reiches und Preußens*, 4th edn, 1915, Halle: Buchhandel des Waisenhauses

Dickson, B, 'The law of restitution in the Federal Republic of Germany' (1987) 36 ICLQ 751

Dowrick, FE, 'The relationship of principal and agent' (1954) 17 MLR 24

Dworkin, R, *Taking Rights Seriously*, 1978, London: Duckworth

E

Erman, W, *Handkommentar zum Bürgerlichen Gesetzbuch*, 9th edn, 1993, Münster: Aschendorff

Esser, J, *Schuldrecht*, 2nd edn, 1960, Karlsruhe: Müller

Esser, J, *Schuldrecht II, Besonderer Teil*, 3rd edn, 1971, Karlsruhe: Müller

Esser, J, Schmidt, E and Köndgen, J, *Fälle und Lösungen nach höchstrichterlichen Entscheidungen: BGB-Schuldrecht*, 3rd edn, 1971, Karlsruhe: Müller

Esser, J and Weyers, H-L, *Schuldrecht II, Besonderer Teil*, 7th edn, 1991, Heidelberg: Müller

Everett, CW, *The Letters of Junius*, London: Faber & Gwyer, 1927

F

Feenstra, R, 'Grotius' doctrine of unjust enrichment as a source of obligation', in Schrage, EFH (ed), *Unjust Enrichment – The Comparatuive Legal History of the Law of Restitution*, 1995, Berlin: Duncker & Humblot

Fifoot, CHS, *Lord Mansfield*, 1936, Oxford: Clarendon

Fikentscher, W, *Schuldrecht*, 8th edn, 1992, Berlin: de Gruyter

Finn, PD (ed), *Essays on Restitution*, 1990, North Ryde, NSW: LBC

Flessner, A, 'Haftung und Gefahrbelastung des getäuschten Käufers' (1972) NJW 1777

Flessner, *Wegfall der Bereicherung - Rechtsvergleichung und Kritik*, 1970, Berlin: de Gruyter

Flume, W, *Eigenschaftsirrtum und Kauf*, 1948, Münster: Regensberg

Flume, W, 'Der Wegfall der Bereicherung', in *Festschrift Niedermeyer*, 1953, Göttingen: Schwartz, p 103

Flume, W, *Allgemeiner Teil des Bürgerlichen Rechts, Das Rechtsgeschäft*, 1979, Berlin: Springer-Verlag, Vol 2

Ford, HAJ, 'Dispositions for purposes', in Finn, PD (ed), *Essays in Equity*, 1985, Sydney: LBC, p 159

Ford, HAJ and Lee, WA, *Principles of the Law of Trusts*, 2nd edn, 1990, North Ryde, NSW: LBC

Fridman, GHL, *Restitution*, 2nd edn, 1992, Toronto: Carswell

Fridman, GHL and McLeod, JG, 'Acceptance of unjust enrichment', in Fridman, GHL, *Restitution*, 1982, Toronto: Carswell

Friedmann, D, 'Valid, voidable, qualified, and non-existing obligations: an alternative perspective on the law of restitution', in Burrows, A (ed), *Essays on the Law of Restitution*, 1991, Oxford: Clarendon, p 247

G

Gebhard, A, *Gutachten aus dem Anwaltsstande über die 1. Lesung des Entwurfes eines Bürgerlichen Gesetzbuches*, 1888, Berlin: Guttentag

Glover, J, 'Equity and restitution', in Parkinson, P (ed), *The Principles of Equity*, 1996, North Ryde, NSW: LBC Information Services, Chapter 4

Goff, R and Jones, G, *The Law of Restitution*, 3rd edn, 1986

Goff, R and Jones, G, *The Law of Restitution*, 4th edn, 1993, London: Sweet & Maxwell

Goff, R and Jones, G, *The Law of Restitution*, 5th edn, 1998, London: Sweet & Maxwell

Goode, R, 'The codification of commercial law' (1988) 14 Monash University Law Review 135

Goode, R, *Commercial Law*, 1995, London: Penguin

Gordon & Frankel, 'Enforcing coasian bribes for non-price benefits: a new role for restitution' (1994) 67 S California Law Review 1519

Grotius, H, *De jure belli ac pacis libri tres : accesserunt annotata in Epistolam Pauli ad Philemonem, Dissertatio de mari libero, & De æquitate, indulgentia; & facilitate quem Nicolaus Blancardus descripsit; nec non JF Gronovii notæ*, 1689, Amsterdam: Janssonio-Waesbergiorum

H

Hackney, J, *Understanding Equity and Trusts*, 1987, London: Fontana

Hallebeek, J, 'Developments in mediaeval Roman law', in Schrage, EJH (ed), *Unjust Enrichment – The Comparative Legal History of the Law of Restitution*, 1995, Berlin: Duncker & Humblot, p 59

Hatschek, J, *Deutsches und preußisches Staatsrecht*, 1922, Berlin: Stilke

Heck, P 'Der allgemeine Teil des Privatrechts' (1939) 146 AcP 1

Hedemann, JW, *Schuldrecht des Bürgerlichen Gesetzbuches*, 2nd edn, 1931, Berlin: de Gruyter

Hellwig, K, *Anspruch und Klagerecht*, 1900, Jena: Fischer

Heward, E, *Lord Mansfield*, 1979, Chichester: Rose

Honsell, H, *Die Rückabwicklung sittenwidriger oder verbotener Geschäfte*, 1974, München: Beck

J

Jauernig, O (ed) (Jauernig/contributor), *Bürgerliches Gesetzbuch mit Gesetz zur Regelung des Rechts der Allgemeinen Geschäftsbedingungen*, 7th edn, 1994, München: Beck

Jaffey, *The Nature and Scope of Restitution: Vitiated Transfers, Imputed Contracts and Disgorgement*, 2000, Oxford: Hart

Jewell, M, 'The boundaries of change of position – a comparative study' [2000] RLR 1

Joerges, C, *Bereicherungsrecht als Wirtschaftsrecht*, 1977, Köln: Schmidt

Johnston, D and Zimmermann, R, *The Comparative Law of Unjustified Enrichment*, 2001, Cambridge: CUP

K

Kaehler, C-M, *Bereicherungsrecht und Vindikation, Allgemeine Prinzipien der Restitution dargestellt am deutschen und englischen Recht*, 1972, Bielefeld: Gieseking

Kellmann, C, *Grundsätze der Gewinnhaftung*, 1969, Berlin: Duncker & Humblot

Klinke, U, *Causa und genetisches Synallagma Zur Struktur der Zuwendungsgeschäfte*, 1983, Berlin: Duncker & Humblot

Klippert, GB, *Unjust Enrichment*, 1983, Toronto: Butterworths

Knieper, R, 'Recht der Kondiktionen: vergebliche Versuche, Bereicherung zu rechtfertigen' (1980) KJ 113

Koch, H, *Bereicherung und Irrtum*, 1973, Berlin: Duncker & Humblot

Kommission zur Überarbeitung des Schuldrechts, *Abschlußbericht der Kommission zur Überarbeitung des Schuldrechts*, 1992, Köln: Bundesanzeiger

Köndgen, J, 'Wandlungen im Bereicherungsrecht', in *Dogmatik und Methode: Josef Esser zum 65. Geburtstag*, 1975, Kronberg: Scriptor

König, D, *Ungerechtfertigte Bereicherung, Grundlagen, Tendenzen Perspektiven; Symposium d Jurist Fak D Univ Heidelberg yum Gedenken an Professor Dr iur Detlef Konig LLM*, 1984, Heidelberg: Winter

König, D, *Ungerechtfertigte Bereicherung: Tatbestände u Ordnungsprobleme in rechtsvergleichernder Sicht*, 1985, Heidelberg: Winter

Koppensteiner, H-G and Kramer, E A, *Ungerechtfertigte Bereicherung*, 1988, 2nd edn, Berlin: de Gruyter

Kötter, H-W, 'Zur Rechtsnatur der Leistungskondiktion' (1954) 153 AcP 193

Krawielicki, R, Grundlagen des Bereicherungsanspruchs, 1936, Breslau: Marcus

Krebs, T, 'A German contribution to English enrichment law (Meier, Irrtum und Zweckverfehlung (mistake and failure of purpose))' [1999] 7 RLR 271

Krebs, T, 'In defence of unjust factors', in Johnston, D and Zimmermann, R, The Comparative Law of Unjust Enrichment, 2001, Cambridge: CUP

Kreß, H, Lehrbuch des Allgemeinen Schuldrechts, 1929, München: Beck

Kreß, H, Lehrbuch des Besonderen Schuldrechts, 1934, München: Beck

von Kübel, F, Teilentwurf Ungerechtfertigte Bereicherung, 1884

Kupisch, B, Gesetzespositivismus im Bereicherungsrecht: Zur Leistungskondiktion im Drei-Personen-Verhältnis, 1978, Berlin: Duncker & Humblot

Kupisch, B, 'Zum Rechtsgrund im Sinne des § 812'(1985) 40 NJW 2370

Kull, A, 'Restitution as a Remedy for Breach of Contract' (1994) 67 S California Law Review 1465

L

Larenz, K, Allgemeiner Teil des deutschen bürgerlichen Rechts, 7th edn, 1989, München: Beck

Larenz, K, Lehrbuch des Schuldrechts, 14th edn, 1987, München: Beck, Vol I

Larenz, K, Lehrbuch des Schuldrechts, 13th edn, 1986, München: Beck, Vol II/1

Larenz, K and Canaris, C-W, Lehrbuch des Schuldrechts, 13th edn, 1994, München: Beck, Vol II/2

Lassar, G, Der Erstattungsanspruch im Verwaltungs- und Finanzrecht, 1921, Berlin: Liebmann

Lenel, O, 'Der Irrtum über wesentliche Eigenschaften' (1902) 44 Jherings Jahrbücher über die Dogmatik des bürgerlichen Rechts 1

Leser, HG, Der Rücktritt vom Vertrag: Abwicklungsverhältnis und Gestaltungsbefugnisse bei Leistungsstörungen, 1975, Tübingen: Mohr

Liebs, D, 'Bereicherungsanspruch wegen Mißerfolgs und Wegfall der Geschäftsgrundlage' (1978) JZ 697

Liebs, D, 'The history of the Roman Condictio up to Justinian', in McCormick/Birks, 1986, p 163

Lippmann, L, 'Studien zu § 119 Abs 2 BGB' (1907) 102 AcP 283

Luig, K, 'Franz von Zeiller und die Irrtumsregelung des ABGB', in Selb, W (ed), Forschungsband Franz von Zeiller, 1980, Wien: Böhlau

M

Maddaugh, PD, and Camus, JD, *The Law of Restitution*, 1990, Aurora, Ontario: Canada Law Book

Markesinis, B, Lorenz, W and Dannemann, G, *The German Law of Obligations, The Law of Contracts and Restitution*, 1997, Oxford: Clarendon, Vol 1

Martin, JE, *Hanbury and Martin, Modern Equity*, 15th edn, 1997, London: Sweet & Maxwell

Mayer-Maly, T, 'Rechtsirrtum und Rechtsunkenntnis als Probleme des Privatrechts' (1970) 170 AcP 133

McCormick, N and Birks, P (eds), *The Legal Mind – Essays for Tony Honoré*, 1986, Oxford: Clarendon

McKendrick, E, 'Restitution of tax unlawfully demanded' [1991] 107 LQR 526

McKendrick, E (ed), *Commercial Aspects of Trusts and Fiduciary Obligations*, 1992, Oxford: Clarendon: Norton Rose M5 Group

McKendrick, E, 'Restitution of unlawfully demanded tax' [1993] LMCLQ 88

McKendrick, E, 'Total failure of consideration and counter-restitution: two issues or one?', in Birks, P (ed), *Laundering and Tracing*, 1995, Oxford: Clarendon, p 217 [1995a]

McKendrick, E, 'Negotiations "subject to contract" and the law of restitution (*Regalian v London Docklands*)' [1995] RLR 100 [1995b]

McKendrick, E, 'Mistake of law – time for a change?', in Swadling, W (ed), *The Limits of Restitutionary Claims: A Comparative Analysis*, 1997, London: UKNCCL, p 212

McLachlin, B, 'Restitution in Canada', in Cornish, WR, Nolan, R, O'Sullivan, J and Virgo, G (eds), *Restitution: Past, Present and Future, Essays in Honour of Gareth Jones*, 1998, Oxford: Hart

Medicus, D, *Bürgerliches Recht*, 16th edn, 1993, Köln: Heymanns

Medicus, D, *Schuldrecht I Allgemeiner Teil*, 9th edn, 1996, München: Beck [1996a]

Medicus, D, *Gesetzliche Schuldverhältnisse*, 3rd edn, 1996, München: Beck [1996b]

Medicus, D, *Allgemeiner Teil des BGB*, 7th edn, 1997, Heidelberg: Müller

Meier, S, *Irrtum und Zweckverfehlung*, 1999, Tübingen: Mohr Siebeck [1999a]

Meier, S, 'Nach 196 Jahren: Bereicherungsanspruch wegen Rechtsirrtums in England' (1999) 54 Juristenzeitung 555 [1999b]

Meier, S, 'Restitution after executed void contracts', in Birks, PBH and Rose, FD, *Lessons of the Swaps Litigation*, 2000, London: Mansfield, p 168

Meier, S and Zimmermann, R, 'Judicial development of the law, *error iuris*, and the law of unjustified enrichment – a view from Germany' (1999) 115 LQR 556

Motive zu dem Entwurfe eines Bürgerlichen Gesetzbuches für das Deutsche Reich, 1888, Berlin: Guttentag, 5 Vols

Müller, G, 'Zur Beachtlichkeit des einseitigen Eigenschaftsirrtums beim Spezieskauf' (1988) JZ 381

Münchener Kommentar (MünchKomm/contributor), *Münchener Kommentar zum Burgerlichen Gesetzbuch*, 3rd edn, 1997, München: Beck

N

Needham, CA, 'Mistaken payments: a new look at an old theme' (1978) 12 UBCLR 159

Nipperdey, H (ed), *Das deutsche Privatrecht in der Mitte des zwanzigsten Jahrhunderts: Festschrift für Heinrich Lehmann zum achzigsten Geburtstag*, 1956, Berlin: De Gruyter

Nozick, R, *Anarchy, State, and Utopia*, 1974, Oxford: Blackwells

O

Oertmann, P, 'Die Bedeutung der Rücktrittserklärung' (1904) 69 Seuff Bl 65

Oertmann, P, *Recht der Schuldverhältnisse*, 4th edn, 1910, Berlin: Heymann

Oldham, J, *The Mansfield Manuscripts and the Growth of English Law in the Eighteenth Century*, 1992, Chapel Hill: University of North Carolina Press

Olschewski, B-D, 'Anmerkung zu BGH NJW 1971, 2307 (12.5.1971)', NJW 1971, p 2307

P

Palandt, O (Palandt/contributors), *Bürgerliches Gesetzbuch*, 56th edn, 1997, München: Beck

Palmer, GE, *Mistake and Unjust Enrichment*, 1962, Ohio: Ohio State University Press

Palmer, GE, *The Law of Restitution*, 1978, Boston: Little, Brown

Parkinson, P (ed), *The Principles of Equity*, 1996, North Ryde, NSW: LBC Information Services

Protokolle der Kommission für die zweite Lesung des Entwurfs des bürgerlichen Gesetzbuchs, 1897–99, Berlin: Guttentag, 7 Vols [cited as Prot]

Pufendorf, *De iure naturae et gentium*, 1672, Londini Scanorum: Sumbtibus Adami Junghans impremebat Vitus Haberegger

R

Rehberg, AW, *Über den Code Napoléon und dessen Einführung in Deutschland*, 1814, Hannover: Hahn

Reichsgerichtsrätekommentar (RGRK/contributor), *Das Bürgerliche Gesetzbuch mit besonderer Berücksichtigung der Rechtsprechung des Reichsgerichts und des Bundesgerichtshofes – Kommentar herausgegeben von Mitgliedern des Bundesgerichtshofes*, 13th edn, 1989, Berlin: de Gruyter

Rengier, 'Wegfall der Bereicherung' (1977) 177 AcP 418

Reuter, D and Martinek, M, *Ungerechtfertigte Bereicherung*, 1983, Tübingen: Mohr

Rickett, CEF, 'Restitution and contract' (1996) NZLJ 263

Rose, FD, *Consensus ad Idem, Essays on the Law of Contract in Honour of Günter Treitel*, 1996, London: Sweet & Maxwell

S

Savigny, FC, *System des heutigen römischen Rechts*, 1841, Aalen: Scientia

Savigny, FC, 'Vom Beruf unserer Zeit für Gesetzgebung und Rechtswissenschaft', reprinted in Stern, J, *Thibaut und Savigny: ein programmatischer Rechtsstreit auf Grund ihrer Schriften*, 1914, reprinted 1959, Darmstadt: Wiss Buchges

Schlechtriem, P, *Schuldrecht, Allgemeiner Teil*, 2nd edn, 1994, Tübingen: Mohr

Schlechtriem, P, *Schuldrecht Besonderer Teil*, 4th edn, 1995, Tübingen: Mohr

Schloßmann, S, *Der Irrtum über wesentliche Eigenschaften der Person und der Sache nach dem Bürgerlichen Gesetzbuch*, 1902, Jena: G Fischer

Schmidt-Rimpler, W, 'Grundfragen einer Erneuerung des Vertragsrechts' (1941) 147 AcP 130

Schmidt-Rimpler, W, 'Zum Problem der Geschäftsgrundlage', in *Festschrift für Hans Carl Nipperdey*, 1955, München: Beck

Schmidt-Rimpler, W, 'Eigenschaftsirrtum und Erklärungsirrtum', in Nipperdey, 1956

Schrage, EJH (ed), *Unjust Enrichment – The Comparative Legal History of the Law of Restitution*, 1995, Berlin: Duncker & Humblot

Schulz, F, 'System der Rechte auf den Eingriffserwerb' (1909) 105 AcP 1

Schulz, F, *Classical Roman Law*, 1951, Oxford: Clarendon

Schwarz, F, *Die Grundlage der Condictio im klassischen römischen Recht*, 1952, Münster: Böhlau

Scott, AW, 'Constructive trusts' (1955) 71 LQR 39

Scott, AW, *Law of Trusts*, 3rd edn, 1967, Boston: Little, Brown, Vol 5

Sheehan, D, 'What is a mistake?' (2000) 20 LS 538

Siber, H, *Schuldrecht*, 1931, Leipzig: Meiner

Siméon, P, *Recht und Rechtsgang im Deutschen Reiche: Lehrbuch zur Einführung in das Bürgerliche Gesetzbuch und seine Nebengesetze*, 1901, Berlin: Heymann

Simonius, A, 'Wandlung der Irrtumslehre in Theorie und Praxis', in *Aus der Praxis schweizerischer Gerichte und Verwaltungsbehörden: Festgabe zum 70. Geburtstag von Fritz Goetzinger*, 1935, Basel: Helbing & Lichtenhahn

Simpson, AWB, *A History of the Common Law of Contract*, 2nd edn, 1987, Oxford: Clarendon

Simpson, AWB, *History of the Common Law of Contract*, 1975, Oxford: Clarendon

Smith, LD, 'The mystery of juristic reason' (2000) 12 SCLR (2d) 211

Spencer, J R, 'Signature, consent, and the rule in *L'Estrange v Graucob*' [1973] CLR 104

Spry, ICF, *The Principles of Equitable Remedies: Injunctions, Specific Performance and Equitable Damages*, 3rd edn, 1984, London: Sweet & Maxwell

Staub, H, *Die positiven Vertragsverletzungen*, 1904, 2nd ed, 1913, Berlin: Guttentag

von Staudinger, J (Staudinger/contributor), *Kommentar zum Bürgerlichen Gesetzbuch mit Einführungsgesetz und Nebengesetzen*, Berlin: Sellier, de Gruyter, Schweitzer

Stern, J, *Thibaut and Savigny: ein programmatischer Rechtsstreit auf Grund ihrer Schriften*, 1914, Berlin; reprinted 1959, Darmstadt: Wiss Buchges

Stoll, A, *Friedrich Carl von Savigny: Ein Bild seines Lebens mit einer Sammlung seiner Briefe*, 1927, Berlin: Heymann

Stoll, H, *Die Wirkungen des vertragsmäßigen Rücktritts*, 1921, Diss Bonn, available at the Westdeutsche Bibliothek, Stiftung Preußischer Kulturbesitz, Berlin

Stryk, S, *Usus modernus pandectarum*, 1717, Halle

Swadling, W, 'Restitution for no consideration' [1994] RLR 73

Swadling, W, *The Limits of Restitutionary Claims : A Comparative Analysis*, 1997, UK: NCCL

Swadling, W, 'The role of illegality in the English law of unjust enrichment' (2000) Oxford University Comparative Law Forum at http://ouclf.iuscomp.org

T

Tettenborn, A, *Law of Restitution in England and Ireland*, 2nd edn, 1996, London: Cavendish Publishing (see now 3rd edn, 2001)

Thibaut, AFJ, *Ueber die Nothwendigkeit eines allgemeinen bürgerlichen Rechts für Deutschland*, 1814, Heidelberg: Mohr und Zimmer

Thibaut, AFJ, 'Note on Ueber die Nothwendigkeit eines allgemeinen bürgerlichen Rechts', in *Heidelbergische Jahrbücher der Literatur*, 1814, Heidelberg, p 1

Thibaut, AFJ, *Versuche über einzelne Teile der Theorie des Rechts*, 2nd edn, 1817, Jena: Mauke Verlag

von Tuhr, A, 'Zur Lehre von der ungerechtfertigten Bereicherung', in *Aus römischem und Bürgerlichem Recht, Festgabe Ernst Immanuel Bekker*, 1907, Weimar

von Tuhr, A, *Allgemeiner Teil des Schweizerischen Obligationenrecht*, 1979, Zürich: Schulthess Verlag, Vol 1

Titze, H, 'Vom sogenannten Motivirrtum', in *Festschrift Ernst Heymann*, 1940, Weimar: Boehlau, p 72

Treitel, GH, *The Law of Contract*, 7th edn, 1987, London: Stevens

Treitel, GH, 'Mistake in contract' (1988) 104 LQR 501 [1988a]

Treitel, GH, *Remedies for Breach of Contract*, 1988, Oxford: Clarendon [1988b]

Treitel, GH, *The Law of Contract*, 9th edn, 1995, London: Sweet & Maxwell

Treitel, GH, *The Law of Contract*, 10th edn, 1999, London: Sweet & Maxwell

V

Virgo, *The Principles of the Law of Restitution*, 1999, Oxford: Clarendon

W

Walter, G, *Kaufrecht*, 1987, Tübingen: Mohr

Waters, DMW, 'The nature of the remedial constructive trust', in Birks, P, (ed), *The Frontiers of Liability*, 1994, Oxford: OUP, Vol 2

Weber, E, *Der Erstattungsanspruch: Die ungerechtfertigte Bereicherung im öffentlichen Recht*, 1970, Berlin: Duncker & Humblot

Weber, M, 'Bereicherungsansprüche wegen enttäuschter Erwartung' (1989) JZ 25

Weitnauer, H, 'Vertragsaufhebung und Schadensersatz nach dem Einheitlichen Kaufgesetz und nach geltendem deutschen Recht', in Wahl, E, Serick, R, Niederländer, H (eds), *Rechtsvergleichung und Rechtsvereinheitlichung, 1967*, Heidelberg: Winter

Weitnauer, H, 'Die bewußte und zweckgerichtete Vermehrung fremden Vermögens' (1974) NJW 1729

Weitnauer, H, 'Die Leistung', in *Festschrift Caemmerer*, 1978, Tübingen: Mohr

Welker, G, *Bereicherungsausgleich wegen Zweckverfehlung?*, 1974, Berlin: Duncker & Humblot

Wendt, O, *Lehrbuch der Pandekten*, 1888, Jena: Fischer

Wieacker, F, *Privatrechtsgeschichte der Neuzeit*, 2nd reprint, 1996, of 2nd edn, 1967, Göttingen: Vandenhoeck und Ruprecht

Wilburg, W, *Die Lehre von der ungerechtfertigten Bereicherung nach österreichischem und deutschem Recht*, 1934, Graz: Leuschner & Lubensky

Wilhelm, J, *Rechtsverletzung und Vermögensentscheidung als Grundlagen und Grenzen des Anspruchs aus ungerechtfertigter Bereicherung*, 1973, Bonn: Röhrscheid

Wolf, E, *Lehrbuch des Schuldrechts II, Besonderer Teil*, 1978, Köln: Heymann

Wolf, HJ, 'Recensione Critica di Dawson JP, *Unjust Enrichment*' (1952) IURA – *Rivista internazionale di diritto Romano e antico* III 382

Wolff, HJ, *Verwaltungsrecht I*, 11th edn, 1999, München: Beck

Wolff, HJ, *Verwaltungsrecht II*, 6th edn, 2000, München: Beck

Wright, 'Pollock on contracts' (1943) 59 LQR 122

Wunner, SE, 'Die Rechtsnatur der Rückgewährpflichten bei Rücktritt und auflösender Bedingung mit Rückwirkungsklausel' (1968) 168 AcP 425

Z

Zimmermann, R, 'Unjustified enrichment: the modern civilian approach' (1995) 15 OJLS 404

Zimmermann, R, *The Law of Obligations: Roman Foundations of the Civilian Tradition*, 1996, Oxford: Clarendon

Zimmermann, R, 'Restitution after termination for breach of contract in German law' [1997] RLR 11

Zimmermann, R, 'Rechtsirrtum und richterliche Rechtsfortbildung' [1999] Zeitschrift für Europäisches Privatrecht 713

Zimmermann, R and Du Plessis, J, 'Basic features of the German law of unjustified enrichment' [1994] RLR 14

Zitelmann, E, 'Die Möglichkeit eines Weltrechts', in *Allgemeine Österr Gerichtszeitung*, 1888, p 210

Zweigert, K and Kötz, H, *Einführung in die Rechtsvergleichung*, 3rd edn, 1996, Tübingen: Mohr

Zweigert, K and Kötz, H, *Introduction to Comparative Law*, Weir, T (trans), 3rd edn, 1998, Oxford: Clarendon